Susan McKay is a journalist and author who has won many awards for her work. She is the author of four critically acclaimed books: *Sophia's Story, Northern Protestants: An Unsettled People, Without Fear: A History of the Dublin Rape Crisis Centre* and *Bear in Mind These Dead*. She was the Northern Editor of the *Sunday Tribune* and has made a number of radio and television documentaries, including *The Daughters' Story* about the daughters of the murdered musician Fran O'Toole of the Miami Showband. She was a founder of the Belfast Rape Crisis Centre and from 2009 to 2012 was CEO of the National Women's Council of Ireland. She has made several series of podcasts with survivors of the Northern Ireland conflict for WAVE Trauma Centre. Her writing appears in the *New Yorker, New York Times, London Review of Books*, the *Guardian/Observer* and the *Irish Times,* and she contributes regularly to broadcast media, including BBC and RTÉ. In 2019 she won a Major Individual Artist Award from the Arts Council of Northern Ireland for a book about borders, which will be published in 2022.

PRAISE FOR NORTHERN PROTESTANTS: AN UNSETTLED PEOPLE

'Susan McKay is one of Ireland's finest journalists ... This book should be read by the Sinn Féin leadership, Irish Ministers and officials in Dublin and Belfast who are trying to make the new model Ulster a reality for all.'

MARY HOLLAND, *OBSERVER*

'This is a wonderful book – distressing and uplifting, mysterious and informative ... Her interviews are both penetrating and sensitive and her comments judicious.'

CAL McCRYSTAL, *GLASGOW HERALD*

'an elegantly written, comprehensive and illuminating portrait of Ireland's Ulster unionist community ... long overdue'

TOM McGURK, *SUNDAY BUSINESS POST*

Northern Protestants
On Shifting Ground

SUSAN McKAY

·THE·
BLACK
·STAFF·
PRESS

First published in 2021 by Blackstaff Press
an imprint of Colourpoint Creative Ltd
Colourpoint House, Jubilee Business Park
21 Jubilee Road, Newtownards BT23 4YH
Northern Ireland

Reprinted with corrections, June 2021

With the assistance of the Arts Council of Northern Ireland

The acknowledgements on pages 337–8 constitute
an extension of this copyright page.

Printed and bound by CPI Group UK Ltd, Croydon CR0 4YY

A CIP catalogue for this book is available from the British Library

ISBN 978 1 78073 264 0

www.blackstaffpress.com

To Mike, Maddie and Caitlin, my beloveds.

And in memory of my dear friend, Mary McPartlan.

'I felt the ground shifting … There needed to
be a steadying of unionism.'

JEAN BLEAKNEY

'This wish for solid ground. This vulnerable
testimony – darkness, storms and floods
frailty, nakedness, sheer exposure – and a love
that answers choral calls for some foundation.'

from 'Type Face', by GAIL McCONNELL

CONTENTS

PROLOGUE

I had been friendly with Lyra McKee for quite some time when something she had written indicated to me that her background was Catholic. I realised that up until that moment, while I had vaguely supposed her to be Protestant, I really had not given it much thought at all. This delighted me. Maybe it is hard for those not brought up in Northern Ireland during or before the Troubles to understand that old reflex that had people scrambling to categorise everyone new they encountered along sectarian lines. Sometimes the name made it obvious, which was helpful. Sometimes not. There were those who were confident they could tell by the set of the eyes. The poet Scott McKendry told me that his father, a shipyard worker, had a colleague who advised him that you could tell by looking at the back of a person's neck. Some would brazenly just ask. Others would ask leading questions about where you lived or what school you went to, leaving the unspoken question dangle. Sometimes you just privately listened out for clues. You didn't have to care one way or the other. You just did it. It thrilled me to realise I was losing the habit.

Of course, Lyra was a unique person who was wonderfully, explicitly, neither, both, and other. Her murder in Derry at Easter 2019 by dissident republicans shocked and horrified people of all backgrounds and beliefs, and even, briefly, brought the politicians and the churches together. She was killed on the eve of the twenty-first anniversary of the signing of the Good Friday Agreement (GFA). We were meant to be at peace. The gathering at her funeral was like a vision of the community united by respect that the agreement was meant to herald and nurture. In the middle of all the pain and anger, there was something healing in that sense of solidarity. For so long people had been imagining, campaigning, and longing for this place – call it Northern Ireland, the North, or the Six Counties – to change, and change for good.

This book is about people who are from a Protestant background, including some whose families are mixed, whether through their parents' or their own choices. In recent years a term has come into use that attempts to corral everyone in Northern Ireland into a binary of ethnic huddles, Catholic Nationalist Republican on one side, Protestant Unionist Loyalist on the other. The term PUL has caught on more than CNR. I dislike it for its sense of circling the wagons, and it excludes a lot of people. The term loyalist needs to be used carefully. It generally refers to working-class unionists, but it is also often paired with or even used as shorthand for 'paramilitaries', which reinforces the false notion that the paramilitaries represent the people. Former Progressive Unionist Party (PUP) councillor Julie-Anne Corr-Johnston said she was a unionist *and* a loyalist. 'I am unequivocally loyal to preserving that union,' she said, 'And ... to the political ideology that was outlined in the Ulster Solemn League and Covenant. Minus the violence of course.'[1]

I was a child when the Troubles flared up and began to destroy all of us. I learned about the society I had grown up in just as it exploded into rage and violent conflict. My education on democracy began with the revelation that I lived in a state founded upon its distortion. I grew up Protestant in the border city of Derry where the Catholic majority had been excluded from power. I had already heard the old cry of 'No surrender'. So, in the late 1960s, as unionism went on the defensive over the demand for civil rights, I learned that an obdurate refusal to compromise was central both to our history and to the Northern Ireland news. We would not yield. We would not bend the knee. What we had we would hold. And if our backs were against the wall, we'd fight.

To understand the people I come from, you have to come to terms with Robert Lundy. Once a year, in the centre of Derry, his effigy is

---

1 https://herloyalvoice.com/interviews/in-conversation-with-julie-anne-corr-johnston/

hung on a scaffold with a sign around his neck that says, 'Lundy the traitor'. It is nineteen feet tall and weighs a ton. There is a parade with bands many of whose names include the word 'defenders'. Then Lundy is burned and there are cheers and shouts of 'No surrender!' Lundy was the governor of the walled city in 1689 when it was besieged by the Catholic forces of King James.

The gates had been shut at the end of 1688 by thirteen apprentice boys determined to keep the city a Protestant stronghold. Lundy did not believe the city could hold out, and urged a negotiation with the Jacobites. The staunch citizens were having none of it. They turned on Lundy who escaped by climbing over the walls, and down through the branches of a pear tree. The gates stayed closed. The siege lasted 105 days during which thousands died of disease and hunger, and people were reduced to eating dogs, cats and rats fattened on the bodies of the dead. But they did not surrender. And that remains the central political principle of modern unionism – more than three hundred years later the advice offered by Democratic Unionist Party (DUP) MPs to the British in their negotiations with the EU on Brexit was to stand up like men and take a 'No surrender' attitude.

As a Protestant, in the traditional unionist scheme of things, you are loyal, or you are a Lundy. There is no middle way. Resist or surrender, and surrender is treachery. Count yourself lucky if there is a pear tree to hand. I interviewed the painter Dermot Seymour, who is from the Shankill Road, for my book *Northern Protestants: An Unsettled People* (2000). As he put it, 'Being a Protestant, for me, is like having no head, in the sense that you are not allowed to think ... without becoming a threat, or a Lundy.'

'The Spanish gentleman' is what Trevor McBride calls Lundy. McBride, whose brilliant work as a press photographer in the city stretches back to the early days of the civil rights movement, has been photographing Lundy for decades now. He admires the artistry that goes into the effigy's creation and contrasts it with the crudity of some of the more recent loyalist murals. He loves the elegantly groomed swirl of Lundy's moustache. In 2019 I watched the Spanish gentleman as he swayed on the frame on which he would shortly be set ablaze. I was moved by his eloquent kohl-rimmed eyes, the white face with rouged cheeks, the lipsticked red lips, the jet black wig against the golden tassels of his tricorne hat. And the flourish of his moustache. His glamour was undeniable.

In the same year, another glamorous figure entered into Northern Irish political discourse. Blu Hydrangea took part in the television series *RuPaul's Drag Race UK*. She is the creation of Joshua Cargill, who was born in east Belfast in 1996. Blu sashayed on set wearing a long black wig and a glittering satin and lace dress with dramatic shoulder tassels that were miniatures of the iconic yellow and black Harland and Wolff shipyard cranes. Cargill was shown explaining that the *Titanic* had been built in the yards, where his father and grandfather had worked. His dad had helped him with the costume. Blu spoke of using the platform of the show, which is watched by millions. 'People look to our country and see repression,' she said in an interview. 'I want to be the opposite of that.'[2] In another interview she said, 'But some people are stuck in the past … they still believe you need to be a Protestant, or a Catholic, that you still need to be straight.'[3] At Belfast's Pride celebrations that year, Blu prefaced her performance of a lip sync to Lady Gaga's 'Born This Way' with recordings of leading DUP politicians expressing hatred to justify the denial of LGBTQ+ rights.

The GFA, also known as the Belfast Agreement, spoke of the 'profoundly regrettable legacy of suffering' and pledged to honour the dead, the injured and their families, through dedication 'to the achievement of reconciliation, tolerance, and mutual trust, and to the protection and vindication of the human rights of all'. The parties to it committed themselves to 'mutual respect as the basis of relationships within Northern Ireland, between North and South, and between these islands.'[4] The DUP was not one of those parties – its response to the agreement was to vow to 'smash' it.

Northern Protestants: An Unsettled People was published when the agreement was new, and memories of the relentlessly violent years of conflict were raw. There was relief, hope for better times ahead. If the killing could stop, anything might be possible. There was also sorrow

---

2 https://www.pinknews.co.uk/2019/10/25/blu-hydrangea-rupauls-drag-race-uk-wedding-plans-twitter/

3 https://i-d.vice.com/en_uk/article/884dwz/blu-hydrangea-icons-and-idols-issue-rupauls-drag-race-uk-belfast

4 https://assets.publishing.service.gov.uk/government/uploads/system/uploads/attachment_data/file/136652/agreement.pdf

and anger, and reason to fear that sectarianism would persist. In the book, I used the phrase 'the people I uneasily call my own' to describe my relationship to the Protestant community in Northern Ireland.

My book's harshest critics inevitably called me a Lundy, and, a term I had not heard before, a 'guilty', meaning someone ashamed of my own people and therefore cringing before its enemies. I was accused of not caring about the onslaught of violence that the Irish Republican Army (IRA) had directed at my community. In the course of one radio discussion a prominent unionist managed to call me both 'wee girl' and 'Goebbels'. But I also found many allies, and in the years that have followed, I have seen a new confidence grow among people from a Protestant background who no longer accept the old divisions here, the old banishings. Far from wanting to defend and maintain, they want to transform the place. They identify with movements that are national, international and global. As far as the local is concerned, they cheerfully call themselves 'Lundys', rebels, 'not staunch' and proud of it.

The institutions set up under the GFA have staggered into their twenty-third year, though they have only been operational for around twelve of those years. When they were resurrected in January 2020 it was after a collapse that had lasted three years. When a new edition of *An Unsettled People* was published in 2005, I wrote an introduction, returning to talk with some of those I had interviewed in 1998–99. David Ervine said that although the vision for unionists was still 'never based on what we want but instead on what we don't want', he believed there was less fear, and less bitterness. 'We have become a more settled people,' he said.

However, in this centenary of the founding of Northern Ireland, unionism faces some unsettling realities. Brexit, championed by the DUP from the start, has had unintended consequences, not least the humiliating revelation that a majority of British Conservative Party members were willing to say that losing Northern Ireland from the UK would be a price worth paying to get out of the EU.[5] Unionism has united, paramilitaries included, to demand the removal of the Northern Ireland protocol by which the British and the EU agreed to resolve the border issue without damaging the Good Friday Agreement, by putting the border in the Irish Sea.

---

5 https://yougov.co.uk/topics/politics/articles-reports/2019/06/18/most-conservative-members-would-see-party-destroyed

There is also the fact that Northern Ireland demographics are at a tipping point. When the state was founded, Protestants outnumbered Catholics by a ratio of about two to one, and ruthlessly discriminatory systems were in place to maintain control. A hundred years later, almost half of the population is Catholic, there are fewer Protestant than Catholic schoolchildren, and the only cohort of the population in which Protestants are in a significant majority is the over-sixties. The 2017 Assembly elections saw the DUP poll just 1,168 votes more than Sinn Féin, which has as its goal the unification of Ireland as an independent republic. The Good Friday Agreement allows the British secretary of state to set up a poll on the future constitutional status of Northern Ireland if it appears that a majority might wish to vote for change.

To make matters worse for unionism, the loss of votes to the Alliance Party is gaining momentum. Although it used to be seen as the 'nice' party for people who were essentially apolitical, it now has a formidable and strategically smart leader in Naomi Long, who grew up in a staunch, unionist, working-class area. Alliance is cross-community, pro EU and takes no position on the constitutional question.

The subtitle of this book, *On Shifting Ground*, comes from something the poet, and unionist, Jean Bleakney said to me. I was interviewing her while we walked along the border between her father's home in County Fermanagh and County Leitrim. She said that in 2017 she had voted for the DUP for the first time. She had panicked, she said. 'I felt the ground shifting …' Unionism, she said, was feeling 'aggrieved, isolated and anxious' and it was losing ground in the face of Sinn Féin's confident North and South republicanism. For Bleakney, the shifting ground was destabilising, but I find in the term also the potential for hope, that the ground can be steadied, maintained in a different, more sustainable way, that it might be the 'foundation', to use Gail McConnell's word, for a place where we can all live in peace.

The book is based on interviews. These were carried out from the end of 2019 until the spring of 2021, a momentous period that included a health crisis, dramatic elections, a pandemic (which inevitably precipitated an even deeper health crisis), the Brexit transition, growing calls from nationalists for a border poll, as well as the introduction of laws permitting same-sex marriage and abortion. *Northern Protestants:*

An Unsettled People, re-published to accompany this new book, contains historical context for places, people, issues and institutions.

The people interviewed in this book all come from a Protestant background. As with my earlier book, I have not looked for the views of people who cannot be so described, and I have not investigated the politics of republicanism or nationalism. Because their voices are often overlooked or dismissed, I have given space in this book to people who are outside of the unionist mainstream. I do not suggest that this reflects their current political power and influence. Indeed, many of them feel excluded and unrepresented. Northern Ireland as it was originally imagined had traditional, patriarchal values and structures. Far too many commentators still look mostly to men when seeking views on the experience of the Protestant community. I had no difficulty finding women and non-binary people who had important and interesting things to say. I kept in mind my late friend Inez McCormack's rule that you had always to ask, 'Who's not at the table?'

Northern Protestants: On Shifting Ground is organised in four sections based on geography. It begins in the rural heart of County Antrim, in the town of Ballymoney. The vote for the Paisley dynasty remains solid there, despite some unedifying behaviour by the current incumbent. There are many Protestant churches. It was relatively quiet there during the Troubles until the parades issues released sectarian fury. It has settled down again. Then the book moves to the far north coast, and the peaceful and religiously-mixed town of Ballycastle, before dipping to the south-east, and the port of Larne, ignominiously the source of the saying, 'Keep your head low like a Larne Catholic'. In 2021, Brexit turned Larne into a border town. This section includes Carrickfergus and the outer edges of the suburbs that stretch south eastwards along the northern shores of the Belfast Lough towards Belfast.

The interviews in the next section are from the city and suburbs of Belfast, where almost a quarter of Northern Ireland's people live, a majority of them Protestant. The city centre has been transformed by peace, but poverty has persisted and deepened in some of the areas that were ravaged by the violence of the Troubles years. Post-conflict Belfast is home to plenty of radicals and progressives and people outside of traditional politics. Loyalist paramilitarism persists, though it has a different energy now.

The third section includes a chapter on the east coast of County Down, from Bangor and the 'Gold Coast' in North Down, to the fishing port of Kilkeel in South Down, looking out across the border to the Republic. It also takes in Mid Ulster, where the Orange Order attempted during the last years of the Troubles to unite the unionist family and resist the Good Friday Agreement. The hub was Drumcree in Portadown, where fierce battles over the right to parade have subsided but never definitively ended.

The final section is about the border. Brexit has heightened its tensions, and turned some of its issues into international ones. This is now the only land frontier between the UK and the EU. There are two chapters, one covering south Armagh, Tyrone and Fermanagh, where the IRA killed many members of the security forces, often then taking refuge across the border in the Republic of Ireland. The last chapter is about Derry, a city in which Lundy is still burned, but also a city that has clamoured for change and in which the flames of imagination have always blazed.

FAR NORTH

CHAPTER 1

Our Own

Once upon a time, when the Reverend Ian Paisley seemed to stand between militant unionism and all harm, Ballymoney was at the heart of his kingdom. It is a small town with a plethora of churches representing every shade of Protestantism, including, even, a Presbyterian cathedral. The motto of the Free Presbyterian Church for 2020 was from the book of Proverbs: 'Where there is no vision the people perish.' When you come in to Ballymoney by train, whether from Belfast or Derry, you pass through countryside so somnolent that it feels like you are travelling back in time, and you are not surprised to arrive into a Victorian red-brick train station, where a metal sign fixed on a high wall instructs those alighting that there are behaviours that will not be tolerated in this town. 'No anti-social behaviour' it says. There is a circle with a red bar across it, a bit like a traffic sign, and inside it stick figures get up to things. One stands, gloomily aggressive in a hooded jacket, holding something that might be a stick. Another seems to be shouting and dancing vigorously. Then there is a woman striking a man on the head, and finally someone roaring into a megaphone. Once you cross the railway bridge, an incongruously modern white spiral staircase takes you down to the car park. A friend from the town told me that when he was a student in Belfast he would take the train home on a Saturday. 'I would be hungover and coming down those stairs I could feel my parents watching from the car below, judging me.'

Joey's Bar, right next to the station, is named after local hero and motorbike champion Joey Dunlop, who died in a crash during a race in 2000. The bar is full of perpetually cheerful beardy bikers. (There is a memorial garden in the town dedicated to those of the Dunlop men who have lost their lives to their dangerous brilliance.) Across the car park stands a store called Winsome Lady. The 1950s-style mannequins in the display window wear cardigans over frocks. Surviving among the charity shops that dominate the main street, there are still small locally owned shops, packed tight with goods. After the first long pandemic lockdown of 2020, I bought a breadbin and some charity face masks in Walker's department store. 'It got awful quiet here during meltdown,' the owner told me.

'ONE OF OUR OWN'

'I am a Protestant, I grew up a unionist. I am a Green Party member. I will be voting SDLP [Social Democratic and Labour Party] in this election. In the light of the shit show created by both the Tory government and Brexit, I have genuinely no idea how I would vote in a border poll now. Climate is still number one.' Sarah Laverty posted this on Twitter in the run-up to the UK general election in December 2019. Twenty-eight years old, and born in Ballymoney, she now lives in south Belfast and works as the policy and public affairs consultant for the National Union of Students and the Union of Students in Ireland. (The unions have been affiliated since the 1970s.) 'I would consider myself left wing, progressive, feminist, socialist. Typically, if you put all those descriptions together in Northern Ireland, people assume that you're nationalist, and if you are from a Protestant or a unionist background, I think there is an assumption that you're more conservative,' she told me. 'Sometimes there's almost a sense that you have distance yourself from the Protestantism, or the unionism, or you have to justify it.'

Ballymoney in the 1990s was, Sarah said, rural, conservative and 'very, very religious'. Her first political influence was her mother. 'She talked to me about homosexuality and race. I'd have watched the soaps with her and she'd be pointing out the hypocrisy of the way women are judged on how they look. I had friends whose mums would be telling them to cover up their bodies. My mum wasn't like that. She was a feminist.'

Sarah wanted to go to Sunday School because her friends went, and her granny wanted her to go to the Presbyterian church, so she did. 'I felt it was all a bit cultish, a bit oppressive. I felt like an outsider,' she said. 'Some of my friends thought I was weird and abnormal. Like, I remember a friend trying to physically drag me to Christian Union, which she apologised for in later life, whenever she'd seen more of the world.'

Sarah's parents' marriage was mixed. 'I don't think it caused them much trouble. My dad was from a well-known big Catholic family in the town and they would have gone and watched the band parades, so they were quite accepted. To be honest, they more got flak for being dole office staff.' However, she does remember her mother telling her that once, when there was a bit of trouble going on in the town, 'maybe parades or something', one of Sarah's uncles came and sat up with her parents in case something might happen. This was most likely one of the summers when the Orange Order fomented disorder over its attempts to parade in Portadown.[1]

Sarah's father got her interested in the environment. 'He took me to bird sanctuaries and forests. He couldn't work in a full-time job because he had a heart condition, but he was interested in nature, and science as well. I was preoccupied with climate change, and a bit of an anxious child.' She was shy too, but took up debating in her final year at Dalriada, the local grammar school. 'It wasn't officially an integrated school and it was mostly Protestant, but it was open to accepting people from different backgrounds,' she said. 'I discovered I had a natural talent for public speaking. We took part in competitions. It enabled me to delve far deeper into things and see issues from both sides.'

Her first protest march was about student fees being raised in 2010 when she was at Queen's University in Belfast. She joined the Belfast Feminist Network, finding it at first 'quite intimidating'. She was drawn to the Green Party: 'It was a real marriage of caring about the environment and the social justice stuff, that was when it kind of fell into place and I realised where my political home was.' She worked on party leader Clare Bailey's successful election campaign. 'For most of my life I'd have seen myself as a unionist, a soft unionist, in that I would have felt that economically Northern Ireland was better off as part of the United Kingdom, that we had a better health system, mainly, and a better separation of church and state.'

---

1 See Susan McKay, *Northern Protestants: An Unsettled People (3rd edition)*, Blackstaff Press, 2021, pp. 116ff

The absence in the Republic of Ireland of a publicly funded health system that is free to users is a major deterrent to northerners when contemplating Irish unity. According to the Northern Ireland Life and Times survey of 2019, 59 per cent of Protestants said the issue would discourage them from voting for unity.[2] A 2020 poll by LucidTalk found that the existence of the NHS would make 54 per cent of Alliance supporters and 52 per cent of Greens more likely to support remaining in the UK while 75 per cent of DUP voters and 55 per cent of Ulster Unionist Party (UUP) voters would choose to remain in the UK regardless of the health service.[3]

But Laverty's unionism was faltering. 'The Republic of Ireland has seen a big shift in terms of its social policies and identities, especially when you look at the referendums on marriage equality and abortion. It is maybe more aligned with my values than it would have been in the past. But really, the main thing I think was Brexit. In the run-up to the referendum I was thinking, how can the Westminster government just allow this to be a pure 50/50 of the population vote? This is insane. Every single part of the United Kingdom experiences being part of the EU differently. And watching how it was all happening made me really feel strongly the whole weight of England's disregard. They never seemed to ask, how are the people who are on a border with the EU going to live day to day? They didn't seem to care.

'The majority of Northern Ireland voted to remain in the EU, yet we have to leave,' she said. In the 2016 referendum Northern Ireland voted by 56 per cent to 44 per cent to remain. 'What really felt galling was that even if every single person in Northern Ireland had voted to remain, it wouldn't have made a difference. It made me feel insignificant, disenfranchised, and disempowered, and it made me start to question whether I was a valued part of this United Kingdom. And really, the answer was no. My boyfriend is from Donegal and he's a republican. He definitely wants a united Ireland. He's asked me – what would you vote, if it was tomorrow? And my answer has been – I would have a hundred questions, literally a hundred questions, which I would put to both sides.'

---

2 https://www.ark.ac.uk/nilt/2019/
3 https://www.lucidtalk.co.uk/single-post/lucidtalk-the-autumn-ni-wide-ni-view-omnibus-poll

Sarah thinks that the unacknowledged trauma that is left over from the Troubles years, when people were terrified and experiencing violence, is holding back progressive politics. 'You get dragged into the old divide. Housing is entrenched in it. Education is entrenched in it. It is really quite draining to be a young person trying to get involved. But you know, people are bored of Green and Orange politics. They really, really are. My generation is bored of it. When Lyra McKee was murdered, it was a huge shock. I remember the feeling of waking up and finding out what had happened to her, and what a lot of people my age talked about was that we felt that one of our own had been taken, except that for us in this case "our own" did not relate to religious background, it meant someone of our generation.'

'I JUST GET THROUGH THE DAY'

Chrissie Quinn sat in her rented flat in an old house in Ballymoney under a framed photo of her sons, Lee, Richard, Mark and Jason. Lee is thirty-five now. Richard, Mark and Jason are all dead. They were burned to death in 1998 when loyalist paramilitaries petrol-bombed the family home on the Carnany estate in Ballymoney. Richard was eleven, Mark was nine and Jason had just celebrated his eighth birthday. The boys were of Sarah Laverty's generation. 'Lee was thirteen two weeks after the fire,' said Chrissie. 'He's reclusive now. He's just on his Xbox constantly. The boys always had a console that they'd play on together. Lee just went into himself after the fire. He just went quiet. I never slept for weeks. I was a shell. We were there for each other but only in the physical sense. We weren't capable. I used to use his brothers' names to him by accident and then I'd see the shock on his face.'

She is in a relationship with Davey Joyce, Jason's father. They were not together when the boys were killed, but met up again a couple of years ago. 'Jason was a lovely wee fellow. He had a massive heart,' Davey said. 'I remember him meeting a wee baby when he was eight and he said, "Och, she's a wee doll." The boys were always together. Richard and Mark were so cheerful. Mark had a laugh that could make anyone happy. People used to call him over just to make him laugh to cheer themselves up. Richard used to say to people, "Lend me a pound 'til my dole comes in."'

I was writing *Northern Protestants: An Unsettled People* at the time of the atrocity, staying at my parents house in Derry, and spending a lot of time at Drumcree. The Orangemen I was meeting there denied their protest had anything to do with a wave of anti-Catholic violence across Northern Ireland. There had already been almost 150 petrol bomb attacks on homes and businesses that week. I remembered hearing the news about the fire that Sunday morning. Shocked and furious, I decided to go to Portadown and hear what the Orangemen were saying. My daughters were little, like the Quinn children. They tried to barricade the front door with umbrellas to stop me going.

Though their chaplain, Reverend William Bingham, had said that morning, 'No road is worth a life', the attitude among the men 'on the hill' was still that what had been done was 'nothing got to do with us'. They were retailing ugly rumours. Willie Frazer tried to persuade me that the fire had been lit from the inside of the house. He had it on good authority, he assured me. Later, after the Ulster Volunteer Force (UVF) connection was confirmed, Bingham said it had been 'wrong to infer' that the Orange Order was involved.

'Religion wasn't a big deal in Carnany,' said Davey. 'You're either a Protestant or a Catholic but that is just how it is in Ballymoney. It doesn't mean much. Chrissie would have been seen as a Catholic. She lived there from she was eight. I'm Protestant – we were made to go to the Presbyterian church, Boys' Brigade, Sunday School and all. My mother still lives in Carnany – she used to gather up one- and two-pence pieces for Jason. All the boys called her Granny and my father Granda. She is seventy-eight now. My father went missing. We put up posters but he was never found. He had issues. My mother doesn't go out now.' He smiled at Quinn. 'I just class Chrissie as a Protestant,' he said. She smiled back. 'I am not,' she said. 'But you know Ballymoney is very mixed. Lee went to a Protestant secondary school and I remember going to a sports day and a lot of the other mothers were from my own school, which was Catholic.'

Chrissie was unsettled. She wanted to move out of Ballymoney, and was considering getting a place in her mother's home town, Rasharkin. Davey said he couldn't live there. 'Rasharkin is Catholic. I'd feel unsafe,' he said. 'They'd burn my van. Chrissie said it would be all right but I think I wouldn't be let live there.' 'Aye, right,' Chrissie said, 'I wasn't all right in Carnany.'

'My mother is Protestant, my dad was Catholic. She is married to a Protestant now. My older sister is Protestant. I don't go to church. Religion means nothing to me,' said Chrissie. She is certain that the attack that killed her boys was sectarian and that she and her sons were deliberately targeted. 'They knew it was my house,' she said. 'As far as they were concerned I was a Catholic. But the boys went to a Protestant primary school. They had been at the Eleventh Night bonfire earlier on the night they were killed. One of the men that did it was at the same bonfire and he put a box of matches into the hand of my mother's partner. My mum's house had been petrol-bombed the night before by the same gang that burned my house.' Many of the Catholics living in Carnany had received UVF Christmas cards with bullets in the post the week before the attack on Chrissie's house. 'Nearly every one of them left,' said Chrissie.

Garfield Gilmour was initially convicted of murder but on appeal this was reduced to manslaughter and he was sentenced to fourteen years in prison. His mother said in evidence that he was 'a well-brought-up young gentleman'. In the aftermath of the fire, Carnany was spoken of like it didn't belong to the town. 'You wouldn't know what goes on in these estates,' one woman told me. But Gilmour, who slept with a machete under his bed, was not from an estate. He was due to inherit a family farm. His mother was a nurse, his father a civil servant. Mr Justice Liam McCollum called him a 'resourceful liar'.[4]

Davey and Chrissie had heard he was back in Ballymoney and living not far from them with family members, but neither had seen him. 'I don't go out much,' said Chrissie. In his evidence, Gilmour named the other men he said were in the car. He said that Raymond Parke and Johnny McKay were the two who got out of the car at the Quinns' house with the petrol bomb while Ivan Parke remained in the car with him. All three men denied involvement, and Gilmour was not regarded as a credible witness.

In November 2019, Raymond Parke's body was taken from the River Bann. It is assumed that he killed himself. 'We don't believe it was his conscience,' said Davey. 'None of them had any remorse. We drove to the Bann after we heard the news. It was misty, like it was trying to clean itself of the garbage that was in it.' Chrissie said it brought her no

---

4 McKay, p. 285

comfort that Parke was dead, though she was not sorry. 'I would have liked justice. I would have liked to see the police go after them,' she said. The couple believe there was at least one witness who saw all of the men in the car when Gilmour drove them back to the scene, apparently to watch as firefighters tackled the blaze. 'But they'd be afraid,' said Davey.

The local council demolished the burned-out house in 1999, and created a playpark for children on the site. 'People in Carnany did care,' said Chrissie. 'There were people threw the flags they had outside their houses on to the street. Women demonstrated with their wains in their buggies.' She said that staff at Lee's secondary school had done their best for him in the years that followed. 'Every Twelfth of July, every anniversary, there are bunches of flowers put up on the railings of the playpark,' said Davey. 'My mother always gets me to send one from her.' The couple do not go to Carnany on that day. 'I go to stay with Lee,' she said. Chrissie does not ever go to Carnany.

Chrissie has had support from mental health services, and is still going for counselling. She wishes she could persuade Lee to go too. 'It was killing me when it happened,' said Davey. 'I can't imagine what it was like for Chrissie. I took to drink. I still do around the Twelfth. It helps you to forget. But not for very long. We could never forget the wains. We are up at the grave brave and often.' Chrissie asked him to show me a photo of the grave at Rasharkin. In front of the stone there is a glass case full of white teddy bears. 'The boys loved teddies,' said Chrissie. 'Those are the ones that were left at Carnany after the fire. It doesn't comfort me to go to the grave. I just get through the days.'

Carnany is on the edge of town, across the road from a small lemonade factory and beside a big Baptist church with a board outside on which a range of warnings about damnation are displayed. It looks over the fast-moving dual carriageway that bypasses the town. The estate has the highest unemployment in the area.

Davey brought me down to see the playpark. The estate is surrounded by Ulster Defence Association (UDA) flags and there are paramilitary murals with heavy antique calligraphy boasting of loyalty and sacrifice for the British empire. One gable wall has a verse in the rhyming style of a Hallmark card: 'The blood our comrades shed/ shall not have been in vain/ We honour Ulster's dead/ and staunch we will remain.' Another has a painting of masked men with guns smashing their way into a house with a sledgehammer, while another man waits in a getaway van. There is a scroll at the foot of the crude painting that says, 'Ulster's present defenders'. The script to the right claims that 'we shall never in any way consent to submit to the rule of the Irish'.

The playpark was brightly coloured and attractive. A huddle of teenagers were sitting under a slide looking at a mobile phone screen, and a couple of younger children were racing about. We stood looking down at the round plaque set into the ground in the middle of the park. It simply had the boys' names in a circle around it: Richard, Mark, Jason. A woman was sitting, still and lost in thought, on a bench outside her house beside the playpark. 'That lady was Chrissie's neighbour at the time,' Davey said. 'She looks after the flowers and takes them down when they're dead.' He brought me over and introduced me. She flinched when she heard I was a writer. He asked her if she would be willing to speak to me. 'What is there to say?' she said wearily, her face bleak. She shook her head.

'A DIRTY, SQUALID, SECTARIAN WAR'

Russell Watton despises what he calls 'two-faced politics'. I met him in his office down an alleyway behind a betting shop in Coleraine. 'I was born in Windy Hill in Coleraine and I've lived in working-class housing estates in this area all my life,' he told me. Watton is a PUP councillor in the Causeway Coast and Glens Borough Council, and a former UVF man. His office is full of photos of people who blew themselves up or got shot or died after years in and out of jail and in and out of sanity. He described the Quinn murders as 'utterly deplorable, a disgrace'. But he insisted that mainstream unionism was inextricably bound up with the growth of loyalist paramilitarism.

'Ian Paisley stood in that town hall there in 1972 and what he said will be stuck in my memory until the day I die. He said the weak-kneed and the yellow-livered could get up and leave the room. If they were not prepared to fight and die for Ulster they were no good to him. And my father was in the meeting and he remembers. What we didn't realise was that there were hundreds of young men that were prepared to do that. There were dozens joined the paramilitaries that week. But the minute we were caught we were called terrorists, we were scumbags, we were low lifes, we were gangsters in suits. The DUP has used the paramilitaries and abused them for years.'

Watton had joined the British army before he became a paramilitary. 'I was in the UDR [Ulster Defence Regiment] but we were ineffective and I was getting angrier and angrier. I was an angry old man at the age of eighteen. I got to the stage I said, to hell with this, and I tried to join the UDA. I was turned down – someone didn't like me – and then me and another fellow joined the UVF,' he said. 'The UDA was massive, maybe forty thousand members. The UVF was far smaller, maybe two or three thousand, and it was tighter, more secretive. And it was militant. It was the militancy we were looking for.' He also said he wanted to retaliate after an IRA bomb killed six old people in Coleraine in 1973.

He left the UDR when he felt he was about to be expelled after four other local UVF men were killed and he became aware the security forces knew he was a paramilitary. 'We were looking for revenge. But the trouble with revenge is you start off with the highest of motives and you end up sectarian,' he said. 'You go into a pub to shoot IRA men but you don't know who is standing at the bar.' He has no remorse, however. 'My mother used to say, you shouldn't have done it in the first place if you regret it. You know what I mean? I don't regret trying to take a war to Irish republicanism. There's no point in saying otherwise. It was a dirty, squalid, sectarian war, this Irish struggle for Irish freedom, absolute nonsense. It was a religious war. The goal was ethnic cleansing. They put fifteen thousand Protestants out all along the border.'

Watton caused controversy when he claimed at a council meeting that during the Troubles it was the paramilitaries who had kept drugs out of the area. He stands over that. 'I mean who kept heroin out of Ballymoney, Coleraine, Portrush and Portstewart? There's four hundred heroin addicts in Ballymena. They didn't build a Great Wall of China between Ballymoney and Ballymena. When I came out of jail twenty-eight years ago, I was told point-blank, if they bring heroin into this area we will shoot them.' Nowadays, he said, people were still reporting drug dealing to paramilitaries. 'Police need hard evidence, is the problem,' he said. 'The paramilitaries will come round and put someone's windows in and they soon get the message they're not wanted. The same with paedophiles – they won't put them in a house in a middle-class area. No, they are dumped into housing estates and no one is told, but the women notice, and they tell the paramilitaries, and those boys will get shot in the knees. Fear puts a stop to these things going on. The people use the paramilitaries, whatever they try to say to the contrary.'

Citing security force intelligence, the BBC reported in 2020 that there were about 12,500 members of loyalist paramilitary organisations in Northern Ireland.[5] Watton said local unionist politicians had no idea what was going on. 'You can sit in that council all day. I'm on the ground. I've worked in the factories. I'm the one that's in the pubs, and wait 'til I tell you, you hear everything in a pub. And you hear everything in a bookies. I'm the only councillor you'll ever meet in a bookies shop.' Every poor area in Northern Ireland has its gambling shops, as well as large, basic pubs with sports on multiple screens. 'I say, if you don't want to tell the police, tell me. I'll tell them. But Special Branch is doing deals with the criminals.'

Watton was pessimistic about the North's future. 'Boris has turned Turk. Wouldn't you think the DUP should have known he would? The Tories have always betrayed us. The DUP put all its eggs in one basket, and they didn't think about political strategy. We've lost ground. We've ended up with a border in the sea and an Irish language act in all but name. Irish is going to be rammed down our throats. That's what people think. And that's going to be a battle a day. They will try it on. They will push it to the limit.

'The DUP is getting some flak over it. Big big style. That is me finished with that party. I only voted for them to keep Sinn Féin out and it's the same for a lot of the grass roots. Protestant working-class people don't have a problem with limited abortion rights. Not wholesale mind you. Gay sex, marriage, nobody gives a damn. There's no point in me saying otherwise. We had a guy come out on our estate, lives around the corner from me. A hard-working fellow came out to me about five years ago, nobody gave two hoots about it. He doesn't bother anybody, he's a great neighbour. Twenty years ago it would've been the talk of the estate. But the young ones now, they couldn't give a shit about it. But see if they put Irish language road signs in my estate? They'll be gone the next day.'

Watton was not impressed that Ulster Scots was to get a commissioner under the New Decade, New Approach deal that got the parties back

---

5 https://www.bbc.com/news/uk-northern-ireland-55151249

into Stormont in 2020. 'Load of crap. I was talking to a fellow from Bushmills and he said, "Why do they want Ulster Scots? I speak it every day of the week and what does it mean to me? Nothing."'

Watton was accused of supporting a delegation of loyalists who turned up at a council meeting in 2019 to protest at the proposed housing of Syrian refugees in a Coleraine estate, though housing does not fall within the remit of local councils. The delegation was led by a former leader of the National Front in Northern Ireland, Mark Brown, who has a conviction for what a judge called a 'vile' and racially motivated assault on a taxi driver. Watton said that far from backing it he had deplored the protest.

He described those who took part as misguided loyalists. 'I met two of them one day in the Diamond, and I said, you're standing with fucking Nazis, come on over here to I show you.' The Diamond is the big square in the centre of Coleraine. 'I took them over to the war memorial and I said, look at those names – people from this town all died fighting fascism and Nazism.' However, Watton had publicly opposed the housing of the Syrians. 'I have 1,253 local people on the waiting list for houses and some of them have waited years and some will never get a house. I can't support fifty families coming in and getting houses in front of them. Alliance accused me of racism of course, but it's common sense.

'I've never seen as much demoralisation and dejection and sense of betrayal,' he said. 'People just feel we are defeated. The DUP lost 48,000 votes in the last election. There's all this talk of people moving to the Alliance Party. They won't. They just won't vote. There's no appetite to get back to violence because there's no clear-cut enemy at the minute. The Scottish independence thing is affecting people too, because if Scotland went independent we are absolutely beaten. I see people, going back into trenches. There's no appetite to go back to the war but I would never, ever rule it out. You just don't know. It doesn't take a big lot. It doesn't take a big lot to kick a thing off.'

Sectarianism still flares up in Coleraine. In 2020 police described the paint-bombing of a house as a 'hate crime' – two Catholics who lived there moved out.[6] A Catholic plasterer working in the town for

6 https://www.itv.com/news/utv/2020-06-16/coleraine-attack-on-house-
    sectarian-motivated-hate-crime

the Housing Executive was awarded compensation after experiencing harassment that was not initially dealt with by his employer. He told the Northern Ireland Equality Commission that he had been called a 'Fenian'. A Union Jack was draped over his van. He was told that if he wanted it removed he could do it himself.[7]

Unionism had been badly led back in the seventies, and it was badly led now, Watton said. 'Arlene Foster has been a disaster. And as for Ian Paisley Jnr, they'd get rid of him tomorrow morning but they can't because of the name. His vote dropped by eight thousand in the last election. Here's one for you. I was told this weekend by a guy that knows these things that he's wearing a pair of shoes that cost £6,000. Who under God would pay £6,000 for a pair of shoes?' No one, obviously. But such ludicrous rumours showed that Paisley's taste for luxury holidays had caused offence.

'I'M JUST NORTHERN IRISH'

The so-called 'brain drain' of young Protestants out of Northern Ireland has long been acknowledged. Each year, several thousand go to college in Scotland or England, and many do not return. Hope Macauley looked set to be one of them. But two years after graduating from the University of Creative Arts in Rochester, the twenty-four-year-old has just returned to her home town of Portstewart and is living five minutes away from her parents, Lesley and Tony. A home bird, as it turns out. But an exotic one. 'My granny taught me to knit, and I loved using my hands and making ceramics when I was at school,' said Hope. 'At uni I began to experiment.' She has already garnered a 'best street style' award at London's Fashion Week, and *Vogue* has called her 'one to watch' and told its readers they 'need to know about' her knitwear label 'now'. Her 'colossal knits', huge, brightly coloured cardigans in ice cream colours and stripes, are selling for hundreds of pounds in Japan and the US. Beautiful, chunky garments, they are made of pure merino wool imported from New Zealand. 'There are no needles involved,' she explained. 'It is a technique, using your hands.' A less expensive range is made with acrylic. The entire family is involved in Hope's business, and there is a team of local freelance knitters.

---

7 https://www.equalityni.org/Footer-Links/News/Individuals/Plasterer-settles-case-for-%C2%A312,500-against-NI-Hous

'I always expected to stay away and live in London,' said Hope. 'I thought I'd work for a fashion designer but after I did a few internships I realised I wanted to work for myself. London is such a fast-paced place and I couldn't afford to live in the city. So I decided that with social media and the internet I didn't need to be there – and I came home. I don't really feel I belong anywhere. I'm just Northern Irish. I'm happy here. I do miss the mix of people in London – there is no variety here. But it is lovely, especially being by the sea.'

Portstewart, along with Portrush, is where Protestants from the western counties traditionally holiday. They are linked by miles of caravan parks. Portstewart is the posher sister. Now a place where students and teachers from the university at Coleraine live, its tall seafront houses face the Atlantic, which occasionally during winter storms hurls rocks on to the road. Both towns are exhilarating in the bright northerly light that flashes off the ocean. Portrush, famous for its golf course, its long white strand, and for Barry's Amusements, has a rougher edge. One day in 2019 I was in a shop on its main street when a drunk man staggered past roaring about 'fucking Fenian bastards'. However, I had coffee that day in a cafe so pink, and with such shiny white china, that it was like being inside a giant mouth.

'I always thought Northern Ireland was too small for Hope,' said her mother, Lesley. 'She fitted in so well to that whole multicultural society in London.' But Hope is happy. 'I have no interest whatsoever in politics,' she said. 'Or religion. Mum and Dad used to bring us to church but I thought it was old-fashioned and uninteresting. There were hardly any young people. I just stopped going when I was a teenager.'

Her parents were in the Methodist Church when they lived in Mid Ulster but returned to their Presbyterian roots when they moved to the north coast. That was, until the church voted to oppose same-sex marriage and to refuse full membership to gay people. 'I couldn't believe that they would vote for gays to be second-class citizens,' Lesley said. 'We moved to a non-subscribing church in Belfast, where we have gay services. I got a lot of publicity speaking out on the radio and local papers. There was a lot of public support for what I said.'

The Macauleys were passionate about integrated education and had been involved in setting up the school they sent their daughters to. 'It was hard going – a lot of parents said they supported it but then wouldn't send their children. The Protestant churches were iffy but so long as the Protestant faith was taught they were okay about it. The Catholic Church didn't support it at all. There was stigma – people said your beliefs would be diluted, which was just a lot of rural nonsense. It was a big leap of faith.' The GFA contains a commitment to promoting integrated education as part of the project of reconciliation, but on its twentieth anniversary, just 7 per cent of children were in integrated schools.[8] The Free Presbyterian Church was more than 'iffy' about the project. In 2012, that church's education convenor, the Reverend Brian McClung, likened integrated education to 'Nebuchadnezzar's plan for the Hebrew captives in Daniel Chapter 1'. He blamed secular education for teaching evolution, respect for sodomy, and promotion of 'open mindedness' in children.[9] The church runs several independent schools based on biblical teaching. It rejects those who treat 'Romanism' as 'a Christian religion'.

Social media presence is a huge part of Hope's business model. She does her own marketing. 'I found it funny once I had a brand,' she said. 'People want to know your opinions and they want you to support causes. I didn't realise people cared. I support Pride, and I promote awareness of the Black Lives Matter movement.' 'We had already used Black and Middle Eastern models in our photoshoots,' said Lesley. Hope's sister, Beth, is gay, and when we met, the family was in a flurry of preparations for her wedding later that week in a local hotel. Lesley wears spectacular shoes and had a new pair ready to go.

In contrast to her daughter, Lesley is highly political. 'Our next-door neighbour when I was growing up was Dominic McGlinchey, the most wanted man in Ireland,' she said. McGlinchey was an Irish National Liberation Army (INLA) leader once dubbed 'Mad Dog'. He was murdered, it is presumed by republicans from a rival faction, in 1994. 'I witnessed the discrimination against Catholics in the unionist state. I understood republicanism. That's why I supported integration. Hope's name is actually Hope Erin – hope for Ireland. In 2010 I stood for the UUP [Ulster Unionist Party] at Westminster – we joined forces with

---

8 Rebecca Black, 'Integrated schools "roadmap to end division" in Northern Ireland', *Belfast Telegraph*, 17 April 2018

9 https://soundofanalarm.blogspot.com/2010/05/lessons-learned-from-past-30-years-part.html

the Conservatives – and then for the Assembly, but I wasn't successful.'

She'd been impressed by the 'movers and shakers' she'd met in the Tory Party. 'They were so much more professional than Northern Ireland politicians. I liked the way they thought big,' she said. 'And I believe in business and the economy.' Brexit, however, was, she believed, a mistake. She feared it would adversely affect her daughter's business. 'Our customers are American, Asian and European,' she said. She joined the Conservative Party in 2011 and is still involved. 'Myself and two other women have established the Conservative Women's Organisation – Northern Ireland,' she said. 'We want to give people in Northern Ireland the option to vote for a party that doesn't have baggage here.'

'COMPLETE WASTE OF TIME'

He's a retired detective, born and reared in Ballymoney. 'Don't be using my real name,' he said. 'I've to live in this town.' I'll call him Jonathan. 'I joined the Royal Ulster Constabulary [RUC] on 30 September 1969,' he said. 'And I served 31 years and 13 days, and at thirteen stations and I must say I was very proud to be a member and I enjoyed every second of it.'

He joined the regional crime squad as a detective in the early years of the Troubles. 'You were going to maybe a different murder scene every day. That was just how life was. I can honestly say without fear of contradiction that the force was very independent. You never enquired, nor were you interested in, what religion the people were. You were there to investigate. You would be talking to some widow, and the tears falling down her face about her loved one being shot, or blown up. And where you got your job satisfaction was maybe five or six years later going over in the court and putting your arm round that lady and saying: Well, justice has been served. That's what it was all about.'

Actually, the assertion that the RUC – membership of which was never less than 80 per cent Protestant – was impartial, was highly contested. Jonathan served at one stage with Johnston Brown, whose book *Into The Dark* described his own experience as a detective who found his work thwarted by a 'hard core' within Special Branch, officers who colluded with informers, effectively creating 'a culture of protecting murderers'.[10] Jonathan said he had not read the book. 'But it wouldn't surprise me

---

10 Johnston Brown, *Into the Dark: 30 Years in the RUC*, Gill, 2005

if that went on, to an extent. I would have certainly been aware that individuals in the community would have received protection from Special Branch in that, when I say protection, I mean they weren't arrested to the same extent as other suspects.' He said these individuals came from all parts of the community: 'Very much so.'

The former colleagues he still meets up with and those he mourns were, he said, entirely decent and put serving the public before their own safety. 'Good comrades would have been murdered and an awful lot of them would be severely injured. Sam Malcolmson was transferred to a hot spot, Crossmaglen, and within twenty-four hours of arriving he was shot through the spine and from that day to this day, Sam's still in a wheelchair. And his mother, when she heard he was shot she took a heart attack and died. Sam has suffered bad. Other fellows I knew from when we were in the Boys' Brigade. One of them was Robert Laverty. It was just a delight to be in his company. But he always expressed an interest in joining the police, and then whenever I joined he obviously was asking me all about it and did I enjoy it and everything else. I said I did. So, a short time later he joined. And lo and behold, we had another fella, John McCambridge, and John decided (by talking to me and Robert) that he would like to join too. And Robert was shot, and so was John. They're buried in the same graveyard, not a big distance apart.

'You'd be devastated but there was an awful lot of people depending on us to try and right wrongs and whilst it was there in your mind that it could happen to you at any time, that wasn't paramount. It didn't affect us on our day-to-day duty,' he said. Investigating atrocities was inevitably horrific. 'I had an awful job one time of being present at the Droppin' Well explosion when seventeen people were murdered. We had to make a temporary mortuary down at the army base and pick up bodies and go down there with body bags and whatnot for two or three days.' The Droppin' Well bombing was carried out by the INLA in 1982 in Ballykelly, a small town between Ballymoney and Derry, which had a British army base during the Troubles. Among those who died were eleven soldiers and six civilians, including teenage girls. He finds it hard to speak about the murder of the Quinn children. It was, he said, 'very upsetting, to say the least'.

Jonathan said he had survived all the trauma because of his wife. 'I can't emphasise enough how good and loyal and supportive my wife was throughout it all. She brought up our daughters because I was never here, and she was always there for me. But there was a lot of marriages broke up because of depression and alcoholism and all of that. I know quite a few policemen and they can see no answer other than a bottle of whiskey. And they can't drink either, because if they take two halves of whiskey they're drunk and they're slabbering all over the place, and they've no health and a lot of people regard them just as being a nuisance,' he said. 'And how do you get help to a man that doesn't want help? This is your problem. You have to get him on a one-to-one and talk to him and make him believe that he is important, that there's help there. And then patience, and deal with him.'

In 2000, Jonathan took one of the severance packages offered after the Patten Commission on policing recommended a transformation of the RUC into the new Police Service of Northern Ireland (PSNI) including a new 50:50 recruitment policy to bring in more Catholic officers and officers from diverse backgrounds, and a focus on human rights. I had attended one of the hearings, in Ballymoney, that Chris Patten held while preparing his report, and I had heard anger and disgust expressed by former RUC officers and others. Jonathan had not gone to the meeting, and said he was not angry but disappointed by the Patten report, which was adopted in 1999 as part of the implementation of the Good Friday Agreement: 'You had reached a stage where you nearly felt as if you were contaminated, that you weren't required. People didn't even like to talk about you. You were forgotten and pushed to the one side and as much blame as possible, down through the years, could be levelled towards the RUC,' he said. 'And when you think of all the good and righteous people that are no longer with us, through no fault of their own.'

He was disgusted by some of the provisions of the Good Friday Agreement. 'They let prisoners out of jail without having served their sentence, yet the wives and mothers of the people that were killed are still serving *their* sentence, grieving every day.' Jonathan said everyone who had committed a crime should face justice and 'pay the price' – including 'rotten policemen'. However, he had no faith that this would happen in relation to the past, because he does not believe the Northern Ireland Executive will pass appropriate legislation. 'Look at the position that our nurses are in. If you're over in Liverpool and in a hospital there, you receive half as much pay again as a nurse here does. That couldn't be fair. No. They've a lot of work to do to get a fair and just country, the way it should be. And we should have integrated education but we don't have it and we won't get it. I certainly would not trust any politician. So, there's maybe a lot of mileage in it for drawing a line in the sand over the past. I can't see you ever getting justice.' He laughed. 'Och, I'm getting like an old dictator sitting here in my armchair!'

Jonathan supported Brexit, but did not trust the British Prime Minister Boris Johnson. 'I have an Irish passport a long time, being that I'm Irish, and a British subject. But if you start to analyse it, and you're talking about the United Kingdom – what is the United Kingdom? Scotland wants to go its own way, so does Wales. Are you going to end up being united to England? I have no great love for the English, and I'm not a unionist as such. I really enjoy going to southern Ireland and I am not averse to some sort of united Ireland if there's justice for everyone in it. But certainly not if someone's going to be discriminated against,' he said.

A Presbyterian, Jonathan saw no good reason for his church's opposition to same-sex marriage. 'What is love? Two people in love, and they adore each other and they're good for each other, and they're happy, why should they not live together and be married?' he said. He had never been in the Orange Order. He did not vote in elections. 'Where would you find somebody that you could vote for? The only person I would ever maybe consider would be somebody like the Green Party. But not the Orange and the Green, dear goodness. The sights that I have seen in the force. No. It would make your hair stand on its end. I would certainly be one that would try and paddle my own canoe, and that's about it. You'll not let yourself down. You aren't depending on somebody else. That's just the way I am.'

'IF IT'S A DISASTER, IT'S THEIR DISASTER'

James from Ballymoney is a caller-in to radio programmes. We met during a heated discussion on BBC Radio Ulster during 2000, one of the last bitter summers of Drumcree. A leading Portadown Orangeman had just called on Protestants to 'get off their bellies'. There were roadblocks throughout Northern Ireland manned by masked men. James had called to speak about his concerns for the boys he taught. He said he'd heard fourteen-year-olds who were Drumcree veterans making plans to build barricades. They were becoming hardened. Teachers were losing authority. He spoke of 'disgraceful leadership' from the Orange Order. I was in a studio in Dublin. I said the Orange Order was making it impossible for progressive politics to develop within unionism and that loyalists were killing Catholics in support of the Orange Order. There was uproar. I was a liar, an ignorant girl, and a 'kind of Goebbels' from Dublin.

James had been horrified by the murder of the Quinns, who were about the same age as his own children. He said a lot of people in Ballymoney today felt the town's reputation had been unfairly tarnished. 'You see Ballymoney isn't really any different from anywhere else in Northern Ireland. It has people who could overreact and behave incredibly violently. It certainly filled me with a sense of shame. One of the most shocking things was the way people tried to pretend it had absolutely nothing to do with Drumcree. Effectively we had open season on the Catholics back then. The Orange Order had lost all sense of direction. It had no idea how to look after the future of the Protestant community. It could not be trusted.'

Now he was concerned that another generation was going to be poisoned by sectarianism.

'Drumcree led on to other things, like Holy Cross, this idea that it somehow did the Protestant community good having this massive show of force over an issue that frankly didn't mean anything.' In a flags-related protest in 2001 loyalists engaged in an abusive blockade as small children were being brought by their parents to school. 'The big opportunity of the Good Friday Agreement, where people could build a new society where we didn't have to kill each other, was being frittered away by those who perceived that they had somehow lost because they were no longer going to be the potential victors.

'Tony Blair made a bad mistake in assuming we had to get the two extremes together. Suddenly Ian Paisley, who had rejected the SDLP, was quite happy to embrace Sinn Féin and sit down with Martin McGuinness. If it had actually resulted in a peaceful and active government, you could accept that sort of hypocrisy. But instead of that, we have effectively had chaos. If one side backs something, the other side opposes it.'

Brexit, he said, was 'utter stupidity' and the DUP had been fools to back it. 'Northern Ireland had come to a place of being at peace with itself where people by and large accepted that there was going to be a border, a pretty invisible border because we were all in the EU together. What the DUP seemed to be determined to do was to actually look for a stark difference between the North and the South. Instead of which they've brought about a border down the Irish Sea, because that is the obvious solution. They made the mistake of assuming they were much more important in the UK than they actually were. They also made the mistake unionism always makes of not planning ahead. Instead of evolving, they went completely back to their roots. They went for humiliating their enemies, even if that meant they were going to lose out themselves. Any unionist with any sense knows this place becomes secure only if you make it a place where nationalists are happy to live.

'And the union has been significantly weakened by the DUP. Some people are saying Irish unity is now inevitable. I'm not entirely certain about that because people would rightly be very scared of the chaos you could have, particularly if it was done with a very strong resistance from the Protestant community, even if they were in a minority.'

James is a unionist, but he finds himself in a position where there is no unionist party he can support. The UUP has 'sunk so low' it cannot come back, he said. 'Before every election the DUP tries to create a sense of panic to get people to vote for them. But the party has effectively been in control for decades now. If things are going wrong, it has to take responsibility. There's a strong feeling in the unionist community that what we need is one party,' he said. 'But if politics here was successful, we shouldn't need to define ourselves as unionists or nationalists.'

James had been saddened to see the evidence accumulate that Protestant boys were still underachieving at school. The curriculum did not serve them well, he felt. 'There was a bit of a fuss in my school recently because a couple of boys chose to do a childcare course. And it struck me as really sad,' he said. 'Life skills matter. We need to start looking at what children really need to help them live happy lives.' His son has moved to London and James reckoned his daughter will leave too. 'Far too many educated young Protestants are leaving because they don't see the future here as being something that is going to meet their needs,' he said. 'I would like to think that by the time I retire I will at least have done something to help make Northern Ireland become a place where my children could be happy to stay.'

'I'D HAVE TAKEN MY STRIPES'

Tom Forgrave lives with his wife, Anne, and their teenage children in the large and handsome farmhouse that has been in his family for three generations, in the lush and tranquil countryside a few miles outside of Ballymoney. The huge green sheds behind their home house 180,000 chickens. Every two months, for two days, trucks arrive down the lane to deliver new day-old chicks. The sun shines in through the open doors of the big kitchen extension where a friendly spaniel romps and there's a range, family photos on the walls and a cookery book open on a stand. It is a picture of settled prosperity and comfort. But the Forgraves are worried people. Six years ago they invested heavily in Northern Ireland's now infamous Renewable Heat Incentive (RHI) scheme, and say that not only have they lost a great deal of money, they have also been unjustly shunned by people who, far from sympathising with them, regard them as paying for their own greed.

The RHI scheme was meant to offer environmentally friendly heating, using wood pellets from renewable sources rather than traditional fossil fuels. It was set up in 2012 when Arlene Foster was Minister of the Environment. Legislation for a similar scheme had already been introduced at Westminster, so officials in Northern Ireland simply copied this. Except that, as journalist Sam McBride discovered, they removed the 107 words that dealt with controlling the costs of the scheme. RHI became known as 'cash for ash' because that, literally, was what it was. Those who installed boilers paid less for the wood pellets they burned than they gained from the government subsidy. This was to have catastrophic consequences for the Northern Ireland economy, and played a key part in bringing down the power-sharing Executive in 2017, after the DUP refused to comply with a Sinn Féin demand that Foster, by then First Minister, step aside until Sir Patrick Coghlin's inquiry into the affair was completed.

The scheme cost tens of millions of pounds. When it became apparent that there was an overspend, one of the DUP's most senior advisers voiced the opinion that he could not see a problem with this, since Westminster was paying. Panic set in when it was discovered, in 2015, that a substantial part of the bill would in fact have to be paid by Stormont. There were botched efforts to rein the scheme in, but some of those who continued to sign up for the subsidies were close to the DUP.

The inquiry alone cost £13 million and there are ongoing legal cases. 'It was an insane squandering of money at a time when the health service was disastrously underfunded and we had some of the longest waiting lists in the UK,' Sam McBride told me. He is the author of *Burned*, the excoriating 2019 book on the scandal, which preceded the 2020 Coghlin report.[11] The report said the scheme should not have been introduced but found no evidence of corruption.

'RHI has been seen as a scam to put money into Protestant farms,' said Forgrave. 'But that isn't how it was. People invested in RHI for the right reasons, not to milk the system. The awful stuff – the heating of empty sheds, houses heated from commercial boilers and all of that – that was the minority. And by the way, Catholic businesses and churches and farmers availed of the scheme too. In 2013 we had reached the point of realising that burning fossil fuels to heat the sheds was unsustainable – the chickens need to be kept at 35 degrees when they first arrive. I heard about RHI and looked into it. It was an incentivised scheme guaranteed by the government for twenty years. We knew a similar scheme had been introduced elsewhere and was working. So we mortgaged ourselves to the hilt, signed up, and invested half a million pounds. There were huge initial costs and RHI income was fully taxable, which we hadn't realised, but the first couple of years went fine,' Forgrave said. Foster had flourished a letter telling the banks that the scheme would be 'grandfathered' for twenty years, enabling people to take out large loans.

By 2017 it became clear to claimants that all was very far from fine, and that the Northern Ireland Executive was planning to renege on its guarantee. In an email later leaked from someone in Stormont to McBride, Forgrave, who already had six boilers and was installing four more, wrote on behalf of the poultry farmers group of the Ulster Farmers' Union (UFU) to the civil servants who were administering the scheme, urging them to delay any changes to the RHI scheme to allow farmers, including himself, to continue to expand. He said that if

---

11 Sam McBride, *Burned: The Inside Story of the 'Cash-for-Ash' Scandal and Northern Ireland's Secretive Elite*, Merrion Press, 2019

cost controls were introduced, such plans would be put at risk. 'We were asking for a period of grace,' he told me. But in 2018 the government at Westminster introduced legislation that removed this guarantee and cut the subsidies.

'They slashed our income by half so that the tariff no longer covered our costs,' said Forgrave. 'In 2019 they forced through additional legislation to slash the tariffs to 10 per cent of what we were on originally. My responsibility was to protect farmers.' The Forgraves had received subsidies worth £750,000 over the first three years of the scheme. 'The media went with the line that I was the man trying to hold on to the scheme, and look at how much money he got,' said Tom. 'My health declined immediately.' 'You haven't been the same since,' said Anne Forgrave. 'You've become withdrawn.' 'It has been all-consuming, sixty hours a week,' said Tom. 'My back spasmed from stress, and I was prescribed antidepressants.

'I spent a month preparing my written evidence for the RHI inquiry and then the inquiry team sent me 2,400 pages to familiarise myself with in advance. I appeared for a full day and I was grilled.' The main beneficiary of the grants in the poultry industry, it emerged, was the massive Moy Park company. Once the scheme was in place, the company had stopped paying in full for the heating costs of its farmers. RHI – in other words the state – was making up the shortfall. Almost two-thirds of its farmers were on RHI. Remarkably, out of the sixty-four people who were called, sixty-three appear in the index of the RHI report, published in 2020. Forgrave's name is not there. 'Not one word of my evidence made it into the report,' he said. 'Justice Coghlin asked the right questions, but the report was a damp squib.

'We're digging into our savings and taking on additional loans to pay off what we owe,' said Forgrave. 'Others have had to sell assets.' As co-chair of a group of Moy Park growers it is in his name that a challenge has been issued to the British government that it breached its contract with those who signed up for RHI. 'Financially, it has really hurt us,' said Anne. 'But that is not the worst part. When I saw Tom being represented as this greedy man on TV and in the papers, I was going, this is not my husband. I do the paperwork for the farm and I know there was nothing whatsoever that was untoward.' 'If I was guilty, I'd have taken my stripes and walked away,' said Forgrave. 'It is toxic.

There's been words said. No one wants to be associated with us. We've had snide remarks. We couldn't put our heads above the parapet.' 'We were brought up to be honest. From a family point of view, we have tried to instill in our children that you must know God's Word, abide by the church's strictures, work hard and show respect,' said Anne.

I asked them about their faith. 'We identify as Protestants, but more so as Christians,' said Forgrave. 'We are Reformed Presbyterians. We declare conversion – it is a profession of faith that each person makes. Our preaching has to be from God's own Word, to be Christ-centred and Bible-founded. We are probably closer to the Free Presbyterians than to the Presbyterians. They are outspoken and hardline – we are conservative but slightly more casual.' I asked them about some of the new churches, including those that welcome gay people. 'God's plan is a man and a woman in charge of a family unit,' said Forgrave. 'Married, with different roles.' 'We pray with our children,' said Anne. 'The schools they go to have Christian Unions and Scripture Unions, and they had Christian primary school teachers. Our eldest is seventeen – she has friends who are breaking away and living the life of the world. She is saddened by that.'

They had heard of the crowds that were going to Pastor Jeff Wright's big, American-style Green Pastures church in Ballymena. 'If you move away from scripture to be popular you won't have deep roots. I'd be afraid with some of these new churches that they lack depth, authority and structure,' said Forgrave. Anne commented that a relation goes to it. 'They do seem to connect to people with problems,' she said. 'And then, a crowd draws a crowd.'

'We have eighteen to twenty families and we sustain a church and pay a minister,' said Forgrave. 'There's a significant commitment. We go to church twice on a Sunday and once mid-week.' 'For now though, because of COVID, we can't do that. So the minister's wife delivers cake to our homes and we gather online and have coffee and cake,' Anne said. 'And prayer,' said her husband.

They do not believe in 'secret' societies, so play no part in the Loyal Orders. 'We actively befriend Catholics and welcome them to our church, but it is hard, as most of them don't come. It has been said that every Catholic thinks a Protestant is a hypocrite and every Protestant thinks a Catholic is an idolator, and there is a certain truth to that.

Certainly, from a whole of Ireland point of view, the Catholic faith is dying and we as Christians should be looking to offer another way to reflect people back to God's given Word, which is what the true church should do.'

The Forgraves are estranged from the state now. 'It is hard to convey our sheer disillusionment with how Northern Ireland is run,' said Forgrave. 'Up to RHI came along we were politically naive. We thought the civil servants were there to work for us and the politicians to represent us. Now we don't even vote. None of them are worthy, and we won't vote just to keep the others out.' He said if he changed his mind he would vote Traditional Unionist Voice (TUV) because he believed Jim Allister had integrity. But he thought it unlikely. 'It is true that there is a brain drain from here, and no wonder,' he said. 'If our kids decide to leave, I will understand.'

'MARTIN McGUINNESS WAS ONE OF US'

At only thirty-four, Claire Sugden had already gone from being a parliamentary assistant to being the Minister of Justice within just two years. She had been in the post for less than a year when the Executive fell in 2017. Nearly three years later, when we spoke, she was frustrated by the ongoing political impasse. We met in a cafe near her home in the Atlantic seafront village of Castlerock, where there is a ruined castle and a fine beach, but most of the old shops and the hotel have been demolished and replaced by holiday apartments.

'My father was English. He was in the British army and he came to Northern Ireland during the Troubles,' she told me. He'd met her mother in a bar, and after they married, he'd joined the Prison Service. He worked in Magilligan Prison, not far from Coleraine, and the Maze. He was one of the last prison officers to be in the Maze before it was decommissioned. Her brother had served as a soldier in Iraq, and a sister had worked for the army. 'We were a Protestant, unionist, working-class, security force family,' she said. 'I was in the Brownies, then the Guides. I was also in a flute band at one stage, Coleraine Fife & Drum. It's probably one of the best ways of learning a musical instrument. It was also close to my family tradition. My mother was originally from a clan in Coleraine and her family was close-knit and collected for the bands and the Orange and all of that.'

Sugden loved playing and marching on the Twelfth. 'To me those days are extremely positive. Even nowadays, I would still go to the Twelfth. It's full of colour, music, everybody's happy. It's a family event. We get dressed up. We enjoy the day. I do find it disappointing when I see that people view it in a negative way. I can understand that from some perspectives but we need to desensitise that.' Her father, she told me, was from a devout Catholic family. 'With no family of his own in Northern Ireland, he tried to join the Orange Order as a way of finding social integration. Obviously he was refused because he was raised a Roman Catholic. My brother, however, would be a member of the Orange Order, but he attends funerals in the chapel, anything to do with my father's family.' Catholics cannot join the Order, and Orangemen are forbidden to attend events in the Catholic Church.

Sugden did politics at Queen's and got work experience with a local MLA, David McClarty, who had been in the UUP but had turned independent after the party deselected him. Sugden felt he had been badly treated. It had backfired on the party, which failed to regain his seat. When McClarty died in 2014, Sugden was co-opted into his seat, and was re-elected in 2016. The UUP had tried to woo her into the party but she saw it as a sinking ship. 'I'm not even sure what that party represents.

'My constitutional belief is that we are better as part of the union, but then my other beliefs are perhaps more progressive, liberal, more left of centre if you like. There's no unionist party in Northern Ireland that represents those beliefs. The DUP certainly don't. I was an advocate of equal marriage. I don't think women should be criminalised for choosing to have an abortion – it isn't a decision taken lightly. The DUP do still seem to be leading their party alongside a religious kind of approach, which I don't think we should be doing, not in the world that we now live in. I think it's okay to have beliefs and we should all respect each other's but I don't think we should impose that. There's a huge gap for that type of progressive unionism. I think Alliance are starting to fill that. I would imagine an awful lot of people who are voting for Alliance probably do believe that we're better as part of the union, but they also believe in other things as well.' Research led by Professor Jon Tonge of Liverpool University in 2020 found that 23 per cent of Alliance voters identify as unionist, though confusingly, 31 per cent said they were

British. Twenty-six per cent said they were Northern Irish, and 33 per cent said they were Irish.[12]

Sugden would not join Alliance herself because she disapproved of the party's neutral position on the constitutional question. 'It doesn't sit easy with me. It is disingenuous. We can't put our heads in the sand. If we were ever to have a border poll, the question will be, do you want to maintain the union of the United Kingdom or do you want a united Ireland? Given the conversation that's emerging because of Brexit, and certainly because of nationalism pushing a border poll, I don't see how far Alliance will get without coming down on one side or the other. I have more respect actually for nationalist parties than I do for Alliance when it comes to that question.

'I think young people associate the constitutional question with Orange and Green, whereas for me it's about the fact that I believe we are better served within the context of the United Kingdom. A united Ireland would actually have severe social and economic consequences for the people of Northern Ireland. My unionism is nothing to do with the fact that I am a Protestant.' She voted to remain in the EU. 'I suppose I would be more aligned to Labour in terms of social, economic values. But it doesn't change my belief in the union. For goodness sake, Leo Varadkar's party might as well be the Tory Party of Ireland!' Varadkar, then the Republic of Ireland's taoiseach, is from the economically right-wing Fine Gael Party.

'Our infrastructure has been built up around us being in the EU. And dismantling that is going to be really difficult. It's a risk, a huge risk. I'm glad that we have more of a cross-community voice now in Westminster to be able to advocate for *all* of the people of Northern Ireland, because I don't think the DUP did that.'

When the institutions were devolved in 1999, the Justice Ministry, which has responsibility for the highly contentious areas of prisons and policing, remained under direct rule. Sinn Féin and the DUP agreed that justice should be devolved as part of the Saint Andrews Agreement of 2006 but continuing wrangles meant it was not until the Hillsborough Agreement of 2010 that this came about. Under legislation introduced that year, the minister was to be appointed not using the d'Hondt system

---

12 Jon Tonge, 'Alliance has enjoyed an upturn ... and it isn't slowing down', *Belfast Telegraph*, 7 March 2020

but by a cross-community Assembly vote. Sugden was offered the role after Alliance turned it down.

'I didn't want to come in with my own baggage and prejudices. I wanted to get out there, meet as many people as possible, listen to all different opinions and then come to a decision,' she said. 'To be honest, that was quite a different approach to that taken by previous ministers in the Department of Justice. My approach was very much about having good relationships with MLAs because I recognised that their scrutiny of me would improve my policy. That was quite difficult for some of the civil servants. I was fighting against a system where they quite frankly made the decisions and I wasn't prepared to allow them to do that. I also wasn't prepared to have the same old voices, most of them from Belfast. I wanted to know what was happening in the rest of Northern Ireland.'

There was one fundamental and unacknowledged problem. 'I think it was difficult for them too to have a young female in the role,' Sugden said. 'It seems to me there is this weird prejudice against young women generally, and, whether it's intentional or not, it exists. I'm pretty sure some of the things that were said to me even by lower level civil servants would not have been said to my predecessor. I had to fight on many occasions, even on things like me wanting my diary to be on my mobile phone. And there were people spreading rumours about me. Sometimes it felt like I was sweating the small stuff, when as a minister I should have been rising above that. They had a very defined way of doing things, quite dated. I wanted to address domestic abuse, mental health, rural issues. I was told they're not within the justice brief. I says, well, they should be, because if we tackle mental health then we're not going to have two-thirds of the prison population with mental health issues, and maybe we won't even have them coming into prison at all.

'I wanted to tackle domestic abuse because it is one of the most prevalent crimes in Northern Ireland, like thirty thousand plus cases reported, and what goes unreported doesn't bear thinking about. Domestic abuse is traumatic, and the trauma often leads to a mental health or addiction issue in the home of a child, and it's almost perpetuating a cycle. I'm a great believer that no one is born bad. I think we are all a product of our circumstances and our upbringing and I think that's what we need to look at.'

Sugden's department led an action plan to end paramilitarism. 'In the three years that we haven't had a government that plan has still continued and that money has been spent. But I am devastated because it was never going to be successful in the absence of a Programme for Government. The reason the paramilitaries are able to be successful for their own ends is because they're able to exploit communities, and they can exploit communities because those communities don't have the things that a government should be providing for them. So is it realistic to say that we can tackle paramilitarism in the absence of public services and good governance? No, it's not.

'Northern Ireland's biggest problem is its inability to govern well and to be efficient. We need a strategy. It's going to take a generation, but we need to start now and we need to start looking at it in a more long-term way. I don't think the problems in Northern Ireland are insurmountable, but if we don't fix them now they could be. We get a considerable amount of money from Westminster every year. Is it enough? If we changed how we do things maybe we wouldn't need as much. And you know, regardless of whether we look to a united Ireland or staying within the union, whatever one you pursue you need to make Northern Ireland work.'

I asked her about the collapse of Stormont in 2017, when the then deputy First Minister Martin McGuinness had announced he was resigning, citing RHI and the refusal to be humiliated further by the DUP. 'I wouldn't say the DUP actively sought to humiliate Sinn Féin but I would say the DUP are arrogant and lack self-awareness,' she said. 'It was one thing after another. That was the government that had the opportunity to do wonderful things for Northern Ireland. I think ultimately what Sinn Féin did was prove to the DUP that they were equal partners in government. And maybe it was a lesson that the DUP needed to learn.'

Despite the fact that the IRA had killed prison officers, and that she had grown up with all the routines of vigilance against this threat, she said she had always had a good working relationship with Sinn Féin, and it was Martin McGuinness who nominated her as Justice Minister. 'They chose me because they knew that they could work with me and they knew that I was reasonable, and my unionism is a very practical type of unionism in the sense that I believe in doing what's best for the people. It isn't enveloped in all of that other nonsense.'

She said of McGuinness that he was 'one of us'. I asked her what she meant. 'He was someone from Northern Ireland who may have called it something else, but his values, how he was raised, he didn't feel unfamiliar to me. I have partaken in a number of cross-community programmes and I must admit I find I have more in common with people in Northern Ireland than I do with people across the border in the Republic of Ireland. It doesn't matter what background you are from or what community you were brought up in, to me there was some affinity there. I had a good relationship with Martin McGuinness, and I do think we feel his loss in this current situation, which is sad.'

The failure to get the institutions back up and running was shameful. 'I think our politicians are exploiting the fears of the people who vote for them. They are showing a complete lack of responsibility around people's lives. At constituency level, I have never been busier because the cracks of not having a government for three years are starting to filter down to the grass roots. The issues that we are dealing with are in some cases a matter of life or death. It isn't just potholes and street lights. Just last week in my office we had to ring the mental health crisis team because we were fairly convinced that one of my constituents was going to take their own life. People are asking me to intervene to get their hospital appointment closer than six months, to get heart surgery. I distribute vouchers for the food bank. It really does concern me that in a Western democracy we're dealing with issues that just shouldn't be there.

'After the peace process settled down what should have happened was that we actually focused on good governance and providing good public services. But sadly the politics just continued to screw it up to be honest. And the political parties need to catch themselves on. They're not there to fight amongst themselves. They're not there to make sweeping statements about pie in the sky. They're there to provide for all of the people of Northern Ireland, regardless of background, gender, race, religion, sexual orientation. Northern Ireland's moving on but the politics isn't. I really hope this Westminster election has been that wake up-call for them. We'll see.'

Sugden pointed to the dearth of women in senior roles in public life in Northern Ireland. 'Northern Ireland is quite backward. We don't support women. Our childcare is appalling. There seems to be a view that women can't be anything other than the typical kind of housewife. In my view, women fail in roles where they act like men. The biggest difficulty the leaders of the DUP and Sinn Féin have is that these women are leaders of parties full of a particular type of man. If women could just be women they might do better. But we're very quick in Northern Ireland to judge women, even on their appearance. The other day, I had a friend who made a comment about someone we used to go to school with – she described her as a tramp. I was absolutely mortified. I'm a big advocate for women all the time.' After Arlene Foster was selected to replace Peter Robinson as DUP leader, MLA Edwin Poots congratulated her, adding that, of course 'her most important job has been, and will remain, that of a wife, mother and daughter'.

Sugden was concerned about what she saw as a growing rage among men in particular and felt the churches could do more to try to address this. 'I have had middle-aged men aggressively come up to me in the middle of a car park and have a go at me. And as politician you obviously think about what happened to Jo Cox,' she said. British Labour MP Jo Cox was murdered by a right-wing extremist in 2016. Although Sugden is in the Church of Ireland, she is not a regular church attender. 'I have a faith. I wouldn't say I have a strong religion. I do like to keep the church as part of my life. So I got married earlier this year, and it was important for me to have the minister conduct a blessing after our marriage ceremony. I felt that it brought some sort of higher feeling to it, a spiritual presence. I do sometimes find peace in that. And there is a community side to it as well as a religious one. My faith is led, if anything, by a belief in the greater good and is based around love. So I'm probably not a very good Protestant, if I'm honest.'

CHAPTER 2

Different Worlds

The last time I'd seen Anton he was wearing glittery blue eye shadow, a velvet coat and patent leather platform boots. He was with his partner, David, in the John Hewitt bar in Belfast. We had all been to Lyra McKee's funeral at St Anne's Cathedral. Anton and David had come over from London. Now it was winter in Ballycastle, and Anton wore no make-up, a woolly hat, walking boots and a big fleecy jacket that used to be his mother's. I was surprised when he told me that the closest he'd come, in Ballycastle, to an overt conversation about his gayness was when the local minister had taken him to task over wearing the platform boots to church.

I'd come to talk with Anton and his aunt, Anna McCallion, a hill farmer on Knocklayd Mountain above Ballycastle. Anton had told me that when he came home from London in the autumn of 2018 to sign a petition in protest against the behaviour of the local MP, Ian Paisley Jnr, he had persuaded her to sign it with him. She had never previously voted. Paisley had been banned from Westminster for the maximum allowed period of thirty days after journalists revealed that he had failed to declare that he had taken gifts of lavish family holidays from the Sri Lankan government in 2013. He had also lobbied Prime Minister David Cameron not to support a UN inquiry into human rights abuses in the country. Had 10 per cent of the electorate of North Antrim signed, Paisley would have been unseated and it would have forced a by-election. However, only 9.6 per cent signed, so it failed. Paisley greeted the news with a 'Hallelujah!' It was no surprise when he was re-elected in the 2019 general election, taking almost half of the votes in the constituency, though thousands did abandon him.

Anton had invited me to stay in his late granny's home, a small bungalow on the mountainside. A hand-painted sign at the foot of the lane instructs: 'No Trespasser'. Anna lived in the house next door. She had cared for her mother for many years and had then taken over the farm. At the end of a winding lane, the houses, behind locked gates, are sheltered by a stand of old pine trees from the wind that sweeps across this north Atlantic coast. Higher still stand the grey ruins of the old limestone quarry that Anton's grandfather used to manage. People come up the mountain to look out for peregrines in the wild sky. Inside, the house is as his granny had left it, full of little china ornaments, flouncy pink sheets, and armchairs laden with lace antimacassars and crochet cushions. When Anna came back from visiting her husband, John, in a nursing home down in the town, she cast a critical eye over the cherry scones Anton had baked for my visit. 'I doubt you left those in a bit long,' she said.

Although he grew up with his parents near London, Anton had spent a lot of his early life at Knocklayd. 'Granny and I would scale the mountain, talking about God and how this world was divinely inspired. We shared a sort of natural religion. We went to the Presbyterian church as well, on Sunday. But Granny didn't see any distinction between religion and everyday life. She would look at the mountain and ask me, "Who made this mountain?" Grace was a big part of what she taught me, that you have to answer to God in everyone, and that reality is addressed to you and you have to act according to your better instincts. She used to say that with God at your back you could do anything.'

His granny also introduced him to make-up and let him give her makeovers. She was a farmer, and she also baked, and organised concerts in small halls around the countryside. She sold second-hand clothing to raise funds for the church, and Anton was fascinated by one of her customers, who was, as far as Anton was concerned, transgender. 'She grew up in a really poor family of girls, and the official story is that they didn't have enough clothes to clothe the only boy, so he wore the girls' clothes,' he said. 'But she continued wearing them and became Sam-MaryAnn, a woman. And my granny would clothe her and give her theatrical hats that had belonged to my great-grandmother.'

Anton was less taken with church-going religiosity. 'It seems to me most Presbyterians have this knowing of God in front of them that drives a wedge between them and their natural reactions. They end up not trusting themselves. A lot of Protestants that I know, I mean religious ones, make me think of Psalm 137 – they are strangers singing in a strange land. I think hardline Protestants are tormented by people asking them to sing a song of Zion, and longing for this heavenly home that's always just beyond reach. Salvation is always deferred. Whereas Granny was present, she was as much part of the life of the mountain as the trees, as the sheep that she so loved, and the cattle. She loved giving people a good time. Sometimes people find it hard to imagine there is a Protestant, you know, a religious Protestant, who actually loves life.'

His parents sent him to Harrow School as a boarder. He is not sure why. 'It was very posh. The uniform was black, because we were in mourning for Queen Victoria. And as a young impressionable person, I was sort of like, this is attractive,' he said. A lot of his peers were from British military families, and they assumed, Anton said, that Irish people were Catholic.

At Queen's University in Belfast, he began to go to DUP events, and LGBT events, being 'thran' in both sets of company. 'It was quite bizarre,' he admitted. 'The LGBT community was anti-church, and the DUP was anti-LGBT, and I used to argue against whatever the orthodoxy was. I stammered when it came to talking about my sexuality. I was just kind of living the life of some distorted soul that was never who I was and never who I was going to be. My problem is that I'm always drawn to – I *was* always drawn to – false security. Eventually I came to my senses, and the gay life took over.' He had moved back to London, gone to drama school and met David.

'WHERE ARE ALL THEM BOYS THAT GOD WAS GOOD TO?'

On the Sunday morning, Anton and I drove to Ballymena, the capital of the North's Bible belt, to go to church at Green Pastures. It was on the site of the Wrightbus company in an industrial estate on the edge of town. This was to be Jeff Wright's first time back as pastor, months after the church had been picketed by about half of the 1,200 workers who had lost their jobs when the bus company went into administration. Alongside the church banner that declared Green Pastures to be 'a family for the lost', workers had draped their work shirts, and held up placards, including one that read 'For the love of money is the root of all evil. 1 Timothy 6:10.' After lengthy negotiations the factory was bought by another company and many of the jobs were saved.

Wright had boasted in a 2017 interview that God had been made a shareholder in the Wrightbus business, a quarter of which was owned by an evangelical trust. Two years later, the workers were protesting about the fact that the company, in which Wright was a major shareholder, had, despite losing money, given millions of pounds in donations to the church, which was engaged in a massive fundraising effort to complete the building of a multi-million-pound complex to which it was to move. Inside, Wright had waxed tearful as he spoke of his sorrow for the workers, while a pianist tinkled moodily in the background.

As we drove in, the car park was already packed, but there to welcome us and direct us to one of the last spaces was Pastor Jeff himself in a high-vis vest. There were a lot of big cars and SUVs. Inside the church, which looked still like a factory unit, people were milling about, families all dressed up in traditional Sunday-best outfits, young professionals in smart casuals, young women in sparkly tops and wearing make-up. There were a few Black people, young men in sneakers with the same eager smiles as the rest. There was a free 'breakfast bar' with cornflakes and coffee dispensers. People broke away from the crowd and advanced towards us with industrial-strength smiles, greeting us, asking if it was our first time. We were shown the welcome centre, given biscuits, directed to the book stall, where the books all seemed to be inspirational American gospel tracts.

A woman told us with shining eyes that we were going to love it. Sinéad had left the Church she was brought up in – when she had needed it to help her it had done nothing, she said, her face darkening momentarily. Green Pastures was different. She took us under her wing, sweeping us up to seats near the front of the auditorium. We said we might need to leave early, and Sinéad said that would be fine, everything was very relaxed at Green Pastures. The huge room and its balconies filled up with the faithful, hundreds of them. There were theatrical lights and a stage that was set up with guitars and drums and microphone stands as if for a rock concert. It was exciting. The band, led by a young woman with long blonde hair and a jumpsuit, moved into place. The singer had a good voice for Christian rock, and soon many of the congregants were flinging up their arms and singing with her.

The lyrics, which were shown on big screens, were militaristic. There were weapons, fights with enemies, unbelievers who were going to be defeated, the triumph of the King. The backing singers swayed with closed eyes. Afterwards, Pastor Lorraine Wright came on, glamorous in denim and cowboy boots, promising that the prayer teams would stand by people, 'whatever you are going through' and then moving on to itemise 'all the different ways you can give'. These included 'filling out the wee form' and 'ticking the wee box'. The big screens lit up with all the ways. Pastor Jeff bounded on to the stage, to whoops and cheers, dressed down in crumpled jeans, a zip-up cardigan and an open shirt. He wore a headset microphone. 'Isn't she lovely, like?' he said. Lorraine is his wife. 'Some girl, some girl.' He thanked people for 'the abuse you took on my behalf'. 'Loyalty is a good thing,' he said. 'It was so with David. The world is going to come against us. But these are revival days. We're here to build a barn for an end-time harvest that God is going to build for the great darkness.'

In Wright's version of the story, he was the brave young shepherd boy who stood his ground when bigger men ran away. He killed the warrior Goliath on behalf of the Israelite armies of the living God, armed only with a sling and a handful of stones. The workers, their unions and the media, were, presumably, the world. The barn was the complex for which Wright was back raising funds.

The sermon continued. God was the CEO, the boss. He didn't have to answer to parliament or look for a vote. 'Wouldn't that be great? Eh?' Wright kept cupping his hand behind his ear and demanding a response. 'Come on, is there anyone out there?' he'd demand. 'Eh? Where are all them boys that God was good to? Aye, come on. They need to wise up, wise up.' God was looking for 'the hardest thing there is, to submit to his authority'. He harked back to 'the days of revival in Ahoghill when the atmosphere in the Diamond was so thick men came out of the bars and fell down on their knees. Eh? Aye, come on.'

He rolled up his sleeves, then pulled a dirty and crumpled hanky from his trouser pocket, blew his nose noisily and wiped his mouth before shoving it back in his pocket. 'Is there enough evidence in your workplace to convict you of being a believer?' he demanded. If you were going to be a Christian you had to be prepared to be hated. He produced another hanky, this one snowy white. He said it was embroidered with 'Pastor Jeff' and that it had been a gift. He riffed about how he knew he was always 'snottering and getting on like that there'. Then he shouted, 'Come on, catch yourselves on, there's steadier people in the bar.' He parodied a person who didn't want to go to church, and talked about how Jesus 'boked up' over people who were lukewarm. He squared up with his fists raised as if to fight. 'You just need a good dig in the head.'

The screens filled up with apocalyptic surging images of clouds in a dark sky. 'Come on! Submit! Throw in the towel! Jesus is looking at you.' Wright shouted, striding about the stage. 'The Word of God will fix you. You need a reset … There's so much suicide going on now …' It went on and on, a rambling, dislocated monologue, consistent only in that he still featured as the heroic boy David. The important message, it seemed, was to do as you were told and get the barn built. Anton and I looked at each other. His aunt Anna was treating us to lunch at the Bushmills Hotel and we were going to be late. But there was no way we could have left without it looking like we were staging a walkout. 'Let's get revival done,' Wright mumbled. The band set up again. When at last it was over, kind Sinéad beamed a questioning smile at us, as if to say, 'Wasn't that wonderful?' We waved and rushed away. 'Ugh,' said Anton.

'I'LL FORM MY OWN OPINIONS HERE'

It was peak lunchtime and there was a long queue for the carvery. But there was plenty – an extraordinary array of roasted ham, beef, pork, chicken, turkey, several types of lamb, venison and even locally reared boar. Anton, a vegetarian, heaped his plate with every kind of potato. People were taking away mountains of steaming meat, dodging collisions with the envious unfed as they wove their way back to their tables.

Anna began by telling me that her generation of the family had almost been prevented from coming into being at all. 'The Dark Hedges that you hear of there, my father was nearly killed at them one time, just before he was married,' Anna told me. 'He worked in Ballymoney, him and his brother and two other men from Armoy, and they were going that particular morning to work when a tree at the Dark Hedges fell across their car and cut it in two and killed my uncle just instantly. And my father and another of the men lay in the hospital in Belfast for I'm sure six months. They had got very severe head damage. But luckily the two of them survived it.' The Dark Hedges is famous now from *Game of Thrones* and is generally thronged with fans. 'I never was at it, to tell you the truth,' Anna said. 'To me it is just a line of trees.' Knocklayd also featured in the series and Anna used to watch the crew as they came and went up her lane preparing to film there. It was sad, she said, the amount of work that went into it for all the filming that they did in the end. They'd invited her up to see the set and have lunch but she declined. She just asked them to fix the potholes their big trucks had made.

'My father was a fair man. One time it was the Twelfth of July, and Daddy met a man coming down from the quarry and he said to him, "What's wrong? It's not stopping time." And the man said, "No, they're hassling me up there and they're putting flags up all over the place." And Daddy just went up and got his stepladder and ripped all down. He told the men there would be no more flags and if it didn't suit them they could just go. He said they were there to do a job and they had no need of knowing what faith the person beside them had. And Daddy was a Freemason and in the Independent Orange Lodge in Stranocum.

'My mother was sadly widowed at forty-nine, so she was left with four children and the farm with cattle and sheep and turkeys and hens and pigs. She had a decision to make, either to sit and do nothing or get on with her life, so she got on with it. That was the type of her, a hard-working woman. Anything she needed, she just seemed to grow it.' Anna grew up going to church on Sunday morning and again in the evening, Sunday School, youth fellowship and mid-week fellowship as well. She remembered in particular a friend who used to sing the chorus of 'I Know Who Holds the Future' (a kind of folksong of a hymn) and accompany himself on guitar. 'There was a verse in it that said that with God things don't just happen "ev'rything by Him is planned". It was lovely. I can see him still. He went on to be a policeman and got ambushed and killed.'

Anton began to boast to me about the prizes his aunt used to win for knowing her catechism. 'It was just part of your life,' she said. 'As we grew up I never had any other notion in my head but to go to church on a Sunday morning.' She married a local man who was a 'very upright' Catholic. They were married in her church, but her husband kept his own faith. They raised their son a Presbyterian, and Anna had only stopped attending church recently, in a row over the upkeep of paths around her parents' grave. 'It doesn't sound like much but it meant a lot to me,' she said.

Anna looked at Anton. He appeared agitated and seemed to wipe away tears. 'What is it?' she asked. 'Oh, I just get sad,' he said. 'You know, with Granny and all that.' Anna sighed, as if torn between sympathy and wanting to tell him to pull himself together. I asked her what she thought about her church's attitude to homosexuality, given that Anton was gay. There was a brief silence in which the word 'gay' dangled. I had said what had not been said before. Anton went very still. 'Oh no, well, I didn't think about it, because nobody ever told me about Anton,' Anna said carefully. 'He just told me about his friend, David. And I just accepted that was it, that was … Anton wasn't my responsibility. He was my nephew. And even though I probably wouldn't have maybe agreed with gay marriage, I could never say that I would turn against some of my relations because they were doing that.'

Anton was moved by the generosity of her words. 'I always felt I was living a double life. I remember when I was getting confirmed and my minister said, is there anything you want to tell us, and I was crying and I said, "No, there isn't anything wrong with me." I remember hearing Iris Robinson on the radio when I was a teenager. She said being gay is an abomination to the Lord. That struck the fear of God into me. That sort of hateful language was never part of my childhood. I went through a bit of a rocky time. I stopped eating and I got anorexia and I didn't go to church any more and I just got cut off completely from all sense.' Anna remembered. 'You were skin and bone,' she said.

In a BBC radio interview in 2008, Robinson condemned a brutal assault on a young gay man in Belfast but went on to say, 'Homosexuality is not natural. My Christian beliefs tell me that it is an abomination … an offensive act and something God abhors.' She said she had 'a lovely psychiatrist' working for her and that he was 'trying to turn homosexuals away from what they are engaged in'. She was chair of Stormont's health committee at the time. She urged people to contact 'this gentleman' and said she'd met people who'd become heterosexual: 'They are married and are having families.' Robinson's husband, Peter, who was then the DUP's leader, defended her. She was quoting the Bible, he said.

Ten years later Peter Robinson was appointed as an honorary professor of the Mitchell Institute for Global Peace, Security and Justice at Queen's, named after the US senator, George J. Mitchell, who chaired the negotiations that led to the Good Friday Agreement. Robinson's incompatibility with the upholding of human rights was overlooked. Paisley Snr, with Peter Robinson by his side, led a crusade in the 1970s to 'save Ulster from sodomy'. Paisley Jnr said in 2005 that he found gay relationships 'immoral, offensive and obnoxious', adding that he was sure most people would agree. Sammy Wilson called gays 'poofs and perverts' in 1992. In 2021 he defended the right to offer conversion therapy.

In 2019, the Belfast Ensemble presented *Abomination: A DUP Opera* by Conor Mitchell at Belfast's Lyric Theatre. Based entirely on actual events and statements, the DUP was gloriously damned by its own hateful words and its hypocrisy. The opera's most extravagant scene depicted Iris Robinson's undoing, as she committed the biblical sin of adultery with a teenager, surrounded by swan-like angels fluttering their gorgeous plumey white wings. As music critic Stuart Baillie wrote, 'It felt like another strike against the monolithic power of fundamentalist politics in the north.'[1]

Anton had lived without organised religion for several years but had reached a conclusion in 2019. 'I just said to myself, I have to go to church. I've got a religious sensibility, and I can't really live without this. So, I joined the Quakers and they're very accepting. They have radical Protestant roots. It's the same whether you are saved or not saved, gay or not gay. I go to Mum's church with her at Christmas and Easter, and I send hymns to Anna and we listen to them,' he said. 'First Corinthians says, "Love suffereth long, and is kind." Jesus often spoke of love in the New Testament. He never once mentioned homosexuality. If we were to go by Leviticus then we wouldn't be eating prawns. I've met young gay people in Northern Ireland who have been disowned by their family and have fallen into suicide and addiction. Religion should be about expanding your vision, not constricting it.'

I asked Anna if she agreed with this view of the narrowness of Presbyterianism. 'I'll be honest, I haven't noticed it. I don't dwell on

---

1 'Abomination and the Anti-Paisley Underground', *Dig With It*, November 2019

that,' she said. 'You know, I didn't know about Anton until today. I'm from another generation. But just because of how I was brought up, I couldn't say, 'No, I don't like Anton now, I don't want him.' And no matter what, if he does something wrong, I would still, and maybe I'm wrong, I would have to still stand by him.' Anton smiled. 'There's fierce love between me and my family,' he said. 'And even if she doesn't agree with certain things, I know that my aunt is a good Christian. So, you know, each to their own at the end of the day. Who am I to judge?'

Anna nodded. 'Everybody's life's their own, whatever they want to do,' she said. 'And I do think it's wrong for the church to get involved in things like that. You go to church to hear the Word of God, not to be judged. There's so few people wanting to go to church now. Used to be you could hardly get a seat. Now in our church it would be down to maybe forty people and it is an ageing congregation. My husband says it is the same in the chapel. The young ones all go off to university and don't come back.'

Anton asked his aunt what she remembered about Sam-MaryAnn. She inclined to the view that wearing women's clothing was just a habit established in childhood. 'She's dead and buried in the parish church, the Church of Ireland, and Mummy's cousins, that she worked to, erected a headstone for her,' she said. 'But they never said MaryAnn, or Sam. They just put her surname on the headstone, and the date of her death.' 'She was buried in a suit, a man's suit,' Anton said.

Anna did not regret signing the petition against Paisley Jnr, but said she did not expect to take up voting. 'I just did it because Anton asked me and I didn't have any love for Ian Paisley because I don't like people doing things that're not right. I didn't like his father either. Somebody told me that Ian Paisley the father was a great man, could get you this, that, and another thing. I just thought, aye, well, I'll form my own opinion here. I mean, everybody said that about Martin McGuinness too when he died. Martin McGuinness was a bad, bad rascal in my estimation. He was an IRA man. I wouldn't like a united Ireland. Don't ask me for why. It's only listening to people, I think, that does know about it. I don't get involved in anything like that. If somebody starts talking about that, I just say, leave me out please.'

It was time to go. Anna had to check on her cattle on the mountain, and Anton and I had arranged to go and visit the Reverend Godfrey

Brown, whose sermons had impressed him as a boy. Anton turned to his aunt. 'Thank you very much. That was a shock for you. I didn't expect such generosity from you,' he said. 'We're good friends, anyway.' Anna looked at him and laughed. 'You say that! Ha!' she replied.

'LIVING IN TWO DIFFERENT WORLDS'

Fired up by his aunt's encouraging words, Anton had new expectations of our meeting with Reverend Brown, who is retired from ministry. We visited him at his home in Ballycastle in an avenue of bungalows with views out over the sea. His wife Margaret served tea in china cups and a stand of fine cakes she had baked herself. Anton enthused and was promised recipes. I told Brown that I had written about his brother, Lindsay, in my book *Northern Protestants: An Unsettled People*. Lindsay Brown had sexually abused boys when he was vice-principal, head of religion, and head of child protection, at Bangor Grammar School, and had been the subject of a damning report in 1998.[2] His brother sighed and said he would not comment.

'We had a very good history in Ballycastle of living well together,' he said. There had been incidents, like the bombing of the Catholic church, and several murders, after which clergy went on television to show solidarity, or held open-air cross-community services. 'It brought us together rather than drove us apart,' he said. There were places where even gestures towards unity had not been tolerated. In 1985, the Reverend David Armstrong had been driven out of his role as a Presbyterian minister in the County Derry town of Limavady after he went to the local Catholic church to exchange Christmas greetings with the priest.

Godfrey Brown was appointed Moderator of the Presbyterian Church in 1988. 'I was only fifty-two,' he said. 'People forget about a behind-the-scenes quasi political role the church has endeavoured to exercise. It involved us in drawing up careful statements for the guidance of politicians, representing the feelings of Protestant people.' He was one of the church men who took part in talks with the IRA and with loyalists in the 1990s, and during the aggressive Harryville picket of a Ballymena Catholic church by loyalists from 1996 to 1998 he was one

---

2 Susan McKay, *Northern Protestants: An Unsettled People (3rd edition)*, Blackstaff Press, 2021, pp. 45–47

of those who symbolically helped to scrub out sectarian graffiti.

Brown felt the church was getting more detached from public issues. I asked him about the efforts made to influence Northern Ireland politicians to oppose same-sex marriage and abortion. He said the church had clear teaching on both issues 'and we are entitled to hold our views'. He was militant in his opposition to abortion. 'Just because a girl doesn't want to have a baby is not really, I think, a good enough reason for destroying a human life,' he said.

In 2018 the Presbyterian General Assembly in Belfast had agreed that same-sex couples could not take communion and that their children could not be baptised. 'We need to be compassionate but also clear as to what the scriptures teach about human sexuality,' Brown said. Anton intervened. 'Can I just say one thing?' he said. He reminded Brown that he had written to him, enclosing a copy of Marilynne Robinson's novel, *Gilead*.[3] Brown said he was reading it. Anton sat forward until he was perched on the edge of the sofa. 'It's just, you are talking about the importance of communicating with people, and what I wanted to put in that letter, but was too terrified, was that I am in a relationship with a man at the minute.'

Brown looked uncomfortable. 'Yes, yes,' he said. 'It's been a big struggle for me,' Anton went on. 'But that book was so important to me, just to bring me back to the central tenets of faith and religion. Because I think it's terribly easy to be caught up in literalism.' He told Brown it was a 'great shame' that the church had narrowed itself into taking rigid positions. He spoke of his granny's 'natural Presbyterianism' and Robinson's generous interpretation of Calvinism. Then he read a lengthy passage from Calvin about looking upon the image of God in everyone. 'The church has a discipline of its own and there are certain things required of those who want to take upon them the full communicant membership,' Brown said. 'It's a case of people living in two different worlds very often.'

'TAKING THE BISCUIT'

That evening, Anton and I called into one of Ballycastle's lovely old pubs: firelight, wood panelling, a collection of clocks, embossed mirrors. We chose a snug with its own hatch to the bar and the whiskey we ordered

---

3 Marilynne Robinson, *Gilead*, Virago, 2005

glowed by the light of the candle on the table. Anton called David and told him excitedly what Anna had said. I could tell that David was sceptical. He had not felt particularly comfortable in Protestant Northern Ireland, Anton said. They had undertaken a border cycle tour in the summer of 2018 and had written about it in an essay for the *Irish Times*.

They had met a young Orangeman in a bar who terrified them with what Anton called his 'cognitive dissonance'. At first aggressive, after quite a few drinks, he had told them what they could already tell, that he was gay. 'He lived in rural Northern Ireland but he would go away to London for weekends to sleep with people and embrace his physicality. Then he'd come home to this pretend life, which led him to fear everybody because they might suspect he was gay. He implied he had threatened to push someone over a cliff once. He had a different voice and composure and everything. And just the most horrendous political views. He was saying dreadful things about Muslims, as if Northern Ireland was inundated with immigrants. I honestly think it's to do with what the Troubles did to society here.'

On their first night, they'd stayed in a Protestant village in south Armagh and gone to the pub. It was the beginning of July and many of the men in the pub had been at 'mini Twelfth' parades, which commemorate the 1916 Battle of the Somme. 'They put on "Take me to a gay bar, gay bar" when David and I walked into the room,' said Anton. 'All these people with shaved heads. David was scared. I wasn't. I know these people are oppressed by things they can't talk about, and they have all this political indoctrination that I got when I was briefly involved with the DUP. Their hostility to us was just a mask for a general anxiety about everything.'

Finally, Anton had spoken about his granda's Orange sash, letting the men know he was a Protestant, and the conversation changed. 'There was so much stammering and they couldn't find the words, but after a while, some of them let us see the humanity in them. One man was describing bathing his child, with his hands in front of him showing us how he lifted the child into the water. And I said, so, what do you think about gay people? And he sort of hummed and hawed and he said, "Well, I wouldn't like it if my son or daughter was like that." Still. I saw that they were not as intransigent as their politicians make out. They were moveable.'

Anton told me he identified with a phrase I'd used in *Northern Protestants*. I'd referred to 'the people I uneasily call my own'. But he was conflicted. 'I feel like my whole inner world is sort of in total chaos the whole time. Even my accent is fluid.' A man who was well on the way to being drunk swayed past the open door of the snug clutching an unlit cigarette in his cupped hand. He nodded in at us. 'Evening girls,' he said. Anton threw his head back, swishing his ponytail, and laughed. 'Oh that just takes the biscuit,' he said.

BALLYMENA

On a Tuesday evening in October 2020, deep in pandemic times, masked shoppers hurried around the aisles of the Tesco store in Ballymena. A young man sneaked into the office where the tannoy system for advising customers about special offers and lost children was kept. He leaned into the microphone. Shoppers raised their heads to a shout of: 'Fuck the Pope', before he was escorted out by staff members.

There is nothing like a local newspaper to give you the sense of a place. The *Ballymena Guardian* was obliquely referred to in the House of Commons when, in February 2021, Ian Paisley Jnr, the North Antrim MP, put it to Michael Gove that the cabinet minister had previously 'boasted' in Paisley's local paper that he could 'sing "The Sash"'. Paisley went on to implore him to scrap the Northern Ireland protocol to the Brexit deal. Gove heard out this appeal for a stake in Brexit's sunny uplands, then confirmed suavely that, yes, 'The Sash' was in his repertoire but so were 'The Fields of Athenry' and 'Flower of Scotland'. Paisley's face registered the snub – this was just one of those things the minister did to please the natives.

Though Paisley did not mention it, the *Ballymena Guardian* had also covered the saga of the dinner that had brought Gove to Ballymena in September 2017. Paisley had invited him as guest speaker, but Gove had later apologised for attending, claiming that he had not known it was a fundraiser for the MP. Paisley had been fined for accepting money from two local councils, and they were also reprimanded.

The week after his comments on Gove's singing repertoire, Paisley was photographed in the *Ballymena Guardian* agreeing that potholed local roads were in a 'lamentable' state. The lead story was about a consultant surgeon at Antrim hospital warning that elective surgery even for cancer had been stood down because staff had been redeployed to deal with COVID cases. The 'tiny' intensive care unit had been overwhelmed. The surgeon said the situation was a result of decades of underinvestment in the hospital. Antrim hospital had featured in shocking reports on the national news when more than a dozen ambulances were queued up outside it and patients who had COVID had to be treated inside them because there were no beds available.

The paper also carried a photo of a smiling young local man now living in London where he was part of a team that had invented a glove that uses artificial intelligence to boost muscle grip. There was a report on a man who knocked someone off their bicycle and then got out of their car to attack him. The judge said he could not tell if this was 'some grudge or vengeance or just general badness'. Another man had been arrested in possession of an offensive weapon, 'namely a Fanta can'. A twenty-two-year-old man with over one hundred criminal offences behind him had self-harmed before entering his ex-partner's home where he placed a photo of the two of them and stole her phone. A restraining order was put in place.

A helpline for children was reported to have seen a 66 per cent rise in calls since the start of the pandemic, many of them about parents who were drinking too much. There were features on sheep and calves with photos of fine beasts reared on some of the best land in the country. A doctor from the town now living in Canada urged the DUP to change its mind about opposing a visit to Northern Ireland by President Biden. He warned that while republicans and nationalists were seen in the US and elsewhere as sympathetic, 'we are all seen as followers influenced by bigotry and hatred.' Another letter writer praised Jo Bamford, the new owner of Wrightbus, for pioneering the development of hydrogen-powered buses. There were ads for drive-in gospel services, careworkers (£9.20 per hour), tractors and shih-tzu pups.

'WHAT COUNTRY AM I REALLY IN HERE?'

'The first Executive opened in 2000 but it was stop–go and then after 2002 the complete hiatus,' said Esmond Birnie. The Executive broke down in 2002 and was not restored for five years. 'And then, unfortunately, I lost my seat in March 2007.' Now an economics lecturer at Ulster University, from 1998 to 2007 he was an Ulster Unionist MLA.

In 2007, in the election that followed the St Andrews Agreement, the DUP finally achieved its goal of eclipsing the UUP, and the Reverend Ian Paisley became First Minister.

'My dad's from Scotland and my mum is from Belfast. I predominantly identify as Northern Irish, but I have a strong sense of Scottish connection. Most of my childhood was spent in Ballymena. In 2008 my wife and I left the Presbyterian Church in Ireland and joined the Evangelical Presbyterian Church. We had certain disagreements about leadership style and worship style. I suppose putting it in crude terms we are more conservative evangelical in theological terms.' I asked him if they were 'born-again' Christians. 'To call our church "born again" is appropriate as this is a biblical term, if you read John 3,' he said. 'The other way of putting it would be that it is more explicitly confessional, meaning you have an actual statement of doctrine and you adhere to it strictly. Most people, when they look at the Westminster Confession of Faith of 1647, never really get into what it says about the Antichrist and the Pope and all that. We have a tighter commitment. Take this dispute about the Presbyterian Church's attitude to the gay issue. People seem not to accept that organisations have standards and if you join, you sign up to them.

'The DUP should have been firmer in asserting that abortion was a red line issue for them. They should have made more of a storm about it,' he said. Perhaps one reason it didn't was that the party recognised that its position no longer fully represented the views of the people. In 2018 a poll by Amnesty International NI found that 67 per cent of DUP voters surveyed believed that having an abortion should not be a crime.[4] 'I am opposed to it in all circumstances except for the vanishingly small proportion where there is a real threat to the life of the mother,' said Birnie. 'I don't find the sexual crime argument convincing. I am disturbed by so-called gay marriage because I feel what we're embarking on is a social experiment here, the full consequences of which we will only see over a very long period of time. I don't think it was necessary because the various financial and other protections were already there, and civil partnerships,' he said.

Birnie initially joined the Conservative Party but became frustrated

---

4 https://www.amnesty.org.uk/press-releases/northern-ireland-abortion-75-uk-public-want-government-change-law-new-polls

by the absence of equal representation for Northern Ireland voters, and joined the UUP in 1996. He had supported the Good Friday Agreement but 'with hindsight' said he should have seen the 'structural weaknesses' that had emerged. I asked him why the UUP had been so decisively overtaken by the DUP in the years that followed. 'The UUP was deeply divided, and the slowness with which the IRA decommissioned was pretty decisive,' he said. 'I suspect the IRA/Sinn Féin made a judgement call that they weren't going to deliver for the Ulster Unionists, but they would eventually deliver for the DUP. By the time they did it, the DUP had wrecked us. With hindsight, again, we and indeed the SDLP together should have made much, much more effort to work together. But we are where we are.

'After 2007 I worked as a special adviser to Reg Empey, the Minister for Employment and Learning. That was a very enjoyable experience. It was the time of the economic recession so there was a lot of pressure. It was very interesting. But it rapidly became clear that whilst on paper it was a four-party coalition, and later on became five parties when the Alliance took on the Department of Justice, it was really being driven by the DUP and Sinn Féin. I can remember in terms of priority Executive meetings, you'd obviously like to be prepared, but the paperwork would arrive fifteen minutes before the meeting. The extent of real input we had to policymaking was quite limited.

'It was very much a cabal. There was a certain amount a minister could do within his own fiefdom or silo but it was just so fragmented and disjointed. You could see that in the long run this form of government wasn't going to work well, and already wasn't working well. Maybe the surprising thing is that it was able to continue for ten years.' The complaint of exclusion by the DUP and Sinn Féin was one the other parties were still making in 2020. 'I left in 2010 when I got an offer from PricewaterhouseCoopers and I stayed there six years before returning to academia.

'There are some very good things happening in the Northern Ireland economy. Since 2012, employment growth has been very substantial. We are doing well in terms of inward investment. We have back-office financial institutions and IT-related companies, many of them American, coming here. That's the good side, the glass-half-full side, but there's also the half-empty side. Maybe it's a temperamental thing. Maybe, dare I say it, I do sometimes wonder whether there's almost like a theological thing to this. I do believe in original sin. You find this in politics and you find it in economics. You devise a response to a problem, but it opens up another problem.

'The classic example is RHI. Its intention was excellent, but because of the way people responded to the incentives we got a hideous outcome. We ended up burning more carbon and with all sorts of weird and wonderful scams. This actually happens quite a lot. We need to have governments, we need to have appropriate economic and social policies, but it's like the dyke is leaking – you put your finger in one place, the water stops coming out there, but then it comes out somewhere else. It is ultimately metaphysics or theology, whatever you want to call it. There's something inherent in the human condition. Human beings don't have perfect foresight about the future. Our motivations, I think, are always mixed.

'Governments can't produce heaven on earth. Sometimes they produce hell on earth. The best you can hope from good, wise policy is that we manage humanity's capacity to be self-destructive, greedy, and abusive. So you know, there's a lot to be grateful for. We're sitting here in a warm building in Northern Ireland, notwithstanding poverty issues around income distribution.' We were sitting in the coffee lounge of one of Belfast's most expensive hotels. 'By and large, we don't have problems of malnutrition. Compared to most of Africa our infrastructure is still very good. I'm often advised, accentuate the positive, tell people about how good things are, and then slip in "but there are a few challenges". Well, I'm not convinced that works. And then it's back, again, to my gloomy view of human nature. I think people just bank the praise and say, well, if we're not doing too badly, we don't need to change.

'What we've had in Northern Ireland is soft budget constraints. Our public, and to some extent our private sector, can make mistakes, but that gets underwritten by the Treasury in London. Over time people begin to get used to it. And that produces what game theorists call moral hazard, whereby if you reward irresponsibility, you encourage more of it in the future. We see it in the Coghlin report into RHI. Those expressions of it's free money, the Treasury will bail us out, fill your boots. Our dependency rate is around about 30 per cent compared to a UK average of less than 20 per cent. Now, it's also high in Scotland and Wales. Some of it is a product of Northern Ireland having a more peripheral, structurally disadvantaged economy, but it is nonetheless a sign of weakness.

'The German sociologist Max Weber wrote about Protestantism and the spirit of capitalism, and a particular outlook in life that encourages people to save their money and have a strong work ethic, and we've got this historical self-image that the industrialisation of Belfast, the Lagan Valley, the shipyards, the ropeworks, the textile mills was all driven by that. The economic history is probably more complex. A lot of the business was developed by people from the outside coming in to Northern Ireland.

'Anyway, something seems to have happened. Something seems to have flipped. You go back to, for example, the Presbyterian Mutual Society (PMS) at the time of the financial crash. That was linked, not to the Paisleyite side of Protestantism, but to the mainstream Presbyterian Church. It would have been fair enough if it had stuck to its remit, but it was acting as a high-risk bank and then it had to be bailed out by the taxpayer. That squares very badly with this sort of attitude of thrift and self-reliance and responsibility.' The PMS had engaged in property speculation. After its collapse in 2008, Stormont extended a £25m no-interest loan alongside other supports. Ten years later, the Department for the Economy wrote off the loan, admitting it was 'unlikely to be recovered'.

Birnie listed a 'whole host of other issues' – the scandal around the Irish Republic's National Asset Management Agency (NAMA); the Red Sky debacle; and the Social Investment Fund, which had been set up in 2011 by the Executive as an anti-poverty initiative but had soon became mired in controversy over a lack of transparency about how grants were awarded, including to groups led by individuals associated with loyalist paramilitaries. And then, said Birnie, there was RHI, 'the poster boy of scandals'.

There was also incompetence. 'We've got to be more efficient. We've got a very low productivity economy and I think there's a tie-in between that and the moral hazard, dependence on the bail out and sort of a predominance of short-term thinking,' he said.

Birnie supported Brexit, even though it had 'complicated' relationships 'both North–South and east–west' and might disrupt the economy in a 'comparatively small' way. 'What concerns me about the European Union is the tendency towards excessive centralisation,' he said. 'And some of the most extraordinarily wasteful policies in modern economic history are firstly, the common agricultural policy, and secondly, the creation of the Euro single currency. I am concerned about the customs checks in the Irish Sea and the business consequences of that. There's obviously a wider political perceptions issue – will unionists start to panic now? If you're watching the lorries being inspected, you might think to yourself, what country am I really in here?'

He is not in any party now. 'On some issues, I'm now far too conservative for the Ulster Unionist Party; on some issues, I'm far too liberal for the DUP. A good person from an Ulster background, C.S. Lewis, said he was a Christian realist, by which he meant, people often are over-optimistic about what can be achieved in terms of politics, economics, or even science and education. All these things can be blessings to people in the very long run. I do believe human history has a direction in terms of the purposes of God.'

'THINE EYE DIFFUSED A QUICKENING RAY'

'If you ever find yourself in Ballymena, get yourself out of it as fast as you can,' said Jan Carson, who sometimes plays her background for laughs. She was speaking on that occasion at the Galway Arts Festival. Another time I heard her, with consummate comic timing, tell an audience that her uncle had been despatched by his church to be a missionary: 'To Cavan.' Just south of the border, Cavan is a two-hour drive from Ballymena. But she is also very loyal to the people among whom she grew up, and, as a writer, she is grateful for the language a childhood steeped in Bible studies gave her. Her novel, *The Fire Starters*, won the European Union Prize for Literature in 2019.[5] Set in east Belfast during the frenetic period leading up to the Twelfth of July, all of its love stories are mutilated by fear. A damaged boy with 'eyes as cold as marbles' is set on unleashing apocalypse, while his father, a former paramilitary, worries about how to tell him that 'violence is a passed down thing, like heart disease or cancer'. A few streets away, but separated by cultural continents, another father contemplates cutting out

5 Jan Carson, *The Fire Starters*, Transworld, 2019

his daughter's tongue because her mother is a siren. 'I am the opposite of literalness,' Carson told me.

'How you learn to understand story follows you through as a writer,' she said. 'My first experiences were biblical, so those kind of allegorical, almost parable kind of story structures sit well with me. But also the kind of bloody violence. My very first memory of big church, which you went to from whenever you were seven, was my minister starting on a two-year sermon on the Book of Revelation. So I got forty-five minutes of Revelation every Sunday for two years. And I always say, look, you're going to end up with a magic realist if you do that. The Bible is thick with metaphors too, and I am very comfortable with those.'

She has also read Gabriel García Márquez, and has spoken of how working with people with dementia (she is part of a research project at Queen's University) has influenced her with their use of sometimes 'odd and wonderful metaphors'. She does a lot of community writing workshops, including one with women who have been subjected to domestic violence, and one in the Royal Victoria Hospital. During lockdown in the summer of 2020, she wrote a series of her 'postcard stories' for isolated older people, and got children to illustrate them. She writes, like a Parisian, in cafés on the Newtownards Road in Belfast.

'Ballymena back in the eighties was a bastion of Protestant culture. Most of our family on my mother's side are Brethren. My dad was an elder in a rural Presbyterian church. We would have gone down to the South in the summer to help out with evangelical campaigns,' she said. 'There was extremely conservative thinking. There wouldn't have been alcohol in the house, and definitely no women in the pulpits. We didn't have drums. There was no line dancing in the church hall. We didn't have friends outside of the church. We had friends that we ran about with in the neighbourhood, but we were always trying to invite them to children's missions. Your whole social calendar was around the church. I was at children's meetings maybe four nights out of seven. The whole of Sunday was church: we went five times for different services and meetings. I'm the proud owner of a fourteen-years-unbroken-attendance certificate. What you get for that in the Presbyterian Church is a giant Bible.

'I went to a Protestant girls' grammar school where a lot of the girls would have been brought up the same way as me. We didn't have to interact with the rest of the world. A lot of parts of my childhood were blissful and really wonderful and I'm very thankful. To feel so known, so loved, so safe, that's a really nurturing thing. It's just that when you start to ask questions the problems begin to come in. There was a tightness to the kind of Presbyterian culture that I grew up with, and I think it's rooted in a real fear of losing control that is not just a spiritual or emotional thing, it's also a physical thing. Since leaving the Presbyterian Church I've attended a charismatic church, and charismatic worship is frowned upon as well, because it's another way of letting your body lose control, in that you would speak in tongues or clap or dance.

'I found myself incapable of loosening the tightness. I still have the fear of the body. I really can't dance. The body is seen as sinful. I love the word "mortified" because in Northern Irish culture it means embarrassed, but includes also the mortification of the flesh that you get in theology. The two things here are linked. There were things that we didn't speak about: illnesses, definitely things to do with sexuality. I remember the minister going through the biblical passage on circumcision and every time he said the word circumcision, he would slam his hand down like a guillotine blade on the pulpit. There is a huge thing within the heart of Protestant evangelicalism in Northern Ireland that is tied up in shame. A lot of people I meet, I feel like they're crippled by it. They can't crawl out from under things that were said over them as children.'

In *The Fire Starters* there are children who are hidden away by their parents and only spoken about in the privacy of a support group. These children include one with wings on her shoulder blades, another who has wheels instead of feet. 'The "unfortunate children" are my attempt to write about my generation, the post-Good Friday Agreement generation, who want to escape their family traditions but are held back, made to feel guilty,' she said. However, there are also those in the novel who are determined to hold on to those traditions, who 'talk of the loud violence their parents knew, as if it is a kind of birthright denied to them'.

There is a tension within Carson between her rejection of the harshness that was instilled in her, and her attraction to its expression in language. 'I love the phrase, "Och, you're powerful good to yourself",' she said. 'If you have an extra bun or an extra half-hour in bed. The implication is that it's wrong to be good to yourself, that you should mortify the flesh and do what you don't want to do. Not only is that a horrible thing to live by but it's inherently unbiblical. There's so many passages in the Bible about people enjoying food, enjoying wine, enjoying company, laughing. It's that dourness I also have always struggled against. Dour even in terms of how we worship, how people dress. I have always been quite a flamboyant, colourful dresser. You're not supposed to draw attention to yourself too much.' At one stage she was wearing one yellow Doc Marten boot, and one red. 'I stuck out,' she said.

'By the time I was fifteen I was passionate about music and literature. There was no encouragement. In fact, I heard it preached from the pulpit several times that it was sinful. I remember sitting through a fantastic sermon on how theatre was wrong. I'm not an idiot – I've read the Bible from cover to cover, and I know it's full of creativity. I think a lot of ministers haven't read the Bible. They just use little extracts taken out of context.

'The community I grew up in had a lot of fear of Catholicism. The biggest thing we were taught about Catholics was that they couldn't have a direct relationship with God, it had to be done through a priest. The thing is, a lot of Presbyterian culture, not doctrine, is very similar. A man in a pulpit tells you what you think about everything. It took me about thirty years to work that out. I've heard people say, if you ask them, what do you think about this? "Oh, I don't know. I'd have to ask my minister about that." I harp on and on and on about why we need integrated education to break down these misunderstandings that get handed down.

'Jesus understood the emotional grip on your soul of telling a story. Yet most of what I grew up under in terms of teaching was prescriptive. The three-point sermon. Here are three things that you should do. I really love Jewish theology because so much of it has story at its core. I like a story that invites engagement – to be told what to do, for me, that's the end of the relationship. When you tell a story and you leave it open to interpretation, it's inviting you as the listener to have an active engagement with it and there's something much more appealing about that. The other thing is I love mystery. The abstract idea of God has always been the part that attracts me.

'I grew up under a pulpit with a burning bush on it that said "*Ardens sed virens*", which is the Presbyterian motto and means burning but not consumed. What an amazing piece of language. It's just beautiful. And then to have that reduced, explained. It kind of made it small. I'm interested in an inscrutable God. That's how the church has failed artists over and over again, because it is not about the unknown and it should be. Instead the model of church is corporate worship, for we all sing the same thing at the same time. Artists want to play and think and work outside the box.

'I have a clear memory of coming into P5 and putting my hand up and asking the teacher what "thine eye diffused a quickening ray" meant. Which I think is the most beautiful piece of language. I'd heard it in a hymn the Sunday before. I still belong to a church. I go to Redeemer Central. It is non-denominational, pretty liberal. I have friends who go there who are from a Catholic background. It's very relaxing. I just go once a week. More and more for me it is that engagement with the mysterious that I want. I think around faith and religion, Northern Ireland desperately needs some new language.

'To be really honest, in the background I come from, we wouldn't have thought any less of Catholics than we did of generally unsaved people. They were people that were out there in order for us to bring them around to our way of thinking. There's such a huge tradition in Protestant culture of sending white Northern Irish people off to underdeveloped countries to tell them how to think and change. There's never been like, why don't we go over to Kenya and learn how community happens over there? Because maybe they're not as screwed up as we are in Northern Ireland and we could learn something.

'I left Northern Ireland to move to the States when I was twenty-five and part of it was this deep frustration with Protestant culture. I had issues with the nationalist side of things as well, but Protestantism was supposedly being done in my name. When I came back I moved into the East partly because it was the heartland of Protestant culture and I needed to come to terms with that.' East Belfast is known glamorously to those who live there simply as 'the East'. 'It has forced me to take a long, hard look at some of the things that are contentious. Like why are parades so important? Why are flags so important? Why are bonfires so important? Two years ago I took a German film crew around on the

Twelfth. I hadn't been since I was about six. And I was like, why have I not done this? Am I afraid of it? And I came away going, it's probably not for me, but I've met some lovely people for whom this is a huge part of their cultural tradition. They're celebrating it in a respectful, family kind of way. It was good for me to challenge preconceptions I have about my own cultural identity.

'A lot of us, people my age here, went through a period of wanting to become completely homogeneous. You go to university. You meet your first Catholics. They're quite like you, and then you want to become a kind of beige Northern Irish person. I'm now starting to find that there are parts of my background and my culture I'm really proud of, and I also want to understand the parts of my culture that I'm not so proud of because there must be a reason why people get that het up and angry over things. I need to listen more.

'If you sat under preaching like Paisley's, there's no room for discourse. It's rhetoric, it's loud, it's in your face. It's designed to not leave room for thought. There's an infantilising kind of element to it. But then you look at religious traditions like Quakerism, and they are comfortable with silence and open-endedness. And then if you look at street preachers, you have to realise that a lot of them fervently believe that folks are going to hell. So of course they're going to get out with a megaphone and shout at their neighbours. Some of it comes from a misguided place of trying to help.

'My new novel is about evangelical Protestantism in the nineties in rural Northern Ireland, which with that theme is no doubt going to be a huge bestseller! I don't think there has been enough of it addressed in fiction. I don't want to destroy things. I still have a great love for that community and a respect for it. I don't want to lambast people, but I would love to start a respectful dialogue about how we can maybe become less intolerant, less tight. For me, unleashing imagination is an act of protest. Just giving people stories that invite them in is actually an act of rebellion.'

'NORTHERN IRELAND COULD HAVE BEEN MONACO'

Confident and smiling, Pamela Dennison strode about the offices and factory floor of her family business on the outskirts of Antrim. She showed me a model of one of her grandfather's inventions – a shaft that harnessed the power of a tractor to other machinery – and chatted to men in boiler suits loading boxes on to forklift trucks. She took a call from a daughter seeking reassurance on some teenage drama. It came as no surprise to learn that although her role is development manager, Dennison can, and sometimes does, drive one of the huge trucks that each day transport furniture throughout Ireland, the UK and the EU.

'We grew up with a strong work ethic and what you learn from growing up you never lose,' she said. 'It's a family dynamic across three generations. My kids are heavily involved as well and I was out with my niece yesterday, and she's three, and she was able to grape [fork] the silage up to the cows with no fear. They're big animals and they're just calved and they're very temperamental, but she was just straight in there and enjoying it.

'My grandfather and his brother set up a heavy-goods vehicle business, and my father set up this company in 1979. My grandfather taught my father that you take a man as he comes, as long as he has a good work ethic and does what he is told. Dad would take on guys in here that would have pasts, the whole shebang: prison, drugs, alcohol, everything. We were taught, don't ask somebody to do something you can't do yourself. I've done every job in this business, and I get respect from the drivers because they know if we're stuck I can jump on a lorry. When the borders really opened in terms of immigration and the Polish influx started, a carload of five of them arrived here and not one of them spoke English. My grandmother put them up free of charge in her bed and breakfast. We got all of them jobs in here. Not all of them lasted, but Adrian did. He's been with us for twelve years now. We know his kids, and his family. He's phenomenal. His brothers have worked with us, his cousins have worked with us, and we classify them as friends. No matter where you go with a Dennison there is some connection to transport logistics, so I suppose it's in your blood. It's become a passion of mine.

'I'm the eldest of four children. My mum worked part time and raised us single-handedly, because my father was always out working. That's what it took. We got to drive tractors in the fields, rear lambs, play in the snow. We ran in and out of each other's houses. Mind you, at one stage there were three children under the age of five in our house. Now, if I ask my thirteen-year-old to empty the dishwasher, it's a row as big as a house, but in my childhood you just had to muck in and do as you were told. When my grandfather died, my grandmother took over the farm and ran a bed and breakfast as well. She helped raise me and we have a very, very close bond. She's eighty-nine, non-verbal and still fiercely independent.' (Margaret Dennison died in 2020.)

'She was of Brethren descent, married into Presbyterianism. My mother was of Brethren descent and married a Presbyterian. We were made to go to church every Sunday, Girls' Brigade, Sunday School. When I was thirteen I rebelled, 100 per cent completely rebelled. Anything I wasn't allowed to do, I would be doing. I couldn't accept being dictated to about belief. As you go through secondary school you meet people from different backgrounds, and your mind becomes open to a whole lot more. There is a conflict between what the Bible teaches and how the church tells you to behave. The church has a lot to answer for in the turmoil of Northern Ireland – it has a closed mind and it has failed to welcome an open-minded society. How you choose to love God is up to you. It's not determined by a church.'

Dennison believed the churches were to blame for their decline. 'When I was twenty-one my eldest child was born out of wedlock and I met an aunt in Ballymena and she said, "Are you getting her baptised?" And I said, no, because it wasn't my belief, and her response was, "Well, good because I don't know a minister that would baptise her anyway." And this is meant to be a Christian lady. First of all, that child has done nothing and is born into love. I've been with her dad since we were eighteen. We're married ten years next month. So I was hurt. Then my sister went to get married in the church we grew up in to a man of non-Christian faith and the minister refused to do it. That really got me. The church is losing members hand over fist, and no wonder. I think religion can be dangerous, very dangerous. I'm not anti-Protestant. I'm just anti-religion.'

She cautioned that polls showing that views on social issues within the DUP were changing did not take account of rural conservatism. 'The majority of DUP voters are Protestants with strong religious beliefs. The party couldn't be seen to bow down to abortion and same-sex marriage so they quite happily stood back and let Westminster change the law because that allowed them not to be answerable to their electorate,' she said. In 2019, British Labour MP Stella Creasy steered an amendment to the Northern Ireland (Executive Formation) Bill through parliament, legalising abortion. This followed campaigns and court cases brought by Northern Ireland activists, and a UN ruling that the UK was breaching its human rights responsibilities. 'There might be grey areas for urban Protestants, but in rural areas it is very much, you cannot do this, you must do that,' said Dennison. 'That is how they were reared, and a lot of people can't see past the end of their own lanes. They haven't opened their minds to other cultures and ideas. Our children go to heavily Protestant schools but they have cousins who are Catholics, and we support the local Gaelic Athletic Club and the girls' team. I'd like to think that they take it as it comes.'

Dennison's firm has extended into the Republic of Ireland for logistical reasons. 'Our head office is here in Antrim and we have a secondary depot in Limerick. It's been very successful for us, especially now regarding Brexit. We use all the ports in Ireland, mainly Dublin, Larne, Belfast, Warrenpoint. I'm the national officer for the Chartered Institute of Logistics and Transport and I'm chair of the Freight Transport Association Ireland. We are the unsung heroes of the economy. And the 'B' word has given us the platform that we've needed.'

Haulage was about to become far more complex and potentially costly. 'At the minute we can move cleanly, clearly, and officially through UK and Ireland. That will come to an end. From my understanding, because it's not clear how the border down the Irish Sea will work, there will be customs-entry requirements. So that's a document with thirty-one different boxes to be completed and a safety and security declaration, which is a thirty-one-page document just to move the goods.' There was a lot of misunderstanding, she felt. 'It is not the hauliers' responsibility to complete import and export forms, but every Joe Bloggs, including some of the biggest manufacturers, think it is. But if you have failed to complete those documents, it will be my driver that will be held. So I will be passing my costs directly on to you. People have no idea of the financial costs that are coming their way.

'The supply chain is seamless now but that's all going to change. There are so many questions about duty to be paid and claimed back, and extra costs. In Northern Ireland you can add an extra 20 per cent compared to what England, Scotland, Wales will have to pay, because they'll just have to pay duty once. It will have to be up to the end receiver to prove that those goods didn't go on into the Republic of Ireland. Then there are fines to be considered, bottlenecks at ports, facilities on boats, perishable goods, and business isn't built on risk – business is built on clarity and assurance and five- and ten-year plans. We can't even work to the end of this year because we don't know.'

Given all of this, I was startled to hear Dennison had voted for and continued to support Brexit. 'Farming and haulage are two of the most heavily regulated sectors under the EU. This sweeping brush that Europe has, they try to treat the UK like the south of Spain. We can't be expected to spread slurry in the same months that France have thirty-degree heatwaves. We're getting sideways rain. There's road transport regulations where France interprets it differently than the UK, and the UK interprets it differently than Ireland. We pay higher fuel duty than anywhere else in the rest of the UK. It's not a level playing field – but that's what Europe is meant to be. And it's not about immigration. It's about what I have to go through just to pay the bills at the end of the month.

'Without a shadow of a doubt Brexit is the right move. It's the British government's failure and, to an extent, the Irish government's, because they have as much to lose as we do, to create a clear and defined path, that is the problem,' she said. 'The only people shouting about the Northern Ireland border were the people in Northern Ireland on the border counties. There was a failure to prepare, and then it was just the perfect storm. Everything went wrong. The politicians here were disastrous. Northern Ireland could have been a Monaco. Theresa May's document offered us "unfettered access". Businesses would have flocked to us, finance, transport, warehousing, IT … '

Full of hubris after the coalition-ending Tory landslide of 2015, Theresa May called a snap election in 2017. It was a disaster for her, and she quickly realised that her only chance to hold on to power was to form an alliance with the DUP, which had ten seats. The SDLP and the UUP had no seats, and Sinn Féin does not attend Westminster. It meant that, although a majority in Northern Ireland had voted to remain in the EU, the DUP could align itself with the most extreme Brexiteers in parliament. They proceeded to oppose every version of Brexit that was proposed, most notably the deal Dennison was referring to, which would have seen all of the UK remaining in the EU's single market, with Northern Ireland enjoying access to both EU and UK markets.

'The DUP and Sinn Féin are both to blame for us losing this,' said Dennison. 'The DUP just failed to understand. They didn't understand the critical nature of haulage and transport in Northern Ireland and as an island nation how integral the supply chain is to the economy. They had the ear of the government and they scuppered it. We could have been home and dry. As things stand, we have no money to finish potholes, we have no money for schools and education, no money for the health service.'

She said Northern Irish people did not identify as Europeans. 'I see myself as Northern Irish first and then, well, it depends who's asking. I'm whatever people want me to be when it comes to business. If I was on holiday, I'm Irish, but I have a British passport and an Irish one. I can't say I'm proud to be British because I'm not. I'm not 100 per cent Irish either,' she said. She and her colleagues had been discussing Irish unity. 'We think if a united Ireland was on the cards, every country in the world would bag us with financial packages. There would be billions from America, the European Union would pump in billions. We think the Brits would be glad to get rid of us so they would fire billions into it, so absolutely, it could work for Northern Ireland.

'Sinn Féin are playing a clever game, and the DUP have no idea they're being played. Sinn Féin sat back quietly and let the DUP scupper their own regarding Brexit, knowing it puts a united Ireland on the agenda. But it's not just Northern Ireland's question. If the Republic doesn't want us it won't happen. Either way, Northern Ireland hopefully can be a prosperous nation once again, but we have a lot of hurdles to get over before that happens. Let's watch this space.'

When Brexit took effect in 2021, and unionism began to unite in a belligerent fashion around demands to 'scrap the protocol', I was keen to know Dennison's experience of the new situation. She was in a new job, on secondment to the Department for Transport in London. 'It's been tough,' she said. 'COVID hit us hard to begin with – we lost 90 per cent of our business overnight with the first lockdown. But we diversified. We started bringing in PPE [Personal Protection Equipment], COVID tests and hand sanitiser for Antrim Area hospital just down the road from us. So out of something bad came something good. Brexit …' she sighed. 'Well, we had prepared for no deal. And then they didn't finalise the deal till Christmas Eve. We were all working eighteen- to twenty-hour days for four to six weeks. It was very time-consuming and it impacted on our bottom line as a business. We got it hard at first. Mind you it was far harder for the food businesses. We've found a rhythm now. We are getting used to it.'

She was dismayed at the 'scrap the protocol' strategy. 'That would make things ten times worse,' she said. 'It would quadruple the cost of duties and it would plunge us back into uncertainty, which is the opposite of what business needs. There is no getting away from the truth – the DUP made a huge blunder when they rejected Theresa May's deal. We could have been the envy of everyone.'

CHAPTER 3

On the Sea Border

'VERY LOST ...'

Claire McAuley has an anthropological love of drag and a fascination with religion. When she was a child in Larne, she learned how to march in the Girls' Brigade, while at Sunday School she was told that if she was bad the devil would come and cut her into a million pieces. Her Twitter handle declares that she will 'defend Larne to the death'. We arranged to meet in the cafe at the back of the leisure centre. 'It's lovely,' she assured me, and it was. There were reproductions of 1950s tourist posters from all around the Antrim coast on the walls, and floor to ceiling windows that looked straight across the coastal path to the glittering sea and, in the distance, Scotland. The staff were friendly women, the coffee was excellent and there was local ice cream. I was disarmed. 'You see?' said Claire. 'I told you.'

'I'm sick of Larne being the butt of so many jokes – I mean look at Mid Ulster,' she said. 'People from Larne never think they are quite good enough. I see it as an underdog and I like it for that. My brother used to get bullied at school and I stood up for him. It's sort of the same thing. Of course it is embarrassing politically – Sammy Wilson during the Brexit debates shouting and ranting. Just awful. I was born in 1984 so my life has been half in the Troubles, half not. I used to say I was a proud loyalist – now I would say my identity is Northern Irish. I definitely wouldn't say I was British. My dad would be ashamed of me for that. My parents are stuck in their unionist ways. My granda was kidnapped by the IRA and the family holds a grudge. My dad said we had to vote no to the GFA and my mum always agrees with him. They are Brexiteers. The way I look at it, Westminster doesn't want you. Ireland doesn't want you. You've been sold a lie. I feel sorry for them. I think as a people we are very lost about our identity.

'We have a very strong link with Scotland, though. My parents' house has the best view in the world: along the Antrim coast and out across the sea to the Mull of Kintyre. There's an innocent side to Larne – nature, the beach, sitting on the rocks watching the ferries coming and going. One of the first dinosaurs was found here. We used to go fossil hunting on the beach. The first signs of life were found along the coast here – they found old flints. Ulster Scots is a bit of a joke though. I say I'm fluent in it because people can't understand my accent.

'Our house had flags – we went on the marches. As a child it all seemed fine to me but by the time I was fifteen I couldn't stand it. I remember a stabbing on Boyne Square in Larne on the Eleventh Night. It felt like it was very paramilitary-run. Drink and drugs, WKD bottles, all a bit dodgy. I was at a parade in the middle of the day and a man in a kilt flashed at us.

'Larne's prosperity was before partition. It has slowly and steadily declined, though my parents say it was swinging in the sixties. But in my experience it was always like this. There is only one hotel left. Dunnes has just closed. McDonald's couldn't even survive here. There is hardly anything but charity shops. When I was growing up, the cinema closed early. You didn't go out and get drunk like a normal teenager – the pubs were too rough. You learned to drive young in Larne. We used to drive around in cavalcades.' She laughed, 'We grew up rollicking, I tell you!

'I was at school with only Protestants. When I went to Queen's I joined the DUP. I was a stereotypical little unionist. They snared me pretty quickly – they said I could be in charge of entertainment. But we didn't have the same idea of what entertainment was, really. I lasted a month or two. Anyway, I soon found that a lot of my friends were not Protestants.

'Larne just got Pride for the first time ever. I came down for it. My dad wasn't pleased. I can't understand my parents' politics really – they are fine about abortion but they don't like women to be in power. I have a gay relation, but my parents are against LGBT rights. He moved away twenty-five years ago to England. We're not supposed to know he is gay, just that he went to England. Almost all my friends have left. My mum is a home bird and she wants us to come back but we won't. I still go to church with her as a bonding thing when I am here.'

We agreed that Larne's Jubilee Crown is no adornment to the town. The eight metre high, gold-painted crown stands garish in the middle of a roundabout – it looks like it came free with a burger and chips. It was put up without planning permission by the local council to mark the Queen's Diamond Jubilee in 2012. Outside the railway station there is another peculiar structure, a framed tourist guide about the writer Amanda McKittrick Ros, who was from the town, and whose reputation is enjoying a reappraisal by feminist scholars. The script denounces her as pretentious, and ridicules her work, while depicting her wealthy husband as indulgent and long-suffering. When Black Lives Matter protests took place in Northern Ireland in the summer of 2020, the slave-trading background of one of Larne's most prominent benefactors was highlighted by, among others, Amnesty International NI. Charles McGarel lived in Magheramorne House, a mansion outside Larne, and paid for the erection of the town hall and the cemetery. The council rejected calls to drop the McGarel name from its facilities.

'I love Larne and hate it,' said Claire. 'There's the Gobbins coastal path – it was a Victorian tourist spot. There were witches in Islandmagee – my cousin lives in one of the houses they lived in and it's definitely haunted. There's an Asda, a diner, the cinema. And some things have changed for the better. Seacourt estate used to be very rough loyalist place – it now has an integrated school. There are a lot of good people here. Larne Grammar is a very good school. Houses are cheap. It's only half an hour to Belfast.'

I asked Claire what she thought about the DUP's 2015 proposal for a bridge from Larne to Scotland. Boris Johnson had recently claimed he would build it. This was seen by many as a joke at the DUP's expense. Engineers pointed out that the North Channel is around thirteen miles wide, frequently stormy, and deep – up to one thousand feet in places. There is also Beaufort's Dyke, a thirty-mile-long channel into which the British Ministry of Defence dumped at least one million tonnes of weapons, from the 1920s till the 1970s. In

1997 the government admitted that this included up to two tonnes of radioactive waste. Claire shook her head. 'My parents would love it,' she said. But we don't have the infrastructure.' In February 2021, after rejecting the DUP's demand for the Northern Ireland protocol to be scrapped, Johnson tossed out the idea that instead of the bridge he would build a tunnel, the 'Boris burrow' as it was quickly dubbed. This time, the mockery was blatant.

'I kind of like that no one wants to come here,' said Claire. 'The Giant's Causeway and Carrick-a-Rede rope bridge are destroyed by *Game of Thrones* tourism now – I don't think our tourism industry has any notion of sustainability. Sometimes I think, let's make Larne great again! Sometimes I just want it to stay as it is, unpopular, unchanging, a little bubble by the sea.' When lockdown began, the satirical online site, *The Ulster Fry*, adapted historic tourism prints to discourage visitors. I sent Claire the one that said, 'Want to go to Larne for your holidays? Of course you don't.' She sent me two emojis: a Union Jack and a fist.

'A VERY SECTARIAN TOWN'

The living room of Anne's flat has a big bay window that overlooks Larne harbour. There is a hum of port activity: trucks revving on metal ramps, beeping sounds, the occasional shout. 'My children thought I was mad taking this flat but I love it,' she told me. 'The port is busy night and day. I'm used to the noise. I have access to the back garden and I have rabbits and a cat and a dog. People say I should learn to say no to my grandchildren, but I don't think so. Daddy worked in the cement factory, Mum stayed at home. I've lived in Larne most of my life and I married here. I started work in Ballantine's drapery on Main Street and then I worked in Woodside's – they used to have stores in Ballymena, Lisburn and Bangor, now it's just in Larne,' she said.

'Larne used to be brilliant – all go, so busy. Busloads came in from Lisburn and all over the place for a day's shopping and then they'd go for a treat to one of the cafes. By the time I retired the place was dead. The shoe shop closed last weekend. The Laharna Hotel has gone. The King's Arms. The Highways. All of them gone. There's nothing now. It's sad. All the wee pubs have closed too. My husband was a lorry driver. It was a blow when Sealink moved out – it's only P&O now.' In

1995 Sealink announced it was moving its ferry operation to Belfast, a significant economic loss to Larne.

'Mind you it's better now than when there was all the bombing and shooting going on,' said Anne. 'In 1974 we were living in the high flats, and my daughter was a baby in the pram. We were on the fourteenth floor. We had to walk down and back up. That was the loyalist workers strike. When the bomb went off in the Floral Cafe on Main Street we watched it from the working kitchen. We were terrified. I wouldn't go near the flats now – they're eerie. The ones in there now aren't right in the head. They look like zombies – I think they're all on drugs. In those days you got a flat and then a local councillor got you a house – that was us. Oh aye, it's a very sectarian town, no doubt about it. My family is mixed – my sister-in-law is Italian Catholic. My best friend this thirty years is Catholic.

'We moved into Seacourt estate in 1970 and reared the children there. The paramilitaries destroyed it. We used to have to bring the kids to my mother's and then we'd barricade ourselves inside the house. We had to move in the end because of them. My daughter is still here in the town, and I have good friends and my grandchildren.' She had been unable to work for a time due to illness and had trouble getting her benefits sorted out. 'I went to the DUP but they didn't do anything for me, so I had to go to the Sinn Féin office in Carnlough and they helped me to get DLA [Disability Living Allowance]. I don't believe in this help-your-own-kind-and-only-your-own-kind thing. After I got sorted out I ran into Sammy Wilson and I said it to him. I chased them last time they came to my door. I never voted last time, which I regret now.

'I voted to leave the EU. I believed Nigel Farage when he said all that money could be used on the NHS. But sure it never came about. You lose faith in all of them. He was just telling lies. It was the nurses got them back into Stormont. One hundred per cent. Yet the politicians paid themselves for those years they weren't working – anyone else would get sacked.'

In the winter of 2019, fifteen thousand nurses across Northern Ireland went on strike. The Executive at Stormont was entering its third year of suspension, so there was no local health minister. The nurses were protesting about potentially dangerous levels of understaffing, and the fact that their wages had, in real terms, fallen by 15 per cent over the previous eight years. In 2014, DUP Health Minister Jim Wells had introduced pay restraints, which meant that Northern Ireland nurses did not get NHS pay increases in line with nurses elsewhere in the UK. Northern Ireland's waiting lists were the longest in the UK.

Anne's anger and solidarity with the nurses and her disgust with the politicians was widely shared. The New Decade, New Approach deal, published in January 2020 as the work plan for the newly restored Executive, was clearly influenced by this. The first priority identified in the document is 'transforming our health service with a long-term funding strategy', and the first commitment is to 'immediately settle the ongoing pay dispute'. There is also a promise to deliver nine hundred new undergraduate nursing and midwifery places.[1]

A MAN FOR 'NO SURRENDER'

When the DUP's Sammy Wilson behaves badly he does so in such a brazen manner that he tends to get away with it. Just 'Sammy being Sammy', those who might be expected to rein him in murmur, with an attempt at a tolerant grimace in his direction, while his supporters rub their hands and chuckle that Sammy 'says it like it is'. During lockdown Wilson posted a photograph of himself licking a chocolate cone in a Larne ice cream parlour, in defiance of the Executive's policy on mask wearing. 'You can't eat if you're muzzled,' the caption said.

When, in September 2020, he returned to Westminster where he represents East Antrim, he was photographed on the London Underground, reading a paper, bare-faced. He claimed he'd taken his mask off to make a call and had forgotten to put it on again, but the passenger who took the photo disputed this. Instead of putting this to Wilson, his supporters claimed the photographer was acting like the Stasi, East Germany's secret police. Wilson openly defies his party leader, Arlene Foster, who is embarrassingly seen to have no authority over him. He called Joe Biden a parrot for Irish republicanism, compared with the eagle, Donald Trump, and said that Northern Ireland's Health Minister, the UUP's Robin Swann, was a poodle for following the advice of the chief medical officer. In 2021, he surpassed himself, calling President Biden a 'bigoted ignoramus'.

---

1 https://assets.publishing.service.gov.uk/government/uploads/system/uploads attachment_data/file/856998/2020-01-08_a_new_decade__a_new_approach.pdf

He's a man's man, Sammy, in the old style. He puffs out his chest, he struts, he makes robust and macho pronouncements and schoolboy jokes. In 2018 he told the then Brexit secretary David Davis to 'stand up to them, man' and that 'if the gloves are off then it is time we went into this fray with a no surrender attitude'. The EU were 'the blackmailing burghers of Brussels', the Irish government were 'cheap opportunists in Dublin'. Before 2019, when the SDLP regained two seats at Westminster, it was left to independent unionist Sylvia Hermon to challenge his excesses. When in 2019 an SNP MP warned that a no-deal Brexit could lead to food shortages for the poor, Wilson was heard to shout, 'Go to the chippy!'

Larne is the capital of his constituency and we met at his office there early in 2020. I arrived early, and had been warned by the friendly woman who set up my appointment that 'he's always late', so I wandered up and down the street. Early measures to try to stall the COVID pandemic had begun to be implemented. The window of one small shop was stuffed with unsold St Patrick's Day paraphernalia, green flags and hats, plastic shillelagh sticks, and ginger-bearded leprechauns. The pharmacy was out of hand sanitiser. I would have to come back the next morning before nine and join the queue, the woman at the till told me.

Wilson's office is in a modest terraced building. A burly man in an Aran jumper, he sat behind his desk in a long room that reminded me of a disused cinema, the framed photos of Ian Paisley Snr and of DUP events over the years standing in for film posters. I sat facing him. We agreed not to shake hands. He was unsmiling. I asked him about the COVID situation. 'This is a crisis the government is handling well,' he said. 'They take a mature view. Not panicking but giving it gravitas.'

He insisted that Brexit would not add to Northern Ireland's woes. 'We were right to support Brexit. The British government is under no obligation to the EU. There is probably no need whatsoever for the border in the Irish Sea. There is scope for the government to dig its heels in and it should. The EU may see the Withdrawal Agreement as legally binding – the British government sees it as a set of principles open to interpretation.' In 2016, the BBC made a programme about Brexit in which Sammy Wilson is heard asking a constituent for his views on Brexit. The man said he was all for it, and added that we should 'get the ethnics out' as well. Wilson replied, 'You are absolutely right, you know.' Wilson said the BBC had taken his comment out of context and that he was 'not a racist'.[2]

Wilson said the British people would not be shackled or corralled. He agreed, however, that now that Boris Johnson was not reliant on the DUP's votes, he seemed to care less about Northern Ireland. 'My view has always been that the biggest threat to the union is not from Northern Ireland or Scotland because good sense will prevail, but from England. People in Northern Ireland don't need to be convinced of the benefits of the union.' This was palpably untrue for those who voted for the SDLP and Sinn Féin as well as some Alliance voters and others. Wilson dismissed evidence of growing momentum in Scotland for independence. 'The Scottish just love to tweak England's tail, sickening the English,' he said.

In Larne, as in many other predominantly Protestant towns in Northern Ireland, there are prominently placed banners these days that say, 'We stand with Soldier F'. They refer to a British paratrooper who was present in Derry during Bloody Sunday in 1972, when the regiment killed thirteen unarmed Catholic civilians. As a result of the findings of the Saville Inquiry (also called the Bloody Sunday Inquiry), Soldier F, as its report designated him, faces murder charges for his actions that day. In 2019, the Larne-based Clyde Valley Flute Band controversially wore armbands with a Parachute Regiment emblem and the letter F on them during an Apprentice Boys parade in Derry. The Apprentice Boys had disowned the gesture. Wilson, however, had attended a rally in Larne supporting the band. He had done so, he told me, because 'it was the right thing to do.

'I am campaigning in Westminster that there should be a mechanism whereby, unless there is compelling new evidence, such cases can't be reopened. I make no bones about it. I want protection for members of the security forces not to be hounded and witch-hunted. The legacy issue is massive and could destabilise the Assembly. Sinn Féin is determined to make its sordid sectarian campaign equivalent to the sacrifices made by the security forces. It wants one-sided legacy arrangements. It is opening the sores of the past that are very much there for some people.'

The legacy of the conflict is without doubt potentially destabilising. Many of those bereaved and injured during those violent years have

2 https://www.bbc.co.uk/news/uk-northern-ireland-35693195

had their needs neglected. Almost two thousand murders have gone unsolved. Several attempts to set up structures to deliver elements of truth and justice have failed. In 2014, the Stormont House Agreement (SHA) was announced, but not implemented. Five years later the British Prime Minister, Boris Johnson, rowed back steeply on its provisions, declaring that he was going to end the 'vexatious' prosecution of army veterans, and that the only other cases that would be investigated would be those with a prospect of 'swift' resolution based on new evidence.

The New Decade, New Approach document surprised many with its promise that the British government would 'within 100 days' legislate for the SHA. The COVID pandemic overtook many of the plans the document laid out, but few believed there was ever any chance that this particular one would be honoured. Unionists had turned against the SHA, seeing it as too favourable to a republican response to legacy.

When Ian Paisley Jnr got suspended from parliament for serious misconduct, Wilson argued there should be no further sanction against him. The DUP evidently agreed. I asked him if the behaviour of his fellow MP was an embarrassment to the party. 'Not at all. Sometimes the rules aren't clear,' he said. Wilson's attitude on abortion and same-sex marriage was blunt: 'Our party is clear on this and if anyone doesn't agree don't join the DUP.'

He defended the bridge proposal. 'There are good economic reasons to have a road link with our major economic partner and it would make a statement that the UK values Northern Ireland enough to have a physical link with it,' he said. 'There is a degree of unease among people who fear that Brexit could end up seeing us tied to the Republic.' I asked him if he thought Johnson had any intention of building it. His answer was ambiguous. 'The PM is known to like making grand infrastructure statements,' he said. He had no fears over a border poll. 'I'd say the chances of a referendum on the border with this government are nil.' A hardline element in the DUP see Wilson as a potential leader post-Arlene Foster. I asked him about this. 'No,' he said, hands on the table, looking me straight in the eye. 'Wouldn't want it, wouldn't get it.'

Wilson had vehemently opposed the notion of a border in the Irish Sea. His trust in Johnson and his government had proved naive. On 1 January 2021, the beginning of Northern Ireland's centenary year, Larne, the capital of Wilson's constituency, became a border town. There was little sign of reaction at first, certainly no organised protest. Then slogans began to appear on gable walls in Larne, and elsewhere. Some of them said 'no sea border', others, more menacing, said 'all bets are off' and 'all border post staff are targets' with a symbol indicating the crosshairs of a gun. Then Agriculture Minister Edwin Poots stepped in. He said that departmental staff and customs workers were at risk, and that trade unions and others had raised concerns over their safety. The department staff were withdrawn, and the local council unanimously voted to pull out their customs staff also.[3]

However, the PSNI then said that it had no reason to believe there were credible threats against any staff, or that loyalist paramilitaries were involved. Trade unionists denied they had raised concerns. Staff returned to work. When Alliance councillors questioned the veracity of the information they had been given, and called for an investigation into why they had been led to believe the situation was dangerous, the DUP mayor accused them of trying to bring the council into disrepute. Unionists voted down the proposal. A TUV councillor spoke of Alliance's 'shame'. Two young men, a mechanic and a farm labourer, were charged with putting up the graffiti.

'FANTASY ISLAND'

'I'm a blow-in to Larne – I'm only here ten years,' said George, who was having a quiet pint in his Larne local, ignoring a drunk busman from Glasgow who was traipsing about the bar seeking attention, slabbering, to use an evocative Northern word. George was formerly a policeman and preferred not to give his name. 'It is a strange place – you can't assume that a Billy here is a Protestant or a Seamus is a Catholic,' he told me. 'There is more mixed marriage here than most places. It's also very, very local around here. They're nosy bastards. I mean that in a warm way. I was in a bar down by the harbour and someone said to me, you're not a harbour rat. I thought it was a compliment but it turned out it means I was not from the far side of the bridge, wasn't a local and shouldn't have seen fit to sit down in a particular part of the pub.

'It was a Catholic led one of the paramilitary organisations around here. No better man. They are full of their own importance. There is one bar they don't have a say in. Though they do have their wee clinic

3 https://www.bbc.co.uk/news/uk-northern-ireland-56364140

from time to time even in that one – you see a couple of them up at the top of the bar and then someone comes in and they go out the back with him and do whatever they do. If the bars don't pay their terrorism taxes they are still liable to be firebombed. The bars they take over they ruin – they won't pay for their drink and so the place ends up closing. Apart from the paramilitaries, most of the crime in Larne is committed by about one hundred or less people in a kind of clan with two or three big families in it. It is just ingrained in them, and there'd be mental health problems there too.'

I told him what Anne had said about the flats. He agreed they had become problematic. 'The high flats are a right den of iniquity,' he said. 'They are mostly social housing for people in trouble. Some of the homeless organisations have flats in there. There's a lot of drugs, partying, fighting. The majority of call-outs for the emergency services – police, ambulance, fire brigade – would be to the flats. Some of the blocks got demolished. There's sea views from the high-up ones but no one wants to live there. It's like a bad prison. It's not like the old street thing where the sons and daughters all moved into the same street as they grew up on.'

Still, George was content to stay in the town. It had changed in more positive ways too. 'Larne's all right. To be honest, sectarianism isn't really the main problem here now. Everyone girns a bit but I've never fallen out with anyone in Larne. The paramilitary thing is more like racketeering, same as you'd get in Birmingham,' he said. 'There's a new dual carriageway to Belfast and houses are cheaper here than in the likes of Bangor out the other side of the lough. There's nowhere much to socialise but sure socialising is gone now anyway – fifty bottles of Bud from Asda and sit at home and watch the football. Brexit might be good for us – if there's this border in the sea they talk about it might boost jobs in Larne with customs staff and security and that. We could do with some jobs. There's hardly any businesses left down the harbour. Just lorries passing through.' I asked him what he thought about the bridge to Scotland. 'Fantasy Island,' he said. 'It will never happen.'

POSTSCRIPT

In July 2020, the Orange Order had to call off its annual Twelfth of July celebrations. I read in the local paper that Orangemen, bandsmen, including the Clyde Valley band, and others, had decided to put their energies into distributing food parcels and helping out elderly people in some of Larne's estates. Loyalists constantly complain that the media never highlight any good news about them. I left many phone messages, sent many emails. After failing to find anyone willing to talk to me, I asked a local community worker if he could put me in touch with some of those involved. He agreed. But the word came back: 'No.'

'DO UNTO OTHERS'

Sleety rain was sweeping across Carrickfergus the day I came to meet Roy Beggs there, blurring the outlines of its blunt Norman castle where it jutted out into the sea. Carrick, as it is usually known, is a few miles up the coast from Larne, towards Belfast. This is where King William of Orange landed when he arrived in Ireland in the seventeenth century. Beggs is the UUP's East Antrim MLA. His office is just around the corner from the castle. As if abandoned there after some military joyride, a Second World War tank is perched at a drunken angle on a steep bank that rises from the coast road into a small park. The tank turned out to be part of an extensive war memorial. I asked a man walking through the park what he thought of the tank, which had been built in the town. He laughed. 'Well, I don't think much of it,' he said. 'It has a bit of a North Korea look about it.' He declined to give his name: 'I don't want to be put out of this town,' he said.

Carrickfergus has always been a military town. It is also the town in which, in 1990, arsonists attacked the building where Sir John Stevens and his team kept their archives while investigating collusion between loyalist paramilitaries and state security and intelligence agencies. And the town in which, in 2012, loyalists rioted and attempted to burn down an Alliance MLA's constituency office.

Beggs' office is tiny and windowless. He is one of just ten UUP representatives returned in the 2017 elections. I had interviewed his father, Roy Beggs Snr, then an MP, at the constituency office in Larne twenty years previously.[4] Then, the party had twenty-eight MLAs. The front door had been surrounded by security lights and cameras back then. None of this paraphernalia is needed now. Some things have not

---

4 Susan McKay, *Northern Protestants: An Unsettled People (3rd edition)*, Blackstaff Press, 2021, pp. 100–103

changed, though. During the election a poster of party leader Steve Aiken on a lamp post in Larne was defaced, an image of Lundy plastered over his face and Ulster Unionist Party changed to 'Unionist Unity Preventer'.

Beggs Jnr started out in politics helping his father, whose career began in the DUP, but who moved to the UUP after a row over allegations of treachery because he cooperated with the local authority of a port town in the Republic of Ireland. In the dominant UUP, his father cut a bullish figure. Beggs Jnr was elected to the first Assembly in 1998. He had hated direct rule. 'I had a huge sense of injustice as to how we were being governed, the lack of democracy in Northern Ireland, legislation going through Westminster and you could not put a comma in the Anglo-Irish Agreement, which unjustly gave Dublin, which had been harbouring terrorists and preventing their extradition, a say in the running of Northern Ireland.'

Like Esmond Birnie, he blamed Sinn Féin for the UUP's decline. Its procrastination over decommissioning had been 'hugely unsettling'. There had been incidents in more recent years that had implied ongoing recourse to guns, he said, so the unsettling effect continued. The DUP had exploited this. 'We always aspire that we will regain our position as the pre-eminent unionist party. We don't think that Northern Ireland has been well served by the Democratic Unionist Party, but the unionist electorate still feels it has to vote for the DUP to keep Sinn Féin out,' he said.

'Take the Brexit issue. I was never a fan of Europe. I disliked the bureaucracy. But as an Ulster Unionist I was concerned that if Scotland was to become independent it would create further barriers between us and the remaining part of the United Kingdom. So I voted remain for the stability of the union. We warned the DUP not to agree to a border down the Irish Sea, but they went ahead. Boris has institutionalised it and Northern Ireland will, frankly, be governed under European regulations, while the rest of the United Kingdom will have freedom to go its own direction.' He saw no reason for a border poll. It would be 'a huge distraction'. I asked him about the bridge. 'Barking,' he said. He reckoned even a design study would cost 'tens of millions'. And, 'If we had access to that sort of money for infrastructure, we'd be much better sorting out our sewage, or tarmacking our existing roads.'

The lack of educational attainment among disadvantaged unionists in his constituency was, Beggs said, his hobby horse. His father had been a teacher as well as a farmer. 'Dad came from a very humble family. But education, hard work and good, family, Christian values basically allowed my dad and his eleven siblings to progress through education and enabled them to find stable employment. A shocking 43 per cent of post-primary school pupils in a particular ward area in my constituency have less than 85 per cent attendance at school, the worst in Northern Ireland,' he said.

I asked him to say more about those Christian values. 'I think the simplest way of answering that one is simply, do unto others as you would have them do unto you,' he said. Christian values had most recently been invoked to oppose same-sex marriage and abortion rights. The UUP regarded these as issues of conscience. 'Personally, as a Christian, I have the traditional view of a marriage being for a man and a woman, but civil partnership is there for those who have other ideas,' he said. 'I struggle with terminating – killing – the life of a young child except in some exceptional situation where the mother's health and well-being would be at risk.'

The south-east Antrim brigade of the UDA was notoriously vicious in its sectarianism and persisted in attempting to force Catholics and people in mixed marriages out of Carrickfergus, Larne and other towns long after the loyalist ceasefire. From the early noughties on, however, it was increasingly more involved in gangsterism, chiefly drug dealing and moneylending. In January 2020, a gang burst into a flat in Carrickfergus and beat to death the man who lived there, Glenn Quinn. A barman, he was said to have criticised intimidation of local business people, and to have been in a fist fight with a local UDA boss.

Quinn, a Protestant, was from a security force family – his father had been in the UDR, and two of his brothers were former policemen. 'It's organised crime. It's about fiefdoms of power and money,' Beggs said. The authorities were 'following the money trail' and had seized houses and property. 'There's also been a significantly higher presence of police on the ground. There's a need to increase the speed of our court system to stop people getting frustrated and going to paramilitaries.' He said there were signs the paramilitaries had stopped trying to control community groups. 'We have to live in hope.'

'SYSTEMS CHANGE'

Lee Robb cuts a dash in Carrickfergus, with her big rings and chunky necklaces and her cropped bleached hair. The day we talked she was wearing a yellow coat and mustard suede trainers. She zips around the town in her grey Mini. 'My granny was a dressmaker and milliner and she always made us clothes,' she told me. 'Then I worked in fashion retail. I love style.' There is more to it than that, though. 'I like to confound expectations,' she said. 'I live on a housing estate. I like to throw people off their assumptions. It opens up a space.'

Opening up a space is Robb's personal and political credo. She said she used to get frustrated by a feeling of decline and sadness that hung over her hometown. She worked for over a decade at the Big Lottery Fund, and had considered moving to Belfast but then realised she would prefer to stay and try to find the positive side of life in Carrick. 'I felt people had disengaged from civic life and we had a town centre that was dying,' she said. 'Paramilitarism was breeding off despair and soaking up a lot of the funding that was coming in.'

Robb sees in Carrick a prime example of 'the tragedy of neo-liberalism.' 'My dad worked in the Courtaulds factory,' she said. 'And I have a very clear memory of the day in primary school that all our daddies lost their jobs at the same time.' The Courtaulds company had set up a man-made fabrics factory in the town in 1951, drawn by the proximity of the port at Larne and the availability of plenty of unemployed workers. It shut in 1981. 'Housing was deregulated and there were terrible planning decisions so you had new middle-class areas getting built that had no connection to the town. Communities were atomised.' She did not want to set up another charity. 'I'm working towards systems change. I'd rather politicians focused on policies that eradicate poverty than deliver food parcels,' she said.

Robb set up a Facebook page in 2017 called Positive Carrickfergus, and allowed it to grow organically. It now has over five thousand members, in a town with a population of around thirty thousand. 'It's part community noticeboard. There is very little arts activity, other than a few dance classes for kids, so we do creative stuff working with organisations like Big Telly Theatre Company. We've held big community lunches in the town hall. There were no community heritage projects so we are working on that. We want to promote active citizenship and participation.' She applied with others and recently got a grant from the Lottery's Emerging Futures Fund for a community interest company.[5] 'We are about creating hope and change,' she said.

MONKSTOWN

On my way to Monkstown Boxing Club, in a big housing estate on the northern shores of Belfast Lough, I took a wrong turn from the bus stop. I asked an old man out walking his dog for directions and he offered to walk with me. He told me about his neighbour in the flats who was 'not a bad lad' but he and his girlfriend had had another row last night and he had locked her out and she was sitting crying on the landing and it wasn't the first time. He pointed out the club with his walking stick. It was in a fine modern building, bright and with no messy graffiti. Inside, the first thing I saw was a poster of Nelson Mandela emblazoned with the words, 'Education is the most powerful weapon with which you can change the world.'

'ARE YOU OKAY?'

'I've got Tourette's so obviously I'm always really agitated and just want to get up and move about instead of sitting still. As a teenager I lost interest in school and studying. I began to get sort of hyper and stuff and I started losing all my focus and concentration.' DeeDee Kerr nearly crashed out of education soon after he started secondary school. It happens to plenty, where he lives. Now, he said, he couldn't be happier. That is after he got a place in Monkstown Boxing Club, which got him back on track. 'My mum and dad were really worried because obviously they want me to do well in life and succeed, but that's not the way it was going to go until I came here,' he said. 'The youth workers are like your friends. You can run about a bit and then sit down again. You can do boxing to relax and calm you down. You have a key teacher and you're in a group of three so you get more time and more attention than you would do in school.'

DeeDee is back in regular school now doing his A levels. He had done an exam in school that morning and had come over to the project to talk to his friends afterwards. 'I'm very good with computers and

---

5 https://www.emergingfuturesfund.com

stuff like ICT and I want to learn about the world so that's why I picked travel and I love learning about the bones of the body and stuff like that. That's why I picked sports. Joining the army has been a thing in my family – my granda and my dad and my uncles were all in it, and I sort of want to take that on, but I'm still debating. I don't know. I'll just see where life takes me.'

He's a prefect now and mentors younger students. 'Maybe younger people coming into the big school are having a hard time getting used to school and I'll go down and speak to them and tell them there's nothing to be worried about. I'll just look at people and I'll think he's struggling just by the way he's walking with his head down and stuff, and you just say to them, are you okay? And then sometimes they might say, yeah or no. It's just having confidence in yourself and knowing that you can sort of help.'

AVOIDING THE 'BUS TO HELL'

'Dream job,' said Amy Johnson. When I met her she was encouraging a cluster of teenage girls with their work on a mental health project. She asked them to keep going and stepped outside with me. 'I always said I would love to work in the community I grew up in, to give back the opportunities I had. I did a degree in youth work at Jordanstown. I might go back some time and do a Master's. I had a really good mum and dad who kind of sheltered me the best they could. You could be exposed to a few things here that other young people that are in middle-class, higher-class areas wouldn't. My parents were strict. I was a social butterfly, not at all academic. My mum always said if there was a bus to go to hell, I would go. I was always down at the youth club.

'The young people that come in here, you can see the potential in them, but a lot of them are just at rock bottom, no self-esteem, no self-confidence, no aspirations, very few dreams or goals in life. They struggle to see life any other way. Young people have a tough time here. So it's really trying to just inspire them to be what they want to be and to believe that no dream is too big, and if they work hard there's opportunity.

'I think it was a lot easier when I was growing up because there was no social media. It is a killer. Between bullying and the constant glorification of celebrities, it's just never-ending. Young people think,

I can't look like that, I'm not going to be like her, so I'm going to be nothing. When I grew up you'd have maybe had some bullying going on at school, but you could escape it whenever you went home. Now you can't. On Mondays we do a thing with our education group where they check, and some of their screen time is like seventeen hours a day. They're sitting up all night on their phone, on Snapchat, on Facebook or on Instagram, and they're coming in in the morning and their eyes are in the back of their head because they've had three hours' sleep.

'I started the young women's group. Boys seem to lash out more, whereas girls are more introverted. We currently mentor probably fifteen young people and a lot of it is about getting them to a place where they're happy in themselves and their bodies and who they are as a person. It is sad to have to do that when they are only thirteen or fourteen. We've had young people that have wanted plastic surgery to change their facial features at age fifteen – just heartbreaking. A lot of our programme is around sexual health and how to be safe. You do worry about them. A lot of young people are ashamed to say they are from an area like this. I try to be a role model. I'm happy that this is where I came from because it makes you who you are.'

MORE THAN A SCHOOL

Paul Johnson runs the club, which started in 1983. His office opened out on to the gym where a boy in school uniform was on an exercise bike side by side with one of the youth workers. They talked as they pedalled. 'It's informal,' said Johnson. 'Not like sitting across the table from a counsellor for an hour once a week for six weeks, after waiting eighteen months for an appointment, even for self-harming and attempted suicide.' This, he said, was what was on offer from the state for young people with serious mental health issues.

Though he is from a loyalist area, as a boy Paul boxed in a club on the nationalist New Lodge Road. 'Boxing has been really good at bringing young people together outside of their segregated and deprived communities,' he said. 'We were previously based down in the community centre, and it wasn't ideal. It was a paramilitary shebeen at the weekends, it was a nursery school in the morning, it was a pensioners' club. We needed a place to call home, and we were very lucky to secure this bit of land and get European PEACE funds.' The

Special EU Programmes Body is one of the six cross-border institutions set up under the Good Friday Agreement to distribute EU regional funds across Northern Ireland and in the border region, North and South. 'We used to be just a boxing club but in 2012 got National Lottery funding for a project called Box Clever, the genesis of which was a report by Dawn Purvis [then MLA for East Belfast]. It showed that young males within the Protestant unionist community were failing to achieve the kind of qualifications they need to survive.[6]

'Education was never a priority in unionist areas,' said Johnson. 'There was always an apprenticeship your dad could get you so you didn't have to do well. I was an electrician for years and did my degree when I was thirty-seven. But now a lot of the big manufacturers have gone and there are better-educated people around looking for jobs. Today it is basically on merit, which is the right way that any society should be, in fact.

'Whenever the conflict was happening, young people were being recruited to the paramilitaries because they wanted to defend their community and our country. It was probably a lie. Today they recruit by selling drugs to a young person. They let them get into thousands of pounds of debt and then the option is either we're going to shoot you or you become a seller. They're getting these cocktails of drugs being flooded on to the streets. The paramilitaries keep a tight rein on heroin because they know the pathway for somebody that's taking heroin is probably an early death. So it doesn't fit the business model.

'Kids were being let down by our education system, going into secondary school with a reading age of probably seven or eight. Absolutely on a trajectory of failure. Teachers don't have the time or the capacity to do the work we do here. Parents were being sent for constantly because of bad behaviour. We do a home visit before they start here so you can kind of get a sense of what issues the parents are facing. They are struggling. One of our students last year was very shy, very quiet, wouldn't engage. We did a home visit with his mum. She couldn't function without a heavy dose of diazepam and antidepressants. She was caring for her own mother, who had just had a major stroke, and was sleeping on a sofa. Our student's older brother was dealing drugs

---

6 https://www.yumpu.com/en/document/view/28757278/a-call-to-action-educational-disadvantage-and-the-protestant-nicva

for the UDA so he was working strange hours. He didn't come home to three in the morning. The two of them were sharing bunk beds. He was coming in, using drugs, and this young person was just in a hellish situation. He got no breakfast. He had no money for his bus fare. He didn't have a uniform. He had one shirt, one pair of shoes, and one pair of trousers and when they got dirty, he was getting called names in school. We got him kitted out and we got his mum some support from Citizens Advice and the food bank.

'At the end of each term, we have a coffee morning, which is a celebration event. So we'll bring parents in. The kids will cater. We have a presentation from each of the key workers about their students and how well they've done. This is a community. This is a family.'

'A POSITIVE VIBE …'

Daryl Clarke is a boxer as well as a youth worker at the club. He's twenty-three. 'I was a bit of a messer. I'm from Carrickfergus, and I live in an estate with a lot of anti-social behaviour, paramilitary influence, drug and alcohol usage, you know. I started off boxing down there, and then I came here when I was thirteen. I just loved the whole set-up. Paul was like a life mentor. We were always doing our boxing sessions, but he also put us through personal development courses,' he said. 'I went to university and I was volunteering here as well, and Paul asked me to help out with admin and funding applications and then I got offered a job here. The ones I went to school with, we just went two different ways. Like I've gone up. I've got my education and I have a good job that I love. My friends that I knew before, they're just doing the same thing that they were doing when we were back in school. Just crazy. Taking drugs, not being employed, not really enjoying life, no motivation. A couple of them have attempted suicide.

'The paramilitary thing is quite intimidating in Carrickfergus. They have a lot of control. A man got killed in my estate recently. Up here is quite similar. I sort of know what to expect and the young people know they can come and talk to us about how not to go down that road. We had a consultation with them last night. They highlighted wanting to do a project on mental health, history workshops, and group relations work as well as outdoor pursuits. We do a lot of residentials. We take them canoeing, we take them down to the Mournes for walks and stuff.

This is their safe space. I just try and give a positive vibe like I would with my mates.

'I've been boxing for twelve years now and I've been away to Florida boxing three times. I went to Spain to fight for County Antrim and I've won the Ulster Championship and won practically everything except one, which is an Irish title. That's next. I want to stay working here. It's a great organisation. If you look at the likes of north Belfast and the suicide rate there, they definitely need something like this. Young men have had these barriers up for so long and the whole stigma around not speaking about their feelings, thoughts or emotions is crazy. They don't have much resilience. There's a lot of bad influences and bad people to be looking at here. We show them good role models. Carl Frampton comes in and out of here. He's from Tiger's Bay, which has the same problems as here, and he's made something of himself. He's a world champion. We have to get them to see they can break through.'

BELFAST

CHAPTER 4

As Good a Place as Possible

The mural draws the eye, not least because one of the cartoonish masked men it depicts is pointing his gun right at you. 'Prepared for Peace,' the script reads. 'Ready for war.' This is the first thing you see when you drive down from the M2 motorway on to the Shore Road in north Belfast. The mural faces the road on the edge of the Mount Vernon housing estate and has been there since the 1990s.

In 2014, a group of working-class women came together to produce a book of photographs of this part of the city. The Protestants among them lived in Tiger's Bay, the Catholics in New Lodge. The once elegant avenue called Duncairn Gardens with its tall red-brick Victorian houses separates them, as does a peace wall.

The photographs show narrow terraces of small red-brick houses that open right on to the street. Some of the houses are semi-derelict, some have been restored by private owners who then, the women note, often charge unaffordable rents. The photographs show the small, modern industrial estates that were meant to provide employment, except that the jobs on offer require higher skills and educational attainment than many local people possess. There are photos of loyalist flags and red, white and blue kerbstones, the captions registering the women's protest that these were imposed on them without consultation and in places where children play. When German bombers attacked Belfast in 1941, killing one thousand civilians, this area was devastated. A photo in the book shows a mural commemorating the Blitz. The caption below states: 'Our areas are more deprived now than they were back then.'[1] They were also the most violent during the conflict. The introduction comments that women were largely excluded from the peace process, and have continued to be excluded during its implementation. The book represents the women's demand for 'the inclusion of their vision' in the public sphere.

Seaview, the home ground of Crusaders football club is on the Shore Road, and on Boxing Day 2019 it was floodlit for the semi-final of the football league in which the home team would face another north Belfast team, Cliftonville. Mark Langhammer, chairman of the Crusaders' board had invited me along. 'Crusaders is rooted in a very loyalist area but pre-Troubles it would have had support from areas like Sailortown, the Docklands, Little Italy, New Lodge, even Ardoyne,' said Langhammer. 'That pretty much stopped after '69 and part of our mission is to re-establish it to some degree. We did a lot of work, including discouraging flag-waving. I counted heads recently and we had seven Catholics on the field.' Langhammer's father's family escaped the Nazis in Sudetenland. His mother was from the Shankill Road. He is regional secretary of a teaching union and served as an independent Labour councillor for several years.

'There's a certain amount of communal banter on the pitch but it's not nearly as bad as it used to be,' he said. 'Back in 1979 Crusaders earned themselves the record for UK police attendance at any match, more than for a Rangers versus Celtic match even. There were a couple of shootings right outside the grounds here. The sectarianism back in the day was pretty raw. Now it's sort of moderated, so you would see our crowd singing at Cliftonville, 'paedos and junkies, paedos and junkies', and Cliftonville singing back, 'feed the Crus' you know from that Bob Geldof song 'Do they know it's Christmas?' That's reflective of the tables being turned economically. But there has been a fair bit of cooperation between the clubs. Things are moving in the right direction,' he said.

'MORE TO LIFE THAN STICKING TO YOUR OWN'

I met Danielle McDowell in the packed Crusaders clubhouse before the game. Cold and early-afternoon-dark outside, it was warm inside,

---

1 Shankill Women's Centre, Lower North Belfast Women's Group, Star Neighbourhood Centre and the Centre for Media Research, Ulster University, *Women's Vision from Across the Barricades*, 2014.

and the atmosphere was boozy and congenial as multitudes of pints were carried aloft over the crowd. McDowell is head of women's and girls' football at the club. She is women's development officer for the Irish Football Association (IFA) and the University of Ulster. She is also a much-capped footballer herself.

'I've always been known as the wee footballer,' she said. 'Even now, when I'm thirty-three. I'm from Rathcoole, which is one of the biggest estates in Europe. I always played football with the boys in the playground, I played it after school, I played in the street, I played it on my own. Anywhere I was, I had a ball.

'My family all went to the Methodist Mission. I absolutely hated Sunday School and Girls' Brigade. There wasn't enough of sport going on. I'd have far rather been in Boys' Brigade. I remember boys coming out absolutely sweating with red faces. They had matches on a Saturday morning and got to run around having a good time being active and competitive. We seemed to always be in doing arty, kind of girly, things. I wasn't a bad child in any shape or form, definitely had that fear factor and respect for both my mum and dad. But I used to try and get really dirty so I needed to get a bath when GB was on because I knew mum wouldn't send me dirty.

'I am very proud and comfortable about my background, but football allowed me to see the rest of the world and see that there's a whole lot more to life than just sticking with your own. From I was twelve years old I was away on trials and there were girls from all over Northern Ireland. I still have many a Catholic friend. I remember hearing people say the word Fenian: Fenian this or Fenian that. I used to say to people, how many Catholics do you know? And they'd say, I don't want to know any, they're all the same. I'd say, well, yeah, they're the same as us. That is something that has been passed down through the generations and people start to believe it, when they have no real reason to.

'Cliftonville and Crusaders is probably the most heated of all the contests within Northern Ireland football. It's a massive game: two local clubs and from very similar parts of the world, though Cliftonville is very much a Catholic club and Crusaders is predominantly a Protestant club, not in terms of the players, but definitely the fan base. To be totally honest with you, I don't know one Protestant that follows Cliftonville. There's been a lot of really good football players coming out of

Rathcoole in recent years, and they are playing with people like Neil Lennon and Paddy McCourt and different Catholic players who've done really well for Northern Ireland. The whole Green and White Army, as they call themselves, the Northern Ireland fans, sing all these players' names.' Lennon was a former Northern Ireland international and Celtic player. In 2019 he was manager of the Scottish team Hibs when he was attacked. Lennon said he was 'fed up' after eighteen years of 'anti-Irish racism'. He had been knocked unconscious on one occasion and had received a parcel bomb. Graffiti had called for him to be hanged. He compared those responsible to the Ku Klux Klan.

'Sport keeps you healthy. You can't drink alcohol or take drugs on a Saturday night and then go to train with Northern Ireland on a Sunday,' said McDowell. 'I always wanted to be my best and get selected. Sports definitely helped me to have the confidence to say no and to not feel inferior or a weirdo or boring or whatever. The barriers for women are still there, they've just lowered a little bit. I read yesterday that 69 per cent of people have seen an increase in women's sport being shown and broadcast or in newspapers. But it's still very much behind male sport.

'I drive the women's team forward to be able to compete with the top colleges in Ireland. The IFA co-sponsors my role and there's a Girls' and Women's Performance Academy to try and prepare our girls for full-time football. The IFA and Ulster University devised a part-time degree in football business and management. The players are all on scholarships so people with limited finances are able to attend university and not leave with thousands of pounds worth of debt. Football definitely helps young girls with their confidence and self-esteem. You just get sweaty and stuck in and nobody cares what you look like, it's about how much you're working for the team. That wee sense of belonging comes into it as well and that wee bit of a support network. In terms of body image, football shows you it's okay to be fit and strong.

'I made my senior international debut for Northern Ireland when I was sixteen and still at school, which was a big deal. I played for the team for twelve years. I played for Crusaders when I was sixteen, and I'm still there. We dominated the league with Glentoran for about thirteen years and I played in the Champions League six times against some of the top professional teams, and players, in the world.

'The Northern Irish thing is more important to me than the British thing. If I'm Irish or I'm British then my forty-seven international caps as Northern Irish don't matter. Like they were Mickey Mouse and I didn't really play for a country, just a little province. So I do see Northern Ireland as a separate country, which I've represented. We're our own people. Like Northern Ireland Protestants 100 per cent have more in common with Northern Ireland Catholics than with, say, Scottish Protestants. If they play "the Queen" at the end of a Saturday night in a social club I'll stand up, and likewise I've been in social clubs in west Belfast and "The Soldier's Song" came on at twelve o'clock and you just stand up and be respectful.' The British national anthem 'God Save the Queen' is almost always referred to simply as 'the Queen' in Northern Ireland. 'The Soldier's Song/*Amhrán na bhFiann*' is the Irish national anthem. 'When in Rome, I think,' McDowell said. 'That's something that Northern Ireland could definitely do with, a sports anthem that all of the community can get behind.

'There was always flags up and kerbstones painted round here and there's still to this day murals on the walls. I think we're probably ten years at least away from ending the paramilitary thing. I remember when I was about eleven seeing a boy being tarred and feathered to a lamp post because he had broken in and stolen from two different pensioners' houses and later one of the wee ladies actually died in hospital because of having a heart attack. I'm not saying that it is justified to tar and feather someone but I doubt very much that that boy would have done that again. I heard the gunshots one night too of someone being shot, being kneecapped, down the side of an entry, for joyriding someone's car. It used to be, we got a sense, maybe, that paramilitaries were actually protecting our communities. They used to go and beat people up for selling drugs to kids. Now they seem to be the ones selling the drugs.'

Tarring and feathering was a form of public humiliation meted out to those deemed by paramilitaries to have offended the rules of the community. The person was covered in tar, on to which feathers were then thrown, after which they would be tied up and displayed in some public place, often with a placard around their neck naming their crime.

'My fiancé's the goalkeeper for Glenavon. He actually played for Northern Ireland as well. It's a running joke in our house that he's only got eight caps and I've got forty-seven. If I'm totally honest with you, I know I just said how great Rathcoole is, but when we get married I don't want to move back there. They have built these lovely new houses but you maybe buy one and then the rest are given out by the Housing Executive to people that don't really care. My friend was next to a house and all they did was party and she had to sell it in negative equity to get out. There's just crazy people everywhere, and drugs, and little kids running around swearing.'

In April 2021, paramilitaries taught children to throw petrol bombs in Tiger's Bay. Along the Shore Road, at Seaview, the Northern Ireland women's team, despite being ranked twenty-five places below their rivals, spectacularly defeated the Ukraine team, qualifying for the European cup finals in 2022.

'PROTESTANTY SORT OF STUFF'

The first Kyle knew was when he got a text from his mate a couple of days before Easter telling him there were to be riots on the Saturday night. There was a list of places and times, including one at a roundabout not far from his Rathcoole home. His mate asked him to share it and he did. Kyle said he wasn't brought up political. 'But the people I run about with I'd hear them going on about Protestanty sort of stuff, you know, Protestants hate Catholics, Catholics hate Protestants, Sinn Féin and the DUP hate each other.'

Almost a hundred police officers were injured during 2021's Easter riots, which happened in Belfast, Derry, Coleraine, and Carrickfergus, with a few skirmishes in other towns. Some of the riots were across interfaces and involved exchanges with nationalists. Others were confrontations between loyalists and the PSNI. There were several fights when householders struggled to stop teenagers commandeering their wheelie bins.

Kyle went along. 'There were people there in balaclavas and black hoods and there were cars speeding about. They were trying to get the police in. So then the Paddy Wagons arrived.' A BBC journalist recorded the moment when the fleet of white PSNI Land Rovers swept in. A man could be heard shouting, 'Here we go – party time,' to whoops and cheers.

'They were setting fire to cars and throwing petrol bombs and stuff,' said Kyle. 'My mate got anxious. He's got anxiety. He went home. I stood and watched it. A lot of people had been drinking and they went home and watched the Carl Frampton fight, and then came back to see the riot. I went to my mate's house and we had a beer. I was told someone had gone on fire while I was away.' Frampton, from Tiger's Bay, has already held two world titles but was defeated in the world super-featherweight title fight in Dubai.

Kyle went back on Sunday night. 'There were people there from Carrickfergus, Carryduff and other places. The ones there that night were far younger,' he said. 'A lot of them were only fourteen or fifteen. I know a few of them – a couple of them are on bail for drugs and stuff.' He returned on the Tuesday. 'I was drunk. I brought a box of empty bottles down, and other people threw them.' He said his mate had asked him to bring the bottles.

'The men who were there were definitely 100 per cent paramilitaries,' he said. 'I was told the commander was there, sitting up at the wall telling people what to do. I was told the politicians wanted the top policeman to resign, but I don't know why or anything.'

Kyle said he did not know why he got involved. 'When I'm drunk, stuff happens,' he said. 'I've nothing against the police. Not yet, anyway.' A few days after the riots his mother shouted up to him that the police were at the door: 'Someone must have touted on me.'

'I don't even like the paramilitaries. When I was younger a boy that was in a UDA family used to bully me. He threw eggs at old people's houses and blamed me. They threatened to do my knees. I told my da and he went and threatened them back. He doesn't like them. They put him out of his house one time because he beat a guy that threatened to shoot him. It was over someone else that owed them money. That's when we moved to where we live now.' He said local paramilitaries were involved in some of the bands and had asked him to join. 'My mother wouldn't let me,' he said. 'My da's mate is in it. He runs the estate he's in. He sells drugs.' Kyle used 'speed and weed' and said he had taken cocaine twice.

His parents were angry. 'My da told me he got lifted years ago at a riot and he got a record. My sister wasn't too pleased either. She is getting married to a Catholic and they have a baby and he is being brought up mixed. They were all giving out to me. My wee brother shouted at me that I was going to go to jail and there were bad people there and they would beat me. He doesn't usually speak to me.'

Kyle said the riots had stopped, 'because of this Prince Andrew, or Philip or something – he's dead'. (Prince Philip had died.) 'I don't think

I will go back out. I only did it to get out of the house. I was bored.'
He is hoping to start a new job soon, stacking boxes in one of the big
supermarkets. After the trouble fizzled out, Carl Frampton spoke at an
online anti-sectarianism rally. He said he grew up next to the interface
and had been excited by riots and had taken part in them when he was
young. 'People have been stirring the pot again, and young people are
being manipulated,' he said. 'It just made me overwhelmingly sad.'[2]

'LOYALISTS DON'T HAVE ANY POLITICS'

An injury had ended Mark Langhammer's own dream of being a
sportsman. He set up an advice centre in Rathcoole and worked there
for thirty years, helping people with housing, welfare and other issues.
'I voted no to the Good Friday Agreement because I thought it would
increase sectarianism. Northern Ireland is a prison. It's not politically
integrated with Great Britain. Unionists wanted to be just wee Prods.
What you ended up with was this bottled-up construction in Stormont
where you had to be unionist, nationalist or other, and it is really hard to
get elected as 'other'. I wouldn't be negative about the agreement because
fewer people are getting killed. But there's still all that "we're beat and
our politicians are useless and Taigs are getting everything" attitude.'

He spoke of the Purvis Report to which he had contributed.[3] In
his view, mixing the social classes was as important as mixing based
on religious background. 'One of the key findings was that Protestants
attended more socially unbalanced schools than Catholics. You have elite
private prep schools, which are attended almost exclusively by Protestants.
They don't exist in Catholic education. When you look at the uptake of
free school meals, it is 2–4 per cent in the Protestant grammar schools and
12–14 per cent in their Catholic equivalents,' he said. 'Our governmental
response to disadvantage is supposedly targeting social need. They shovel
a bit of money towards the poor areas. Lots of money over a long time
will make a difference, but only a tiny one. If you force the social mix it
costs nothing, but middle-class kids do a bit better, the working-class kids
do vastly better. But you have to argue this with wealthy parents.

---

2 A version of this interview appeared in Susan McKay, 'The North – "Riots stopped
  because Prince Andrew or Philip or something – he's dead"', *Irish Times*, 17 April 2021

3 https://www.yumpu.com/en/document/view/28757278/a-call-to-action-
  educational-disadvantage-and-the-protestant-nicva

'In Catholic working-class areas there are a lot of social networks. Teachers quite often come from the area. In the equivalent Protestant area the teachers by and large live elsewhere, in a middle-class area. There is more cohesion among Catholics. Say we had flooding – in the Catholic districts of my constituency I would get the head of the tenants' association coming to me and saying we tried to ring the Department of the Environment, but they're overloaded and they can't come out; we got sewer rods and lifted the drain ourselves but that didn't work; we tried this and we tried that, and now we are trying you. In the Protestant area I would have got 60, 70, 80 calls, all from individuals basically saying, "What the fuck are you doing about this water?"'

He felt that change was coming, and welcomed the prospect. 'There will be a border reckoning sometime soon. My children have moved to the Republic for work. When they were teenagers they lived a freer life than I did at their age. They didn't have as many boundaries. But they both still came to the conclusion that there was something constraining about Northern Ireland. A lot of younger people who don't see a viable political route for their idealism are finding other routes – social causes, the environment, and climate change,' he said.

Fears that there would be significant loyalist violence in response to the threat of constitutional change were based on an exaggerated view of their capacity, he felt, and an underestimation of the role of collusion between British intelligence agencies, the police, and loyalist paramilitary groups. 'Loyalist resentment boils over into things like flags and marching. They can cause a bit of mayhem, and, yes, they could kill people,' he said. 'But the extent of it depends on the succour they are given by political masters, and the degree to which British military intelligence and Special Branch want there to be trouble. Left to their own devices, they will be policed in ever-decreasing circles. They don't have any politics. They don't want normal British politics. They don't want normal Irish politics. They don't really want power sharing. Their outlook is largely nihilistic. They don't have a world view.'

'PARANOIA IN THE PSYCHE'

I met DUP councillor Dale Pankhurst at the Christmas tree at Belfast's City Hall, and we talked as he drove me around interface areas of north Belfast. He was angry because a newspaper had associated him with the intimidation of a young Catholic woman, which he denied.

The woman and her four children had been forced to abandon plans to move into the house allocated to the family by a housing association in the Tyndale estate on the mountainy outer edge of north Belfast. The windows of the house were smashed, a Union Jack was flown from a drainpipe and KAT (Kill All Taigs) was daubed on the front wall.

'The problem is there are still those on both sides that just want to cling on to violence, you know. Well, more so on the republican side, obviously,' he said.

'Tyndale's where I'm living at the moment, in my grandmother's old house. There's a bit of damp in it. I live with my girlfriend and our child. Recently, there has been some new builds allocated out. Around three weeks ago people were talking about republicans getting these houses. So, of course, I went to the housing association and to the police, well, not officially the police, I went through the local neighbourhood constable. I told him about the rumours and that it might be best to have a wee look at this before you do anything, because the last thing you want to do is move someone in and then them getting seriously injured or else the house being severely damaged. I think threat assessments were carried out. A few couples moved in, and then their homes were attacked. I don't know much more than that,' he said. He added, however: 'Given the history of north Belfast, Tyndale is a staunchly loyalist area and there are security force members who live there. So, of course, people think, where will the information go if this person's a real hardline republican?' Pankhurst had also expressed the view on social media that locals should get houses before anyone else and that 'our areas cannot become dumping grounds for all sorts'.[4]

A year earlier, Pankhurst had claimed during a BBC TV interview that he saw no evidence of a sectarian motive after a similar incident. Behind him the spray-painted words 'All Taigs Out' could be seen on the garden wall of the house.

North Belfast is notorious for its housing problems, chiefly the chronic shortage of public housing and disputes about sectarianism in its distribution. Research consistently shows that people would prefer to live in mixed-religion neighbourhoods. In 2017 this was the choice of

---

4 'DUP councillor Dale Pankhurst posted Protestant areas "cannot be dumping ground for all sorts"', *Irish News*, 2 December 2019

78 per cent of people surveyed by Northern Ireland Life and Times. Yet 94 per cent of housing in Belfast is segregated.[5] In 2009 a UN committee expressed concern that 'the most disadvantaged and marginalised individuals and groups, such as Catholic families in Northern Belfast', were suffering disproportionately.[6] In 2017 the Equality Commission (ECNI) found that while there had been some progress, Catholics were still waiting longest for social housing.[7] The Equality Coalition, a group of NGOs, published a report on sectarianism in 2020. Its author Robbie McVeigh noted that the Good Friday Agreement had introduced a statutory duty to measure inequality brought about by institutional discrimination.[8]

Pankhurst, however, told me that nationalists 'exaggerated' their need for housing, while unionists were 'honest'. He said he did not like to use the terms Catholic and Protestant when it came to housing, because 'you have Catholics who are unionists and Protestants who are nationalists, well allegedly.' His family stories were harsh, though he said he had a great and happy childhood. His granny, a messenger for the RUC, had talked about having to go up to republican police stations in a Saracen tank, getting 'bricked' along the way. His mother had told him about having to throw herself to the ground on Duncairn Gardens during a gun battle, and how Westland where she grew up was known as 'Dodge City' because of incidents like the IRA shootings of 'two Christian fishermen' taking a short cut through the estate. He showed me houses defaced by paint bombs, including one where a man had his Christmas lights torn down, and pointed out the shifting flashpoints.

We drove through Glenbryn, infamous for the Holy Cross protests of 2001. Pankhurst was only six, and said he did not remember anything about it but had seen a TV show that was, he believed, biased. The dispute, which started over a flag, ended up with an ugly blockade at which loyalists hurled bags of urine, a blast bomb, and sectarian abuse at schoolchildren his age. In his account of the affair, the PUP leader Billy Hutchinson, while trenchantly criticising the loyalist violence,

5 Ann Marie Gray et al, NI Peace Monitoring Report No 5, Community Relations Council, 2018, pp175–8
6 UN Committee on Economic, Social and Cultural Rights, forty-second session, Geneva, 4–22 May 2009
7 https://www.equalityni.org/KeyInequalities-Housing
8 https://caj.org.uk/2020/02/17/sectarianism-the-key-facts/

also questioned the motivation of the parents of the children. They were determined, he said, to 'march them up to the school'.[9] Television footage went around the world showing small children crying and clutching their parents' hands while adults, their faces distorted by rage, lined the pavement to shout at them. Hutchinson wrote: 'loyalists were depicted by the media as white supremacists.'[10]

Loyalists frequently blame the media for how they are perceived. In November 2020, a few days before the anniversary of the tragic death in 2001 of sixteen-year-old Glen Branagh from Tiger's Bay, a photograph was posted on a loyalist Twitter account of a mural dedicated to his memory. The post explained that the boy had 'died on active service … when a pipe bomb thrown by Republicans exploded whilst he was trying to remove it from outside local houses.'[11] Branagh, known to youth workers as 'not a bad lad' and to his friends as Spacer, had been inducted into the UDA's youth wing in 2000. There was a problem with the loyalist account of his death because Branagh had actually been involved in a riot when the pipe bomb he was throwing at nationalist youths across the peace line exploded in his hand causing catastrophic head injuries from which he died. The UDA had denounced journalists for reporting this, though it was on CCTV.

Pankhurst loved flags. He remembered an incident when he was a toddler on his father's shoulders. They were going to Beatties fish and chip shop and he spoke of his delight at the flash of red, white and blue above him, but this was quickly followed by the explosion of some sort of device. His father grabbed him into his arms and rushed him home. He recalled loyalist feuds – 'bullets whizzing up and down the street' – and his sister having a screwdriver put to her knee 'by criminals masquerading as loyalists'.

He showed me where an old RUC station had been demolished and houses for nationalists built on the site. Unionists saw this as 'ethnic cleansing', he said. And, back to the contemporary, he pointed out the site of the old Girdwood barracks, where, after years of disputes about who to house there, a community hub to serve people on either side

9 Billy Hutchinson with Gareth Mulvenna *My Life in Loyalism*, Merrion Press, 2020, p. 253

10 Ibid., p. 254

11 @LoyalistPhoto, Twitter, 11 November 2020

of the interface was built instead. 'The problem is they keep the gates open at night, so you have Protestant youths and loyalist youths come down from that end and nationalists and republicans come up from that end and they normally fight with each other at what is supposed to be a peace centre,' Pankhurst said.

'It's paranoia in the psyche,' he told me. 'Community relations are at an all-time low and loyalists especially, and unionists, feel the Good Friday Agreement and the legacy of the peace process are geared against them. The major fear is a united Ireland. It's the big bogeyman. Unionists and loyalists just don't want it. People are really angry that this place is being used as a football by the Irish government, the British government, and indeed the European Union. It has just been chip, chip, chip, across a range of things: legacy, parades, housing. You have this spectrum of grievances that unionism has at the minute – they are not being dealt with properly. And then, of course, the Brexit grenade right in the middle of it all doesn't help.

'If you put yourself in the position of a working-class unionist who goes to work from nine to five, comes home and sits down to his tea, and all you have bashing out in the media is that another soldier's been lifted, another legacy inquest has been opened up into a Provo that was shot dead in disputed circumstances, while there remains I don't know how many murders committed by the IRA that still haven't been resolved in any way, shape or form – that's just one tiny piece of the puzzle. Then you move on to parades. Every summer you've got another interface.

'It's incredibly sad that we're twenty-one years after peace supposedly come to this country, and yet we have thirteen- and fourteen-year-olds who were born years after the Troubles ended, and they're engaging in violence. In Lower Oldpark, round about Halloween time, I approached one of the young guys and I said, "Clear off, you're not from round here. What on earth are you doing down here?" The usual response is, I'm just down fighting this guy because he was texting my girlfriend or something last week. But this young fella turned round and said, "I'm down here to protect my community." I couldn't believe it. I just said, "For goodness sake, wise up and go home. All's you're doing is causing trouble for all the residents round here."'

Pankhurst spoke of his passionate attachment to his cultural traditions. 'My dad puts his flag up religiously on 1 July and takes it down Black

Saturday. I can remember him showing me my granda's collarette and apron from the Black and the Orange,' he said. 'I always loved going to the bands. I love traditional blood and thunder. It's just the old-style bold Orange flute. I'm in Whiterock Flute Band. It's traditional – it hasn't changed its style in over fifty years since it was created. I mean, "The Sash", "Lily", "No Surrender", "Dolly's Brae". We still have the old goatskin bass drum, and the thump of that thing is absolutely amazing. It's half a Lambeg. That's a Lambeg shell cut in half and then the two skins put on each side. We also have the traditional Balmoral-style hats, which is like a bonnet with a big orange plume that sticks out the side at a ninety-degree angle. It's brilliant, I love it.'

It was loyalty to the flag that got him into politics, he told me. 'The Parades Commission is not liked within loyalist and unionist communities. Any time that Sinn Féin have gone to them and said, we've a problem with this parade, they have acted upon what Sinn Féin demands. I was outside City Hall the day they voted to limit the flying of the union flag. I was eighteen. I can remember the atmosphere changing like the flick of a switch once the vote came out. All of a sudden there was just mayhem. I can remember lads going up and punching the life out of a Land Rover just out of sheer anger. There were certain people tried to get me involved in rioting, and I point-blank refused. I saw my mates being criminalised and their futures ruined.' I asked him who the certain people were: 'Just men with scarves over their faces', he said. Paramilitaries? 'Potentially,' he said. 'And that's when I thought, throwing a brick or a bottle isn't going to make much of a difference any more, you need to get involved in politics. A year later I joined the DUP.'

There was considerable anger at that time against the DUP over what many loyalists saw as its failure to defend the flag when Belfast City Council voted to limit the number of days the Union Jack could be flown from City Hall, in line with British government guidance on designated days. 'The local government elections in 2014 were my first election, and we got it rough and heavy on the doors,' said Pankhurst. 'People were saying, I wouldn't vote for you if my life depended on it. One individual let his dog out on me. There's me sprinting down his big, long driveway with his Staffy running after me. I think it was the first time I outran a dog, a bit like Usain Bolt. The loyalist people in north Belfast are sort of unforgiving. If you double-cross them you know you will be shafted in the next election. There is no second chances with it. That's why I'm a people politician – unionism and loyalism first.

'The politicians right at the top of this game may live in big houses, but they don't realise the damage they're doing to the working-class areas, where a flag is all that people really do have to cling to. Even bread and butter's hard to come by every day. It's more than just a piece of cloth, you know. I can remember studying flags and symbols at Queen's. I can remember reading books and stuff about it.' Pankhurst was about to start studying for a PhD at Queen's. 'It's my identity. It's what rallies people around the cause of being British. Certainly there are more English people than there are anybody else in the United Kingdom, but I'd say Northern Ireland is the most loyal.' Jayda Fransen, one of the leaders of the far-right Britain First group had told BBC Northern Ireland's *Spotlight* something similar in May 2019. She said Northern Ireland was the 'last stronghold for Britain', and she loved its flags. 'For a patriot it's paradise,' she said. She said that you would get called a racist in England if you flew a Union Jack.

'The Tories would shaft us in a heartbeat,' Pankhurst said. 'I have no lust for the Tories. The only time Tories want us is when they are looking to put soldiers on the front line for them. I absolutely don't agree with their politics, their austerity cuts. I'm more left of centre because I'm from a working-class background. The Tories will use the union to get to their own power, as Edward Carson would say. London's never been our friend.

'I'm loyal to the queen and the crown and my country. None of those things have ever shafted me. Parliament has, but I'm not loyal to parliament. And I don't think any loyalist is. A unionist is someone who likes the economic benefits of being part of the union, but also the political, cultural and social aspects as well. But loyalists take it that bit further.'

He had a meeting to go to in City Hall, but before we finished, he returned to the Tyndale incident. It turned out that the woman who had been unable to move into the house had contacted him for help. 'I've got texts on my phone from the partner of that woman,' he said. 'Hold on a wee second.' He held out his phone for me to read: *"I really appreciate you helping regarding the matter A. raised with you.*" He started going on about his links to the Ulster Defence Regiment and all,' said Pankhurst, 'so I replied: *"It doesn't matter … you should be able to live anywhere on any side. I have a duty of care as an elected rep for every one and have to report everything I hear …"* The other person texted back: *"Okay, no problem, mate. I totally understand and me and A. really appreciate your help."*'

'All's I was doing was trying to protect them,' Pankhurst said. 'I think they've got intimidation points, so they'll be okay, like.' Those on waiting lists for public housing are allocated points according to their needs. Having evidence of intimidation would gain you points and boost your chances of getting a house elsewhere. According to Pankhurst he had simply done his bit to find a Belfast solution to a Belfast problem. 'They'll be fine,' he said. 'They'll be looked after.'

'YOU JUST SOW A WEE SEED'

'I hate the term cross-community,' said Eileen Weir. 'In the Shankill Women's Centre we have Indian communities and we have Chinese communities, we have a lot of different communities. And we've always had a mixed workforce here. We were doing all this long before the Good Friday Agreement, but we had to do it under the radar in those days. Now women would book their taxis from all over west Belfast and the taxi drivers bring them to the Shankill to us on a Thursday morning. The women will tell you, as well, there's better shops on the Shankill than the Falls.'

The two roads run parallel to each other, separated by a peace line that is mostly open now, though still capable of being closed if there is any trouble. Both roads were somewhat severed from the city centre when the M1 motorway was built. The Shankill starts at Peter's Hill and sweeps outwards and upwards to Woodvale, beyond which is the Crumlin Road. Alan McBride, who used to work in a butcher's shop on the Shankill, told me it had always been superior to the Falls for shopping, with small grocers, butchers, hardware, drapers and fruit and vegetable shops. There are quite a few boarded-up buildings now. He felt that the road has, in a way, never recovered from the IRA bomb detonated there in a fish shop in 1993, killing ten and injuring fifty-seven, among them his wife Sharon and her father Desmond Frizzell, the shop's owner. 'There's no life in it now in the sense that there aren't the bustling crowds there used to be,' he said. He listed the names of the old traditional shops and grocers: Moore's, Glover's, Stevenson's. Some are still in business. McBride no longer lives in the area but is still partial to the Ulster fry for £3 in Mikala's Kitchen.

'We had the president of Ireland here on Good Friday,' said Weir. 'Right enough, our walls were graffitied, we were intimidated: Brexit, get Ireland out of Ulster, you know, all the normal stuff. We got Belfast City Council up to get it all off before the president came and we went ahead, and it was a great visit,' she said.

It was a different story when Mary Robinson came to Belfast in 1996, and visited Windsor Women's Centre, also in a working-class unionist area. Loyalists firebombed the centre after her visit. In 2018 I had sat in on some of Weir's weekly discussion sessions and was amazed by the warmth, openness and solidarity the women showed towards each other. They were from some of the areas that had suffered most during the Troubles. The political violence was gone, but otherwise their issues were the fundamentally the same as they had been during the conflict. The women were struggling with the complexities of health, housing, employment and welfare systems that kept many of them and their families in a constant state of stress. Being poor was a full-time occupation. Weir presided, a warm and skilful facilitator.

'I'm a true Shankill Road woman,' she said. 'There were plots behind our street, and people came from everywhere to get their flowers and their cabbage and scallions and lettuce and tomatoes. My mum worked in Ewart's mill. My granny and my aunts and uncles and all lived in the same street. That used to be the way. My mum's sister married a Catholic, so all my cousins were Catholics. I used to play as a child in Ballymurphy.

'I left school at sixteen with absolutely nothing. I joined the UDA. It wasn't illegal. When there were no-go areas, I made sure that the elderly people got their milk and their bread and butter. It was caring for the community, and that's what I thought the whole of the UDA was doing. Then I got a job in Gallaher's tobacco factory and got heavily involved in trade unionism. I was a shop steward for eighteen years.' She had worked in Ballymena and had to intervene to stop displays of flags in the workplace – workers retaliated by wearing red, white and blue clothes.

'I got an education through the union movement. I went on to the women's advisory committee and I got to meet a lot of people, North and South, because we were amalgamated. We supported an Irish language primary school. We supported the campaign against strip-searching. Within the Protestant community, strip-searching was a republican issue, because most of the women in Armagh prison were republican women. So I had to work out for myself what was right and what was wrong. I campaigned secretly because otherwise I would probably have been on a lamp post with tar and feathers round me.

'I took redundancy in 1995 and started coming into the Shankill Women's Centre. I did a personal development programme and you have to set your goals, and one of mine was to transfer my skills into the community. Education had let the women down. They were coming in here, they were sitting smoking and they were just talking, but nothing was changing. They all lived in the one community, so they weren't getting any wider views. I started working with those women. I suppose that course changed my life.' Weir's skills attracted the attention of well-known republican community activist Mary Enright. 'She had tortured me for two or three years to become a facilitator, and Mary would be somebody that was a good mentor to me,' Weir said. 'I was wary. I had this thing at that time of not being able to spell and write. In the end she put it to me very plain. She said, "Right, Eileen, this is just the way it is. We need more Prods to deliver this because all the Fenians in west Belfast are all doing it and you are being left behind." And I said, "Right, okay, Mary." And that was that.'

After that, Weir was called on to mediate in some extremely difficult situations. One was the Holy Cross protest. 'I live there. I live in Glenbryn. I was sent up to see if there was anything Shankill Women's Centre could do. Those women in Glenbryn had begun an innocent protest, which was hijacked by paramilitarism. It got blown up out of proportion. I could have seen them from my front window. I was approached by a very prominent community worker. "I didn't see you at the protest, Eileen," he said. And I went, "I know, you didn't." She told the man it was hypocritical to demand the right to parade past Catholic houses in Portadown and call it the 'Queen's Highway' and then deny Catholic parents the right to bring their children to school past Protestant ones.

She also knew the women caught up in the so-called Shankill feud. 'I was a Shankill Road woman and they were all Shankill Road women. You either went to school with them or you had worked with them at some stage,' she said. The feud was sparked when UDA leader Johnny Adair held a march on the Shankill along with members of the Loyalist Volunteer Force (LVF), which had broken away from the UVF in order to back the Orange Order at Drumcree. The UVF retaliated. At least seven people were murdered in the months that followed, and about eight hundred people were driven out of the UDA-dominated Lower Shankill into the UVF-dominated Upper Shankill.

'So I was sent in to the UDA area, to Gina Adair, Johnny Adair's wife. She said, "No, we're all right, we can look after ourselves." I also went to the women who were put out of Lower Shankill. They'd have been seen as UVF. I said, I'll come in and do some personal development with you, we'll make it fun. So they said, yes. And after doing that work with them I said to them, now you need to consider your name, because they called themselves FODDD, Families of the Displaced, Dispersed and Distressed, I said it is bringing you back constantly to what happened. It is traumatising you. So about three years later, they changed their name. And they're now called Families Beyond Conflict. That's what you do, you just sow a wee seed and leave it with them. You don't try and tell them what to do.

'I probably agreed with 80 per cent of the Good Friday Agreement. It was a chance, it was a hope, for a future that wasn't perfect, but at least it was something. I didn't agree with the prisoners getting out because most of our loyalist prisoners of war were already out. And what happened was a lot of ordinary criminals claimed they were loyalists and got out. And now we wonder where the drug dealers are coming from.

'We talk about everything here. We talked about what would happen if we became a united Ireland. The women wanted to know would you be better off, or worse off. Nobody knows, nobody can tell us. The next question was, but what would happen to me as a Protestant? I said, "Nothing should happen to you. It should be a shared Ireland for everybody with nobody left out. You'll not get any special treatment, but you'll not get any worse treatment than anybody else. It's trying to build an equal society, where one religion doesn't fear the other religion. The plan is that you will still be able to do and celebrate what you want to celebrate, and still have your own culture." And the Catholic woman beside that woman said, "Yes, and that's the way it should be.'"

Northern Ireland society as it currently exists is rife with inequalities. 'I've never seen poverty so bad around here,' Weir said. 'We never had food banks on the Shankill, never. I could probably count ten now between here and Ligoniel, just up the road. People are proud, and people just can't afford to be proud any more. It's soul-destroying. Having to use a food bank and admitting that they can't manage. We have working poor. We have people doing two jobs and still have to use food banks. The welfare system doesn't work, and the reforms mean they need to get two jobs. But then they lose other benefits. I mean, it's the typical cleaning jobs, you know, low-paid, hard work, sundry jobs. A lot of women have gone into caring again. There are a lot of people out there that are struggling.'

Over 100,000 Northern Ireland families depend on universal credit (UC), the relatively new aggregated benefit brought in to replace a range of other supports. Its inflexibility means it is uniquely unsuited to the work patterns described by Weir, particularly when women are juggling jobs involving zero-hour contracts, meaning that they do not know from week to week what their income will be. There is also a benefit cap meaning that you can only receive a limited amount from benefits regardless of your needs.

Under this regime there has been a dramatic rise in destitution – and the shocking, Dickensian-sounding word is appropriate here. Destitution means not being able to afford basic necessities like heat, light, food, clothing and hygiene products. According to Cliff Edge Coalition NI, a group of community advice and support organisations, almost a quarter of Northern Ireland children live in poverty and, obviously, the figure is far higher in certain areas. When the Northern Ireland Executive published its draft budget in 2021, it proposed slashing the funds available for groups supporting welfare claimants – without putting in place overall funding at a level that would promote economic recovery.

Dr Ciara Fitzpatrick of Ulster University and the Cliff Edge Coalition told me this would be devastating for people already caught in a system that was demeaning and marginalising. 'This all goes back to the neo-liberal ideology of the UK government and the Northern Ireland Executive has not done enough to protect people. We are back to the

Victorian notion of poverty being the responsibility of the individual, and it is leaving people powerless,' she said. 'It is going to cause a tsunami of ill health, including mental health.'

Those who are hardest hit are lone parents, 90 per cent of whom are women. One woman told me that in her experience UC was cruel, aggressive, stigmatising and debilitating. It had pushed her deeper into debt, and made it impossible for her to work. Eileen Weir was angry that the system depended on women somehow managing to pull their families and communities through hard times. 'During the Troubles women in both communities actually kept the communities alive,' she said. 'And it looks as if that's happening again. But again being penalised at every turn.'

Julie-Ann Corr-Johnston is an articulate and outspoken young loyalist feminist. She was elected to Belfast City Council for the PUP in 2014, the first woman to represent her area and the first openly lesbian unionist councillor. I had heard her speak about how she had not always been so confident. She said she had been self-harming and suicidal. It was the Shankill Women's Centre that empowered her, she said. She lives with her wife and their children in north Belfast and is still a community activist, though she lost her council seat in 2019. She described poverty as a greater threat to the union than republicanism, and shared Weir's view that unionist politicians have let their people down.

'Then they've the cheek to turn round and call us resilient,' said Weir. 'If we were resilient we wouldn't have the rates of suicide that we have. We're not resilient. There's a woman in one of my groups and she has lost two daughters and a granddaughter in the last four years to suicide. We also have the trauma that has come down through the years. We never got a peace dividend in the areas most affected by the Troubles. There's a lot of the Good Friday Agreement was never implemented. We haven't really dealt with the past or equality issues, or women's representation. There's no Civic Forum, no Bill of Rights. I ask women – what's different for you? And one of the things that they say is: We fear our own community now more than the other.

'There is a dictatorship within our own communities. A lot of people didn't want to be bothered doing things any more. They'd had enough. So a small minority, many of them ex-paramilitary men, claimed to speak for a community and kept control. Funders supported them without asking questions, and people were afraid to challenge them. That's something I do. If it's an all-male platform I stand up before it starts and ask where the women are. Don't get me wrong – there are some former paramilitaries doing great work.

'I think working-class women are streets ahead of anyone else when it comes to changing this place. But we're not getting any recognition for it. We are about to build a women's centre. PEACE IV's funding it in conjunction with Belfast City Council.' The European Union has invested millions in funding community infrastructure since the Good Friday Agreement and has committed, despite Brexit, to continue PEACE Funding until 2027. 'The new centre will be on the old bonfire site in Lanark Way, right on the interface with the Falls,' said Weir. 'We never would have thought of that in the past. That's how far we have come.'

'CHANGE'

'Sharon's death in the bomb was a huge event that changed everything. We were a young couple with a wee girl and a life in front of us,' said Alan McBride. 'But I get frustrated by the way people in this country constantly refer to people by what happened to them in the Troubles. I am "Alan McBride whose wife was killed in the Shankill bomb in 1993". Yet I have done so much more with my life since, and as well, there was a whole life before that. And I think when you start to pigeonhole people by what happened to them, sometimes there's an inability to get beyond that. And so you become the professional victim. Sharon was helping her father in his shop when two IRA men walked in with the bomb, which exploded almost immediately.

'It's almost as though you are not allowed to change, and to change your mind. And if you were outspoken on victims' issues and you change your outlook, it is really difficult. Whenever Sharon was killed I took placards and stood outside Sinn Féin offices. I confronted Gerry Adams. I chased him around America. I had a hatred of Gerry Adams, and not just republicanism, but loyalism as well. It was difficult then to come out and actually say something different because it's almost as though everything you've been saying before was not true, and so what you are saying now might not be true either. You could argue that point, and yet I just see it that I was at different stages in life. I don't regret that campaigning work I did.

'There was a Gerry Adams that was talking about peace and a Gerry Adams that carried the coffin of Thomas Begley,' he said. Begley was one of the bombers, and was killed in the blast. 'I came to understand in later years that there was a struggle going on within Adams. But when I was confronting him as he came off a plane in Dublin airport I was not aware of that, nor was I even in a place where I was ready to hear it. It was easier for me to see him as a pariah. I was standing up for innocent victims. So now when I see people taking those kind of positions I might challenge them but I would never say that they're wrong for doing it. Sometimes when you are on a quest for justice you've got to speak out. My thing is now that if the question is about making a difference, how are you likely to make the most difference? I know for me that came whenever I was able to talk to people across a table and get to know them.

'After Sharon died I used to read and write up in the graveyard at Carnmoney, where she is buried. I began to change when I met a republican who had been in prison when the Shankill bomb went off and he said some of the younger republicans were celebrating almost, and he told them off. He told me that what happened that day on the Shankill Road was wrong and that he was deeply sorry. I knew he meant it, and that was the first time I'd heard that. And I was never quite the same person after that.

'One of the things I thought about was sectarianism and the influence my uncle Cecil had over me. He was a Christian. I actually suspect he was gay. Lovely, beautiful Christian man, but also very bigoted in his views. I realised we live in a society that is so abnormal, and that played a part in people joining organisations and going out and doing the things that Thomas Begley and Sean Kelly did. Not that it made me soft on them because I have no time for either of them. But at least it helped me to understand that it's just too convenient to try to put all the blame for the Troubles on people like that.

'Basically I'm a unionist. I'm a unionist who has also been a nationalist. Whenever I was a cross-community youth worker I heard a version of history that I'd never heard before. I heard about gerrymandering and all that, and I became more Green than Orange. When Sharon was killed I had to think really hard about where I was.

'I'm an Alliance voter now. I don't see a confident unionism out there, a unionism that talks about the merits and benefits of the union and of being part of this great United Kingdom. There's a terrible lack of generosity too, not to mention the homophobia. There is this thing that we, meaning unionists, have given and given and got nothing back. I don't see it, whether that is politically or culturally, socially or economically. I just don't see what we have given. If anything, there is a sense of entitlement that must sicken people in other parts of the UK.'

McBride supported the Good Friday Agreement, but regrets that it has left Northern Ireland with a system that insists that politicians have to identify along sectarian lines as unionist, nationalist or other. 'There's a serious lack of vision when all you can say is "Vote for us because we're not themmuns",' he told me. 'That is so uninspiring. Unionism is going to have to move beyond its narrow tribalism, to become inclusive. It is cut off even from its working-class voters. When a unionist gets a big job the first thing they do is move into a middle-class area, whereas Martin McGuinness and people like that lived among the people for all their days. Unionism is going to have to show that it is progressive to want to stay in the United Kingdom – that the NHS is worth protecting, that we can work with our neighbours in Ireland and in Europe to build a better future.

'I'm a romantic unionist – I just love being part of a group of islands that are so diverse and so incredible. So I don't want to lose that. But unionism has become a term that is so tarnished that even people like me who want to remain in the UK don't want to use it to describe ourselves. Quite a lot of Alliance people are like that. Also, I am a pragmatist. And I mean, economically, I want to be able to have a house and a car and a job and a standard of living. And to be honest with you, those things matter more to me than the flag that's flying above our country. And if because of Brexit, Northern Ireland is not flourishing and the South is, why would you not want to be part of that? I absolutely would – for me, for my daughter, for my family. I guess people would say you would sell your soul, and you're right, I would. Having a life matters more to me than flying a flag.'

PAVING AN ALTERNATIVE PATH

We met in Forthspring, an interfaith community based in an old Methodist church right up against the peace wall between the Springfield and Woodvale roads in west Belfast. Reverend Karen Sethuraman is warm and welcoming, with a generous smile. She was bustling around, in denims and a sweatshirt, in the middle of moving her base to rooms in the building. She was excited by the potential of working on the interface. 'Something like 80 per cent of people in Northern Ireland say they are spiritual but only 30 per cent go to church regularly. The mainstream churches find that sad but for me it is exciting that 80 per cent of people are spiritual,' she said. 'My role is to do work which supports my mantra, which is, "Love God, love your neighbour".'

The high interface fences of this part of Belfast dominate the local skyline, looping through areas of dense working-class housing that looks the same on either side. The Good Friday Agreement goal of dismantling the fences by 2013 was not realised. Some, in fact, were reinforced and made taller. In places they have become tourist attractions. Sethuraman is driven by the potential they present as locations in which to break down distrust and bring people into a sense of belonging together. Much of the work that has been done in this regard has been led by women. However, a 2020 survey by the Department of Justice found that Protestants living along peace lines were considerably more fearful about the prospect of them being dismantled than Catholics. Almost 40 per cent said they felt their community would disappear, and 18 per cent even said they would move away.[12]

'The faith I grew up in was fuelled by fear,' said Sethuraman. 'I was born in 1972 and lived on Hyndford Street, the same as Van Morrison, in the heart of east Belfast. My mum brought me up on her own, and she was a person of faith so I was brought to church every week, to the Elim Pentecostal. I invited Christ into my heart when I was eight, because I was afraid of hell. In time I moved to the Baptist church because it had a vibrant youth group and my friends went. Church bored me, but towards the end of my teens I had a deep sense of call. I had already learned that I could not be a church leader. I lost sleep because I thought I would be called to Africa as a missionary, because that was what women were allowed to do, and that was not what I wanted.'

Sethuraman is now a Baptist pastor, under the Baptist Union of Great Britain. Her ministry is not recognised by the Baptist Church in Ireland, which will not ordain women. 'I don't feel called to be a maintenance

---

12 https://www.justice-ni.gov.uk/publications/public-attitudes-peace-walls

minister with a church and a flock,' she said. 'I am a pastor in the community and in the streets. I can marry people and bury people, and I can reach out to the people like me who never fitted in to the church of For God and Ulster.' She considers herself to be in the tradition of the Anabaptists. 'They had the courage to step out of the institutional church to create community and do life,' she said. 'They paved an alternative path and got persecuted for it.' When Sinn Féin's Deirdre Hargey was mayor of Belfast, she chose Sethuraman to be her chaplain.

She studied theology at Queen's University and was shocked by the sectarianism she encountered in her training for ministry. 'I was told I should not be seen with Catholic clergy, and there was a lot of emphasis on converting Catholics,' she said. She had one teacher who excited her with talk of embracing mystery and the things she had been shut out from in the staunchness of her childhood. She got a job as a youth worker with a Baptist church. But she was never going to fit in. 'It got to a point when I realised I had to either sell my soul to Northern Irish Protestantism or be true to my own faith. The elders, all male, wanted me to present them with a strategy for evangelism, to get more people into church, but I knew my most effective work was outside of all that.'

She left, and plunged into what she calls her wilderness years. 'The church treated me appallingly. They said what I was doing was not the work of God. I was the loneliest I have ever been,' she said. 'It nearly destroyed me.' But she rallied, and decided to strike out on her own. 'I have always had a heart for people who don't fit in, people like me, people who are spiritual but have been rejected by their church. I speak a lot about gender equality, and I meet a lot of LGBT+ folks who have been hurt in that way. There is work to be done redeeming and repairing the damage. My faith goes beyond what I think. I would be slaughtered within the church for my stance on so many issues. I am pro-life *and* pro- the right to choose. I'd like to see more people living the experience of anti-sectarianism. I believe in the work of reconciliation, but the whole "you must forgive" thing makes me nervous – it isn't a good starting point.'

She celebrates her love for her family on her busy social media accounts, often posting about her grief over the recent death of her mother, whom she adored, and who died after cancer treatment was delayed because of the COVID crisis. Her husband, Karu, is a Malaysian

Indian. 'He's from a Hindu background but he became a Christian in Malaysia and went to a Catholic school,' she said. 'We have three children – Megan, Erin and Johah – and during the Black Lives Matter demonstrations we posted a picture of our mixed-race family.' She said they had all experienced racism in Northern Ireland. When her daughter heard Vice President Elect Kamala Harris say she was the first woman of colour in the role and she would not be the last, Erin declared that she wanted to go into politics and to be the president of Ireland.

After Lord Kilclooney, formerly known as John Taylor, once an Ulster Unionist minister, referred disparagingly to Harris as 'the Indian', Sethuraman invited him to dinner with her family. He did not reply. She also wrote to the House of Lords in protest. He was not sanctioned. She is highly political, and if she had not been 'hounded', as she describes it, by her calling, she would have chosen to be a human rights lawyer. 'Finding the middle ground is not the answer,' she said. 'I stand on the side of the people who have experienced injustice, and with my neighbour.' Her children, when asked are they Protestant or Catholic, cheerfully reply that they are neither. 'For many people here ecumenism is a bad word – but in a post-conflict community on a small island, I really don't think so.'

Sethuraman is interested in alternative theologies that offer healing. 'There is a theology around reconciliation through lament,' she said. 'I am not sure the churches here know how to grieve and lament. There are so many hurt and broken lives on all sides of the community here. I want to know, where is the church in that?' she said. In 2021, Suthuraman took part in a public debate on Irish unity, hosted by the Ireland's Future group.

After I left her I went to No Alibis bookshop to collect some books I had ordered. Walking down Botanic Avenue I was behind two men, one of them Black, the other white. Holding hands, laughing and chatting, they were absorbed in each other, stopping briefly, in step like dancers, to kiss lightly.

'CHANGE IS ACTUALLY POSSIBLE'

As a journalist, I was often in the Shankill estate, and it was always an anxious experience, sometimes a frightening one. This estate was, until the end of the loyalist feud in 2000, dominated by a particularly brutal

UDA faction led by Johnny Adair. For a time the whole of the lower end of the Shankill was known as 'Adairland'. His house on Boundary Way was known as the Big Brother house, while the green in the middle of the estate was called Johnny Square. His big cannonball face glared out from the most prominent gables. It used to be a desolate place where you felt watched, and knew that anyone who spoke to you was being watched too.

The UDA's heavily armed and drugged-up paramilitaries no longer strut about it, though many of the old murals commemorating killers are still in place. One such painting takes up the entire gable wall of Stephen Donnan-Dalzell's house, dedicated, in gothic script, to 'Stevie "Top Gun" McKeag'. Born in 1970, deceased in 2000, he is described as 'sleeping where no shadows fall'. Top Gun wore a gold chain around his neck with a golden gun charm dangling from it. A prolific sectarian killer and second in command to Adair, he died in his house of an overdose of cocaine and painkillers, an arrow from a crossbow embedded in his living room wall. In 2019, his son was jailed after he attempted to evade the police by driving recklessly at high speed through the streets of east Belfast in a black BMW.

Donnan-Dalzell, who uses the non-binary pronoun their, lives in an end-of-terrace house in the middle of the estate. Their house looks on to the back of the great crumbling edifice of the old Belfast courthouse on the Crumlin Road. 'On any given Sunday there's upwards of one hundred tourists a day outside looking at the mural,' said Donnan-Dalzell. 'It's McKeag's family that I have married into, incidentally. His sister is my sister-in-law, but I don't really talk about that with them. They are entitled to grieve for their dead. I just tread lightly because I'm an outsider here, even though I am a working-class Protestant.' A tattoo runs the length of their arm. It is a quote from a talk Lyra McKee gave about LGBTQ+ youth: 'Do not tell me there is no such thing as hope.' Donnan-Dalzell had it done in the weeks after she was killed in Derry. In their early thirties, they are of the same 'ceasefire babies' generation as Lyra.

'I work in a homeless hostel. It's a hard job but I really enjoy it and I'm good at it. I have the right temperament. I think I've a big heart. So I have the tattoo, literally wearing my heart on my sleeve. Lyra was very much the best of us. Our generation was never supposed to know this heartache and pain. To say that one of my friends was murdered by the IRA is a surreal thing. It made me feel I needed to try to do better, and be better, and make this place better. Because that's what she did, she came from a place of understanding rather than judgement,' they said.

'People tell me all the time, it's hopeless, this work. I'm helping people navigate things like universal credit and applications for social housing. They may be in the throes of addiction, things like heroin or diazepam. These are the most vulnerable people. Not only are they homeless, they have mental health issues, no family support, they're in and out of jail, they're in and out of hospital. There is violence against women. It's just multiple complex needs.'

Donnan-Dalzell felt the area had changed. 'When people talk about the Shankill or the Falls, they picture a grim scenario. This place was a hotbed of sectarian strife. But working-class Protestant communities get seen as backwards and bigoted, and they're not. The people here are unionists – they don't want a united Ireland, but they're not scared to go into Catholic areas and they don't think that Catholics are monsters. They have Catholic friends and work with Catholic people and people from different backgrounds. There are things they think are important that might look sectarian but it's not that they want to be up to their necks in Fenian blood or anything like that, it's because that's how they were brought up. That's their culture, that's what they call home. I've lived here with my husband William for two years now. He's lived here most of his life. Me and William have never had any issue living here as a gay couple,' they said, admitting, 'I don't know if that would be the same if I was a Catholic.

'Growing up, I would have been quite loyalist but also very ignorant. I didn't want anything to do with Catholics or the Irish language. When I was nineteen and realised I was gay, I suddenly saw that I was now an outsider myself. The DUP did not represent me and didn't want to. I had to find my tribe, I had to find a political voice. And that took a long time. I began to realise that the DUP were probably the worst thing to happen to working-class Protestant communities. There's still very much that "us and them" mentality among the community that I come from. It's not that they're voting DUP because the DUP are homophobic, or because the DUP are pro-Brexit, it's because the DUP are not Sinn Féin. But once I was gay, I was now "them", and not "us".

'I very quickly started to become afraid because my mum and dad were very devout in their belief as born-again Christians. We would have gone to church every Sunday, and Sunday School. It was drilled into us from a pretty early age that gay people shouldn't be allowed near kids, gay people are a danger to society, they're perverts, all that really negative stuff. So whenever I came out – on 15 May 2008 – it was probably the worst day of my life, to be honest with you. It was like, Oh. My. God. I left a letter for my parents and got a bus into town and then got a phone call from my mum who was the angriest I've ever heard her, telling me to come home. I just knew straight away that I was going to be walking into a hell storm of heartache really. And that lasted about three years.

'I tried to end my life, I ran away from home, I had constant arguments with my mum because she just couldn't understand where she had gone wrong. She was having to reconcile, well, if these people are so terrible how come one of them is my son who I love? I didn't know who to turn to. Eventually I went to Cara-Friend, which is for LGBT+ youth and started to find my feet, and that was the making of me in terms of developing self-reliance. My tribe turned out to be the centre ground really: the Lundys, the Greens, the Alliance Party. When Naomi Long won Peter Robinson's seat in 2010 I realised change is actually possible. And it gave me a lot of hope for Northern Ireland.' Donnan-Dalzell stood for Alliance in the 2014 local elections.

'I think the hardest time really was when the flag vote happened. My parents viewed it as the republicanisation of City Hall and there was me, a member of a party that had gone along with that,' they said. The Alliance Party had led the move to limit the flying of the Union Jack to certain days, in line with other parts of the UK. 'Looking back on it, I think I was very arrogant and self-righteous. I was only twenty-four, like, I didn't know my arse from my elbow. That said, I used to go out with a fellow whose brother served time in jail for rioting over the flags. And his life choices are severely limited as a result. And for what? I mean, he's not blameless, but he was easily led, as young men often are.

'I stood in the area I grew up in. I had to convince my family to vote for me. It was just about eighteen months after the flag vote. You were getting chased out of people's driveways. I got spat on by someone. It taught me a lot. Mainly, that I am entitled to my politics, but so are other people. And you don't get anywhere by denigrating people because they vote a certain way. I know the Orange state stripped away the rights, entitlements and expressions of identity of nationalists and republicans and Irishness here, and that was abhorrent and entirely wrong. But you can't start a new Ireland by doing the same thing to working-class Protestants.

'My mum and dad worked in the RUC during the Troubles and lost friends and saw some horrific things. So I need to be more mindful, I think, of why they feel that they need to vote for the DUP. I try not to get into politics with my mum. (My dad passed away.) I'm thirty-one. I'm very lucky that I grew up in a time when the Troubles were coming to an end. One of my really good friends, she lives in London, and she is a die-hard republican from Armagh, a big GAA supporter. We're both lefties. But certain conversations are uncomfortable because she doesn't think there's any such thing as a good soldier, or a member of the RUC that was a decent person. And when she says those things she's actually talking about my parents.

'You have to try to empathise. Like, there are people voting for the DUP on the Shankill estate who lost relatives in the Shankill bomb. It's hard for people to look past the constitutional issue because it's not just about their place in the union, or their place in a united Ireland. It's about the people they buried, it's about the things that they have had to witness, it's about the bodies they have pulled out of rubble. It's really deeply personal. We haven't recovered as a society from the mass trauma of the Troubles, and the health infrastructure is just not there to deal with that.

'Unionism should be inclusive. Believing in the power of working together, that's what a union is. I'm a trade unionist. I believe in Northern Ireland being a part of the United Kingdom, and I think the UK being within the EU strengthens our position as a country. Brexit will just decimate the UK and Ireland. I just want to live in a place that thrives. I would prefer it to be within the EU, and I would prefer it to be within a United Kingdom, but whether we have a united Ireland or not, unless there is significant social change in how the most vulnerable are treated, it doesn't make a difference.

'There is a long way to go before we actually have proper peace here. Unionism is having an identity crisis. Under Arlene Foster the DUP have kind of crashed into the ground. They are only one seat ahead of Sinn Féin in the Assembly. They have lost two Westminster seats. They massively overplayed their hand during the hung parliament to the point where they are now irrelevant. Unionism has a lot of soul-searching to do to find out what it is now.'

'LEFT TO THEIR OWN DEVICES'

The Stevie McKeag mural features in a poem by Scott McKendry who grew up in the Shankill estate during the 1980s. 'Duck, Duck, Goose' is about the greylag geese that briefly stop off on the green each November, 'fleeing the Icelandic freeze; swapping the aurora borealis/ for murals in memory of Stevie McKeag/and Bucky McCullough'. The geese found unlikely protectors in the paramilitaries:

> When a local finally stuffed one for Christmas dinner,
> a scrawl went up on the courthouse wall:
> Let it be known
> As with tourists
> The gooses are to be left to their own devices.[13]

McKendry and the novelist Phil Harrison have a Belfast gospel hall in common. They found this out after Harrison spoke at a symposium on 'The Protestant Imagination' in 2019, during the C.S. Lewis Arts Festival. Harrison talked fondly about how he had practically grown up in the hall near his childhood home in Ballysillan, further up the mountain flank of west Belfast than the Shankill. 'Three times on a Sunday, Monday night Every Boy's Rally, Tuesday night prayer meeting, Thursday night children's meeting, Friday night youth club.' He loved it. 'It shaped my identity and sense of myself as Protestant, evangelical and working class,' he said. McKendry looked perturbed. Over coffee and giant scones he told me he had hated his time at the hall. The three of us met again at McKendry's house in south Belfast, where Harrison mocked the extensive array of fancy soaps and potions in the bathroom.

'The estate is very tame these days,' McKendry said. 'When I was really young we were allowed to run around like chickens. No one wanted to go into the estate, so it was almost like you were in the safest

---

13 Scott McKendry, *Curfuffle*, The Lifeboat Poetry Pamphlet #8, 2019, p. 15

place in the world. Though it was also completely mental. From I was very, very young, I've always been attuned to class, and especially accents and different sorts of body language and the way people dress. Not just, like, that person's middle class, that person's working class. I mean the whole strata. It used to be someone would say, "I'm from the Shankill", meaning the Shankill Road, and someone else from, say, Tennant Street a bit further up the road would say, "No you are *not*. You're from the estate.",' he said. The Shankill estate was built in the 1960s. 'Then, in the estate itself, the person who was regarded as the lowest of the low was the single mother with no brother and ten kids nearly in rags running around. And then at the top you had maybe someone who was a paramilitary or someone whose father and uncles were like hard men. And then everybody else in between.'

Harrison's mother was a primary school teacher in Ballysillan. He had been brought to services in the hall 'from my eyes were just about open ... It's a Brethren hall. It is a strange little thing, completely fundamentalist and evangelical and conservative theologically, and yet very anti-authoritarian as well,' he said. 'There's no minister. There's an eldership of usually six men, always men. Women have to wear hats in the services. But every one sits round Quaker-style. It's all centred round the breaking of the bread. The way into that was through baptism, a dunking in a tank under the stage. I was ten when I got baptised.'

His mother had been brought up in that world. 'My dad hadn't at all. He was abandoned as a child. He spent the first few years of his life in an orphanage. And eventually the Harrisons came along. They were sixty years old. They came to foster this little girl, and she had kind of taken my father under her wing. Apparently he screamed and cried so much they had to take him too.'

Knowing this had contributed to Harrison becoming a writer. 'I'm interested in how people find ways to justify their positions in the world through the stories they tell. When I look back at my dad's story, essentially he doesn't know who his parents are. He has a name but he has no interest in finding it out because as far as he's concerned the Harrisons are his parents. I have three younger brothers and a younger sister. And we all have this kind of Harrisonness, the Harrisons about town. I have, from a very young age, been conscious it was a one-generation thing. That American idea that you make yourself up, which is also a Protestant idea, has always been part of me. I didn't have some big generation thing going back that I had to live up to. My dad came from nowhere so I could also come from nowhere in a sense.

'But getting back to the hall,' he said. 'I always loved the floor. Do you remember? It was parquet.' 'Yes. Sort of bouncy parquet,' said McKendry. 'I would have been ten when I was brought to the hall. It was just a way to get me out of the house. We had moved to Ballysillan. It was kind of leafier and there were a lot of old people, and the kids in the street, to me, were just so naive and gentle. In some ways it was nice but it was also kind of weird. I was used to being able to roam free in this place that was kind of closed off. So there was a guy – the son of my aunt's friend's friend – who was the same age as me. My ma was, like, let's get him some sort of friend here. So I was sent to the Every Boy's Rally because he used to go. My ma was thinking, we have to get him some kind of social life, he's going to be a weirdo here, like. This is him.'

Harrison laughed. 'Little did she know, it's a losing battle,' he said. McKendry continued, 'There had been a kind of history in the family of what we call hermitage. When I was sent to the hall no one ever talked to me that much. I remember looking at the boys who came from the bigger houses on the front of the road, and thinking, "Look at this arsehole."' 'I was always very conscious of it when hard kids came in,' Harrison said. 'I would have been them, if you know what I mean,' said McKendry.

'So,' Harrison asked him, 'Growing up on the Shankill, you didn't see yourself necessarily as a church or a Christian-type person, but did you see yourself as a Protestant?' 'Protestant just meant not Catholic, or living within a kind of unionist or loyalist community,' said McKendry. 'People who went to church were called Christians, or born again. And it was funny, they were seen as these amazing people who could do no wrong. They were better than us, and we were lower than them, but at the same time we were proud of that. Proud to be in the gutter,' McKendry said. 'I suppose it's a kind of defence. We smoke, our fathers go out and gamble, everyone gets drunk all the time. The backdrop is the Troubles but it's something that happens in every city where you have that kind of ghettoised space. We didn't want for anything. Christmases, the sofa was absolutely piled with stuff. My da was always working. I had an uncle who went to university and went to live in

Doagh. That was a completely different world altogether. The sun was always shining. They used to go for walks with a blanket and a hamper and sit and eat a ham hock with boiled eggs and wheaten. It was picturesque.

'When I was in the estate, I was sent to Sunday School a few times and the guy who picked us up in the bus who was born again used to shout really loud at the kids and he used to wreck my nerves. I was probably just quite sensitive. So, by the time I went to the hall, I was already deeply suspicious of these sort of organised activities.'

McKendry produced a photo he had taken of the hall. 'I just took it walking past. I didn't want to take it full on, in case Samuel Orr walked out.' Orr is the evangelical pastor in Harrison's powerful novel, *The First Day*. His relationship with a woman who is a Beckett scholar and a poet leads to the birth of a child, biblical violence, and themes of retribution and forgiveness. It mingles human love and the love of God sacrilegiously, tenderly. 'She opened the door to him and wordlessly touched his face. Her hands moved over the surface and he closed his eyes. *And the earth was without form, and void; and darkness was upon the face of the deep. And the Spirit of God moved upon the face of the waters.*'[14]

Harrison remembered the 'epilogue' to evenings in the hall, when orange squash and biscuits would be served along with 'a talk about why you should give your heart to Jesus'. He still got a 'sense of vitality' from his roots, and enjoyed being 'well versed' in the Bible. 'My definition of Protestantism moves from Luther through Kierkegaard,' he said. 'The central tenet is you have to stand on your own before God. It is a radically existential idea and inexorably personal. It pushes us to challenge authority. Then Sartre came along and updated it to "You have to stand alone before the empty meaninglessness of the universe."'

Theologically, Harrison had left that world behind. 'My journey into writing was a journey out of faith. I did a Master's in theology and literature in my mid-twenties trying to make sense of, if I'm not Christian any more, what am I? That moved me into embracing liberation theology and then I realised there's different types of truth. A story has more than descriptive power, it has actual power to create.' He had recently started psychoanalysis. 'My father inherited certain traumas that made it difficult to be around him at times as a child. I can now

---

14 Phil Harrison, *The First Day*, Fleet, 2017, p. 37

look back and think I can understand, but when you are seven years old you don't. I became attuned to changes in psychological atmosphere, and what was going on just below what seemed to be going on. I'm not interested in hero narratives. It is more, what are the things that stop people getting the things they want?'

'A good part of my life has been taken up with rejection of this Christian religion,' said McKendry. 'But then it dawned on me one day, I'm some kind of post-Christian. If you don't think that something has to give to help people who are suffering, you're a complete bastard. For years I would have said religion had no influence on me. And then you realise your whole life's been backdropped by this massive cultural force that kind of governs everything.'

McKendry's first ventures into writing were as a child. 'Playing with my teddy bears and making up wee sort of narratives for them and stuff,' he said. Harrison asked if he remembered their names. 'Gizmo, who was the kind of leader of the teddy bears, and then you had Aynsley, his sister who was a blue teddy bear with a clock on her belly. And then Dessie, the younger. And then there was Magic Murphy, the gorilla,' he said. Harrison laughed, 'This could be a loyalist gang: Gizmo, Dessie and Magic Murphy. I think I've seen them in the *Sunday Life*,' he said. McKendry said this phase ended abruptly. 'I remember I was about eight and I was doing one of my wee sort of plays, you know, like giving them all voices. And I could hear my ma and da laughing from their bedroom. I went in and I was like, "What are you laughing at?" And my da says, "Nothing." I was like, "No, you fucking liars, you are laughing at me." I was ashamed for years. So the teddies got put into their bucket and under the bed.'

After leaving school, McKendry trained as an electrician but was declared bankrupt during the recession in 2011. He signed up, aged twenty-eight, as a student at Queen's. There, with Ciaran Carson as his mentor, he began to write poetry. 'I think I was drawn by the precision of the form,' he said. His pamphlet *Curfuffle* was a Poetry Book Society selection for 2019. The poems are brutally eloquent, with a fierce cultural commentary running through them, from the carry-on in the hut at the Twelfth bonfire site, to a satire on the secret inauguration rituals of Loyal Orders. In 'Keepers of the Pedigree', Pebbles Flintstone is sworn into the Order of the Water Buffalo: 'I, Pebbles Flintstone, of my own free will, in the presence of The Lord Almighty, / will have no truck with Donald Duck, no Looney Tune, no Tom, nor Jerry …' [15]

Both writers are politically minded. 'I can slabber, as we say, about the DUP all day,' said McKendry. 'I used to ask myself, is it religion? Is it politics? I came to the conclusion it is just basic tribalism. I wouldn't call myself Ulster Scots, but I do have an Ulster-Scots background, like every single person who can trace their ancestry here back more than two generations. But I'm not going to claim this planter background, because I was born on a council estate. There's absolutely nothing privileged in my background, apart from my da having a job in the shipyard. My granny's sister did some research into our lineage and it turns out there was this very rich farmer called Campbell who got my great-granny pregnant. My ma's da was a proper communist.'

'I don't think the DUP are Protestant at all,' said Harrison. 'They are obsessed with money and authority, which are deeply un-Protestant in the Lutheran sense. I didn't grow up wrestling about trying to escape my class. In our church there were some kind of aspiring middle-class people who drove in a nice car down from the Cavehill Road, and then there were people who lived round the corner. There was no hierarchy. Luther said the "covetous man" was the enemy of mankind, and the kingdom of heaven was always at odds with the pragmatism of capitalism. The sin that caused Satan's fall was the very substance of what is now our economic system.'

He sensed that the staunch were relaxing a little into the twenty-first century. 'My partner is Catholic from a Gaeltacht in the Republic and my parents, who are still conservative evangelicals, have no concern at all.'

---

15 McKendry, p. 11

CHAPTER 5

East

'TINPOT MAFIA'

'Andrew was always prone to depression,' said Jenni. 'He had no consistent male role model. A lot of it was to do with his father. His father could have helped him in so many ways but he didn't. He just disappeared off. Andrew was a great footballer but all through those adolescent years he was smoking dope constantly. He messed up at school, and when he was twenty-four he was admitted to hospital with drug-induced psychosis. He got treatment and eventually he was doing really, really well. He got a nice girlfriend and he was playing really good football. He was in one of the top local teams and was becoming a sort of amateur celebrity.'

Jenni is a friend. A vibrant woman, and a dedicated trade unionist who works as an administrator, she was always full of life and cheerful plans for travel or outings. Except when her son, Andrew, was in or heading towards one of his psychotic episodes. Then she became fraught and depressed. She smoked heavily and could hardly be persuaded to leave her house.

'Then one night there was a party in one of the houses on our street and someone smashed up my car,' she told me. 'Everybody knew who had done it, and after I went to the police, the guy was coming to my house in the middle of the night, shouting. The police said they could do nothing. So Andrew had come across a guy who was a local UVF commander who had just got out of prison, for God knows what. And this guy told Andrew he'd sort it out. And they got the guy put out by the Housing Executive.

'After that, they had the squeeze on Andrew. He got a call asking him, "Would you like to come and play for our team?" Andrew felt it was an invitation he couldn't refuse, although he'd always maintained that he would never play for them, because they were paramilitary, and everybody knew they were. So, he went and played with them and he was like their George Best. He was their golden boy. And, of course, he started dabbling in the drugs because they're all taking cocaine. So he started getting into debt, at the same time as he was getting addicted. And then once you get into debt with them, there's no such thing as a payment plan. No. It was, "Well, you could start selling for us." That was like giving George Best a case of whiskey to sell.

'Initially Andrew might have sold a bit of it. But before long he was taking more of it than he was selling. So the debt then started to grow. One day I was in his car with him and the police stopped him and searched the car and found cocaine and arrested him. So I phoned one of the UVF leaders and he said, "Leave it with me, love." And he sent a solicitor. The police were saying to Andrew, "If you help us out, we'll help you out." But Andrew wasn't going to say anything. Anyway, he was released and later on was charged with possession.

'Soon after that Andrew was behaving strangely. He took my car and sold it and a friend of mine saw some big UVF guys driving it through the town. She took a photograph. You could see their faces – I knew them. So I brought it to the police. They said, "Do you want us to charge your son with stealing your car?" I said, "No, I'm just letting you know the registration number and that this car is now a drugs car." They were fairly nonchalant.

'Andrew's football had gone to the dogs and he'd been dropped. I had been round to the house he was renting several times and the windows were broken. His friend told me, "He doesn't have any money, he doesn't have any heat, he doesn't have any electric." And I said: "Why not?" And he said: "Because they've taken his debit card from him, so he has nothing." They'd taken his car, too. And it became obvious Andrew was heading into a psychotic breakdown again, and it got so bad he thought that I was involved in this persecution: that I was sleeping with one of the UVF leaders, I was the enemy, and I was trying to poison him. He was completely paranoid.

'They had instilled this terrible, terrible fear into him. He owed them a lot of money. So I got back to them and said, "Listen, you'll get your money whenever we have the money but stop giving Andrew drugs." Of course that was ignored. And I had to section Andrew and he was in intensive care in a locked unit. Then I went to one of the ones who claims he has nothing to do with the UVF but is out on social media all the time holding forth about how hard done by loyalist communities are. And all I got was, "Business is business, and it doesn't matter who Andrew is, or what he's done for us, or anything else." And I said, "But you don't understand. This is a severe mental health breakdown." He just shrugged.

'I said, "You know, from what I can see, you're intimidating all these kids. You're on the road to Notown. You have no ambition. All you can aspire to is a caravan in Millisle or Benidorm, or a holiday in Dubai, and, you know, I'm paying for your new teeth that you can see from the moon, and I'm paying for all of it, because I'm the one that has to pick up the pieces. I'm the one that has to run around and pay the debt. And you've got a four-wheel drive, and you're supposed to be a community worker; but I've paid for that. You've nothing to offer this community."

'After that, I fronted up a Facebook page for parents of addicts. I took a Diploma in Drug Counselling. It's just a group of mothers who will talk about enabling and detachment and all the things that you're supposed to do but, in general, what we had in common was it is very hard to get help.

'The UVF have this whole area divided up and they are all commandants of their own wee patch. Some of them, their fathers and uncles were murderers and extortionists during the Troubles. This is the new generation. One of the ones round here was in prison but he's out now, driving a Porsche. This is what I mean. That's what they aspire to. They might drive a Porsche, but they live in a little house with steel shutters on the stairs in a working-class housing estate.' Jenni showed me some of the houses, with cars that could hardly fit into the paved-over front gardens. I had been in such houses during the conflict, interviewing men who wanted sympathy because they had to 'live like this', when the way they conducted their 'struggle' was smashing down the doors of people who had no such security, and killing them.

'And they're ringing up young lads wanting them to go down and intimidate some of the non-nationals that have moved in down the town. You know, "Away down and throw a tin of paint over some poor Bulgarian woman's house. Or start a wee riot. Set a bonfire. Burn the road." The area had a small but growing population of immigrant families, and a spokesman for the Belfast Islamic Centre said racist leaflets were regularly distributed by a small minority of people. 'It's tinpot mafia,' said Jenni. 'Then these ones that think of themselves as leaders laugh among themselves because they stir up trouble and then they get government money to make it go away. There's no such thing as God and Ulster – it's God and my back pocket, as the wee lady from Ballymena used to say.'

Wendy Erskine's short story, 'To All Their Dues' deftly captures the way intimidation becomes normalised without being acknowledged. Soon after Mo opens her beauty parlour in east Belfast, a red snooker ball smashes through the window. The butcher next door brings in some glass repair film. "'Kids, huh?" the butcher said. "Kids," said Mo. "That's good of you. I appreciate it. That's great." "Just pay it," he said. "Ain't really that much, just pay it."'[1]

Not long after the incident she is visited by a man. 'It's all about community,' he informs her. 'Communities don't run themselves. Businesses like yours, they're vulnerable … There's a lot of people out there who are not nice people, and all we are really doing … is offering you our help. As a member of the community.' When she resists he makes it clearer: 'You need to watch it.'[2]

Under the Executive's community relations strategy, 'Together: Building a United Community', an attempt was made to create areas of religiously mixed public housing. One of the schemes was in east Belfast. In 2017, four Catholic families who lived there, left their homes and told the Housing Executive they had been intimidated out by loyalist paramilitaries. The following year, banners displaying photographs of IRA atrocities were put up around the scheme along with the hashtag 'stand up against sectarianism'. I thought about this when, in 2021, the

---

1 Wendy Erskine, 'To All Their Dues', *Sweet Home*, The Stinging Fly Press, 2018, p. 7
2 Ibid., pp. 12–13

DUP's Ian Paisley Jnr referred to 'the Catholic IRA'.

'You should see them on Remembrance Sunday,' said Jenni. 'They all go to up to Belfast to the UVF graves at Roselawn, and they get dressed to kill. Recently they've been going like *Peaky Blinders* in the old flat caps and the twill. Then they go to the pub where there's a bottle of vodka and a bottle of Bush and lines of coke and they all get totally obliterated.'

In 2020, in advance of Remembrance Day, when wreathes of red poppies are laid at the cenotaph at City Hall in Belfast, an incongruously large rectangular wreath appeared. Against a base of white chrysanthemums, UVF was spelled out in the traditional poppies. It was removed after protests from the Alliance Party.

THE DEATH OF 'BIG O'

On a Sunday evening at the end of January 2019, a group of masked men armed with knives attacked Ian Ogle at the top of his street on the lower Newtownards Road in east Belfast. The forty-five-year-old, who had lived in the area all his life, was stabbed and beaten and kicked as he fell to the ground. A few days later, his twenty-eight-year-old daughter, Toni, spoke to a crowd of around a thousand, mainly local, people at a candlelit vigil at the spot where he died. 'I'm going to make sure my daddy didn't die in vain,' she said. 'Me and my family are going to the courts to get justice. These people don't even deserve to live among us.' In March, to mark International Women's Day, local women held a march on the road with banners that read 'Justice for Ian Ogle'. Toni again addressed them. 'I feel like east Belfast is going to rise up,' she said. 'No more bullying. We have had enough. It is time to take a stand against these thugs, look after each other and take east Belfast back.'

What made this rebellion so striking was the fact that Ian Ogle had been killed not just by thugs, but by thugs, some of whom may have been associated at some stage with loyalist paramilitaries. The Newtownards Road and the area around it had been one of their strongholds during the Troubles, and the walls still bear crude murals boasting of their prowess against 'the enemies of Ulster' or their 'sacrifice at the Somme'. Toni continued to campaign defiantly in the months that followed. She told a reporter in October that year that it was an insult to commemorate the twenty-fifth anniversary of the loyalist ceasefire 'when so many are living in fear'. I met her a year after her father's murder, in a cafe on the road.

'Daddy went up to the top of Cluan Place and he was standing talking to the pastor. Then they must have heard something. We were in the car and when we got to the corner there was a crowd and it was chaos and my brother Ryan's friend was screaming that they had sliced Daddy. I never saw horror like what I saw in his eyes. I just knew it was really bad. The neighbours started to come up the street and someone ran down to get towels to put on the wounds. Then the police came and I was screaming. I pulled out my phone and I made a video. See if I knew my daddy was dead, I wouldn't have taken it. Ryan was holding Daddy and he was shouting, "He's making a noise." I was covering my ears and I wouldn't listen. Now I know it was the gurgling of Daddy's last breath.

'My daddy was the thirtieth Protestant loyalist killed by loyalists since the ceasefire. We found that out after,' Toni says.

'"Big O" they called my daddy. He was a big character. He was actually quite well known and famous, so he was. Everybody loved him and he loved himself and he was all about the attention. He called himself a loyal Prod because he was in the East Belfast Protestant Boys. He played the flute and he was very talented. At a young age he had got involved in the UVF. My daddy says he obviously joined up when he thought at the time there was a cause. There was a hell of a lot more going on back then. There's been an image painted that he was sectarian but he's not. My daddy had Catholic friends and Ryan's seeing a Catholic girl and my daddy actually went up to her house to meet her family. I've many Catholic friends; my daddy's been in my house chatting away to them. So he's not sectarian, but he obviously doesn't agree with the republican movement.'

She showed me photographs of her father. When he was young he was strikingly good-looking with his shaggy Rod Stewart hair and his big collared shirts and his flares. Towards the end of his life he had put on a lot of weight and had a look about him of a man both worried and medicated. He had suffered intimidation, she said, and it led to anxiety and depression.

'He went to prison over the flags protest in 2013. There was a bit of trouble and he got caught up in it. He was outspoken. He would have liked the flag to go back on City Hall all the time. A lot of young kids got in trouble during that time and got criminal records and it was the same again over the bonfires in 2019. One of my wee relations was at Avoniel because of the commotion. We tried to tell him not to go but he went and his picture was published by the PSNI and I was absolutely furious. I wrote to the politicians and I said, how come members of the UVF and UDA were standing in a crowd and the PSNI has published a picture of a fifteen-year-old boy? I'm very like my daddy and he encouraged me to debate. I disagreed with him over bonfires. I'm twenty-eight now and I grew up with them. He loved them and he was always out collecting wood and that. I said no, it was bad for the environment and it should be just beacons now.'

In 2019 loyalists built a large Eleventh Night bonfire of wooden pallets and tyres in front of the leisure centre at Avoniel, which is run by Belfast City Council. There was a general appeal from officials for bonfires to be lowered in height and for tyres to be removed, and this was done at Avoniel. However, the council said the bonfire was too close to the centre and should be removed entirely. The loyalists refused and a stand-off ensued. Threats were issued to contractors hired to clear the site, and to council staff. Mervyn Gibson, Grand Secretary of the Orange Lodge of Ireland and a Presbyterian minister, addressed the crowd that gathered to encircle and protect the bonfire. He called for calm but blamed 'a republican-dominated council'.[3] The bonfire was allowed to go ahead, and loyalists hailed it as a great victory.

'The ones that get the kids out and into trouble are telling them not to cooperate with the police,' Toni said. 'My wee relation got a message from the paramilitaries telling him he was to go to them and they'd tell him what to say. These wee boys are impressionable, you know; they see these men and think, wow, look at their clothes, look at their cars. And I'm like, but it's dirty money. Go and get yourself a job. I'd like to know why they're still recruiting teenagers into paramilitaries when there's no need for them. They were only kids themselves when the ceasefire came so what are they in it for? It's basically them grooming kids to sell drugs and to me that's no better than paedophilia. I heard they get them to come for punishment beatings and then they make them take part in punishments as well. I heard there was one wee boy and he got into so much debt with them he killed himself, but I don't know the

---

3 https://www.bbc.co.uk/news/uk-northern-ireland-48919485

ins and outs of it.' There was a rape, too, the perpetrator alleged to be a paramilitary leader, but before it could be investigated, the woman killed herself.

'Cluan Place used to get really bad riots. It is an interface; it's the border with Short Strand. In 2002 there were five people shot. But they've put so much money into improving the houses; I mean fireproof roofs and bulletproof windows and gates on to the entries and boundary fences. My mummy was actually really struggling where we were so we were offered a three-bedroom house in Cluan and it was fantastic. It's really hard to get into a Housing Executive house. I was able to just walk to the top of the street and get the bus up to school.

'There were still riots and stuff. But we were just kept away from it. A couple of times my mummy had to get my granny to come down and to get us out of the house, but it didn't affect us. Obviously, the flag protest, Cluan Place got absolutely battered, so it was a nightmare then. But Cluan Place hasn't seen any bother for a long, long time.'

The Newtownards Road Toni described was rough. She talked of bars in which local paramilitaries, 'off their head on drink and cocaine', get into fights. She said it can be 'a wild Western' with bystanders getting beaten with bottles and glasses, and barstools being thrown about. Then local paramilitary leaders hold court martials and decide who is to be punished.

'After Daddy died I cried and cried and cried that night. I couldn't stop. Then I couldn't cry any more. I was numb.' There was much speculation about who killed Ian Ogle. 'This place was in uproar. It was rising up. Then there was the women's march against criminality and that was brilliant. And let me tell you, when my daddy was murdered, the support from the nationalist community – I mean Short Strand, the Markets, Twinbrook, Ormeau Road we had cards sent from – it was amazing. And there was a vigil for daddy and that day two ladies came along from Short Strand and they were crying.

'My cousin said I hope you are not offended by the flags, because there's a Rangers flag, and one of the ladies said, no, no, if that's what he liked. And a fellow from Markethill came and he put an Ireland jersey on the fence. And we were like, how are we left behind in the peace process when this has happened? Loyalists just killed a loyalist and Catholics are coming in peace. Tell me, would you have had this years ago? We've come a long way. And even though I lived on an interface and there was always something going on, me and my family, we're not sectarian. We've turned out all right.

'My daddy knew his history. My daddy could tell you about the Reformation, Martin Luther. My daddy knew everything – he was an actual loyalist. He wasn't one of these ones who came out and said St Patrick was a Prod, you know what I mean? He had the 36th (Ulster) Division at the Battle of the Somme tattooed over his whole back.

'When I was a teenager, I was always under the impression I grew up in a society where the only people got into trouble were housebreakers or perverts, paedophiles, people who maybe had beaten women. Basically, I say now our community is an absolute mess. I know there's been good work done in east Belfast and you can never take that away from the people who are absolutely busting their balls to do the best they can for the community. But that's overshadowed. And how do you solve one issue without solving them all?

'See these ones that walk round saying the PSNI are harassing hard-working, innocent loyalists? That sickens me. It's the paramilitaries and the criminals. Honestly, it's all propaganda with them. The reason loyalist communities are held behind in the peace process is because criminal elements portraying themselves as loyalists are holding us back. They say they are defending our community but really they are terrorising it.'

Toni invited me to a public meeting she had organised in a local hall a few weeks later. It was chaired by Mervyn Gibson, and among the two hundred or so people there were local DUP MP Gavin Robinson, and local GP and PUP councillor, Dr John Kyle. Toni was the key speaker. 'I keep beating myself up about what happened,' she said. 'I keep thinking, what could I have done to stop this?' She said she would not stop campaigning for the truth to come out. 'If standing up for justice for my family means I am a tout, then I am a tout,' she said. She had been told by some of his former friends that her father would be turning in his grave at her behaviour. 'Well, I am my daddy,' she told the meeting. 'That is why I'm going to continue this fight. Because as long as I'm still breathing, Ian Ogle will never be dead.'

'OCH, I'M BUSY THAT DAY'
'Armagh is calling Londonderry, Tyrone to Fermanagh, Antrim

to Down. Steadfast o' Sons of Ulster. Rally for God and for Ulster. Rally for people and for country. Like past generations do not flinch when into defence we are called. Keep close the cry of our people, no surrender.'

In November 2019 this was the notice that went out inviting people to get tickets for the grand finale in the Ulster Hall of a series of rallies that had been held all over Northern Ireland in the run-up to the general election. The aim was to 'stop the betrayal act' and resist the imposition of the 'economic united Ireland' that would, it was claimed, follow from a border in the Irish Sea. The rallies were an attempt to unite the unionist family in opposition to the Brexit deal that would keep Northern Ireland in the EU single market while the rest of the UK left it. Speakers at the rallies included politicians from all the unionist parties. The message was simple: 'Vote unionist'.

The archaic language used by the organisers to summon up all the ancestral ghosts was strange to see on Twitter and Facebook. The Ulster Hall was iconic – here, Sir Edward Carson had rallied men in 1912 to resist Home Rule. His illegal army, the UVF, went on to smuggle guns into Ulster. Here, the Reverend Ian Paisley had rallied men in 1986 to resist the Anglo-Irish Agreement by joining Ulster Resistance, the group he set up in protest against it. After the guns it smuggled into Northern Ireland were used in sectarian atrocities, the DUP distanced itself. Here, David Trimble, leader of the UUP, had battled Jeffrey Donaldson and other internal opponents of the 1998 Good Friday Agreement, before Donaldson, Arlene Foster and others defected to the DUP.

Paisley had got over 100,000 Protestants, unionists and loyalists out to hear him in front of the City Hall in 1986. He declared that civil war was imminent and called on God to deal with Prime Minister Margaret Thatcher: 'Take vengeance upon this wicked, lying, treacherous woman,' he prayed. There were similar performances by Paisley at Drumcree. In 1998 he had declaimed that the authorities had better let the Orangemen complete their parade before the Twelfth of July, the day he called 'the decider', because otherwise 'anybody here with any imagination knows what's going to happen'. In the early hours of that day, the UVF murdered the Quinn children.

In October 2019, loyalist blogger Jamie Bryson had posted on Twitter a blurry photo of a pier, with the comment, 'Having a walk along the harbour in Donaghadee tonight. It was here in 1914 that the Ulster Volunteer Force landed guns to resist the Home Rule Bill that was to be imposed upon us by a treacherous British Parliament.' He had claimed that, if in the course of delivering Brexit the British tried to separate Northern Ireland from the rest of the UK, this would 'inevitably see a grass roots PUL resistance that would make the Anglo-Irish Agreement and flag protests look like small tremors.'

Leaders of the contemporary UVF and other loyalist paramilitaries attended the 'betrayal act' rallies. When schoolboy Joel Keys was invited to take part in a pageant at the Ulster Hall rally, he had some initial concerns. 'I raised it with them, what if certain people turn up, meaning people you wouldn't want to be seen with,' he told me. He meant paramilitaries. 'The response I sort of got was, it's a public meeting, we won't turn anyone away.'

Joel is Toni Ogle's cousin, and it was his late father who had tattooed the Battle of the Somme on to Ian Ogle's back. 'For me Ian was sort of the last connection I had to my dad,' he told me. 'Toni and her mum, my auntie, are really brave to speak out against those groups of people, knowing the risks.'

Joel had agreed to play the part of Robert Quigg, who like many of the UVF men of 1914 had gone on to join the British army, and to take part in the Battle of the Somme in 1916. Quigg had been awarded the Victoria Cross for rescuing seven soldiers trapped in no-man's-land.

'I was a bit apprehensive in case they were going to be aggressive and staunch, and it would be hateful. But it was very professional and they didn't try and control what I was saying at all. I loved it. As Quigg, I was defending democracy and saying, if I'm going to put my life on the line for your right to vote, you should be going out and voting no matter what,' he told me. He sent me his script: 'When the United Kingdom is under threat, it is the duty of every Ulsterman to step up and save it, just as I saved as many of my brothers as I could at the Somme,' he'd written.

I had gone along to the Ulster Hall, but got short shrift. My request to attend was met with a cold and abrupt, 'Absolutely not.' I told Joel this. He felt on balance that it was right to exclude the media. Unfavourable coverage could have cost unionism votes. The hall had not been full, he said, but the atmosphere had been fantastic. There were Unions Jacks everywhere, with a vast one behind the stage. (When it was pointed out afterwards that it was upside down, the organisers said this was deliberate. The flag was 'in distress'.)

Journalists had been excluded from all of the 'betrayal act' meetings, but the deputy editor of the *News Letter*, journalist Ben Lowry, had been invited to witness the Portadown meeting. This was held in the Carleton Orange Hall, scene of many torrid Drumcree meetings. Lowry reported that just over three hundred people attended, 90 per cent of them men, and that the speakers included Bryson, the DUP's then MLA Carla Lockhart, and the UUP MLA Doug Beattie. Lockhart called for unionist unity in the December election. Bryson, who spoke at all the rallies, warned that if the legislation went ahead, 'we are in the final days of the union'. He said the Belfast Agreement had been passed because of 'the politics of hostage' – unionists had to support it 'because if not the IRA might kill us'.

The same thing was happening again. 'The loyalist and working-class unionist community – we have been criminalised, dehumanised, mocked and sneered at … then they wonder why they have created this monster.' In the chair, Orangeman Robert Wallace offered that, from 1641, threats to Protestants had been resolved by 'men on the ground'. Bryson said loyalists had a right to defend themselves. Wallace asked the audience 'whether there were any lengths to which they would not go to resist the destruction of their country'. The answer was no, and then they sang the national anthem.[4]

Joel loves flags. 'In my estate, Taughmonagh [in south Belfast], see an election coming up, or the Twelfth, any excuse, there will be flags on every lamp post. Some even hang them from their houses. It's not us trying to intimidate anyone. It's just us expressing love for the country that we're in. It's an expression of who we are,' he said.

'My stepdad is very good. If you don't have a great relationship with your parents you can get drawn towards paramilitaries and criminal groups, and drugs. Protestant working-class boys perform the worst in education and I think the family thing plays a big part in that. There's a difference in culture between Catholic families and Protestant families. An Alliance-type person was explaining to me that in the old days there was discrimination against Catholics and they had to try extra hard to get on, and they still have that in their culture.

---

4 Ben Lowry, 'Loyalist Protest Meeting in Portadown Against Boris Johnson's "Betrayal Act" was packed and angry', *News Letter*, 25 November 2019

'In order to succeed in school most of the work happens at home. My little sister Grace comes in and she's told to get her homework done before she's allowed to go out and she huffs and she puffs but she gets it done. I don't want to be slagging other families, but I think a lot of parents are afraid to push their kids in case the kids take it out on them. And then shouting at your kids if they don't do well, that's pointless. As a parent you should look at that and go, well what can I do to help?

'If you look at the republican areas, there's a lot more of their youth willing to get out and do things. I was on that *Top Table* TV programme on the BBC a while ago and I met one of the Sinn Féin youth members and I added them on Facebook, and you see posts they put up where they have all the kids out protesting for what they believe in. I don't have very much faith I could get a single person in my community out if I wanted to do something like that. I'm in unionist groups on Facebook and whenever there's things like a protest mentioned, everyone's all, yeah, yeah, yeah. And then whenever a date is set, people are "Och, I'm busy that day." There's a stereotype in the Protestant community that the BBC is biased against us and no one I know will speak to them, but I didn't experience that at all.

'I think my mum's always voted DUP, but for the same reasons that a lot of people do, which is just, you know, my mum did or my granny did and I don't have a problem with them. She just goes off and votes DUP out of habit. This last election was the first I was old enough to vote in, and I decided to campaign for the DUP, for Emma Little-Pengelly in Belfast South. The Ulster Unionists would have been the ones I was sort of swaying towards but then they took a remain stance on Brexit, which was upsetting for me.

'The biggest issue people talked about was getting back into Stormont and helping the health service. The pro-life thing and gay marriage didn't come up as much as I expected. I'm a Christian, but I feel that my faith should only affect my own behaviour. So I support decriminalisation of same-sex marriage and I didn't agree with the DUP using the petition of concern to block it. I used to be completely against gay people and I used to probably be racist as well. This is why I'm such a big believer in freedom of speech. I was able to go into school, express these views and the teachers were able to say, well, why do you believe that? It encouraged me think and to change my view on all sorts of things.

'I don't think the working class of both communities really hate each other. A lot of unionists will shout things like, fuck the Pope, but see if you ask them, what about this Catholic or that Catholic, they'll say, "Oh yeah, they're fine. Most of the Catholics I work with are fine." Some of them are married to Catholics or going with them. The things they shout would be classed as sectarian, but is there hatred behind them? I don't think so. It's just sort of, "Look, I'll just shout this because it's fun and it creates an atmosphere." I think we all shout things we don't mean. I only know one person who really hates republicans and he had a load of family members who were lined up and shot by republican extremists. So his attitude mightn't be right but it is not unreasonable. It's like most Catholics aren't going to come up to you and say, "You stole our land."

'I don't have a problem with a border poll and I don't get unionism's opposition to it. I'm going to vote to remain in the United Kingdom anyway. I believe that's where we're best suited, best served and best placed and I think the vast majority of voters would agree. So a border poll doesn't scare me. I don't know why we would want to flat-out deny one. And if the people of the country come back and say we want to join the Republic of Ireland, why would I want to stop a democratic vote? Boris Johnson wasn't looking out for our interests. If we end up with customs at our ports and all that, I think that's us finished. I don't think that there'll be any comeback for unionism. That will be us lost from the kingdom.'

During disturbances on Sandy Row in Belfast in April 2021, Joel was arrested. He told me he had been there because he was passing and saw a thirteen-year-old he knew and had gone in to try and extricate him: 'He's a good wee lad – he'd just got bored.' Joel had become disillusioned by the DUP. 'I'll be voting for an independent next time.'

'HOLY COW'

'People seemed to make an icon out of it or a holy cow out of it, but it was just an agreement,' said the Reverend Mervyn Gibson, Presbyterian Minister, Grand Secretary of the Grand Orange Lodge of Ireland, and a former RUC officer. He was speaking about the Good Friday Agreement. 'Is Northern Ireland a better place now than before 1998? It is, obviously. There isn't the same level of violence and no one would want to return to that. Do I think it was the agreement that did that? No. I think republicans realised they were never going to win. They saw probably how easy it was to get what they wanted in the political arena through subterfuge, while keeping their military machine intact. It is the army council still makes the decisions,' he said. We met at his manse on a street just off the Newtownards Road.

'The Orange Order took a stand against the Good Friday Agreement. I would have been, up to then, an official unionist supporter,' he said. He meant Ulster Unionist – the term he used dated back to earlier splits. 'But there were things like prisoners being released for no good reason, which was morally wrong. They were going to decimate the police force, again for no good reason. It was just to appease republicanism. It wasn't because of bigotry or anything the RUC was kept Protestant, it was because Roman Catholics didn't want to be part of the state, or were terrorised by the IRA.

'There was nothing guaranteed about decommissioning in it. I talked to Trimble the day it was signed. He tried to persuade me, but he didn't. I stood outside a school in east Belfast handing out leaflets, saying please vote no because it supports terrorism. Loyalist paramilitaries were standing outside the same gates telling people to vote for it,' he said. This was a reference to supporters of the PUP and the Ulster Democratic Party (UDP), which had roots in the UVF and the UDA but wanted to transition into politics. The Orange Order and anti-agreement unionism retained the loyalty of elements of paramilitarism, including the breakaway LVF that was conspicuous at Drumcree. The perception of these shocking alliances had damaged Orangeism.

Along with Jeffrey Donaldson, Gibson was one of the DUP's negotiators in the Haass talks. US diplomats Richard Haass and Meghan O'Sullivan chaired negotiations involving all the political parties in Belfast in 2013 to attempt to resolve the still potently fractious parades issue. 'I was quite honoured to be asked by Peter Robinson to do it because I was never a member of the DUP,' said Gibson. 'I think Haass came over here with the expectation he was going to listen to everyone, write something and we would take it or leave it. He realised pretty quick it was a five-ring circus. Haass was obviously a brainy individual, but it just frustrated him that he couldn't get something as small as Northern Ireland to agree to something. He couldn't hide his disappointment but

Meghan O'Sullivan could. You couldn't play poker with her. She just had one of those faces.' It was widely speculated that the Orange Order had urged the DUP to reject the compromises reached.

In October 2020, after a summer without the traditional Twelfth of July, Gibson gave an interview to the *News Letter*'s Sam McBride. It was remarkable in its realism. He conceded that times had changed: 'It isn't 100 years ago where the Orange was the backbone of unionism.' He had abandoned the dream of a united unionist party and commented that, 'sadly, sometimes the first thing unionists do is look for the Lundy in the room' and that this would have to stop. 'We've to get over ourselves on that one,' he told McBride.[5]

'THEY ALWAYS SEE THE NEGATIVE'

Aadi is Black. He loves cricket. He is an engineer. He was an early supporter of the civil rights movement. He is also a former loyalist paramilitary, and he asked me not to use his name because his family had suffered enough because of him over the years. I met Aadi during a Northern Ireland Human Rights Festival event in east Belfast. The cheery, multicultural brochure said the event would discuss 'PUL approaches to human rights'. It was in the hall in which Toni had held her meeting, but whereas that meeting had been packed with mostly local, working-class people, there were just twelve people in this audience.

'I was born in the West Indies,' Aadi said. 'My mother's from here. My father was a marine engineer and his boat was in here for dry dock, for getting repairs. And that's how they met. They lived here at first but then they went back to the West Indies and set up home there, and then five years later I came along and they sent me to my grandma's over here to get an education when I was five years of age.

'I was brought up with my grandmother off the Woodstock Road and that's where I feel like I learned my values and my character. In the sixties, in the seventies, there was just one other mixed-race family I recall in the area. There were possibly a couple of Chinese, but not very many. I had no trouble. I think part of that was I was good at sports – cricket and things – and I was good at mixing with people. It opened doors for me. And my grandmother was a big protector. I doubt she

---

5 Sam McBride, 'Orange Order leader: For the Union's survival I may have to
   accept a changed Northern Ireland – and I will', *News Letter,* 26 October 2020

would have let anything happen to me. She was from Clydebank in Scotland and she was very church-centred. I had to attend the Church of Ireland. I had to respect people. Nothing came easy to me. I had to work for my things, I had to save, I had to study.

'My parents were killed in a car accident in Europe when I was twelve and that was sad, but my grandmother made up for it – she was a strong lady. They left money in trust for me and I went to university in England. I was more interested in world politics than local politics. You know, Malcolm X, Mandela, Steve Biko, and then Kennedy, Churchill. I lifted my eyes, whereas the majority of people that I would be associated with, their horizons were just local. They went to school because they had to, and saw themselves as plumbers or shipyard workers who'd get a job, get married and live where they grew up.

'I came back because of my granny. When the civil rights movement started up here I went to demonstrations. But I soon realised there were some people pushing a bad political agenda. In east Belfast, there would be very few of us at the university. In many ways, working-class Protestants were just as restricted as working-class Catholics. If you weren't in the Orange Lodge, you didn't get a job in the shipyard. If you weren't in the Masonic, you didn't get a job in the civil service. On this side of town they saw civil rights as a threat to the state.

'But there's this arrogance about unionism. They don't think that they have to explain their case and they just don't. It's just, what are you talking about? The minute you start questioning it, they pull up the drawbridge, or they say, oh, that guy doesn't get it, he's a Lundy. I have been very disappointed in unionist leadership. Even from 1968 and '70 when they did introduce changes, it was done begrudgingly. It's really sad, but I don't see it changing, probably until there's a border poll. I think it will probably fail the first time. But after that, the unionist population might realise that if they want to maintain the union, then they're going to have to explain themselves.

'I started out with the vigilantes, which was basically young whippersnappers looking after the streets. The excitement was staying out at nights and walking about. Obviously other guys started to get organised. Then things got out of hand – the street rioting became more vicious. So people got together, a lot of them ex-British soldiers or police, and set up the UDA. At one stage there was something like twenty thousand people – men – in the organisation. And soon the view was taken that it was better to go on the offensive than just being passive.

'Very quickly, I was set out as someone who understood politics, so I was pushed as the acceptable face of the organisation. They didn't want me to know anything about the other stuff. We always were trying to rein in the other guys, but that was difficult because our own politicians weren't presenting our views and the security forces were failing to protect working-class areas. Later on, I was involved with the UDP. But we could never get people to vote for us, even within our own organisation. And now, all these years later, we're going backwards. I mean 40 per cent of the people in my area just don't vote. Those who vote, vote for the DUP but don't trust it. It doesn't reflect working-class people. They vote for it because the party plays on their fears of a united Ireland.

'I didn't go to those "betrayal act" meetings because they're pointless. We should remember a lot of working-class people went to jail, their lives ruined, can't get employment now, families broken up – on this unionist ticket. We've got to get a clear idea of why we want the union: positive things, not what it's against. The reason there is hardly anybody at a meeting about human rights is that the attitude is still the same as back in 1968. You mention rights to the unionist community, they see that as the nationalist community using it to wedge them away from Britain. I've tried. But they always see the negatives as opposed to the positive.

'If there was a border poll and people voted to leave, I would accept it because that is democracy, but we would not be unionists any more and I would probably leave. I would either go to England or back home to the West Indies. I would be sad. For all the faults with Northern Ireland, and in Ireland as a whole, it's a great country. People are great. They laugh with you and they laugh against themselves. In England you don't know your neighbour, even if you live for years beside them. In Ireland everybody knows everybody. So it's more comfortable for me here. It's like the West Indies: they know your father, they know your grandfather, they know your history.

'I go home every five years or so to watch cricket and see family. The only thing is that when we were back there last year, I noticed that my wife wasn't as comfortable as I would be. The expectations of the people are really low and it's a bit bleak. It's certainly not safe for tourists and people not from that community.

'The UDA stopped in 1995 and that, that should have been the end of it. What we have now is just gangsters and thugs. There's not the same political development in unionist communities that there is in nationalist communities. There are the same issues – bad housing, bad education, bad job prospects, poor political parties, poor public services. But unionist communities always take the view that if you oppose those, you seem to be a traitor. So it's difficult for them.'

A UNITED IRELANDER

David Porter lives in an apartment in Lambeth Palace, facing out across the Thames to the Houses of Parliament. He is the Archbishop of Canterbury's chief of staff. The palace is an extraordinary architectural parcel of buildings, some of which date back to the fifteenth century, while others are Gothic Revival and Tudor and the new library was just completed in 2020. It is a far cry from the narrow terraces off the Newtownards Road where Porter grew up. Even the crenellated gate lodges are far, far grander than the Lord Street gospel hall where he learned his Presbyterian faith. But although in his role of 'holding a space for dialogue' his primary task these days is helping his boss to avoid a split in the Anglican Church, he is still deeply engaged with 'the narrow ground' of Northern Ireland.

The quote is from Sir Walter Scott, who wrote in 1825, 'I never saw a richer country, or, to speak my mind, a finer people; the worst of them is the bitter and envenomed dislike which they have to each other … and they have such narrow ground to do their battle in, that they are like people fighting with daggers in a hogshead.' It is also the title of A.T.Q. Stewart's brief, powerful and gloomy 1977 book, and Porter uses the phrase frequently. (In 2001, Stewart concluded that 'the whole of Irish history is an arsenal of abuse'.)[6]

'Identity and belonging have been contested for over four hundred years in the north of Ireland. All of us are victims of the narrow ground,' Porter said. 'We are all complicit, but some are culpable.' I liked this

---

6 A.T.Q. Stewart, *The Narrow Ground: Roots of Conflict in Ulster*, Faber, 1977;
The Shape of Irish History, Blackstaff Press, 2001

distinction. I have never cared for the idea that 'we all have blood on our hands'. In his sixties now, Porter remembers the years when the North was crashing into the Troubles. His father was a vigilante. 'I grew up in the junior Orange Order. I remember going on a bus to Ballykinler and getting stopped by the paras. We all sang "Nick nack Paddy whack, give a dog a bone, paras 13, Bogside none."' The reference is to Bloody Sunday. 'People don't realise how much anti-Catholicism and fear of the other is preached. Two things drag us back: that and middle-class morality. The failure of the leadership of the Orange Order to give direction is appalling. It is bad for Christianity. As someone said, and I can't give their name, the worst sort of sectarian Orange bigot is the Oxbridge-educated one.'

During the violent Drumcree years, Porter, who is now a Baptist, was one of the founders of the Evangelical Contribution on Northern Ireland. 'We had a deep passion to challenge the whole concept of "For God and Ulster",' he said. 'We called it out. We said it was idolatrous. We also pointed out that the rituals of the Royal Black Preceptory are those of British Israelism. The idea of being God's chosen people is actually a heresy. The glory of God could be realised in a united Ireland as much as in Northern Ireland. God is more interested in good neighbourliness.' Unionists were 'on the wrong side of history' in this twenty-first century.

'I've been a united Irelander since I was in my teens. People believe they are as "British as Finchley", but they aren't,' he said. This claim was made by Margaret Thatcher in 1981. 'The British government has treated us like any other imperial colony from which they were trying to extricate themselves. We have to face reality. The route to save the union is also the best strategy for preparing for life outside the union.'

'NOT PREPARED'

'That's it, dead straight, dead straight, you're doing great there …' There's nothing like three men dedicating themselves, unasked, to directing me into a parking space to drive me to cursing, but I could already hear the preacher crying out, 'Thy word will be like a hammer, will be like a sword that it will pierce to the heart,' and I was duly subdued. My friend had given me a ticket for the drive-in prayer service. She had been having a hard time and her boss, who is in the

Plymouth Brethren, had given her the ticket out of kindness. 'He wants me to know it is all part of God's plan,' my friend said. 'He means well but, quite honestly, if this is the best God can do, I want to change my plan. There have to be better deals.' The car park was across the road from the Connswater shopping centre, behind C.S. Lewis Square, which has an arts centre, a bookshop and seven statues from the writer's fictional Narnia, chief among them the lion, Aslan.

There were two preachers, both in three-piece grey suits with white shirts and grey ties. They were standing on the back of a truck, with a banner that read, 'Amos – Prepare to meet thy God.' The pitch was for souls. The story of the ant and the grasshopper was given a COVID application – *we* might have been on lockdown but the ant was toiling away, locking in its provisions. 'The harvest is past, and the lamentable cry of the prophet is we are not saved ... Go to the ant, thou sluggard!' I was sure the preacher was pointing at me. 'I fear that some of you are not prepared,' he said. God had a problem with the attitude of the man who had spent his summer eating, drinking and being merry. 'I speak tenderly,' the preacher said. 'Are you prepared to die? I am very conscious that one of us will be next. If you die in your sins you will perish. You will go down to hell with the devil and his angels for all eternity. If you reject the Lord, he will reject you. These are the solemn realities. Now, I want you to listen to Raymond.'

These sermons terrify me. I looked to the right to the car beside mine. Two older ladies in berets looking implacably ahead. Saved. Safe. Raymond warned us that he was going to speak of things that were 'stern and sober'. God was a meticulous record keeper with 'an eye as a flame of fire in every place'. He knew our works and was noting them in his book with his pen of iron. Raymond said he was going to read Revelations, chapter 20. 'I would doubt if it has been read much, if at all, around C.S. Lewis Square,' he said, rather snidely. Lewis was a Christian and his books are packed with biblical imagery, but evidently his faith was not of a strong enough stripe for Raymond, or maybe the preacher disapproved of what was being done in Lewis's name.

Then Raymond plunged us deep into Revelations, the angel from heaven chaining up the dragon devil and casting him into the bottomless pit of hell, the lake of fire and brimstone, the torment day and night forever for those whose name was not in book of the lamb slain. I thought of Jan Carson, who had attended two years of Revelations sermons. 'I'm glad my records have been blotted out by the blood of Christ,' Raymond said. Two little girls sped by on skateboards. Raymond said that if any of us wanted to put our name in the book, we should speak to the preachers after. When it was over, he urged us to take care departing. 'There is one car at least will have to be got round,' he said. He pointed. I froze in my black Republic of Ireland registered car ... 'Let us pray,' said Raymond. He and the other preacher stood on either side of the exit, Bibles in hand, waiting for repentant sinners.

'STUFF ABOUT SWANS'

I returned to the square to meet Sammy Douglas, former DUP MLA for Belfast East, in the coffee bar in the EastSide Visitor Centre, beside the statue of Aslan. He is on the board of the EastSide Partnership and this centre is one of its projects, a hub for the culture and arts scene that is flourishing here. To walk the Newtownards Road from the city centre is to see all the social divisions of Belfast, from the run-down working-class terraces of the lower end to the increasingly gentrified middle with C.S. Lewis Square and other arts venues and studios, and further out, towards Stormont, Ballyhackamore, now one of the city's most fashionable areas, where old wealth meets new.

The Visitor Centre has guides to walking tours of Van Morrison's Belfast and of the 'street art' of the Newtownards Road, meaning for the most part the loyalist murals. You can book yourself into an Airbnb in George Best's childhood home in the Cregagh estate. Arts officer Rachel Kennedy runs a dynamic and edgy programme. This has included the very popular Drag Queen Story Time, which had drag artistes reading stories to children in local libraries. There is an annual C.S. Lewis arts festival, with which Jan Carson, one of the many artists now living in the area, is often involved. The partnership was set up by the Department for Communities to promote community regeneration. Partnership projects include one on tackling poverty and one on educational under-attainment. The square also has, in a set of converted shipping containers, Freight, one of Belfast's coolest new restaurants.

'I would describe myself as Obama describes himself, as a community organiser,' said Douglas. 'I'm originally from Sandy Row. Some people call it the heart of the empire or what's left of it. I've been living and working in east Belfast for nearly thirty years. I'm sixty-six. I grew up before the Troubles in a small kitchen-house with a photograph of the queen in it. The Eleventh of July, the bonfires, the Twelfth of July were all a major part of my life.

'One of my uncles married a Catholic and his son grew up as a Protestant and was shot dead by the IRA going to work one morning. My sister was nearly killed in an IRA bomb. The IRA left a pram bomb outside the bar she was in and I saw the ambulance guys carrying her out and she had a white jumper on and it was full of blood. I wanted to kill just to avenge. Looking back, I was an angry young man, and the people who did that were angry young men too, and the police on the street, the soldiers, they were all angry young men.

'Everybody in our street was in the UDA, the UVF or the Red Hand Commando and there were some Orange Volunteers as well. I had brothers who ended up in prison. One of them was involved in the UDA right up until the Good Friday Agreement. He took his own life and I suppose, looking back, he was a troubled soul. There was a lot of that. You go into clubs, and you see people who have major problems with alcohol or drug abuse, including prescription drugs, and many of those people have been paramilitaries. I remember when Jonathan Gray died of a drug overdose. Lovely young lad, but he got involved in the UDA. His father was Jim Gray – Doris Day, as people called him. He couldn't go into the funeral service. He couldn't cope with it. Then he was murdered himself, by other loyalists.

'Just before the election in 2011 Peter Robinson asked me if I would stand. I was shocked. I said, "Look, I'm a member of the British Labour Party". And he said, "What's your problem?" He said Jeffrey was a member of the Ulster Unionist Party. So I decided to give it a go because I believed he had a vision for Northern Ireland. I got elected. Peter put me on a committee working up plans for the transition of paramilitaries. He was one of the most intelligent people I ever met. He's a huge loss to politics. People say about Ian Paisley having a good relationship with Martin McGuinness and he did, but they forget that Peter Robinson was with Martin McGuinness for over seven years and they travelled the world in partnership. Our problem at the moment is that there's a lack of that positive leadership. There's a lack of respect.

'The flags decision in 2012 came as a shock to us. A lot of people said to me after, "I didn't even know that they flew the Union Jack." I got a lot of anti-DUP anger from paramilitaries and just people coming into my office and tearing up DUP leaflets. It was certainly the darkest period in terms of politics. I went to a meeting in a hall near here one night. This was a baying crowd that was angry. They said, right, you can lead us, and they got me to lead them up the Newtownards Road to the Alliance office, carrying a big flag. I was probably a bit afraid to say no because there were people from east Belfast, Sandy Row and the Shankill, all pointing in your face. I negotiated with the police. I said they're just having a peaceful protest.' A few days after this, protesters burned out the Alliance offices.

'I ended up in hospital with palpitations, pains in the chest. I collapsed. I got psychiatric counselling. I said to my wife, I'm not going to take this abuse, no job is worth it. Things settled down a bit but I still had people standing outside my office with the Union Jack and a poster saying "DUP sell-out". I went down to talk to one of them. He was from Ballymena. The next day I saw him up on top of the police Land Rover, and he was arrested. I saw the poisonous side of social media – somebody would say, let's have a protest, and within an hour you had five hundred people. Do you see the Good Friday Agreement? I don't think we would have had it if we had had social media at that stage. So I'm off Facebook now. I'm still on Twitter, but I only post stuff about swans and Victoria Park and C.S. Lewis Square.

'I'm no longer an MLA but I am still a member of the DUP. I voted for the agreement and to be honest one of the reasons was the prisoners getting out. One of the biggest successes was that paramilitary groups were funded and they kept the peace at the interfaces. The flags protest brought in a batch of young people, people you couldn't control. There's a lack of leadership in loyalism now and the danger I see is some charismatic figure coming to the fore: a Johnny Adair of this world, or a Billy Wright, who can attract that sense of loyalty. I don't see anybody at the moment. I grew up as a loyalist. I feel loyal.' He laughed. 'I'm not quite sure what I am loyal to or what the thing is that keeps us together. The queen's a wonderful woman. A global figure. But when she dies, I can't see the same loyalty to the royalty.

'I recall a discussion we had in the party about same-sex marriage.

We had thirty-eight MLAs at that stage, and Peter Robinson was there. I said, I have a daughter, and I love her to bits and she's gay. And I said, I would prefer that she was straight. And you know why? Because we're living in a homophobic society. And there was silence.

'The counselling helped. I talked about difficulties with my father growing up – he was a very dominant sort of person and a heavy drinker. He totally controlled my mother. She was terrified of him. I had to spend a good part of my childhood over with my granny in west Belfast. I remember the police coming to the door, and having to walk, maybe at nine or ten o'clock at night, because there were five children and you couldn't afford a taxi. I remember waking up my granny's in a big double bed and my Aunt Jenny brought me in a bap, and tea in a big blue and white mug.'

When Sinn Féin's Martin McGuinness resigned as deputy First Minister in 2016, effectively collapsing the Executive, one of the reasons he gave was the intolerable arrogance of the DUP. A few months later, in the run-up to the 2017 Assembly election, the DUP leader Arlene Foster rejected Sinn Féin calls for an Irish language act, with the words, 'If you feed a crocodile it will keep coming back for more.' The remark backfired. There was a surge in support for Sinn Féin and for the first time in the history of the Northern Ireland state, unionists failed to secure a majority. Foster later said she regretted making the comment, not because it was offensive, but because it had allowed Sinn Féin to 'demonise' her.

Douglas saw this as evidence of Foster's 'spectacularly poor' judgement. 'A woman I know, from a nationalist background, she's a civil servant, she said to me shortly after the crocodile remark, "You know my politics, Sammy, I was never a supporter of republicanism, but see when I heard that I just thought, fuck the DUP." I know people who wouldn't have been out waving a Union Jack but they were happy enough to try and make this place work – they have got more aggressive. I think we're in a very dangerous place. My fear is that the whole thing could collapse tomorrow. If it's in the interests of the parties they will walk away from it. The loyalist paramilitaries said their war was over because they believed the union was safe. Thing is now, there is the potential break-up of the union.'

The Northern Ireland Life and Times survey for 2018 strikingly found that one in two respondents said they defined themselves as neither nationalist nor unionist. The 2019 survey showed a degree of retrenchment. While 39 per cent still chose 'neither' identity, and it was still the largest designation, the proportion claiming a unionist identity rose from 26 per cent to 33 per cent. However, as Katy Hayward and Ben Rosher note in their analysis of the change, unionists did not indicate any 'growing intensity' about their identity. Among nationalists, by contrast, there was a steep rise in those claiming a 'very strong' allegiance to their identity.[7]

'Unionists don't trust the British government,' said Douglas. 'The biggest threat to the union at the moment is the rise of nationalism in England. The DUP had its supply and confidence deal, they were big allies, but all of a sudden they ditched us. I agree with Peter Robinson – when you take out insurance on your house it's not because you think it's going to burn down, but to protect yourself for the future. Unionism needs to sit down and come together and have a discussion about where we go from here. I know a lot of people fear a united Ireland. But it is a bit like death. Most people don't fear being dead, they fear the process of dying. Irish unity wouldn't be as bad as the process of getting Irish unity. You could actually probably live quite peacefully in a united Ireland; it is just that the ten years of it becoming a united Ireland would probably be pretty awful.'

---

7 https://pure.qub.ac.uk/en/publications/political-attitudes-at-a-time-of-flux

CHAPTER 6

Such a Thing as Hope

LOYALISM, 'THE CONFUSED CHILD'

'When the UVF shot Bobby Moffett and they killed him in broad daylight on the Shankill in 2010, they killed the PUP as well,' said Dawn Purvis, who resigned her leadership of the PUP after the killing. She had been chosen as his successor by party founder and its first leader, David Ervine. He died in 2007, aged fifty-two. 'David Ervine always said the DUP would be responsible for the break-up of the union, and he is being proved right,' she said. 'He said the DUP couldn't make Northern Ireland work because, in his words, the party just hated Taigs. History has shown us over and over again, the British government don't care about anybody apart from the British government. So the DUP got into bed with the Tories and then got sold down the Swanee.

'Our history just repeats itself. That destabilises loyalism. It has lost the sense of identity that it had at the time of the peace process. There's been no real positive leadership from the PUP for quite some time.'

It is remarkable that many who write and talk about the party make little or no reference to Purvis, the last of the party's leaders to attempt to realise Ervine's radical vision, nor to why she failed. Billy Hutchinson was elected to the first Northern Ireland Assembly alongside Ervine. Hutchinson's memoir scarcely mentions Purvis, but conveys scepticism about her given reason for resigning, and implies that she did not direct the party's political will strongly enough. According to Hutchinson's account, David Ervine's brother Brian stepped in as leader and 'tried in vain to steer the PUP ship back into steadier waters, but the brand had become confused. No one was exactly sure what the PUP was any more.'[1] Hutchinson became the party's leader in 2011.

Purvis continued, 'So loyalist working-class communities are looking to the DUP for direction and for leadership and I really don't think it's coming. When Brexit happens, it is going to be an unmitigated disaster. I think that's what we're at: the beginning of the end now. I think you'll see Scotland having their indy [independence] referendum. I think eventually you'll see a border poll in Northern Ireland, in Ireland, and it doesn't bode well for unionism. The British government are fed up with this squabble in their backyard and they'd do whatever it takes to get rid of it. And the DUP isn't preparing people.

'I remember at the time of the St Andrews negotiations talking to members of the DUP in north Antrim and saying, you know, Paisley's going to do a deal. And they said, "No, he'll not, no, he'll not. The Doc won't sell us out." When he did do the deal there were people in tears because they felt so betrayed. He had deserted them.' The St Andrews Agreement was the 2006 deal that paved the way for the DUP to go into a coalition with Sinn Féin. 'The same thing is going to happen here. If we have Scotland for the Scottish, England for the English, Wales for the Welsh, that leaves the last remnants of the Brits in Northern Ireland. Northern Ireland for the British. What does it mean? What does it mean when that happens for people who hold on to this notion of identity that they can't explain, but it's something that they hold on to, like somebody's trying to steal it from them?

'The DUP are not having those conversations. And people are going to feel isolated and betrayed by that, and when they are frightened and isolated they kick out. You get that sense at the minute with these "betrayal" rallies, that people are circling the wagons again, they're becoming insular again, taking refuge in that old notion that if you're not with us you're agin us. Anybody like myself who has a difference of opinion around unionism and the future of relationships in these islands is being classed as "latte-drinking liberal elites".' This term was used by Bryson, who demanded unionist unity while sneering at anyone who

---

1 Billy Hutchinson with Gareth Mulvenna, *My Life in Loyalism*, Merrion Press, 2020, p. 272

did not share his narrow view. When Gareth McCord, the brother of a Protestant victim of the UVF, disrupted a loyalist protest that had attracted just two people in Belfast in April 2021, Bryson called him 'deranged'. Just as Paisley had claimed in the past that it was ecumenism that was destroying Protestantism, the new loyalist 'thinkers' saw liberalism as the ruination of unionism.

'I do get concerned that rednecks like that can wind people up to a point where they're creating lines of difference once again, a bit like the Millwall supporters: nobody likes us and we don't care,' said Purvis. 'But society does care, because nobody wants to go back to the days of riots and bombs and killings. And if a stone is thrown the DUP will be the first on the airwaves to criticise them. So loyalists are like the confused child once again: "Hold on a wee minute, you called this the 'betrayal act'. You said that Boris sold us out. You have wound us all up to this point and then you slap us down."'

Purvis is from the south inner city of Belfast. 'At the start of the Troubles my family had been put out of York Street in north Belfast and they moved into Donegall Pass. I have lived there ever since, thirty-eight years in the same street. Growing up you had a geographical boundary in your head as to where it's safe to go and where not to go. You grew up with violence. It was a really tight-knit community. There was tartan gangs then.' These street gangs of youths from the 1960s wore red tartan scarves like the Scottish gangs that supported Glasgow Rangers football team. They were known by their neighbourhood – in Purvis's area they were the Pass Tartans. They engaged in sectarian stone throwing and street fights with 'green tartans' from the nationalist community.

'There was the UDA and then the UVF. And you sort of knew who these people were. There were women involved as well at that time,' she said. It was women from the UDA who beat Ann Ogilby to death in 1974, not far from where Purvis lived. 'Yet I had a very happy childhood. Mum was a single parent in the late 1960s and she was seen as a fallen woman. She worked hard, looked after us well. We were latchkey kids, reared on the streets.

'I remember umpteen occasions when soldiers kicked our door in, lifted us out of bed and put us against the wall because there was no time to evacuate the street. The next minute there was bits of car landing in the street and then it was, "Go on, back to bed, you've school in the morning." If there was rioting with our Catholic neighbours on Lower Ormeau or the Markets, everybody was rallied to get the stones and the bricks. It's really strange, because there are people in Donegall Pass in mixed marriages to people from Lower Ormeau or the Markets. And of course we have quite a large Chinese community as well.

'I was married to the guy next door when I was twenty-two. The tradition was, boys to the Gasworks, girls to the stitching factory. My sister had started work there after she left school and then it would have been my turn but it closed down, and the Gasworks closed down. My husband was a trained electrician. I was just doing various jobs: hairdressing, domiciliary, catering. I started finding my voice at that time, becoming more and more involved in the community. I had two small children so I set up, with others, a mother and toddlers group. The IRA bombed our street in 1992 when we lived behind Donegall Pass Police Station, and I was suffering from post-natal depression. Our house was completely wrecked. I remember looking up at the sky through what used to be the roof, feeling, is this ever going to stop?

'Then I started hearing these shadowed-out men on television talking about a peaceful future and a way forward. I liked what they were saying. They knew what it was like to be involved in violence, to go to prison, and they were saying, no, there's a better way. After the ceasefires I was asked did I want to join the PUP. They supported a woman's right to choose. They supported an end to academic selection, and proper education for our children. They believed in community co-operatives and equality. And I'm going, wow, this is great, this is me, this speaks to me. At the first meeting I said, I will just stay in the background and make the tea – but of course I left that meeting as branch secretary. And it became my life for sixteen years. I grew up politically. I became the first member of my family ever to get to third-level education. And I was able to see the injustices within our own community, and look at politicians who lorded it over us for forty years. I had never seen our local Unionist MP, Martin Smyth'. Smyth, who was also a Presbyterian minister, was the UUP MP for Belfast South from 1982 to 2005.

'From '98 to '99 there was a lot of euphoria about,' said Purvis. 'We got the referendum, the elections to the Assembly, the shadow Assembly up and running. There was a lot of anticipation. We were going to get an Executive that would be making its own policies and delivering for the people. The border would become irrelevant and so would unity. But then very quickly loyalism was embroiled in a bloody feud initiated by people who turned out to be agents of the state and drug dealers. They were opposed to the peace agreement and they were fighting with loyalists who were proponents of the peace agreement. And that was a horrible time.'

In 2001, former RUC detective Johnston Brown confirmed on a television documentary that RUC Special Branch (who dealt with intelligence) had destroyed a tape police had made of one of Adair's gang admitting his involvement in the murder of solicitor Pat Finucane in 1989. Brown said that a high-level decision was taken to sabotage the murder inquiry because of the role of informers and agents. It was a vicious world in which killers felt they were untouchable.

'My youngest son, it affected him badly,' said Purvis. 'He stopped eating. He lost three stone in weight within six weeks. He couldn't swallow his food. And I couldn't understand. So eventually a child psychologist saw him and it came out he was frightened for me. He thought that Johnny Adair was going to shoot me. So I took some time out. It put things in perspective.

'None of us ever thought the DUP and Sinn Féin would become the largest parties. But that's what happens when people see their political leaders as not managing the process properly, and that's I think what happened with Trimble and Mallon. It seemed like a carve-up. I mean, the first thing the Assembly did was vote themselves a pay rise and a pension. No thought for how that looked to people who were waiting on a peace dividend. There was no peace plan, there were no creative ideas for integrated education and sharing the space and moving forward. And that's what people wanted.

'Support for the agreement started to just haemorrhage away. There were some good things, like the Patten Commission, and reforms to the RUC. So things were going in the right direction, but Trimble was a disaster. He had to be dragged kicking and screaming to it every time. This is a man that won the Nobel Peace Prize with John Hume. Let's go! But instead of being the driving force, out there selling this as something that unionism should embrace, it was always bad news. He didn't lead. He didn't bring his party with him.

'And that meant the DUP just started to gain. They gained Arlene, they gained Jeffrey, they gained Peter Weir, they gained Simon Hamilton. Then they started to change their message. They recognised that Paisley was a bit off-putting in the media because of his rabble-rousing. So they started to use him less and started to talk about a fair deal for unionism. People latched on to that, because they saw the agreement as disadvantaging unionism. Now, of course, it absolutely didn't. Equality, human rights – what's not to like? But it was sold as: they're getting everything, we're getting nothing. People looked at Trimble and saw a loser, and the DUP became the largest party.

'I didn't have a great interest in electoral politics. My focus was on party structures, development, policy, growing the number of women within the party. At Queen's I was learning about the welfare system. I became equality spokesperson within the party, and we developed a policy on gay and lesbian equality and we were doing progressive things.

'For a couple of years then I was out doing academic research, into things like the role of ex-prisoners in conflict transformation. I was chair of the party. In 2006 the UVF came up with their end-game process, which was great. The St Andrews talks were leading to a plan for devolution to be restored again. And then David Ervine died. My world fell apart. I think for the peace process, for loyalism and for the PUP it was devastating. I had no idea he had nominated me to take over from him.

'At his funeral on the Newtownards Road, you had Gerry Adams and Peter Robinson embracing Jeanette Ervine, real symbols of reconciliation, and the PUP benefitted and I was returned as an MLA. I was divorced by this stage. My boys said, you always went with your heart when you looked after us, it's time you went with your head and followed this. We'll support you. Of course they had their granny to spoil them to death!

'But the UVF had not decommissioned and the PUP still had a massive job to do – to bring paramilitarism to an end, to bring class politics into working-class areas, to help regenerate and really transform those communities because of the neglect for decades. So I set to work. Not easy. The PUP was male-dominated, and as far as the UVF is concerned, you're a woman, you've never been involved, you've no prison sentence, you've no credibility. In 2009 I read about the decommissioning of weapons in the papers. The relationship was breaking down. It was obvious the next step was demobilisation but they didn't want to talk about it. I was the only woman in a room with about fifty men. I was the PUP leader, but they were so paranoid.

'Then in 2010 I was at a wedding in Donegal and I got a call from a journalist – actually I got twenty-two missed calls first. And he said, Dawn, I'm just ringing to get your reaction about the alleged involvement of the UVF in the murder of the man on the Shankill yesterday. And I was, like, what? So I just said, "Completely wrong, absolutely condemn it." I'm not an apologist for anybody's violence. And I heard from journalists and others that this was a man who had basically put it up to a UVF leader because they were threatening his sister. They had beaten her son and put him off the Shankill. The PUP was my political home but I just thought, I can't carry on like this. These people were not going to go away. They had too much control.

'I tendered my resignation from the leadership and from the party, and asked them if I could remain as an independent MLA for the remainder of the term – there was a year left or something. Because there were a number of things that I was working on, including a report on educational disadvantage among Protestant working-class boys that I wanted to see through. I ran again as an independent in 2010 but I was beaten by Sammy Douglas for the DUP. As far as I am concerned, for Northern Ireland to be safe and prosperous, unionism has to disappear and so does nationalism.'

'WHAT NEXT, DAWN?'

'My mum always says to me, "What next, Dawn?"' Although she was distraught about the end of her political career, Purvis was not going to give up on her passion for justice. She went on to become the director of the new Marie Stopes Clinic in Belfast, providing contraceptive services, non-directive counselling and medical abortions for women in early pregnancy.

Growing up, Purvis had seen the unacknowledged struggles of women in her community. 'Domestic violence was rife and no one did anything about it,' she said. 'And I used to hear women talking in whispers about such and such a girl who had "gone and got herself into trouble".' She remembered the day a teenage girl she knew got her to accompany her to meet a dishevelled-looking man at the bar to whom she gave some money. Purvis later learned that this was a notorious illegal abortionist. Abortion in Northern Ireland was subject to a potential penalty of life imprisonment under legislation passed in the Victorian era.

The PUP supported the right to choose and as an MLA Purvis had called for the 1967 Abortion Act to be extended to Northern Ireland. However, the leaders of the DUP, the UUP, Sinn Féin and the SDLP claimed there would be 'strong opposition' in Northern Ireland and that such a move would damage the peace process. 'We tried to set up a pro-choice group in the Assembly,' Purvis said. 'Just one MLA, Alliance's Anna Lo, said yes. The DUP's Jim Wells wrote back and dug his pen so deeply into the paper that it was torn!' Wells, who went on to become health minister, had called the 1967 act 'legalised carnage'. Purvis said she felt defeated. 'We thought we'd never get our rights,' she said.

The Marie Stopes clinic became a target for anti-abortionists. 'On the day we opened we had the mainly-Catholic Precious Life on one side of the road and British National Party protesters and Protestant evangelical anti-choice people on the other,' said Purvis. 'They'd book up all our appointments. At Christmas they placed an empty manger outside. They'd show women gross photos. They'd tell them they'd go to jail.' When Purvis arrived at work in the morning there would be a hooded figure with a banner waiting at the door, and there would be protesters waiting for her when she finished in the evening. As with the UVF, so with the protesters: 'I realised there are some things you can't fix. There was nothing I could do to make these people stop what they were doing. The work itself could be very emotional,' she said. 'One woman gave us flowers and told us about how her sixteen-year-old friend had killed herself after she had not been able to get an abortion.'

After decades of campaigns by pro-choice activist groups in Northern Ireland, abortion was finally legalised by a vote at Westminster in 2019, while the Executive at Stormont was collapsed. Labour MP Stella Creasy steered through an amendment to the Northern Ireland (Executive Formation) Bill, with an overwhelming majority supporting it. While Sinn Féin had abandoned its long-held opposition to abortion, the DUP had declared the issue a 'red line', and later in 2019 it recalled the Executive for an emergency debate in an effort to thwart the new law. The leaders of the main Northern Ireland churches, all of them men, along with the Irish Council of Churches, issued a joint statement supporting the DUP's efforts.

Abortion was legalised in Northern Ireland in March 2020 but the Minister of Health, the UUP's Robin Swann, did not commission the new services required for the law to take effect. During the pandemic, women still had to travel to obtain abortions. In 2021 the Northern Ireland Human Rights Commission was given leave by the High Court for judicial review of decisions by the Secretary of State for Northern Ireland and the Department of Health, challenging failures that have left Northern Ireland in breach of its human rights obligations under UN and EU conventions.[2] Before the case came to court, the Secretary of State intervened and ordered the Executive to implement the law.

Purvis had moved on to become chief executive of a housing charity in North Down. 'I'm still quite active, but all outside of politics really,' she said. 'I'm chair of Healing Through Remembering, which looks at how we can deal with legacy, and of Positive Life, which supports people living with HIV, and I'm on the board of the John and Pat Hume Foundation for peaceful change and reconciliation. I find a lot of what is going on in unionism right now completely backward-looking, and I wouldn't set much store by some of the people running these "betrayal act" rallies. A couple of them came into my office when I was leader of the PUP wanting to talk to us about adopting "olde English" as a language.' They pronounced it 'oldie', she said, and told her it had been used in County Derry by the guilds of London. She laughed and took a swig of her tea. We agreed I would say it was a latte.

'I TRY AND TRUST PEOPLE UNTIL I KNOW I CAN'T TRUST THEM'

'I remember after my brother Edgar died, my father turning to me and asking, "What are we going to do?"' said Anne Graham. 'I was shocked. Up to that, he had been the dominant person in the family and he'd have consulted with Edgar. They'd have seen me as a kind of office girl – I was a civil servant. They'd certainly never asked my opinion.' I kept running into Graham at interesting meetings in Belfast. She always

---

2 https://www.nihrc.org/news/detail/update-on-human-rights-commissions-legal-challenge-on-access-to-abortion-services

spoke, and what she said was always thoughtful and at a bit of a slant from what others might have expected from her.

The first time was at a seminar in Belfast in December 2019 in memory of her late brother, Edgar Graham. It was held to mark the thirty-sixth anniversary of his murder by the IRA, just around the corner on University Square. He was on his way to give a lecture on constitutional law and a gunman shot him in the back of the head. He was a member of the old Northern Ireland Assembly of the 1980s for the UUP and a law lecturer, and he was twenty-nine when he died. The meeting had been organised by the victims and survivors group, South East Fermanagh Foundation (SEFF), and many prominent figures from unionism were there, including former First Minister, and now Lord, David Trimble, and Arlene Foster, DUP leader and the current First Minister.

One of those who spoke was Calvin Reid, a serious young student in a dark suit, part of a group of young men all similarly attired. He said that 'little to nothing has been done to commemorate this great man' and other 'victims of terrorism, innocent victims and members of the security forces'. The responsibility for legacy, he said, 'is with my generation'. Reid would go on to launch a debate in the weeks that followed after he claimed that Queen's had become a 'cold house for unionists'. In the speech with which he welcomed winning the Nobel Prize in 1998 along with John Hume, Trimble had conceded that Northern Ireland had, in the past, been a 'cold house for nationalists'.

In 2015 a journalist who requested information on the religious affiliation of students at Queen's was told that the university population was 'broadly in line with the available census data for 2011 … Of those who declared a religious affiliation, 35.8 per cent of students at Queen's identified themselves as Protestant, 50.6 per cent identified themselves as Catholic, with 13.6 per cent other/not declared.'[3] The statement added that the proportions of the general population aged eighteen to twenty was 48.5 per cent Catholic and 43.3 per cent Protestant. A petition calling on the university to 'end the sectarianism towards Protestants and Unionist students at Queen's' attracted just over three thousand signatures in early 2020.

---

3 'About 50 per cent more Catholics than Protestants enter higher education', *News Letter,* 20 January 2016

The Northern Ireland Peace Monitoring Report for 2018 cited Department of Education figures that showed that Catholics were more likely than Protestants to continue into higher education (45.8 per cent of Catholics to 40.2 per cent of Protestants).[4]

Graham focused on the loss of her brother's intellectual and political potential. She spoke of Diplock courts, of internment, of allegations of shoot-to-kill policies. 'He stood four-square for the rule of law,' she said. 'Those were dark times.' She quoted the late human-rights advocate, Kevin Boyle, who had written about her brother's 'singular absence ... of prejudice or rancour' in a letter of condolence to the family. She lamented also the killings of other lawyers, Pat Finucane and Rosemary Nelson. When others in the room became fierce and spoke of 'evil forces' at work, she pulled things back, but she warned that she did have a sense that the moment was perilous: 'I hope and pray that, as Northern Ireland is yet again convulsed by rancour and division, people, and particularly politicians, will consider carefully what they say and do, so that we never again sink into the abyss of hatred and intolerance which led to Edgar's death,' she said.

The next time we met was again at Queen's, this time when Linda Ervine was giving an illustrated lecture on the role of the Irish language in Northern Irish history and culture. Ervine has an open-hearted love of the language and runs Turas ('journey'), an Irish language school at East Belfast Mission in the staunch heart of the Newtownards Road. The fastest-growing cohort of Irish language learners in Northern Ireland is now among Protestants, including several early school leavers who have gone on to further education after attending Turas. Ervine is from a communist background. I had heard her describe the conflict in Northern Ireland as squalid and sectarian.

She is the president of the recently founded East Belfast GAA club, whose members come from all sections of the local community. The GAA has played a powerful role in creating a sense of identity and local pride in the nationalist community in both parts of Ireland. In 2019 Sammy Morrison, a leading member of the TUV, wrote about the absence of such cohesion within unionism: 'If you are a nationalist young person you go to a school which reinforces your identity, play

---

4 Ann Marie Gray et al, Northern Ireland Peace Monitoring Report, Number 5, October 2018, p. 163

sports which reinforce your identity, and many learn a language which reinforces your identity,' he wrote. 'What gives a young person from a unionist background a sense of identity?' He warned that the loss of unionist votes and seats was a problem that could not be solved 'by lapsing into Derry syndrome (i.e. let's all rally together, shut the gates and whoever isn't standing with us is a Lundy)'.

Ervine saw culture as something that could be shared. At the Belfast meeting she spoke of place names and of how when the Irish language declined in the seventeenth century it was middle-class Protestants from Belfast who saved it. She linked the love of Irish to many historic unionist figures, and said that in 1896 the Grand Chaplain of the Grand Orange Lodge had declared it a disgrace that children were not being taught the language of their country. Her slideshow included Queen Victoria, who said her favourite 'motto' was 'céad mile failte', and so it was put up everywhere to welcome her to Belfast in 1849. Presbyterians had spoken of 'our sweet and memorable mother tongue'. Stern Protestant opponents of Home Rule spoke Irish; the UVF had it on their banners in 1914. 'We are steeped in this language,' she said. 'Protestants who reject it don't know their history. Catholics who claim it as theirs alone don't know it either. Language doesn't vote, doesn't sectarianise, doesn't fly a flag.'

Graham had listened intently, and when she contributed to the discussion afterwards she praised the event, and said that it was sad that even at Queen's 'we've been told Irish is offensive'. Everything was political, she said, 'but it doesn't have to be party political.' Afterwards she told me she had been dismayed by how Irish had become a 'hot and heavy subject' around Queen's. 'I'm a very open-minded person and I'm a good linguist. I thought, well, I have Latin, French and German, I can pick up the Romance languages, so I decided to try Irish. I'd heard of Linda Ervine and I thought I could be an example to people in a small way. I try to work in a positive way.' She'd contacted Ervine who sent her to a class on the Falls Road. She was getting on well.

'It is a pity that Irish has been weaponised by both sides,' she said. 'I have an Orangeman friend and he said he couldn't cope with having Irish language words on road signs – I said, you'd get used to it. Nelson McCausland said an Irish language act would be the silver bullet republicans will use to bring down unionism. I've been surprised to find a few friends who are also learning – they aren't threatened by it.'

The DUP's East Londonderry MP, Gregory Campbell, is infamous for making demeaning references to the Irish language. While an MLA in 2014 he began a speech with 'curry my yogurt can coca coalyer', a parody of *'go raibh maith agat, Ceann Comhairle'* ('thank you, chairperson'). He was banned for two days but at the DUP's annual conference later that year he held up a yogurt pot, said he thought he would have curry for dinner, and that if there was an Irish language act he would use it as toilet paper. The audience found this blatant sectarianism highly entertaining.[5]

Graham told me that when she was a girl she had loved to walk along the shore at Lough Neagh. She had learned about the history of the Mass rocks and the holy well there. She felt a connection to the people who had worshipped at the ancient pre-Christian church. The rural community she'd grown up in was integrated, she said. 'People relied on their neighbours.'

'I try and trust people until I know I can't trust them. I go to ecumenical meetings. I have come up against people who say, "Catholics are two-faced, you know". It is true that there have been apologies that aren't apologies for Edgar's killing. I wouldn't say that I am Irish, but I should point out that I was not and never have been in the unionist family. I'd be a woolly liberal in many ways. I used to argue with Edgar about shoot-to-kill – he was anti-capital punishment but he stood up for the security forces. I was told that our Uncle Harry stopped speaking to me because he thought I was veering towards Alliance.

'I am not sure about the "cold house" thing, though I did send a message of support to Calvin,' Graham said. 'Queen's don't wish to note what happened to Edgar. They seem to feel it is bad for the image of the university. They said there would be a bursary and a plaque. I wrote the wording for the plaque sensitively but they didn't put it up, even though the money had been collected for it among lawyers. They were very rude to me. I don't care any more. I heard that students cheered in the student's union when Edgar was killed. I was glad when that building was demolished. Someone said Edgar was feeding information about nationalist students to loyalists. Someone blamed Edgar for not condemning Pat Finucane's murder – slight timeline problem there!' Pat Finucane was murdered by the UDA in 1990, seven years after Edgar Graham.

---

5 https://www.bbc.co.uk/news/uk-northern-ireland-politics-30167847

'I am wary of anyone using Edgar's murder for political purposes. I wouldn't celebrate anyone getting shot. It devastated the family – my mother never recovered. The health service was no use to her and her church wasn't supportive. They just put people on Valium in those days. There was talk of electric-shock treatment. I thought that was wrong. She had reactive depression. She blamed herself because she had got Edgar to come home from England after Daddy had a heart attack. My father took dementia and died five years after Edgar. My mother died seven weeks later from a chest infection. I am an orphan now.'

'FULL LUNDY'

The setting for our next encounter was quite different. 'Radical Female Voices in Unionist Communities' was held in March 2020 at Áras Uí Chonghaile, the James Connolly Visitor Centre in republican west Belfast. There are pockets in the area in which Irish is the first language, and some call the area a Gaeltacht. Connolly, one of the executed leaders of the 1916 Easter Rising, had lived close to the centre. When he officially opened the stylishly refurbished building in 2019, President Michael D. Higgins praised all those 'who in their diverse ways' subscribed to Connolly's socialist legacy. One of the quotes from Connolly framed in the hallway reads: 'We believe in constitutional action in normal times, we believe in revolutionary action in exceptional times.'

The speakers at the 'Radical Voices' event were Dawn Purvis and Sophie Long who had written her doctoral thesis on loyalism. Long, also formerly in the PUP, now works for the Joseph Rowntree Charitable Trust. She began by joking that she was 'completing my way to full Lundy' by learning Irish in England. 'It is a beautiful thing,' she said, 'when women get really pissed off.' She spoke of the need for 'a complete transformation of how things are organised here' given that Northern Irish society was rooted in 'violent masculinity and not valuing women's lives'. Unionism was in decline. 'It will tighten its boundaries and it will become harder for women to find a voice,' she said. Hence the drift of young Protestant women to Alliance and the Greens. Purvis agreed. 'Unionism is a continuum. You have Jim Allister on the right – his TUV doesn't want a Catholic about the place,' she said. She was referring to old Lord Brookeborough's advice in the early years of the state to Protestant employers. 'Then you have the DUP whose policies are just anti-everything. The UUP has a lame-duck leader and doesn't know where it is.' There was no place within that continuum for feminist voices. She said that her own sons were raised as feminists. 'They look at the unionist parties and think they've been dug up out of somewhere,' she said. She warned that 'more young women were not voting than voting'.

Purvis praised the work of the woman whose website, *Her Loyal Voice*, was giving working-class loyalist women a platform. I had met the founder Ellen – she prefers not to use her surname – several times to talk about women and unionism. She is from a loyalist background in north Belfast and told me she had become interested in the history and politics of loyalism because her late father had been involved in the UDA. 'When I started looking around I found a lot of books and articles about republicanism, including republican women,' she told me. 'I couldn't find anything about women's involvement in loyalism.'

As a researcher who loves hearing people's stories, she decided to set up the website and has also conducted a survey to which 530 women responded. 'The women have a lot to say, and they feel they are not being listened to,' she said. 'They don't feel the unionist parties represent them, though those who are in the PUP do feel they have a voice. The issues they raise range from the constitutional status of Northern Ireland to equality, poverty, housing and education.' She said many of the women supported abortion rights and the right to same-sex marriage. Ellen told me that two things had made her sad. 'One is the amount of abuse the women get, especially on social media, after they speak out. The other is that they really feel that they cannot any longer express their Britishness. They feel they can no longer talk about love for their culture and identity, from band parades to the flying of the union flag. They feel they are being asked to give up their identity, their connection to their heritage. The women feel they are being treated as second-class citizens.'[6]

Graham had again spoken from the audience at the Radical Female Voices event. 'My grandfather was a soldier at the Somme,' she said. In 2016 republicans had commemorated the Easter Rising, while unionists had commemorated the Battle of the Somme, aggrieved that while their forefathers were going 'over the top' as British soldiers in

---

6 https://herloyalvoice.com

a world war, Connolly and his ilk were seizing the moment to rebel in Dublin. Graham, however, was simply marking cultural difference. 'I am not from an Orange family and I am a unionist with a small "u",' she said. 'Most of my friends are garden-centre Prods.' This term, attributed to Professor Greta Jones, is applied to tranquil suburban dwellers who vote unionist but are less preoccupied with politics than with cultivating their own gardens, literally as well as in the Voltairean sense.

'My brother was murdered by the IRA so it was a little bit of a stretch for me to come here,' said Graham. 'I wouldn't have done so twenty years ago.' She said she lived in suburban south Belfast, which was right next to the working-class Taughmonagh estate. Her question was, 'What can *I* do to reach out to loyalist people?'

There was no clear answer. Both Purvis and Long suggested the relationship between the classes in unionism had been corrupted by the exploitation of the working classes. Long said unionist supremacy was gone but the notion of it remained and with it the delusion of 'we are the people'. Historically unionism relied on loyalists to do the fighting. The betrayal rallies had been part of a long tradition. 'We saw middle-class unionism mobilising working-class loyalists as if for war, but this time it was, "Your Country Needs You – Vote DUP!",' she said. In 2021 Ian Paisley Jnr claimed in parliament that Northern Ireland had been 'screwed over' by the Northern Ireland protocol. Later, on the BBC's *Newsnight* programme he said, 'We've given blood for the union, in terms of our soldiers, and what do we get back? A slap in the face with a wet kipper.'[7]

'YOU CONNECT'

Molly Leggett, who is twenty, has no doubts at all that Queen's is a cold house for unionists. She said that when people in her halls of residence found out she was a member of the DUP 'they started banging at my door at night and shouting things at me'. Someone else got threatened for wearing a poppy on campus, she'd heard. She is the chairperson of the Democratic Unionist Association (DUA), the youth wing of the DUP at the university. 'Teachers will dig in at certain politicians in the

---

7 Andrew Madden, 'We have given blood for Union: Paisley launches scathing attack on Boris Johnson over post-Brexit supply issues', *Belfast Telegraph*, 15 January 2021

party and it is nearly like trying to make you feel embarrassed about your British identity, which I think is very unfair. I feel that every day going in. I think actually unionist societies as a whole – ourselves, the young unionists, the conservatives – we've all sort of come together really. We feel a bit isolated on campus.'

She works part time in the Ulster Scots museum in Belfast's city centre, so was particularly interested in a module on her course on history and society. 'One of the readings was about Nelson McCausland when he was culture minister for the DUP. They basically made him out to be a horrible man because of his views. But then we had another reading and it was based on the hunger strikes and it was, like, all these guys are great for doing X, Y, and Z,' she said. 'Just the complete deference. It was shocking. A lot of students felt very uncomfortable. Then we had the "Brits Out" incident, where it was written on a sign at a freshers' stall. The Students' Union president said everybody is welcome and respected at the uni but there is a fear factor. Students from a Protestant unionist background don't want to express who they are, so they just take a head-down approach. Get out the door as quickly as you can, get the degree and leave. And I think that's nearly the way I am now. Obviously I've met really good friends through the DUA but I do think it's a cold house for unionists and that's why.'

Molly lives in Belfast during the week, but her 'home place' is the family home in County Armagh. She identifies strongly with her family traditions, including Orangeism. 'I'm from just outside Portadown, out in the sticks a wee bit. I go to the Church of Ireland with my granny all the time. I love it. My family are very connected with Altnaveigh Orange Lodge in Newry in an area that through the Troubles had a lot of issues, which my dad came up through. They have Altnaveigh Sunday to remember the men that were murdered by the IRA in 1922 – I think it was the Irish Civil War. It's a lodge that's very close to my heart in that way.'

The Altnaveigh massacre was one of the most notorious incidents of the Irish Civil War. On a June morning in 1922, around thirty IRA men drawn from Monaghan, Louth, Armagh and Down walked across the border from Ravensdale in Louth to Altnaveigh, a small Protestant settlement overlooking Newry. There had been many skirmishes between the B Specials in the North and the IRA, featuring attacks on barracks, isolated murders and the burning out of houses. This time, the IRA gang murdered six Protestants, including a woman, and attempted to kill more. Dozens of houses were also burned out. There have been repeated attempts to burn the hall down.

'I feel a very strong connection to the Orange Order. I came up through the future leaders programme. A lot of younger people feel disillusioned with the Orange Order and they do think that it's sort of for older people. My wee brother and my granda and everybody in my family is involved in some way. It promotes our culture and identity. I like to go to the Twelfth of July with my entire family. There's people that I wouldn't see for a full year and that's the way that I get to see them. It's like a safeguard too – you feel like you can meet people that believe the same thing as you do. You connect.'

Molly said she was 'devastated' when abortion and same-sex marriage were introduced in Northern Ireland by Westminster. 'I am a devolutionist and what I was so hurt by was, you know, waiting lists in the hospitals, the education system. My wee brother and sister are still at school. My mum's a nurse – she's waiting as well for her pay rise. There was a lot of things that they could have stepped in for, and they stepped in for two very controversial issues in the middle of the talks process. But the issue of abortion has united Protestants and Roman Catholics at Queen's. We've had about twenty sign-ups in the pro-life society, and these are people that are from families that would be predominantly voting on republican lines. So that is good.'

'MY GRANDFATHERS' FOOTSTEPS'

It was Jordan Greer who introduced me to Molly. He had brought her into the Future Leaders Initiative. She described him as being 'really chilled and already a Worshipful Master'. When I had contacted Greer, a DUP constituency assistant, he was courteous and helpful. We met first in the order's Schomberg House Museum of Orange Heritage in east Belfast. It has a life-size King William on his white charger, along with battle scenes and models of battle re-enactments. This heritage is extremely male, by the looks of it. Greer is in his twenties, and newly married. 'The leaders' programme is basically about recruiting young people and exploring capacity building,' he said. 'I encourage them to grow their confidence in terms of media skills. It's part of the Brother

Drew Nelson Legacy scheme. He was the Grand Secretary and sadly passed away quite recently. He saw us as the future of the order. He felt we should not change our principles, but we should take a more modern approach. The order is for the unionist family. We need to promote the importance of the union.

'Both my grandfathers were in the Orange Order but not many of my friends my age would have joined,' said Greer. 'They'd have been involved in Orange culture through being in a band maybe. But I had a very keen interest in history, which sort of drew me in to it. I'm following in my grandfathers' footsteps. I joined the Ulster Special Constabulary Loyal Orange Lodge in Sandy Row district when I was eighteen. It's a memorial lodge to the B Specials, which one of my grandfathers was in. Also, it's close to Queen's where I was a student. I was chaplain and deputy master.' The B Specials was an auxiliary force to the RUC, notorious for anti-Catholic violence. When it was disbanded, many ex-members joined the UDR.

'I'm from a Presbyterian background but I am now in an independent church,' said Greer. 'It would stick to the very core Christian fundamentals on moral issues. I wouldn't like to say American-style – evangelical would probably be the best way to describe it. They have a good youth set-up and kids' programmes.

'Now I am worshipful master of my local lodge, Tildarg True Blues LOL 632, a stone's throw from my house outside Ballyclare. The younger members only really turn up on the Twelfth of July. Most of the men that go to the meetings would be over the age of fifty apart from our new deputy master. So we have two young men at the top now. Obviously the older men are there to guide us. The main challenge today is the secularisation of society amongst people under the age of thirty. There'd be less religious affiliation and less political affiliation in terms of defining yourself as a unionist. Younger people don't really feel that connected to their heritage, which is really our problem.'

'WHERE ARE ALL THE UNIONISTS?'

Another Jordan, Jordan Moore, saw the problem for unionists differently. The recent Queen's graduate, who studied politics, wrote a piece for the *Belfast Telegraph* in December 2020 in which he argued that the problem was that the young people who believed in the union were 'embarrassed at their leading parties'. He was a working-class unionist who had grown up proud to be British. 'I remain a devoted unionist and my love of the union could not be more substantial,' he wrote. 'However, neither could my disdain for the policies of the leading unionist parties and this prevents me from voting for either.' His politics were left wing and liberal and he saw these values as being in no way incompatible with unionism. However, the DUP and UUP clung to conservatism 'as if it were a matter of life or death'. He expressed disgust at Sammy Wilson's support for Trump, and the UUP's electoral pact with the Conservatives in 2010.[8]

'When I attended Queen's I often thought, "Where are all the unionists?",' he wrote. He had found out that, like him, unionists at the university hid their political views 'through fear of alienation and ridicule'. He found that others who, like him, supported abortion rights and same-sex marriage, and believed in evolution, were now either not voting, or voting for Alliance. He was concerned that the DUP and UUP did not seem to realise they needed to address this alienation if they were to survive. Some young unionists have decided to attempt to do this within the political system. They include UUP member Michael Palmer, chairman of Ards and North Down Ulster Young Unionists, who is gay. He saw the centenary year of 2021 as an opportunity for unionism to 'remould' itself as 'a positive, welcoming, all-embracing political force'.[9]

In January 2021, Scott Moore (no relation to Jordan), a student of international politics at Queen's who describes himself as a 'Strabane liberal', Tweeted that although he was a Protestant from a unionist background, he no longer identified as either. 'I find few things in politics more repulsive than the outlook of the DUP, UUP and TUV.' Why, he asked, would he vote for parties that had been complicit in, or culpable for, homophobic bigotry, denying women access to abortion, and refusing to act on climate change. He said the parties were harming young people and losing voters, and instead of recognising the reasons for this, they just got 'angrier and angrier'.

---

8 Jordan Moore, 'DUP and UUP leave many young unionists feeling embarrassed', *Belfast Telegraph*, 1 December 2020

9 Michael Palmer, 'I am gay, unionist, and proud – and 2021 will give us the chance to show off the diversity of our cause', *News Letter*, 21 July 2020

He was immediately attacked for his use of the word 'repulsive' by unionist politicians. The UUP's Doug Beattie accused him of being 'sneering and condescending'. Other tweeters piled in, mocking him as 'not all there', which he took to be a reference to his being autistic. The worst insult one person could come up with was, 'Bet you sit down to pee'. This reminded me of a hearing a rioter at Drumcree shouting at the police, 'Away home and change your tights.' Extreme evidence of toxic masculinity. Moore was not deterred and went on to highlight the DUP's silence after MP Gregory Campbell posted remarks claiming there were too many Black people on a *Songs of Praise* broadcast.

I asked him if he was surprised that senior politicians had responded so forcefully to him. No, he said, and sent me an article about a campaign he had participated in as seventeen-year-old sixth-former in 2016.[10] The previous year, the Commission on Religion and Belief in Public Life had said that Northern Ireland schools should stop requiring students to take part in religious worship during school hours. Moore agreed, and had spoken in a debate on the issue. A TUV councillor had declared that his efforts were 'like the policies of Chairman Mao, Stalin and Hitler'.

Professor Jon Tonge of Liverpool University led a survey after the 2019 Westminster election that found that while the DUP retained a large majority of its core voters, 'unionism has a significant problem in not attracting pro-union members of the electorate to vote.'[11] There are 500,000 non-voters and 30 per cent of them support Northern Ireland remaining in the UK. The survey suggests that the most socially progressive group in Northern Ireland is non-voting young Protestants. Scott Moore has joined the Alliance party. He has also defiantly adopted the word 'repulsive'.

In April 2021, Doug Beattie brought a motion to the Northern Ireland Assembly to ban conversion therapy – the process of trying to change a person's sexuality. The motion noted that LGBTQ+ people did not need 'a fix or a cure'. The DUP proposed an amendment protecting 'legitimate religious activities'. This was rejected. The TUV

---

10 https://www.secularism.org.uk/news/2016/04/sixth-former-compared-to-stalin-for-campaigning-against-mandatory-prayers-in-school

11 Jon Tonge, https://www.liverpool.ac.uk/media/livacuk/research/heroimages/The-University-of-Liverpool-NI-General-Election-Survey-2019-March-20.pdf

voted against it. Moore welcomed the motion, which passed by a large majority. However, he was appalled that Steve Aiken had advised UUP voters in the next Assembly elections to give their next preferences to these other unionist parties.

I had asked Aiken about the dearth of women in representative roles in his party. He said they were making efforts to get more women involved. But when I asked him what feminist measures he had in mind he looked at me with startled incomprehension. 'Feminist?' he said.

'IS THAT A REAL LANGUAGE?'

I met Stephen Carson at Linda Ervine's lecture. He had done his undergraduate degree at Queen's and was, when I met him, deep into a PhD there. 'I never felt Queen's was a cold house for unionists,' he told me. 'That is just scaremongering. Right enough, it is a culture shock for some people to see all those green tops,' he said. He was referring to the hundreds of Catholic boys who come up to Queen's from the country and live raucously in tiny, sub-standard and overcrowded houses in the Holylands area. They roam about in large, loud groups wearing bright green GAA tops as if it was their uniform. 'It's like your granny when she gets her cataracts done,' Carson said. 'But you get used to it.

'A man in the young unionists was saying to me the "cold house" thing is a self-fulfilling prophecy,' said Carson. 'Protestants will be put off and won't come, and those who do will feel more isolated. Things have happened in the past – the Students' Union took a stance for a united Ireland. I don't agree with that – I think it should be neutral.'

Carson was involved in An Cumann Gaelach, the Irish Language Society at Queen's. After hearing Ervine speak, he stood up and said that he was a Protestant learning Irish too, and that Ervine's work was a huge encouragement. He was rushing away that night to get back to the library to work on his thesis. When we met again in a cafe at the Europa bus station, he was between the library and an Irish class. 'Some of the boys were surprised that night and said to me they never knew I was a Protestant,' he told me. 'But they were by no means hostile. They love the language and they just want people to learn it.

'I had no interest in Ulster Scots until I started to learn Irish. The Scots language came over in a big way in the Plantation, from the lowlands. Irish loaned words and other words came back,' said Carson.

'Ulster Scots is very influenced by English now. People like to bash it and they shouldn't. It is part of our identity and we should cherish and respect it. Like Irish it belongs to all of us. I live in Armagh in an area called Drumadd, from Dromad Uí Chianáin, O'Keenan's Ridge. The two languages are mixed up together, both part of our identity. Both have a proud literary history. Both are also politicised but English is politicised too. What is important is that we challenge that by everyone speaking the languages. Then they can't be used divisively.

'I grew up in the suburbs of Armagh,' he told me. 'Dad was a plumber, Mum worked for the education authority. My school was traditionally Protestant but I'd say is about 15 per cent Catholic now. We used to do EMU projects at school.' Education for Mutual Understanding was a community relations programme that involved visits between schools of different denominations. 'You would come home and go, "Mum, we went to this school and there were Catholics in it!" As if they were exotic. Only to be told, your parents' best friends were Catholics, your neighbours are Catholics, all the kids I mucked about with are Catholics. So, my first awareness of all this was finding out I already knew a lot of Catholics.

'Armagh is fairly mixed. Rugby and football clubs are mixed. Staff at the shop I worked in were mixed. As people grow up together they learn respect. My parents grew up in the Troubles and they mixed a lot with Catholics then too. I was born in '96 – the Troubles haven't touched my life. My generation has been so fortunate – we haven't seen bombings and shootings. That's not a right, that's a gift and we have to protect it. My parents' generation couldn't even go out to the cinema or to a pub. I used to wait on my mum after school at my gran's and TG4 would be on and we'd be watching *SpongeBob SquarePants* in Irish. I had no other exposure to Irish from I was a child till I was eighteen.

'I started to learn Irish at Queen's. How it came about was I was living with two fellas in student accommodation and we got on really, really well. Donal and Conall. Conall had gone to *bunscoil* and Donal was doing a degree in Irish. I was still asking, is that a real language? They laughed and said they hoped so. Then I did a hill-walking course and there was a man there who was an Irish speaker, and he'd tell us the names of the mountains, and I thought, you have told me a story and explained something. I was rubbish at French at school but it turned out I was good at Irish. I could talk with Donal and Conall. They liked that – they never put me down or made me feel stupid. Making mistakes is the way you learn. I started to go to classes at Conradh na Gaeilge. People here hesitate to do things that are seen to belong to the other side. But in my class there was a Norwegian, two Americans and a Chinese student. I thought, well if they can learn it, why can't I?

'Then my mother was doing research on our family tree and it turns out a lot of our relations are from the west coast of Scotland. My great-great-great-granny only spoke Gallic. There is only an A4 sheet of paper between Gallic and Irish. As a Protestant unionist that gives me a sense of connection between the islands – Scottish, Gallic, Irish, Cornish, Welsh, Breton and Manx. I see it as an anchor; it has given me roots. You need that. It has allowed me to place myself,' he said. 'My identity now as a unionist is cultural. It is based on the languages that link these islands. I don't think an act of union is as powerful as that, the sense of people travelling between these islands for a thousand years.'

Carson was halfway through his doctorate in chronic obstructive pulmonary disease and it was weighing on him. 'I have a healthily passionate dislike of science at the moment,' he said. 'I am more interested in Irish. I might end up as a translator, or teaching science in an Irish language school. I don't think the doctorate is a waste though. My granny used to say, "education is a load easier carried than a set of tools".'

'A RATHER UNPLEASANT WAY TO RUN A PARTY'

Tim Cairns got his taste for politics tramping the streets of Belfast with his Cavan-born grandmother, who was a militant campaigner for Paisley. He and his parents had attended Paisley's huge 'Ulster Says No' rally against the Anglo-Irish Agreement in 1986. Still at school, he joined the UUP but, disliking the Good Friday Agreement, he joined the DUP in 2001 as a policy officer. Others who got involved during this period included Timothy Johnston, now the party's CEO and a powerful behind-the-scenes figure.

'The ultra-conservative evangelical aspect of the DUP didn't appeal to me. I was a Baptist at that time and we are Church of Ireland now. I was uncomfortable with the homophobic slurs you'd hear,' he said. Cairns went to Canada, attended a 'liberal evangelical theological college', got married and had children. He returned with his family when the DUP gave him another job in 2011. 'The DUP had changed. The uber-conservative folk were still there, but there were signs of a recognition that to be electorally successful they'd have to be a bit more moderate. I felt the DUP was the party best capable of maintaining the union and most adept at negotiating.'

However, Cairns is unimpressed by the present leader, and felt Peter Robinson had chosen her to succeed him because she was 'anyone but Sammy [Wilson]. I don't think that she really has that strategic brain. Timothy Johnston, whether you love him or you loathe him, and whether you think he's a good political operator or not – I don't happen to think so – he's very much the politics of the immediate. How do I get over this immediate crisis? To hell with the future. And in fairness to him, he's good at managing fires that are burning today. But a good firefighter will say, I might lose this section of the wood here, but we can save this whole side of the mountain.'

It was not perhaps the best choice of metaphor for Cairns to use. He featured significantly in the inquiry into the RHI affair, his evidence on the DUP prompting chairman Sir Patrick Coghlin to comment that this seemed like 'a rather unpleasant way to run a party'. Cairns said that politics was 'a grubby world' and admitted he had been willing at times to fit his story into the party's narrative. He had been SPAD, a special adviser, to Jonathan Bell when Bell was the minister with key responsibility for the scheme. Cairns' relationship with Bell had become difficult. He told the inquiry that during a trade mission to New York, the minister had become drunk, causing them to be thrown out of a bar, and had then sung 'Breakfast at Tiffany's' at full volume. He also said Bell was not across his ministerial brief. Bell denied these allegations.

Cairns, now outside of politics, except as a broadcast media commentator known for occasional flurries of intense emotion on air, felt there was a lack of talent in the upper echelons of the DUP. He described Paisley Jnr as 'an absolute idiot'. I asked him why he thought Paisley Snr had gone into government with Sinn Féin in 2007, affectionately if patronisingly referring to a man once known by him as 'an unrepentant terrorist' as 'my deputy'. Cairns said Paisley had wanted to prove wrong all those who had said he would never be the Prime Minister of Northern Ireland. He said Paisley had trouble staying awake during meetings by that stage. 'McGuinness was kind to him. Whereas any other political opponent would have seized on that elderly frailty, McGuinness helped him cover it up. There was probably a gratefulness there. I was in the First Minister's office for a few years, and Martin McGuinness was very affable. I think Paisley got carried away with it all.'

Cairns has retained huge admiration for Robinson. 'He's quite a cold person, but he was an operator,' he said. 'Him and McGuinness had both been round the block. They worked well together.' He did not think Northern Ireland could recover from the conflict unless the education system became fully integrated. 'We're seeing folk in their twenties being very bitter, and sectarianism deepening. There's a lack of political vision and leadership and people are getting entrenched. There's a sense that things are going backwards.'

DOWN TO MID ULSTER

CHAPTER 7

See You in Valhalla

Helen's Bay is one of Northern Ireland's 'most sought after areas', its houses selling for millions of pounds. Estate agents rhapsodise in glossy brochures about homes with dressing rooms, en suites, and triple garages. One mansion has 'beautifully screened grounds, ideal for housing rare-breed animals or for those with an equestrian interest'. References are made to proximity to top schools and golf courses. The joke I was told twenty years ago still works – the people are divided into 'the haves and the have yachts'. Kilcooley estate in Bangor by contrast falls within the top 20 per cent of Northern Ireland's most deprived areas, with houses that sell for well under £100,000. One such house 'enjoys mahogany effect uPVC windows' *and* has an 'enclosed rear'. It also boasts access to a local restorative justice programme that addresses 'community conflict with a focus on paramilitary attacks'. Investors are advised that such houses can be acquired with sitting tenants paying £500 a month in rent. It takes just ten minutes to drive from one to the other, though almost no one does. The extreme gap between Northern Ireland's wealthiest and its poorest citizens is on full display up here in the north-eastern corner of Ulster.

'I'M A UNIONIST NIGHTMARE'

'The Brits don't want us and nor does the South. Can you blame them? Imagine looking at your profit-and-loss account and having Northern

Ireland on it. I despise the DUP and Sinn Féin. I'd rather stick red-hot needles in my eyes than deal with arseholes that got paid for three years and didn't work. I hate flags and bonfires and all this paramilitarism and poison. If I had my way I'd ban it all. If the UUP and the SDLP and Alliance all got together and talked about an all-Ireland movement which is about prosperity for all our young people, I'd be up for it. But as things stand, there is no one I can vote for.'

Oliver runs a large and thriving business in North Down. He did not wish to use his real name, he said, because it might damage his ability to carry out his philanthropic work. We met at his office where he was dressed down in jeans and polo shirt. He looked vigorous and sporty. 'My grandfather set our family up in business,' he said. 'He was the driving force, the patriarch. We've had several businesses blown up by the IRA over the years and we have always come back and done something else.

'There was never a bad word in our house about Catholics,' he said. 'I went to prep school and I met boys there who have become lifelong friends. Some of them are from the South and I used to go and stay with them and that was how I got into hunting and shooting and fishing.' His conversation is littered with references to his friends: a 'captain of industry', a 'top surgeon', a 'perfectly ordinary guy', a 'great girl'. He could not stand snobbery, he said. He lived in a village on the Ards peninsula. 'We sent our kids to a prep school because our local primary school had red, white and blue kerbstones outside and we just thought, this isn't happening. And they were in school with kids from Poland, Russia, Catholics, mixed race … and now we are very friendly with a mixed-race family. It's a very nurturing environment and, yes, the kids are wrapped in cotton wool but what is wrong with that? Then they went to grammar school and now they are at uni in England. The youngest just left and he said to us, "I won't be back here." If they choose to stay away, I won't blame them.

'I'm a unionist nightmare. My family has always been unionist but to me they are like King Canute – they think if they just say no often enough it'll not happen. I am an Ulsterman and an Irishman and I have more in common with a man from the Republic than someone in London. The South is far more go-ahead than here. They have gay marriage and abortion …' he slapped his desk hard. 'A woman should be in charge of her own fucking body. The DUP is inextricably bound up with the Free Presbyterians.

'This place, Northern Ireland, has 1.8 million people, about the same as Leeds, but we've ninety MLAs and all these councillors and special advisers. These people collectively blew half a billion on RHI. There is no integrity, no accountability. They are looking for half a billion for these Troubles pensions. That is just untenable. Then we've got the Irish language. You want to learn Irish? Knock yourself out. But I hate the way it has been politicised and weaponised. Where does it stop? Of course, you also have this thing of what Green gets Orange has to get too.

'The NHS. I mean it is wonderful but it has become a sacred cow. You can't criticise it. But we can't afford free healthcare from the cradle to the grave. Free prescriptions and all of that. It is not sustainable. And there are far too many managers. High-level taxpayers need a break too. I pay £50,000 a year in rates and I don't even get my bins lifted. There's a lot of greed here among the business classes too, a lot of speculation, a lot of fraud – a complete lack of moral compass.

'The old Northern Ireland was nothing to be nostalgic about. If I had been a Catholic in the 1960s there is every chance I'd have been on a civil rights march. I mean, correct me if I'm wrong but my understanding is these people didn't even have a vote. What the fuck was that about? There's a lot of Catholics would never have joined the IRA if unionism had proved ready to change back then. And of course the IRA's violence then begat the violence from the other side. It's awful. Getting it to change seems impossible too. By dint of its own stupidity and arrogance the DUP has hastened a united Ireland.

'But you know, it's between the devil and the deep blue sea for us. We love Northern Ireland. Your normal person here is a normal person. And we have a lifestyle here that costs a hell of a lot less than it would in England – I mean school fees are a fraction of what they'd be elsewhere. We do a bit of charity fundraising and we have a lot of fun.' He showed me photos of a ball. He was all dressed up as an Indian, dancing Bollywood style.

'MISTAKEN IDENTITY'

'It has been a long hard fight, there is no end in sight, and to be honest with you, you get tired,' said Alex (pronounced Alec) Bunting. 'They didn't think they'd have to give us a pension because they didn't expect us to live this long.' In constant pain for thirty years, a wheelchair user, and with deteriorating health, Bunting is one of those who have been campaigning for more than a decade for a state pension for those who were seriously injured in the Troubles. In August 2020 a High Court judge in Belfast ruled that the Northern Ireland Executive had acted unlawfully in delaying paying out the pension that had been approved at Westminster nine months earlier, and was part of the New Decade, New Approach deal.

Sinn Féin had held out against the proposed arrangements because those injured in the course of incidents they had initiated were to be excluded from eligibility, and others would have to make their case to a panel. The party's Martina Anderson reacted with fury to the High Court judgement. A former IRA bomber, she had gone on to serve as Sinn Féin's MEP and head of outreach to unionism. On Twitter she claimed that the pension was 'mainly for those who fought Britain's dirty war in Ireland', and who had been involved in collusion. She later deleted the Tweet, and apologised for her 'clumsy' comments.

'Flip me,' said Bunting, shaking his head. 'I was disgusted when I heard that.' His wife Linda, sitting with us outside their adapted bungalow in the suburbs of Bangor, said she had been appalled when she heard about it. 'She's one of the old guard,' she said. Bunting said that a senior Sinn Féin person and ex-IRA man had said, '"we won't leave any of our comrades on the battlefield." Michelle O'Neill was willing to let abortion and gay marriage through but not the pension.'

He told me about the day his ordinary life was destroyed. 'On 21 October 1991 I owned a taxi business in Belfast. I was on the early shift. There were two jobs – taking some disabled kids to school and taking a lady into her work in town. I said I'd take her first and then I'd see if I got back in time to take the kids. Town was blocked because of a security alert and the woman was going berserk that she was going to be late. 'There was an almighty flash – the car door opened and my leg went flying out in two pieces and then me after it, like I'd been shot out of a cannon. I hit the ground, blood spurting over my face. A doctor was passing and he helped me and got me to hospital. Thirty-seven pints of blood were put through me. I was on life support. There's a funny story actually. The police told me a lady found half of my leg

194

in her backyard – she put a bucket over it. They thought they'd have to take the other leg off too because of the shrapnel from a box of change I kept under the car seat. There is still a £1 coin behind my right knee.

'The IRA had put a bomb under the driver's seat. They said it was a case of mistaken identity. There was a reserve peeler [part-time policeman] had lived in my house before we did. There'd been a UDR soldier killed at the bottom of our street two weeks before I was blown up. They must have got their information wrong. They don't care. You're just collateral damage.' The woman who was his passenger was also badly injured. 'I used to see her the odd time and she just cried,' Bunting said. He often thinks, he said, of what it would have been like if the car had been full of the children.

'Alex was twenty-nine when it happened. Since then our life has basically been hospitals and operations,' said Linda. Alex asks her to show me his daily medications. She heaps the boxes on the table. 'Fourteen different tablets every day, including morphine, and an injection once a week,' he said. 'I've had numerous operations. I've had to have my stump shortened twice. I've three crushed vertebrae. I've nearly died several times, and my doctor is worried about me at the moment. I am in pain all the time. I sleep about two hours a night.' 'Since the last time he got the stump shortened he can't walk so he is in the wheelchair all the time now,' said Linda. 'My hands and shoulders are destroyed from pushing myself,' said Alex.

'I was in hospital for a year. Then I couldn't cope outside so I had to go in again. I was deaf. We couldn't live in our old house and we couldn't find a bungalow. I'd lost my job and Linda had to give up hers to look after me. One of our boys, Colin, was very badly affected by it. He really struggled. He was taking seizures.' 'He stopped sleeping and then when he did fall asleep he was shouting,' said Linda. 'Eventually we rang Alan McBride at WAVE,' said Bunting. 'He'd known the boys when he and his wife Sharon used to work for the Boys' Brigade. He got him counselling and it all came out.' 'It turned out he was on the school bus that day and he saw the wreckage of the taxi on the road and thought his daddy must be dead,' said Linda. WAVE Trauma Centre is one of the main NGOs that support and advocate for people impacted by the Northern Ireland conflict.[1]

---

1 http://wavetraumacentre.org.uk/

When he realised he would never be able to get a job to support his family again, Bunting fell into despair and attempted suicide. His sons were fifteen and ten years old at the time. 'Linda said to me, "What are you doing that for after all you've come through?"' he said. 'So many of the injured have died now. We have been trying to get support since Eames/Bradley in 2009.' He was referring to a report for the secretary of state on dealing with the legacy of the past prepared by a committee chaired by Lord Robin Eames, former Church of Ireland Archbishop of Armagh, and Denis Bradley, vice chairman of the first Policing Board and a former Catholic priest.[2] 'We've had to go on to the streets to get signatures for a petition and we've been to the Dáil and to Westminster and Stormont and now the High Court. And you know, all the worries I've had, the others in the injured group have had them too. Life has been very hard.' The executive at Stormont has since been ordered to pay the pension.

'WHAT FLAGS?'

It took a while to organise a meeting with Dee Stitt. First he was off to Vietnam, then Spain. While I waited, he urged me to do my research. 'Google me,' he said. 'There's reams about me in the media. They call me a drug dealer, a murderer, a racketeer. There's no evidence for any of it. I don't even like using the words crime and loyalist in the same sentence. Say some wee lad had committed suicide – the rags would say I made him do it.' Loyalists are certain that but for the media their goodness would shine.

We had met before, the last time in 2018 at the site of the Eleventh Night bonfire in Kilcooley. No one would speak to me until I spoke to Stitt. Except for one man who had stormed up to me and said, 'We hate you. You're all liars. Fake news. Doesn't matter what we say. You do nothing but victimise us and deny us our rights. You're as bad as the politicians and you're paid by the politicians.' Stitt had been affable by comparison, his opening line: 'Shake the hand of the man that rocked Northern Ireland.' He was supervising boys who were trying to rebuild the bonfire.

---

2 https://cain.ulster.ac.uk/victims/docs/consultative_group/cgp_230109_report.pdf. It was a classic Northern Ireland committee of the great and the good, consisting of nine men, including international advisers, and just two women.

In a bid to build the tallest in the country, they had overreached. Under the headline, 'Vain UDA boss Dee Stitt is once again a laughing stock after his prized bonfire collapsed on Friday night,' the *Sunday Life* reported that 'The red-faced Charter NI chief executive is being ridiculed on social media, having earlier claimed the pyre was a "military operation, being constructed by structural engineers for safety".'[3] As crowds gathered to watch the disaster, the report said, an ice cream van arrived on the scene. I had asked Stitt about the paramilitary Ulster Freedom Fighters (UFF) flags on lamp posts around the green. Such flags were illegal. We were standing under one of them. 'What flags?' he'd said. As I drove out of the estate, I was followed by a white jeep that turned back once I was on the main road.

A month later the former armed robber had resigned from his job with Charter NI, a government-funded body that was meant to provide training and employment opportunities in deprived areas. He had been under pressure over his UDA connections, which he alternatively boasted about and denied. Having been photographed with First Minister Arlene Foster in 2016, he later claimed she had 'ruined my street cred'.

We met this time at the Cuban-themed cafe he runs in an industrial estate outside Bangor. He came in sweating in gym gear – leggings, shorts, sweatshirt. 'I've been training from I was in prison. My wife and I do this every morning now, it's called the 45-minute insanity burnout,' he said. 'We are partners in crime.' His watch pinged and he showed me that it said he had just burned 439 calories. 'I've been to Cuba three times – I have friends over there. One of them, his father was a regional minister, Carlos you call him. They have a beautiful house. I took the pictures we have on the walls here – these aren't where he lives. These are in the backstreets.' Judging from photos he posts of gin and tonics against a fine lawn, Stitt had a nice house too.

'There's a good community spirit in Kilcooley, and good relations with the PSNI. Very little summary justice is handed out. There's a waiting list to get into it,' he said. He reminisced about gun battles that took place in his youth, describing one as 'a crackin' story' and 'folklore in my community'. He had joined the UDA at fifteen and was

3 Ciaran Barnes, 'UDA boss Stitt a laughing stock as bonfire collapses', *Sunday Life*, 8 July 2018

jailed for armed robbery at twenty-one. 'I got out as part of the Good Friday Agreement,' he said. 'Drumcree was the start of the erosion of loyalist culture. Beginning of the end. Now no loyalist band gets to walk through a nationalist area – it's all gone now.' He had been involved in the decommissioning process. 'I was an interlocutor – big fancy name,' he said. 'I had a certificate that enabled me to go all over Northern Ireland and collect weapons and explosives from all the dumps – M60 machine guns, AK-47s, sniper rifles, pistols, grenades, explosives, blast bombs, all the tools.'

The media had ruined Charter NI for him. 'Everything was rosy in the garden for about four years. Then they got stuck in. How could this terrorist be a fit person to handle public funds. Andy Tyrie, he's the UDA's supreme commander and he's eighty years of age, he said to me, "See the ferocity of the press against you, Dee, what have you done, killed the queen's corgis?" At the end of it all they were calling for my head. People in the DUP were feeding it. I was being used as a scapegoat to take attention away from the RHI. What an organisation and they destroyed it,' he said, shaking his head.

Stitt said his business was now the cafe and a fish and chip shop in Newtownards. 'And very successful we are,' he said. A workman got out of a van outside and walked through the cafe to the toilets. As he emerged, Stitt said to him, 'You just love that wee toilet, don't you?' The man grinned. 'Aye,' he said, heading out the door.

Unionism was in a very weak state, Stitt said. 'The UUP ones that came into the DUP ruined it.' This view was widely held among traditional DUP voters. The reference was to Arlene Foster, Jeffrey Donaldson and others who left the UUP over their opposition to the Good Friday Agreement. It was why Donaldson, in some ways the most credible potential leader to follow Foster, might have difficulty pleasing those at the rougher edges of the party.

'We've got sold out – yet again,' said Stitt. 'I wouldn't rule out a return to violence because the loyalist community will never accept a united Ireland. Sinn Féin is the still the political wing of the IRA. The language coming out of them is totally alien.' He clapped his hands. 'I don't know, I haven't a crystal ball but I wouldn't think they'll take it lying down. The DUP is useless, full stop. All of them are as weak as water. Except maybe Sammy Wilson. At least he has backbone and morals.'

'DEGREES OF SANITY'

I attempted to go to one of the early 'betrayal act' rallies, in a small Orange hall outside Bangor. I walked in without controversy, took a seat, and looked about. There was the usual sense of stepping back in time – that smiling photo of the young Princess Elizabeth, lots of photos of men in sashes, notices inviting donations to the war memorial fund. Among the men in the hall, there was a scattering of women, and youths in tracksuits and hoodies were manspreading on benches along the walls, elbows on knees, grey-lit as they gazed into their phones.

I saw Jamie Bryson enter, and join a knot of men, bobbing up and down on his toes, hands in pockets, darting glances around the room. I got up to speak with him, hoping he might enable me to stay. We exchanged pleasantries about Twitter. A big angry face loomed in, hand on my arm, 'Are you Susan McKay?' Yes, I said. 'No journalists,' he said. He began to try to steer me towards the door. The youths looked up from their screens. 'Don't be grabbing at her, she's going,' Bryson said to the man. To me he said, 'Hold on – I'll see what I can do.' He went over to a group of men at the door, but when I looked over, it seemed they were just chatting. He didn't return. A tall man sombrely dressed in black approached me and, standing too close, told me to leave. Another man saw my discomfort. 'Leave her alone, she's being dealt with,' he said. The tall man headed over to the Bryson group. Shaking his head, the man who had spoken up for me said, for my benefit, 'Jesus Christ – it's a journalist, not the Gestapo!'

Bryson returned. 'If it was up to me you could stay but this is not my meeting,' he said. 'This was organised by veterans.' One of the other men said, 'It's just there'll be mad things said and you'll record them and report them.' I laughed, and agreed that this was so. Bryson smiled, 'There's degrees of sanity,' he said. 'Aye,' said the other man. 'There'll be talk of bombs over Luimneach,' Bryson said, and they laughed. Earlier that month, another loyalist had said, by way of indicating how angry the loyalist people were, that he had heard someone else say, 'We'll see how hard the border is if bombs start going off in Limerick.'

Apologising again for my expulsion, Bryson invited me to come and meet him and a few others at the Con Club in east Belfast. Later on he sent me a message: 'Apologies for that balloon, he shouldn't have been aggressive – a point I made to him forcefully'. We exchanged a few messages in the weeks that followed, but the idea of meeting up fell away.

'LOST SOULS'

On the last weekend of August 2020, Brett Savage was to go camping in the Mournes. It was his favourite place. He was a skilled climber and he felt free in the mountains. He had been to Everest base camp. He used to bring his mother, Dolores, home a stone from every place he went. The last one she got was from the Atlas Mountains in Morocco. When he didn't turn up to meet his friends that Saturday morning, and didn't answer his phone, they went to his flat in the West Winds estate in Newtownards. There they found Brett's lifeless body. He had hung himself. His rucksack was there, with his climbing gear, packed, ready to go.

'Brett had his demons and sometimes something, just some smell or sound, would trigger them and then these moods would just come over him in waves,' said Dolores. 'I could just see it in his face – anger and stress and trouble. All he could do was just lock himself in his flat for a few days.' He would watch *Star Wars* videos. When he felt better, he would drive over to his parents' house. 'He'd go straight to the fridge and raid it.' He was thirty-two when he died.

Brett was a former soldier in the Royal Irish Regiment. There was no military tradition in his family but joining the army was the choice of many young working-class Protestant men, and the battalion has a base in Newtownards. 'He had always wanted to be a soldier,' Dolores said. 'His teachers told us he was a dreamer at school.' Dolores and her husband, Noel, had sent Brett and his younger sister, Holly, to an integrated school because they wanted them to have open minds.

At sixteen, Brett left, and by seventeen he was signed up. After training, he was sent first to Iraq, and then to Afghanistan. While he was there, he and other soldiers from his unit were trapped for fifty-five days in what became known as the Siege of Musa Qala. The British soldiers were hopelessly outnumbered by several hundred Taliban fighters and came under sustained gun attack. Brett was injured, and witnessed the deaths of several of his comrades. 'I saw a lot of fucked-up shit,' he would say afterwards. The soldiers were told to keep two bullets in case they were about to be captured in which case they were advised to shoot themselves.

'When Brett came home he got out of the plane and threw himself down and kissed the ground,' Dolores said. 'Then he gave me the biggest hug ever.' It did not take long for his parents to realise their son was suffering. 'He used to just sit in the house, crying. Noel brought him to the doctor who said he had post-traumatic stress disorder. 'But the army just basically said, well, you've got your arms and legs, go back to your regiment. We couldn't get help for him.' The traumatised young man was returned to service. He was also later allowed to join the Reserves, and was despatched to Cyprus.

The PTSD became more complex. By 2014, Brett was in a bad way. He spoke about it in a video interview admitting that he had been 'crazy, taking drugs, drinking …' and, his mother said, 'lashing out'. He frequently had black eyes and cuts from fights. He could not hold down a job. At one stage he became homeless, sleeping in his car. Fortunately, his family had finally made contact with an organisation, Beyond the Battlefield, a charity based in offices in a small industrial park in Newtownards, and run by ex-soldier Robert McCartney to serve the thousands of ex-service personnel who live in Northern Ireland, some of whom served there during the Troubles. After the peace process, they were, according to the charity, 'no longer needed or wanted'. Others have had Brett's experience of being plunged into situations of extreme violence in conflicts about which they knew little. 'I did twenty years and I have four medals,' McCartney told me. 'If they do wrong I shout at them just like in the army. I take no nonsense.'

I had gone to a protest in Portrush over the Royal British Legion's decision to close Bennet House. This was a big Victorian terraced house looking out over the Irish Sea at which care and respite were offered to ex-service people, from both sides of the border, and their families. The protest was on the grassy slope between the house and the sea. The crowd of several hundred men and women heard speeches about how important the place had been to many who had served in 'Operation Banner', the name given to the British army's campaign in Northern Ireland, and also abroad. A preacher quoted Matthew 11: 'Come unto me, all ye that labour and are heavy laden, and I will give you rest.' Several of those I spoke to opened their overcoats to show me a line of medals on their chest.

McCartney told me that by his estimate thousands of former members of the armed forces have problems arising from their experiences. 'Around four hundred attempt suicide every year, and out of those, thirty succeed,' he said. A friend of Brett's used his personal protection weapon to shoot himself a few weeks before Brett's suicide. When he heard Ian Paisley Jnr claiming that 'we've given blood for the union, in terms of our soldiers ...' McCartney was disgusted. 'They give paramilitaries money to stop them moneylending,' he said. 'But for their own soldiers, they do nothing.'

Beyond the Battlefield had helped Brett sort out the terms of his discharge from the army and to get his military pension. It helped him find a place to live, and it offered him counselling. He had seemed to be getting better. But the damage went very deep, and was compounded by the attitude of his former employer, the Ministry of Defence, and the years when it had seemed no one but his family cared.

'The army gave Brett no help,' said Dolores. 'They just didn't want to know. He loved being a soldier, but he was far too young to be sent to a war zone. These young boys go out there and come back and they are just lost souls. I think the politicians should do more to help too.' Brett's father could not cope with losing his only son. 'Noel kept saying, I need to be with him, I need to look after him,' said Dolores. 'His heart was just broken.' He suffered a massive stroke, refused treatment in hospital, and died two months after his son.

Brett's sister, Holly, cannot stay with her shattered mother, because a local paramilitary took against her and she was banished from Newtownards. 'But I got a car and I go up and see her and her wee girl, Olivia, in Bangor,' Dolores said. 'Olivia is all that is keeping me alive to be honest. But at least Brett has got rid of his demons now.' She sleeps with his T-shirt under her pillow. 'Noel had given it to him,' she said. 'It says, See You in Valhalla.'

'NUMBSKULLS'

'We were in pubs, well actually one pub, one very tough pub,' said Bill Wolsey. 'Now we have a pizza chain and various properties. We are developing a hotel in Dublin, and some more pubs.' We were drinking tea in a corner of his decadent country-mansion-style Merchant Hotel in Belfast's Cathedral Quarter. It used to be a bank. 'In the nineties, we could see the peace agreements were coming, but more importantly we knew the people were ahead of the politicians. Tourists were starting to come. We thought, this can only grow. We also felt that there was a demand for a five-star hotel that was less formal than the two five-star hotels in Northern Ireland at the time. We wanted to aim for a younger market in the ABC socio-economic group.

'About 60 per cent of our guests would be local people, and of the other 40 per cent, the bulk would be the Republic of Ireland. And then French, Italians and Americans. Our prices mean you eliminate a lot of people who don't have the money to come here, but you do get grandmothers taking granddaughters, granddaughters taking grandmothers, for afternoon tea. But by and large, people with money. I remember Porsche telling me that they sell more per head of population here than anywhere else in Europe. There's a sizeable middle-class in Northern Ireland. We also have a very well-educated population and they are constantly demanding opportunities that are of a high level. Our food is Michelin standard.

'My parents were old-school socialists. They were Methodists. My dad boxed for Ireland. He used to say, if you stood twelve monkeys on the Union Jack, they'd get elected. He told us, you must always think about education, housing and work. That's what's really important.

'There was never enough work here. My dad probably lived in England for, maybe, ten of the first fifteen years of my life. I saw him at Christmas and in the summer. I remember leaving him to the train station and when I'd turn to walk back home, I would smell my hand and get the smell of my dad. He was a maintenance fitter and a proud member of the Transport and General Workers' Union. My parents gave me a moral compass and I'm eternally grateful.' Wolsey wanted to be a footballer but an illness put paid to that ambition.

After training in catering in London, he returned to Northern Ireland, borrowed his parents' savings and bought a pub in Bangor that had dropped its asking price dramatically. 'It was a very dodgy pub – Stiff Little Fingers playing upstairs and boys that would have chopped your fingers off downstairs. We inherited two years of hell,' he said. 'But I became successful.'

I had heard Wolsey speak at a public meeting organised by People's Vote, an anti-Brexit organisation led by young people to call for a second referendum on EU membership. 'I regularly say the middle classes here went off to play golf in 1968 and never returned. Anyone who put any thought into it knew that compromise was the way forward. So when Brexit came along and the DUP backed it, I spoke out because I could see nothing but danger for Northern Ireland.

'The DUP thought it would strengthen the union. I thought the complete opposite because it would hit us economically and once you become poorer, the population starts to question the legitimacy of where they are. For one thing, we received far more in grants from Europe than we contributed. So I felt that, for a whole raft of reasons, it was time the business community stepped up there. The deal that Theresa May put forward could have been really beneficial for Northern Ireland because it promised us access to Europe without penalties and we were able to trade seamlessly with the rest of the UK. That was an opportunity that should have been grasped.

'Instead we have nothing but uncertainty. Does that give energy to those people who want us to return the conflict? That's one question. And the second thing is that any business needs to put in a five-year plan. The biggest danger now is that the Tories will start to look at where they can make cuts. In Northern Ireland, we have too many hospitals, too many schools, too many civil servants and as sure as hell we have too many politicians. We're already quite a poor region, which has been managed by politicians who are afraid to take any decisions that may upset the electorate. The DUP overplayed their hand massively and forgot that if you can be bought, you can be sold.

'In business it isn't just what you make; it's also what you put back. I work for charities for disadvantaged people and prisoners due for release. We give them a three-month training course within our company and it's something that I'm proud of. I do think there is social mobility here. If you are at an elite school and you're rich, but thick like cream, your father can give you the initial start and it's far harder for someone who comes from Ballysillan.' (This is the working-class area in which Wolsey grew up.) 'However, now as we're in a much more competitive business environment, talent, in my mind, always, always comes through.

'I live just outside Holywood and I have two sons who have worked in the business since they were about nine. That was how they made their pocket money. And now I have a nine-year-old daughter. My wife's the marketing director in this company. We encourage everybody throughout the whole company to speak their minds. Politically I find our situation in Northern Ireland depressing. The inertia that left us three years without a government,' he said.

Wolsey had denounced the Stormont shutdown in an interview with the BBC in which he said, 'We have replaced the men of violence with the women of intransigence.' 'If the RHI debacle had happened in business the banks would have called, and the person who had been in charge of that would have been told, you are no longer in charge – move. It is a classic example of nobody having the courage to stand up and take responsibility for a disastrous decision,' he told me.

When the Executive proposed locking down the hospitality sector during the second wave of the pandemic in 2021, Wolsey believed the move was disproportionate and disastrous for business. He filmed himself sitting in a beautiful room in his house, calling the politicians 'numbskulls'.

A PRAGMATIST

Terence Brannigan is the chairman of Tourism Northern Ireland and is involved in a slew of other businesses as well, spanning healthcare, technology, investment advice and start-ups. 'So quite a broad portfolio,' he said. He lives with his family in a house his wife chose on the 'Gold Coast' after they moved back from England. He was dressed in a very fine suit and elegant shoes when we met in a Belfast hotel that is reputed to serve Northern Ireland's most expensive pint in its rooftop bar.

He appears at ease with wealth and influence but he was born into a struggling family in Belfast in the 1950s. 'I remember sitting on the stairs crying my eyes out because I could hear my mum and dad arguing about money. We were evicted from four different houses because we couldn't pay the bills or couldn't pay the rent. We ended up we didn't have a house at all.' The family was split up, and three of Brannigan's siblings ended up in institutional care. 'It was dreadful,' he said.

He joined the radical student movement, People's Democracy, when he was at school. 'I believed in equality. I understood there was gerrymandering, that in places it was more difficult for a Catholic to get a job than a Protestant, but looking at the plight of my own family, we weren't in a better position than our Catholic neighbours.'

University was out of the question – the family needed him to earn. He went into business young, moved to England, and was rapidly promoted. 'I became a director and we did a management buyout that was the largest in the UK in 1987 and today Compass Group is the largest catering company in the world,' he said. 'I was chairman of CBI [the Confederation of British Industry]. Then I bought a business here in Northern Ireland and started to pick up some public appointments.'

One of these was to the board tasked with developing the huge site on which the old Maze/Long Kesh prison stood. I asked if it was Peter Robinson, then the leader of the DUP, who chose him for this role. 'It was OFMDFM [Office of the First Minister and Deputy First Minister] – Peter Robinson and Martin McGuinness,' he corrected me. 'The site is 347 acres. That's twice the size of *Titanic*. It sits on the A1/M1 intersection. So east, west, north, south, and it is within half an hour of the ports and airports. It does not get better than that in terms of economic opportunity. We had a significant interest internationally from the private sector wanting to invest. There could have been three thousand jobs there.'

However, the legacy of the conflict intervened. In 2013, the plan ran into trouble with unionists, because included in it was the development of a centre for conflict studies. There was EU funding and the renowned architect Daniel Libeskind had already prepared a design. Libeskind was chosen to design a memorial on the 'ground zero' site of the World Trade Centre in New York. He is also famous for the Berlin Jewish Museum. Architecture, he has said, 'articulates history'. The centre was to be based in the old H–Block building that had housed the prison hospital. 'There were concerns it would be used by republicanism as a shrine given its history because you had the hunger strikers there,' said Brannigan. 'You also had loyalist prisoners. You had prison warders and prison governors murdered as well throughout that period. So it is a very emotive and sensitive area.' Robinson came under pressure. 'When Peter felt he did not have the support of his party he sent what's known as "the letter from America",' Brannigan said. Robinson had a holiday mansion in Florida at the time. The letter collapsed the project, blaming Sinn Féin for insensitivity towards victims of the IRA. McGuinness then withdrew his support for the development of the site. The grand plan is now abandoned, the old prison is falling into disrepair. Planning permission lapsed in 2018.

In his youth, Brannigan believed that unionism did not care about its working classes, maintaining their loyalty through fear that otherwise Northern Ireland might cease to exist. But he is now a member of the DUP and a huge fan of Peter Robinson. 'He looked from the outside to be a right-wing unionist. But he's actually quite an in-depth thinker,' he said. 'And he was a great strategist. Peter knew the best way to secure the constitutional future of Northern Ireland as part of UK was to make it a place where soft nationalists would see it as being in their best interest for the status quo to remain.'

In 2018, Robinson issued the first of a series of warnings that 'the battle for the union is on', describing as 'chloroformed' those who could not see that 'the opponents of the union are charging our lines'.[4] Brannigan said unionists needed to look across the border where Sinn Féin had become the third biggest party. This had happened because the other parties had become divorced from the issues people cared about. 'Up here, the demographics are changing and I don't just mean nationalist/unionist – I am thinking of age,' he said. 'Young people genuinely don't care in the main about the Orange and Green but they do care about social issues and economic issues.'

Brannigan had been disappointed by Foster. 'The party took the wrong position on Brexit. I was absolutely adamantly a remainer. However, I'm a pragmatist. We must make the best of it.' He was open-minded on the question of a border poll. 'I am a democrat,' he said. 'I believe in the principle of consent, so the day that people determine here that the constitutional position should be changed I will accept that and I'll embrace it.'

'EXPLORING THE MYSTERIOUS AND THE MAGICAL'

Colin Davidson has his studio in what may have been stables at the back of his house near Bangor. It is what is known by the advertisers as 'a gentleman's residence', substantial and imposing, with a gravelled drive on which family cars and a sports car are parked. In the studio, a huge log fire was blazing, and an eloquent portrait of Seamus Heaney stood

4 Peter Robinson, 'Some refuse to talk about the elephant in the room …', *Belfast Telegraph*, 3 August 2018

on an easel by the window. 'People often ask me, when did you start to paint?' he said. 'My answer is always the same, when we all start to paint and draw – when we grab a brush or crayon and start to scribble on the wall. I just didn't stop. Whenever everybody else went out and started to kick a ball around about the street, I drew.

'The grammar school I went to didn't take art seriously. As an artist, you carve your own route out, and there needs to be a huge amount of self-will and, even possibly, in a very tunnelled way, a certain element of self-belief. I have struggled with confidence throughout my life and I suppose the stammer, which still rears its head now, was very restrictive to me as a kid, and was really bad through my teens. Confidence and self-belief were a million miles away then. I used my drawing and painting to, I suppose, communicate.

'I went to art college in York Street. That was a tough personal time for me. I remember struggling with who I was, and just with this really crippling sense of not being as worthy as anybody else. I suppose that's what my life has been fighting against.

'I grew up in a Protestant Christian family, but by the time I was in my early twenties I found it difficult to find an identity for myself within any church or organised religion. Identity is a minefield and I think very deeply about it. What sort of tore at me a bit, through my teenage years, was the fact that I had a definite sense of being Irish. I didn't feel British. I remember my parents praying that God would keep me safe before I headed into the Falls Road in the eighties to buy a set of uillean pipes. Not a thing many Protestant teenagers would have contemplated. I wasn't willing to be told, back then, what my identity was. Whenever I needed a new reed, I went to a place off the Newtownards Road that sold bagpipes and they nearly chased me out the door.

'I became absorbed in Irish culture. I read Joyce, I was big into Yeats. I remember going down on the train to Dublin in my early teens and having an excitement about crossing the border. Not quite that I was coming home but that I was going to somewhere that gave me the inspiration for who I wanted to be. But I think sometimes there needs to be a realisation that the Irish language, which I love with all my heart, and the emblems of Irishness were used as weapons in a psychological war against the community that I grew up in. And whilst I may have personally dealt with that, there are thousands people in our community who have not healed. They are still struck with fear when they see an Irish flag or read the Irish language because it was associated with terror and war and killing and death. Our political representatives need to be reminded of that. Equally, the Catholic minority in our community was, for many years, treated like shit.

'I set up a design firm of my own in the mid-nineties. It was successful. But I remember issuing myself with an ultimatum of sorts and saying, look, if you're destined to do anything truly original in your career as an artist, don't miss the chance. I was working on very set briefs for city councils, drinks companies, PR firms, hotel chains. Whilst it was creative, I realised that the most exciting work for me, personally, was the work that I was doing in my spare time when I came home, which was painting. I'm really a loner at heart I suppose.

'In January 2000, I started to paint full time. One thing I've always painted and drawn is my home town, Belfast. I did a series called No Continuing City in 2004: big paintings of Belfast from high viewpoints. It was interesting from a formal point of view – exploring pattern and space and colour and light – but also there was this kind of emotional and intellectual experience behind it. I was witnessing this city emerge from what I knew it to be during my childhood and my teenage years: a city in decline, a city that was being destroyed.

'I still, no matter what I'm doing, come back and do a Belfast painting once a year. I go up on to Cave Hill or Black Mountain. It's kind of a touchstone for me now. It's to see what I've learned, too, because all the paintings have progressed and are different. And, of course the change in Belfast is phenomenal. I'm immensely proud of the Belfast that I go into now. I love the regeneration of the Cathedral Quarter, all those bars and restaurants and music venues and busy streets. It has become a centre of cultural and historical importance. When I was at the art college thirty years ago it wasn't an area you wanted to walk down. Now it's where everybody goes.

'You have to celebrate it. Whenever I'm there listening to a band play in the Harp Bar, and it's packed, and people are chatting with people who they don't know and they've only just met, the idea of being a Protestant or Catholic doesn't exist, which I find a wonderfully refreshing. I just love getting a fix of it from time to time. That, for me, in some ways is who we've always been. It's at the heart of what we are.'

Davidson has become known for his portraits, which he calls 'big head paintings'. The first was of the musician and songwriter, Duke Special. 'I loved his look, and something just made me want to paint him. I'd always seen Peter as being thoughtful, considerate, almost vulnerable, and then suddenly he had the dreadlocks and the eye make-up.[5] I identified with something in him as a human being, a sense that I felt the same way. I loved the confidence and the vulnerability – that duality, that tension. I painted him and I got more attention for that one painting than for anything I'd done before. It won a few awards. And then Peter introduced me to Glen Hansard, who I painted, and then I got involved with the Lyric Theatre. They were looking for art for the foyer, and I was looking for direction.'

He has gone on to paint many of the North's leading artistic figures, including Brian Friel, Seamus Heaney, Michael Longley, Ciaran Hinds and Liam Neeson. He also painted the queen, and President Michael D. Higgins. He is in high demand as a society portraitist, his sitters including the likes of Brad Pitt. He mentioned that he had given private lessons to Pitt, with whom he got to visit the Rembrandts in the National Gallery in London, out of hours.

To my mind, his most powerful work, however, is the collection of portraits he began in 2010, of people who were victims and survivors of the conflict. 'The Silent Testimony work came, I suppose, because of a personal passion,' he told me. 'I had read the Good Friday Agreement and voted yes in the referendum. I realised this was going to hopefully be positive for most of us, and for us as a society. I naively had the view that it was going to be positive for people who were going to be let out of prison too. But there was nothing in it for victims and survivors; save for a few lines which basically said that at some point we'll have to do something about this.

'And as time went on, you know, I realised that actually nothing politically was being done. There was a lot being done by groups like WAVE [Trauma Centre], but discussing the past became decidedly uncool. Whenever I started making the head paintings in 2010, I realised that I might have found a way, as an artist, to explore and comment on how I felt about that. My idea was simply to paint people who suffered loss, and instead of commenting on the past, to actually comment on

5 Duke Special is the stage name of Peter Wilson.

now. It's still about right now. It was just to afford the gravitas that is usually bestowed upon someone of great public standing or celebrity on someone who isn't known outside of their family and friends, but who has a story that hasn't been heard before.

'I decided to do that with eighteen people, from as many different backgrounds as you can think of, who suffered loss in as many different ways as it's possible to suffer loss through a conflict, at many different ages. I'm eternally grateful to WAVE for partnering with me on it as well and to the Ulster Museum, which asked to be the first to show it.' The exhibition has since toured internationally and has been shown at the UN headquarters in New York. In the summer of 2020 Davidson lent his support to the pension campaign that Alex Bunting spoke about, regularly posting the portraits along with appeals for the politicians to take action.

'People have a need to acknowledge our past, and what is left behind, without resorting to the usual hyperbole of politics. There were no references in Silent Testimony to whether my sitters suffered loss at the hands of the IRA or the UVF or the British army. We were looking at fellow human beings. People went in and were struck by the fact that we weren't told who the Protestants and Catholics were, and some of them said to me they were ashamed at themselves for even thinking they needed to know. That actually goes to the very heart of what the enduring problem in this place is. We still haven't got over the "them and us". In fact, I wonder if we've even scratched the surface.'

'EMANCIPATING MYSELF FROM RESTRICTIONS ARISING FROM SHAME'

She launched herself as a furious and utterly original dramatic artist in England, got some of her best breaks in the Republic of Ireland, and is now back in Northern Ireland where she has just made her first feature film, and has another currently shooting. Stacey Gregg is a restless iconoclast, perched for now with her wife and child in Bangor on the North Down coast, but holding on to their flat in London just in case they want to leave again. 'I'm an Irish playwright who's at home in London, Dublin and Belfast. A lot of my identity has straddled binaries: gender, nationality, class,' she said. 'I'm comfortable with that. I pursue it. I'm happiest in the in-between places. 2020 is a terrible year to have made a film but it was an absolute blast. It's a psychological drama and a contemporary ghost story set in Belfast. There's a score, and I worked closely with the composer. Art forms don't seem discrete to me. I'm quite eclectic.

'I've never stopped trying to write about my Northern Irishness. Having lived in groovy parts of London and Brighton, it is hard to deal with the aggression about gender that persists here,' she said. 'You can't grow up here and not be political. I'm very aware that Protestants don't get a good rap. I feel uneasy when people mock working-class Protestants – it shows a poverty of empathy. There's a flavour of condescension. I find value in being from a people who were seen as the oppressor in the relationship. It's uncomfortable and I feel it's a moral duty to understand that discomfort.' There is transformation afoot, she senses. 'Northern Ireland has unclenched somewhat. Young people are just more respectful and open. Attitudes to consent really have changed.' That suits her: 'I've been emancipating myself from restrictions arising from shame.

'Digital natives have access to ideas that go far beyond those imparted by the traditional cultural sources that informed their parents' imaginations,' she said. 'There is a fluidity to their sense of persona and identity. And there are so many women knocking it out of the park doing work that is exciting and interdisciplinary, bringing new ideas into drama without becoming polemical – like Phoebe Waller-Bridge, Sally Rooney, and Michaela Coel on TV, and then writers like Maggie Nelson, Ariel Levy and Deborah Levy. Also, and very importantly, women have started being their own executive producers, and that makes such a difference. They're insisting on having control.' Not before time – according to the Writers' Guild of Great Britain, only 14 per cent of primetime TV slots in the UK are occupied by work written by women.[6]

Born in 1982 in an outer suburb of east Belfast, where 'everyone's mum', including hers, worked in the Ulster Hospital, she feels sad when she goes back there because the distinguishing feature now seems to be a huge park-and-ride facility for commuters. 'My dad was in the navy and he moved us to England for a while to get us away from the Troubles, but they missed family, so we came back. The week we moved

6 https://writersguild.org.uk/equalitywrites/

into our new house someone was killed on our street. Then there was a retribution killing ten years later. Even though they'd taken us away to be safer, and now we were back, Mum and Dad's attitude seemed to be, "It happens".

'I could have spontaneously combusted with resentment at school. The school I went to wasn't interested in the arts. They were regarded as 'pretentious'. Queerness was definitely not acceptable.' A brace of DUP politicians in the making taught her or were her peers. 'Sammy Wilson was one of my teachers, as was Michelle McIlveen; and Gavin Robinson played my dad in *Romeo and Juliet*. I had a cover relationship with a boy who was gay,' she said. 'There was a schism between working-class Protestants who were not homophobic, and the fact that they voted for the DUP, which is.' Her parents were DUP voters.

She was impatient to leave, applied to Cambridge – 'for the craic' – to study literature, and got a place. She had a year out on a scholarship to an American high school on the way, which saved her, she believes. 'Otherwise they'd have crushed me. I became aware of my working-classness at Cambridge. I was the poorest person I knew. It was another way of not fitting in. I had a lot of rage. I was isolated and volatile. I nearly quit, and I nearly got thrown out after organising a rent strike as a student leader. I've always been involved in protest movements. I remember a sympathetic tutor saying to me, "Do you not have some friends in Paris you could go and stay with for a while?"'

She has always been drawn as a writer to what is new, unsettled, shifting, out on the edge, or beyond it. 'I was fuelled at first by the galvanising energy of anger,' she said. Influenced by Sarah Kane and Steven Berkoff, Gregg's final project at Cambridge, and her first play, was *Ismene*, which took the Greek story of Antigone and wrote into it the story of the murder of Robert McCartney in Belfast, and also the death of her granny. 'I wrote it through grief. I knew I wasn't going home – home had been embodied in Granny, my tough matriarch.' She wrote 'Yer Ma's a Hard Brexit', a fierce monologue about Brexit, set along one of Belfast's peace walls. In *Choices*, she pulled apart the taboos that surround talking about issues like IVF and abortion, particularly in Northern Ireland.

With *Scorch* she took on what has become known as 'gender fraud'. She explores the painful break-up in the real world of a relationship that started online, in terms of the gaps between what is real, what you want to be real, and how your reality, and your gender identity, is perceived by others. In *Perve* her themes include false rumours and how a photograph taken during what seems to be an innocent moment of intimacy can be transformed by a betrayal into online slut-shaming. And now, with *Here Before*, she's taken on Belfast, love and ghosts.

Perve won a Stewart Parker award, which was special, since it was through the mentorship of his niece, Lynne Parker, at the Project theatre in Dublin, that Gregg got on to the Rough Magic SEEDS programme and got to the Berlin Theatre Festival: 'That visit lit me up like a Christmas tree,' she said. Ruth McCarthy, artistic director of Outburst Arts, has been another of her champions, and Gregg is offering a mentorship through Outburst for a young, queer filmmaker in Northern Ireland. 'I wish there had been something like that around for me,' she said. Her work has been performed in Dublin, London, Belfast and Edinburgh and is winning some of the top awards.

'Over and over the work that I make for theatre fucks with the fourth wall. I hate theatre that is well behaved, that tells a liberal audience what they already think,' she said. 'I'm always sniffing after the subversive.' One reviewer said of a piece set in a women's prison, 'It grinds hard against the rigidity of the theatre landscape.' While working on *Scorch* she wrote that, 'the idea of cisplaining makes my blood run cold'. However her work is not polemical. 'Most of my ideas come from dreams,' she said.

'I love moral complexity and this I relate to my queerness – there is no such thing as the binary. My creativity emerged from the cognitive dissonance of growing up queer in a milieu that found me unpalatable and odd. I didn't fit in and performance was a way to deflect attention away from me.' She spoke out for gay rights at school without talking about her own quest for a gender identity in which she could be herself. She recently described herself as agender.

She wrote about her granny in a piece described as mixed-media memoir, *Hatchet Jinny*, which was performed in 2018 as part of the Queer Outburst Arts Festival in Belfast. 'I wanted to write about her and about hard love. It took me a long time to come to it. That's what she gave me. There's a pragmatism and an economy to it. You know where you stand. My wife is from Essex and she appreciates those same qualities.' Her mum fretted about what people would think of the family when Gregg's first full-length play, *Perve*, was put on in the Peacock Theatre in Dublin. 'My parents are proud of me but they wouldn't say so because they wouldn't want to give me a big head! I gave my dad Jeanette Winterson's *Why Be Happy When You Could Be Normal* and he understood it.

'I think most of that Protestant privilege is essentially gone or going, but the residual entitlement remains, and can become brittle and defensive. I became aware that I'd inherited some of this, and part of going away was to dismantle it; yet in the same way I'm sensitive to power hierarchies because of my queer antennae, so this bizarre, Protestant entitlement helps me understand why some behave as they do; how unless you are given the tools to identify and scrutinise, it can take root and solidify into something very unattractive,' she said. 'And that wilful dismissal of anything imaginative as "pretentiousness", that refusal to be open to change.'

For now she is happy to be back. Her wife had longed to live by the sea, and they are loving the experience, and their son has started preschool. 'I dress him in colours,' said Gregg.

'RUGBY BOYS'

'The rugby rape trial really radicalised young women here,' said Gemma Louise McSherry. 'We saw ourselves as that nineteen-year-old girl. We recognised the swaggering sense of entitlement in those guys, and their complete lack of respect for her. They were found not guilty of rape. But what we heard from that courtroom made a lot of us recognise something. It was that sexual abuse is about more than being dragged down a dark alley by a stranger. We have all experienced it.'

She was referring to the 2018 trial of two professional rugby players from Northern Ireland, Paddy Jackson and Stuart Olding, for rape, and two of their friends, Blane McIlroy and Rory Harrison, for related charges. All were acquitted on all charges. However, widespread disgust at the attitudes revealed by their social media exchanges sparked the emotional launch of #IBelieveHer and protest marches all over Ireland.

McSherry is twenty-seven, in the same generation as the young woman who was the complainant, and she is familiar with the culture exposed in the trial. 'I have talked about this with a lot of young women who went to these grammar schools that have rugby boys who are seen as celebrities. There was a lot of slut-shaming that went on and some of it was by rugby mums and dads. Some of the teachers, including evangelical Christians, are part of the problem too. Their attitude was "boys will be boys",' she said. 'The boys never seemed to get called out, and the girls' complaints were mostly dismissed.' She said several young women had talked of incidents involving the sharing of intimate photos without consent. Teachers had gone on to reprimand not the boys who had abused trust by sharing the private images, but the girls, for having allowed such photos to be taken in the first place. McSherry remembered her own shame when she was set up to believe a rugby boy she fancied had invited her to a match only to find out it was a hoax and he and his mates had been ridiculing her earnest texts, and calling her ugly and a 'Paki' because she had swarthy skin.

From what she witnessed herself and from the accounts she has heard from others in rugby-dominated grammar schools, McSherry described a culture of gender-based bullying and sexual abuse perpetrated by an elite set of boys, some of whom have gone on to be violent men. In some cases, if women spoke out, their fathers or other male relatives had used their power and social standing to fend off accusations. In some cases that were reported, top barristers were employed. The behaviour she described ranged from derisory sexualised nicknames, to walking upstairs behind girls and rating their legs, to sharing intimate photographs without consent, to stalking, domestic violence and rape.

Gemma's own school was Regent House in Newtownards. Her social background was not typical. 'We were relatively working class, as opposed to the middle-class majority at Regent,' she said. 'My mum's side are very Protestant, my dad's side are very Catholic. My dad came from one of the only Catholic families in a very Protestant estate. I got baptised as a Protestant and sent to Protestant schools though I also got brought to Mass and Irish dancing classes.'

In 2020 McSherry wrote several hard-hitting articles, including one about three young men who were her peers at school. In May that year Jeff Anderson had pleaded guilty to sexually assaulting a woman, assaulting another woman occasioning actual bodily harm, and eleven counts of voyeurism involving secretly filming women for his own sexual gratification. He got a three-year sentence suspended for three years. 'He was a classic rugby boy,' said McSherry. 'He was popular. His parents were rich and he lived in a mansion. At the age of eighteen he was driving a brand-new black SUV to school. I was fifteen and a theatre nerd and when he invited me to a party I was flattered. He said my friend would be going with us. He picked me up. I was all dressed up in my leather leggings and thick make-up – he was in a tracksuit. There was a pizza in a box on the back seat. He drove past my friend's house and brought me to an empty house where there was a lot of drink set out. It became clear we were not going to a party. He started asking me intrusive sexual questions. He didn't do anything other than that but it was just so uncomfortable. Eventually I left and walked home feeling mortified. I never spoke about it.'

She wrote about James McQuillan, who in January 2020 got a nine-month suspended sentence for assault, threats to kill and breaching a non-molestation order in relation to his then girlfriend, Ciara Hindman. Ciara now campaigns for reforms to stalking law. McSherry also wrote about Dylan Rogers, a former Ulster Under-19 rugby player. He was jailed for nine years in Spain in November 2019 for attacking and raping a woman. He held her captive in an apartment and she had to escape to seek help. 'These kind of guys are known to girls at school as predators and creeps,' said McSherry. 'After my pieces were published I had a lot of messages from women from all around Northern Ireland who had experienced horrific misogynistic abuse and violence, mostly unreported. One woman said she had been raped at the age of fourteen. Some of them said they wished they'd spoken out sooner.'

One man who responded to her work confirmed that in his rugby career in Northern Ireland 'locker-room talk was rampant' and 'serious offences were waved away to protect these men with bright prospects and family-secured futures'. Several other men wrote about brutal and racist rugby 'initiations'. McSherry also got called a slut, a whore and a tramp.

'No one is saying that playing rugby makes you a rapist,' she said. 'But that small-town celebrity culture does cultivate toxic masculinity. It has horrific consequences for girls and women. These guys are adored from a very young age and they develop a belief that they can do as they please without consequences, and their parents will always get them out of any kind of trouble. The schools they go to prioritise them even though they may well be academically mediocre. They think they are going to be top rugby stars but most of them end up in accountancy.'

SOUTH DOWN

Kilkeel on the south coast of County Down is a fishing port at the foot of the mountains of Mourne. The road into the town from the north dips steeply down and then veers back up again to a stately street with Victorian banks and a town hall. On a stormy day in winter 2019 there was hardly anyone out and about. The big blue Schomberg Centre had posters up for highland dance and Lambeg drum classes, and it also offers capacity building for marching bands, and a young ladies group. But it was closed. There was a shop selling every imaginable variety of pork sausage, and a fish shop. I saw a couple of African men with plastic bags full of groceries, heading down to the harbour.

Crossing the street, I met Jim Wells, a tall figure dressed formally in a dark suit and tie, both of us tilting against the camber of the hill. We greeted each other like friends and made no reference to our most recent encounter on the BBC Radio Ulster's *The Nolan Show*. The new laws on abortion and same-sex marriage were about to be introduced and we had battled for almost an hour. It was acrimonious and wearying.

Wells' devout views were too extreme for even the DUP. He had lost the party whip in 2018 after vociferously criticising leading figures. He said afterwards that he felt he had been 'fed to the crocodiles'. Abortion in his opinion was never permissible – he had compared the number of abortions to the number of people murdered in Auschwitz and Buchenwald. He claimed in 2015 that children should not be brought up in homosexual relationships because they were 'far more likely to be abused and neglected'. He later said he regretted that these words had been uttered.

'CALL OF THE SEA'

'The call of the sea just got me and I couldn't get away from it. It's in the blood, it's in the family, and through the generations,' said Brian Chambers. 'My father never tried to steer me any which way. "Do what you've a passion for, enjoy what you do and you'll find it is not like work," he said. So I abandoned my plan of going to university to study marine engineering. I finished school in 1990 and just a few weeks later we launched the boat and I've been a full-time fisherman since. My father fished for prawns but then at an early age, simply for the security of his family, because fishing can be a very up-and-down livelihood, he got a job in the RUC for a steady income. That was around 1973.

'My parents knew there was a threat there and we got a bit of bigotry. There was one day we were going to sea and some local boys, that I actually went to school with, threw stones at us, going out round the pier. One night, we'd been at sea and our car had been vandalised in the car park beside the pier. Just wee things like that. This would have been Protestant boys, angry that the RUC were maybe stopping a parade here or there. Things flared up in what is called the "mad month", in July. And then in September they're getting on the school bus with you, as if nothing ever happened. But my father had to check under his car morning and night in case there was a bomb attached. One very close friend of his was shot in Newcastle. A gunman just walked up behind him and shot him in the head and disappeared into the crowd. That was the IRA.

'One thing about the fishing is that once you go out round the pier, politics and religion are all forgotten about. More so than what I see in any other industry. I've had breakdowns and called people to come for me, give me a tow, and you never ever think of who it is you're calling – it's just John or Seamus or Mick or Paddy. It's the same in Ardglass, Portavogie, Clogherhead, no matter where you go, once you round the pier everyone's equal. Everyone knew who everyone was in a small community. When there's been a disaster everyone has helped.

'Another family tradition is the Orange Order. My father was in it and I am too. I'm in an accordion band and so was my father. We've been over and played at the Menin Gate in Ypres in Brussels. We've done a tour of the Somme. My son, he's just learned to play the drum now as well, in a band. It's a great way for young ones to learn music without having to pay to go to classes. My daughters were in the band too but they have moved away now to university in England. They went to do courses they couldn't have got over here. I doubt if they'll come back.

'I'd be pretty easy-going about the border. From we began fishing crabs, a lot of our crabs went across the border to Donegal and to Cork. So, it was never, ever an issue at all. It was just, put it on a lorry, take it to the factory, sell it and you got paid within a week. There was no paperwork, no red tape. Going back twenty-five years ago, when the brown crab fisheries started to develop in Northern Ireland, there wasn't really the market here. I was totally pro- getting out of Europe, from a fishing point of view. Now the lines are starting to blur, with a border down the Irish Sea. I never signed up to that. When you're part of a country, I don't feel there should be a border within that country.

'I'd be worried now if we're going to be selling lobsters to Dublin or Cork and they're going to be held up at the border. It's a live product that has to be in premium condition. And then we have shellfish going out of the country in first-class, pristine, living condition into France and if those lorries are going to be held up at Calais or Dover in queues of lorries, we could be in a lot of trouble. The shellfish are stressed and they deteriorate the longer they are in the tanks. So there's a bit of me would have doubts now about Brexit but then there's a certain bit of thranness in me that would say – well, no, it's best for the fishing industry.

'I've always voted. I have it in my head that men fought and died in the world wars to give us democracy. If Hitler had won the Second World War we mightn't have been as democratic as we are. It always annoys me when people refuse to wear their poppy. At the Somme you see the rows upon rows upon rows of gravestones of young men – 18, 19, 20. Those men gave their lives. A complete generation was lost and I just feel that we owe it to them. I think the shutdown at Stormont was a complete dereliction of duty, a complete national disaster, so I do. People are sick of the two big parties but when it comes to an election, we do seem to have the mentality to go back into the trenches.

'One of the best politicians that we had – that never got a fair chance as a leader – was Mike Nesbitt. The election before Mike resigned, he said, Vote Ulster Unionist first, and vote SDLP second, because he saw we needed a change, and the DUP weren't doing it and Sinn Féin weren't doing it. But the SDLP didn't back him up. And that holed Mike Nesbitt below the waterline, and he couldn't recover from that. Sometimes here, it's not a matter of voting for who you want, there's a mentality of voting to keep the person out that you don't want. It's not a good place to be.

'Myself and my brother have three boats. We've a scallop boat, a prawn/scallop boat, and a smaller vessel that fishes crabs and lobsters all year round. It's a dangerous industry. If you're careless, the sea'll have no mercy with you. If you make a mistake, the sea will unfortunately punish you severely. But if you respect the sea, and keep all the safety rules and the safety equipment up to date, it's manageable. A cousin of mine actually was lost. That hit me a bit hard, to be honest with you. That was in 2005. We were about a week, or more, trying to retrieve his body. Everybody was out searching, all the trawlers, the helicopters from both sides of the border. We got his body back. My cousin was a Catholic. There was a mixed marriage in the family. He was twenty-four. The boat is still out there and I know exactly where it's at, and every time you're in around that area it comes back to you. It hits the community very hard. There were three generations of one family lost in Kilkeel. The hardest thing about it was they were due to decommission the boat and get out of the fishing and that's why the wee grandson was there.

'There's many's a day we go to sea and we come home with nothing. If you were to calculate out how much you get per hour, you just wouldn't even entertain going to sea. It is as simple as that there. There's many's a day you go to sea and you know, from experience, you know from the conditions, it's not going to be a good catch today, and maybe if you were to take into account the diesel, the insurance, the bait, the expenses, you'd be better not to go to sea. But you still have to go to sea because fishing's fishing. You have to keep trying. And if the fish aren't there, go and look for them somewhere else. And you know there are mornings I'd be out at sea and you'd look back at the shore and the sun rising up above the Mourne Mountains and you are just overwhelmed to contemplate the majesty of God.'

'NOBODY LOVES US'

Alan McCulla runs the Anglo-North Irish Fish Producers Organisation, Sea Source, from offices down on Kilkeel's harbour. 'There's one lesson that I have learned sitting as a fishing representative here in Northern Ireland and that is that nobody loves us,' he told me. 'London doesn't love us. Dublin pretends that it loves us but it doesn't love us either, and we're by ourselves.' He said this cheerfully.

'I'm fifty-two years old and my dad was a fisherman, so it was fishing that brought me up, here in the Kingdom of Mourne. I came to work at the harbour twenty-eight years ago. There's about eight thousand people in Kilkeel, and about one thousand employed in the fishing industry and industries connected to it. We directly employ fifty, we manage fishing opportunities, and we do a little bit of political representation. We're involved in fish sales. We have two small factories, we have diversified into off-shore energy and we're expanding into North America. All sorts of crazy things. We have always got challenges. Brexit's one of them. But the opportunities more than outweigh the challenges. So, it's something that we're looking forward to.

'In 1973 Kilkeel had forty-eight trawlers, the year the UK and Ireland joined the EEC. Fishing was the lost child within the whole European project. UK waters and Irish waters became European waters. Part of the bribe (as I like to put it to people) was that Brussels started throwing money at the industry. Fishermen took it to build new boats. By the early 1980s the fleet here in Kilkeel had grown to well over one hundred trawlers and we had a Common Fisheries Policy. Probably back then nobody really read the fine print. It was a good time, there was plenty of fish to be caught, there was plenty of money coming in, everybody was happy. Then the good people in Brussels decided we'd too many boats chasing too few fish. By the late 1990s Brussels was throwing money at us to scrap the boats they had encouraged us to build. We are back to forty-eight now.

'So the fishing industry was in the doldrums and for a few years it was touch-and-go as to whether this company was going to survive or not. We had to sit down about fifteen years ago and take a long, hard look. And the decision was – we can't depend on anybody to help us, only ourselves. So, the fishermen here decided to start selling their own fish, which doesn't sound radical but was revolutionary.

'We're here, we're getting stronger, and I'm the eternal optimist. The Republic of Ireland is our neighbour, we can see it from outside the office here,' he said. Kilkeel looks to the south across the Irish Sea towards the east coast of the Republic. The Carlingford ferry now takes just fifteen minutes to cross the fjord, and the invisible border that separates Down from Louth, North from South. 'We're fishing in the same waters, we're fishing for the same species, we're supplying into the same market,' said McCulla. 'Kilkeel is the biggest fishing port on the east coast of this island. It's the main hub for repairs and all of the ancillary industries. We've got visiting vessels come from the Republic to get work done here in Kilkeel. We buy a lot of produce from the Republic and bring it here to Kilkeel for processing, and likewise there's a lot of the product that our members will land here that's exported back South. So, there's a lot in common. What's not in common, and what has been our biggest bugbear, is a mechanism called the Hague

Preference. Under this, fishermen in Northern Ireland have had to surrender fishing quotas to their colleagues in the Irish Republic. And they're not going to give it back again.

'I'm a northern Protestant, and that is important to me. I'm a unionist. Around the Twelfth of July you would have seen boats putting up the Union Jacks and the Red Hand of Ulster. But, generally, politics didn't come into it round the harbour. There are fishermen who are unionist, nationalist, Protestant, Catholic, whatever way you want to describe them. What they have in common is they make a living from the sea. Some of my best friends around the harbour here I'm sure wouldn't be ashamed for me to describe them as staunch republicans. We've learned, the hard way, that if we want to make progress, we need to stick together.

'If anything, there are nearly more Filipinos and Ghanaians working in the industry here than locals now. We're very cosmopolitan. Local people stayed ashore. Their families want them home for their tea, and they want a steady income. So, we had a crew shortage. We started to recruit abroad in about 2004. Around the same time there was the tsunami in the Indian Ocean and this community raised money and partnered with a village in southeast India.

'We have offered the foreign workers houses on shore, but they choose to live on the boats because they want to maximise the money they have to send back to their families. Every year we bring in an NGO called Human Rights at Sea. They go on to the boats. They look for things that are wrong and they produce a report, which we take very seriously.

'Here's a fact about Kilkeel. We have a factory here, an American-owned factory, it's called Collins Aerospace. Something like two out of every five seats that are made for Boeings and Airbuses in the world are manufactured here in Kilkeel. They employ about one thousand people from the community and elsewhere. So Kilkeel is prospering, but if you walked up the main street, you wouldn't think it.' In the summer of 2020 the company announced it was to make about a quarter of its staff redundant.

'I am proud to be British. I want to stay British, full stop. But history has taught us that English politicians will throw us in front of the bus at the first opportunity. We need to start thinking about what's best for Northern Ireland, not what's best for somebody in Scotland, or England, or Wales, or the Republic of Ireland.'

'THERE WERE BLACKS, JEWS, PAKISTANIS, YOU NAME IT'

I'd been at Henry Reilly's for about an hour when the misunderstanding emerged. His daughter, Sarah, had brought sandwiches from a deli in town, and joined us for lunch. She was wearing a sparkly top and she seemed really happy to meet me. 'I told Sarah you are writing a new series called *Mourne Girls*,' Reilly said. There was a pause. 'You're not Lisa McGee,' Reilly said. McGee is the author of the brilliant and hilarious TV series *Derry Girls*. 'No,' I said. 'We thought you were Lisa McGee,' he said. Sarah was gracious about the disappointment.

'I joined the young unionists when I was sixteen and Enoch Powell became our MP,' said Reilly. 'Jeffrey Donaldson worked for him too. Enoch would have been in this house quite regularly on constituency business. I would have brought him round locals who wanted to see him about things from grants to potholes. Enoch was curious. I remember telling him about a young fellow whose father had been assassinated by the IRA in his yard. I said, we have to do something. Enoch said, you're absolutely wrong. What we must do is just accept this and never flinch or show any weakness.'

The UUP had invited Powell to Northern Ireland after he was sacked by Edward Heath from the British cabinet for his notorious 1968 'rivers of blood' speech. His inflammatory anti-immigrant stance made him popular with an intolerant and angry element of the unionist population, and far from acting as a deterrent, this encouraged the UUP to hope it would boost the party's support base. He was elected MP for South Down in 1974. 'The way Enoch influenced me was that I was 100 per cent integrationist,' said Reilly. 'Enoch lost his seat in '87 to the SDLP, one of the saddest days of my life. I'll never forget it. Myself and some of the old hands went down to the house and Pamela and Enoch were giving out a drink, and he said to me, do you want ice? And I said, no, it's just water. And he said, well, try telling the captain of the *Titanic* that.

'My father was a farmer and a potato merchant, sold potatoes over to Cyprus, Morocco, all over North Africa for years and years. They'd have been shipped from Belfast port or latterly out of Warrenpoint. But that all fell away with EU rules – what they call the free market prevailed.

'In 1989 I was elected as a councillor. At that time DUP was a bad word down here in South Down. They were just seen as fundamentalist

Paisleyites. That's completely flipped now. The DUP's the biggest party down here. But the DUP now are what the UUP were then, without the big-house brigade. When I was in it, the landed gentry across Northern Ireland were the backbone of the Ulster Unionist Party. The Duke of Westminster, all the big estate owners, all the big farmers, the likes of Sir Josias Cunningham. And they had real steel about them in terms of patriotism. Money meant nothing to them. Whereas the DUP seem very, very influenced by material gain. Though saying that, my best friend in politics is a DUP councillor, a really top bloke.

'This used to be a unionist area but after local government reform in 2015 we were gerrymandered into taking in exclusively nationalist areas. That has been a disaster. They're putting up huge bilingual signs with Gaelic on the top. English is secondary now to the council. It's just completely sterile now of any link to the United Kingdom, while they push and push all these aspects of Irish culture. I'm a proud Irishman, but I'm British, I'm a citizen of the United Kingdom, but the council just eliminated the symbols of my statehood.

'There's only eight Unionists out of forty-one councillors. We get on well most of the time on everyday issues, but then you get the likes of the play park in Newry named after Raymond McCreesh,' he said. In 2001, the park was named after the late IRA hunger striker who was believed to have taken part in the Kingsmills massacre in 1976, in which ten Protestant workmen were killed by the IRA. Unionists have made unsuccessful attempts to get the council to change the name of the park. 'That's still painful for a lot of people here who suffered at the hands of the IRA,' said Reilly.

'I was in the Ulster Unionists till I was fifty. I'm sixty now. But they were becoming pro-European. The UUP headquarters even flew the EU flag alongside the union flag, at a time whenever fishermen were having their boats decommissioned. I had always been anti-EU anyway because of Enoch's influence on me. I started drifting away. I supported the Good Friday Agreement. The IRA wanted out. They were becoming a spent force. And the way that the loyalists were attacking them made them feel vulnerable. So it wasn't a surrender on our part, it was a surrender on the part of physical force tradition. But Unionists made a mess of the agreement.'

Reilly described how he was deselected from the UUP amid acrimony.

'Then somebody highlighted my anti-EU credentials to Nigel Farage and I got a phone call one day in 2007, and I ended up joining UKIP [United Kingdom Independence Party]. I really enjoyed it. I topped the poll down here on three occasions. The EU influence on the fishing industry is so brutal that people here understand it wasn't some benign cow giving free milk. It was a destructive organisation that ruthlessly imposed its directives on communities. No accountability. There was a good social aspect to UKIP as well. I loved going over to England to the conferences.

'The thing that used to really get me was this label of being racist and fascist. They were more devoted to individual liberties and freedoms than any other party. There were Blacks, Jews, Pakistanis, you name it,' he said. Then he clashed publicly with David McNarry, then a more prominent UKIP convert. 'I was expelled in 2015 and I lost everything as a result of that,' he said.

'So then Jim Allister phoned and he thought I could take South Down for the TUV. Jim's actually a gentleman. But I regret joining them now. The TUV just was not me. I would enjoy having a pint of Guinness and a puff on my cigar or whatever, but within the TUV that would be sacrilegious, that would be a sin. Even at the conference the shutters were pulled down on the bar. They were mostly all Free Presbyterian evangelicals. Nothing wrong with that, mind you, I would have a strong Christian faith myself. Anyway, I resigned a year later. And now I call myself an independent.'

'A GOOD NEWS STORY FOR YA!'

The Christmas tree said it all, according to Chris Wallace. In December 2019 I heard the Kilkeel businessman on BBC Radio Ulster describe the tree that had just been put up in the town as a sorry affair. He saw it as clear evidence of Newry, Mourne and Down Council's neglect of the town.

'The facts are, the total spend in Kilkeel for the tree, the lights and the whole Dickensian festival was just shy of ten grand. Now if we look up the road to Newcastle, it got a spend of £26,400 just for the tree and its lights, and other grants then on top of that. Now whether that is sectarianism or their councillors just work harder and together, I can't say,' he told me. Newcastle, the largest town in the area, is predominantly nationalist. Wallace had more urgent concerns, too, which he also spoke about on the radio. One of his baby twins, Charlie, was born with a rare heart condition that had required intense periods of hospitalisation. Wallace spoke out in support of the striking nurses.

I met him soon afterwards at his big, bright new house on the coast road between Kilkeel and Annalong. We sat in the kitchen, after he had shown me the living room, a cheerful mayhem of toys. 'I fully support the nurses,' he said. 'And it is obvious the people of Northern Ireland are behind them and are fed up with the politicians.' He and his wife have spent long periods in Great Ormond Street Hospital in London, as well as in hospitals in Northern Ireland. 'We have got excellent care everywhere, but in England the nurses have more time to spend with their patients. Here, they are the cleaner, the dinner lady, the administrator and the nurse. And meanwhile up in Stormont the politicians are taking their money and not doing their jobs.'

Wallace was just ten when the Good Friday Agreement was signed. 'My nanny was an Ulster unionist businesswoman and our family has always been au fait with politics. We are proud of our culture and our background, but we also respect that the other side of the community has its own pride too. My parents sent us to an integrated school so that we wouldn't get bitterness bred into us. I am proud to say I am a born-again Christian, and that influences my politics. I am a Christian first and foremost, and I vote for the individual rather than for the party.' He admired Jim Wells. 'He says it like it is,' he said. 'He's a Bible-believing man and you know where you stand with him. There are no back doors.'

Wallace said he did not judge people. 'They'll meet their own judge,' he said. He added that his family had been pleasantly surprised to get support from local Sinn Féin politicians. 'Hand on heart,' he said, 'they messaged me weekly to ask how our child was doing and offered us the support of their Westminster office.'

Wallace described himself as 'extremely pro-Brexit' though the government had 'made a shambles of it'. His own furnishings company had lost out on a major contract in the Republic of Ireland because of uncertainty around Brexit timings. Fabric from the UK was going to cost significantly more and he would have to do a lot more costly administration. The Theresa May deal had been infinitely better for

Northern Ireland than the one Johnson ended up with, he said. The Prime Minister had led the DUP 'down the river'. The worst thing was, he said, 'no one can give us certainty'.

I heard from Wallace in the early days of the COVID pandemic. In April 2020 he sent me a newspaper report about how he and his wife, Emma, had already made and donated thousands of masks to local hospitals and were about to turn thousands of metres of fabric into scrubs. He was quoted as saying the NHS had saved their son, so they had decided to use their business to help the NHS, which had been struggling with PPE shortages. There were photos of little Charlie, with his family and among nurses. Other businesses from the area had contributed to the effort. Wallace added a message to me: 'There is a good news story for ya!' he wrote. 'The whole Mourne community rallying around.'

CHAPTER 8

Here Endeth the Lesson

'IF YOU DON'T VOTE DUP YOU'RE AN OUTCAST'

'People are surprised sometimes I have done so well,' said Amy. 'Because I come from a loyalist estate.' She's a senior housing manager now, but when she was a teenager came close to dropping out of education. 'I suppose it was down to my mum that I stuck it out. Unless you have support behind you, it's very hard to change your mindset. I remember mum saying she'd take up another job – she already had two – and she did, she got work in a chippy. All of the jobs she had were low paid and long hours. She put me through school and university and then my two brothers after me. Mummy says now, I'm very proud of the three of you.'

Amy lives in a housing estate in a small Mid Ulster town with many flags. She asks me not to use her full name or that of her town. She asks me not to park close to her house. Mid Ulster is volatile, and she has learned to be careful. She keeps her head down. 'I've lived in this estate all my life. I've reared my own family here. This town was always quiet enough but when I was a teenager the Drumcree carry-on was happening over in Portadown and of course that drew us like a magnet. We had cousins over there and that's where I sort of knocked about. Rioting was very exciting and it was like a recreational thing. Everyone went crazy.

'When we heard the police in Portadown had blocked the road down from Drumcree, all the Protestants thought, well, they're supposed to be a force for us, and now they're turning their back on their own community. So there was us shouting, "SS–RUC" at them and calling them Catholics. My mother would have been at work and thought I was safe in school or at home and I was away on the bus to Portadown. I was skipping off school, drinking, anti-social behaviour. I got involved with the wrong crowd and my life started to go on a real downward spiral very quickly.

'I had got into a renowned grammar school when I was eleven. It didn't really invest much in young working-class Protestants. The class distinction was definitely very much made from the start. There were two different uniforms that were a different price and obviously my mum bought me the cheaper one. And somebody actually said to me in school, oh that blazer you have on has a funny tinge off it – that must be the cheap one. I just took my blazer off and refused to wear it ever again. I covered my uniform with badges and I drew all over my tie and I instantly rebelled. I was a great hockey player. But every time I went for hockey trials, it was always the police officer's daughter who got the position or the minister's daughter.

'There was an attitude that kids like me where I lived shouldn't be invested in, even if they had brains. I failed all my A levels. Mum opened my results and cried. She just looked so disappointed. But I got into a course in Belfast, me all alone with a suitcase and I had never even been in the city, and I got a degree and I did well,' she said. Amy believed the stigma about people who live in public housing has persisted. 'I can understand why young working-class Protestant men think no one gives a shit about them.' Amy and her husband are both working and they could move to a more middle-class area. But Amy sees no reason to. 'My oldest boy is seventeen. He has come home a couple of times and mentioned about us living here and how his mates are saying this and saying that. I said to him, listen, this might be a housing executive house but you have a good home here, our neighbours are good, your granny and granda are around the corner, your mum and dad are not in debt. Don't you worry about what your mates say. I'm not moving out to suit your mates. And you're a smart kid.'

Snobbery is not the only prejudice Amy has had to negotiate. 'It's not good for a woman to be seen to be doing well in loyalist communities,' she said. 'The men don't like it. We have to keep our heads down. But what happened to me came for me completely out of the blue. I wasn't aware that I was even being discussed on social media. But then I got a message to say that a lot of derogatory stuff was being said about me. So I looked it up and it was mad. They said I was moving foreigners into loyalist areas. They said these people were wearing GAA tops, that they were vandalising bonfire sites. Then a picture of me went up. Somebody said I looked like a dog. My address went up. It went from maybe four or five people commenting to about thirty young men commenting. It was quite threatening.

'I started to look at their profiles and photos and I realised I've lived here all my life, but I didn't even know who they were. They were all just like keyboard warriors. Then one day I was walking down the street and this young guy actually said to me, "Hey, Amy, how are you doing?" And it was one of them. And then I saw another of them serving at the filling station out the road, and I shouted at him, "Are you the wee fucker who has been targeting me online? Say it to my face. I'm standing here now. Come on." He near shit himself and he walked away into the garage.

'I went down to the police one morning after something really bad went up, and I was very, very worried. One of the response officers just sort of leaned back in his chair and said, "Well, would you never think of moving out?" And I said, "Are you serious?" And he went, "Aye, would you never think of moving out?" I said "You want me to move out of my home because I'm being targeted by men who I don't even bloody know?" I said, "What about you going in and dealing with these boys? Are these people touts? Is this the reason you are not lifting them?" It was a good eight weeks or so that went on. And then as quickly as it started, it stopped.

'The law does not recognise that hate crime can be carried out within communities of one identity. Last year over six hundred people got moved out of Housing Executive houses, and mostly because of internal hate crime. Sure, most of us are living segregated for God's sake! What Catholics would want to target me around here? There are Eastern Europeans in this town but they just keep their heads down and they are white. There was a Black family and somebody spread a nasty rumour about them and they disappeared. So everybody mostly around here would be white. But Protestants aren't the only bigots in town. There was to be an integrated school and all the Protestant churches were up for it but the Catholic priest just flat out refused. I said to my husband, "And here endeth the lesson".' The Catholic church opposes independent integrated education but in 2021, parents in County Antrim rejected a proposal from the council for Catholic Maintained Schools to close Seaview Primary, voting instead for it to become integrated. This was approved by the DUP Minister of Education Peter Weir.

'I voted to stay in the EU,' said Amy. 'I saw what the funds it gave us have done. Working in public service, I also knew the inward investment of migration. Sure, the hospitals would collapse without it. But none of my family, none of my friends voted to stay. I am not aware of one other remainer in my circle of friends. Why? A border as high as you can get it and all the foreigners out. And no united Ireland. They just did what the DUP said, and sure now it has all backfired on the DUP. But round here if you don't vote DUP you are an outcast. A girl said something to me one day assuming I was going to vote for Brexit and I said I hadn't made up my mind. She looked at me like I had horns on my head.

'My husband is an Orangeman. Mad for his flags. I agree with the Orange Order to an extent. But society has moved on – they need to drop the anti-Catholic stuff. My husband would say it's not an anti-Catholic organisation, it's a pro-Protestant organisation. See when we sit down to watch the news, I shout at the TV. My husband shouts at the TV. I said to him, if anybody else could hear you or me they would think we were off our rocker.

'My middle child, he's fifteen and he is in a WhatsApp group for young people interested in Alliance. He's like me, all for equality issues. There are three hundred or so in the group. He had a fight with some boys that are Free Presbyterian because they were saying anti-gay stuff. Fights with his daddy too. My youngest boy isn't sectarian exactly, but he is afraid of Catholics.

'I don't even want to think about a border poll. Oh my God, world war three. I really do think loyalists are back in 1912 right now. I read that Britain First has set up in Northern Ireland. And I was, like, going, holy shit, that's all we need.' British far-right extremists involved themselves thuggishly with the Drumcree protests, and Britain First took a significant role in the flags protests of 2012 and 2013.

'Protestants here will never take a united Ireland,' said Amy. 'Would I? No. I don't think so. I know nothing else other than being British. Somebody asked me the other day was I Ulster British and I said, well, I'm British, but if you're asking me if I'm more British than the British, like mega, mega British, well I'd never classify myself as that. But if a united Ireland was coming down the line, I probably would tell you I am Ulster British. If there was an all-Ireland solution, a government in the North and the government in the South, I still would not want Irish language signs at the end of my street. And that is coming from right in the pit of my stomach.'

'WE ARE ALL HUMAN'

'I love politics. When I was a teenager my peers had Peter Andre and rock band posters on their bedroom walls. I had election posters and the Doc,' said Carla Lockhart, the DUP's MP for Upper Bann. She still has the Doc on her wall – a large portrait of the late Reverend Ian Paisley in his religious robes and dog collar hangs behind her desk in her constituency office in Lurgan, County Armagh. Lurgan has an undeclared border on its main street – Protestant one end, Catholic the other. It was the hub of the dissident loyalist LVF and there is a dissident republican element also.

The office is full of boxes of chocolates (gifts from constituents), bowls of them on a table by the line of chairs where people wait to see her. Lockhart has had a lot of online abuse directed against her appearance. 'I have a thick skin but I didn't like my family seeing it,' she said. When she publicised the abuse, she got support and solidarity from political women across the board. She in turn spoke out against those abusing Sinn Féin leader Michelle O'Neill. 'Online harm is going to be one of my main issues in parliament,' she said. 'There'll be a law – at the moment it's the Wild West. I'm all for free speech but not if it jeopardises safety.'

Lockhart is glamorous and stylish. When we met she was wearing a navy blue suit with gold buttons and a knee-length skirt, and patent loafers. 'I can't be bothered with heels any more,' she said. Her blouse is dazzling – pink and blue with rhinestones and diamante buttons. Her hair is sleek and groomed and she is wearing bright blue eyeshadow.

'I was brought up on a Tyrone farm and my dad would have canvassed for the DUP and he had great time for Dr Paisley and Peter Robinson when they were at the helm,' she said. 'It was sad when the families fell out.' Despite Paisley's great age and failing attention span, his family resented the party having evidently precipitated his retirement as First Minister in 2008. Peter Robinson, who had been deputy leader of the party since 1980, was referred to by Eileen Paisley in a TV documentary as 'the beast'.

'I was born in 1985, and from I was knee high I was out with my father,' said Lockhart. 'When I was fifteen I got to do work experience with the party and I stayed with Peter and Iris – it was amazing. I remember the last day I was so tired I slept in and Iris shouted up the stairs was I ready to go, and I was still in bed! Peter Robinson inspired me. He was one of the most strategic politicians around. You felt safe when he was in charge.

'There is definitely a male dominance in politics. Women have to work twice as hard. You see these men in suits and they ooze confidence, and you see women rushing in and they have had to deal with a thousand other things like childcare before they even get to work. But I am not in favour of quotas or anything like that. If someone is selected it can't be just because it is a woman – they have to be capable. I have had to work very hard for everything I have achieved. I remember I failed the 11 plus and a teacher said I'd let myself down and my family down.'

The teacher's inappropriate judgement is typical of the extraordinary onus put on Northern Ireland children to 'pass' this exam in their final year at primary school. Passing it means you could go to a grammar school, the traditional route to third-level education. Adults refer back with real pain on how it felt to fail, or boast of some achievement and add, 'Not bad for someone who failed the 11 plus.' Following a review in 2001, Sinn Féin wanted the exam scrapped but the DUP reprieved it as part of the St Andrews Agreement. In 2004, a Sinn Féin education minister abolished it but there was no agreement on a replacement to deal with the transition from primary to secondary education. Grammar schools introduced their own privately-run tests and these tended to divide along traditional sectarian lines. Inevitably, some parents can afford coaching for their children, while others cannot, so the current situation also contributes to social inequality. The DUP is devoted to the principle of academic selection for children at this stage in their education.

Lockhart had gone to the local technical college and then to Ulster University. 'When I was twenty-one Peter urged me to replace a councillor in Craigavon who had sadly died, and so I was co-opted and then I got elected. Council is a lot of work, some of it meetings about meetings. At twenty-one, I was the youngest mayor of Craigavon, while holding down a full-time job, and I had also just got married. It was an amazing year. Though it was also the year I had my first miscarriage.'

She went on to run David Simpson's Westminster election campaign and 'managed to get him elected'. She was elected as an MLA in 2016. 'I was just cutting my teeth – and then the Assembly collapsed. People were frustrated. It looked as though RHI happened on our watch. In hindsight, my personal opinion is people like humility. There should have been lots of apologies. This was the only constituency in which we increased our vote. The three years that the Assembly was down were absolutely soul-destroying. People frowned upon you because they felt you were being paid to do nothing. It damaged us.'

Then came the DUP's big moment, when the British government needed them. 'The DUP had the balance of power and it was good for Northern Ireland,' said Lockhart. 'We were able to negotiate the confidence and supply agreement and bring funds to all in Northern Ireland.' Under this deal, Northern Ireland got £1 billion in extra funds over five years.

A year later, 'David had some personal issues', as Lockhart discreetly put it. Simpson had all the most traditional DUP credentials. He was highly respectable, a sixty-year-old businessman (he runs a meat factory), married for thirty years and with a family, a devout Free Presbyterian, Orangeman and member of the Royal Black Order. He even sang country and western, in the gospel style of Willie McCrea. Opposing same-sex marriage, he had said at Westminster, 'In the Garden of Eden it was Adam and Eve, not Adam and Steve.' But he was also, to use his own language, an adulterer.

In 2018 a Belfast tabloid revealed that he had been having an affair with a younger woman, a DUP councillor who worked in his office, and was also married (her husband worked at the meat plant). Simpson resigned from the Loyal Orders and from his seat. Lockhart was selected to replace him and held the seat in 2019. 'We are all human. We all make mistakes,' she said. 'I wouldn't criticise him. It was a difficult time. David is still a friend and a political mentor.'

Lockhart is a prominent anti-abortion campaigner. She described the legislation introducing abortion to Northern Ireland in 2019 as 'wrong, constitutionally and morally' and the introduction of guidelines for the provision of abortion in Northern Ireland in June 2020 as 'one of the darkest days in Northern Ireland's history.' Her allies in this struggle span sectarian and political divisions. 'Life is sacred from the cradle to the grave,' she said. 'I was brought up in a Christian home and I have always believed that the most basic right is the right to life. I had two miscarriages and then I had Charlie sixteen months ago. I was really disappointed that Westminster went over the heads of people in Northern Ireland. My fight now, along with my MLA colleagues, is to try to repeal the law.'

I asked her about the Amnesty Northern Ireland poll that suggested attitudes were becoming more liberal even among DUP voters. 'I haven't seen that,' she said. 'But experience shows if you make abortion legal at all you end up with a situation like in England where one baby is aborted every three minutes.[1] The 1967 act was meant to be tight. A life is a life. It isn't in our gift to take it. I would like to see a perinatal palliative care hospice here. But you know, in some cases women are told a baby won't live and when it is born it is fine and goes on to have a good life.'

Lockhart said her faith was important to her. 'I don't go out and beat the Protestant drum every day but I am steeped in being a Protestant,' she said. 'I am very proud of our heritage and culture and I'm involved in the Orange Order. The Drumcree issue is not over. It still means a lot to the people of that lodge and the wider community. Their desire is still to complete the walk. There is a deep sense of anger that civil and religious liberties were taken away. It caused a deep hurt.'

The Orange Order persists in its demand to be allowed to parade 'home' from the church at Drumcree. In October 2020, along with a photograph of Drumcree Church, the Ulster Civil Rights Network posted on Twitter: 'Unionists in NI are treated just like the Black population of South Africa under apartheid. In Portadown and many

---

1 In 2019, Department of Health and Social Care figures showed that 200,608 women in England and Wales had abortions in 2018.

other areas Protestants are blocked by Republicans from even using public roads to peacefully walk home from Church just one day a year, such is the discrimination.'

The demographics of Portadown have changed, and much of the old housing traditionally occupied by Protestants is now rented out to people from Eastern Europe who work in local factories. The man who had been the Orange Order's spokesman during the Drumcree years, David Jones, had become a local councillor. He joined UKIP, notorious for its anti-immigrant rhetoric, but left after finding out 'from a third party' that party leader Nigel Farage, having snubbed Jones, had accepted an invitation to speak at a rival DUP event. After that Jones stood as an independent.

'Lurgan is still a very divided town. The vast majority of people have moved on but as we saw last week, there are just a few who still want to take the life of a security officer.' Lockhart was referring to threats from dissident republicans who had also recently orchestrated low-level rioting in the town. I asked her if she had any concerns about the fact that there are still local loyalists who declare ongoing loyalty to the late LVF leader, Billy Wright, whose stronghold used to be in her constituency, and who is still lamented on murals. 'Not getting into the specifics of Billy,' she said. 'But they do need to leave the stage. Let's move forward.' She corrected herself: 'Billy Wright'.

'FINEST SONS'

I spoke with one of the men who still regarded Wright as his lost leader, and 'one of Ulster's finest sons'. We communicated on social media. He wanted no meeting, no name, not even a phone conversation. He maintained Wright had been central to the 'defeat' of the IRA in Tyrone and Armagh, first in the UVF (before it went 'lefty' under the influence of David Ervine), and then in the breakaway LVF. The LVF killed Catholics and burned down Catholic churches during the core years of the Drumcree dispute.

On his social media sites, he posted clips of interviews Wright had given in which he boasted of getting information from the security forces, whose hands, loyalists believed, had been tied.

'The TUV for me are the only party that actually stands by their principles,' the social media warrior told me. 'I think a lot of DUP voters would find them more relatable, and the least likely to be bought off. The DUP seem to fold very easily to the demands of republicanism, but unionists feel there is no other way to have a good presence in Stormont and Westminster than to vote for them – it is just tactical. Loyalism has been let down at every level, concession after concession.' That unionism had been overly generous and had been stripped was central to the message of Jim Allister's TUV. He constantly referred to 'appeasement' and the 'insatiability' of republicanism.

A LucidTalk poll in the *Belfast Telegraph* in February 2021 showed significant numbers of voters saying they planned to stop voting DUP in favour of the TUV. The poll saw DUP support plummet from 31 per cent to 19 per cent, while the TUV's rose from 2 per cent to 10 per cent. Given the PR system, a lot of these votes would return to the DUP as second preferences, but it was nevertheless an ominous sign for the party that was itself once seen as the hardline alternative. As a one-man party at Stormont, Allister constantly harangued his former colleagues for failing to be sufficiently staunch in their unionism, for compromising, appeasing, putting in peril. He said the Irish Sea border meant the 'emasculation' of Northern Ireland. He had become the ghost of Paisley past. Such was the DUP's lack of direction in early 2021 that it began to take its leadership from Allister, joining him in taking the British government to court for allegedly breaching the 1800 Act of Union and the Good Friday Agreement, and in boycotting cross-border cooperation with the Irish government. Lord Trimble supported the challenge. The UUP followed.

The Portadown loyalist said 'our' paramilitaries were a deterrent to 'so-called dissident republicans' who were actually 'just a proxy used by Sinn Féin'. A change in the constitutional status of Northern Ireland would provoke young loyalists and 'would cause an eruption of violence equal to if not worse than that of the past.' According to this strand of unionism, the riots of April 2021 were inevitable because 'the community' had seen how the threat of dissident republican violence had caused the land border to be replaced by one now dubbed 'the violence appeasing sea border.'

'YOU'D LOVE TO PUT YOUR ROSE-TINTED GLASSES BACK ON'

'Once you start learning about injustices, you keep seeing them everywhere and sometimes you'd love to go back and put your rose-tinted glasses back on,' said Ashleigh Topley. 'But then, equally, I feel like I'm able to make a difference and educate people in my circles that maybe aren't aware of the way things have been and hopefully open their eyes.' Ashleigh was on maternity leave when we met at her house, her baby daughter in a bouncy chair tossing toys about the room, her other daughter at school.

'I've lived in Portadown all my life,' she said. 'I had to go to the Church of Ireland and Sunday School and all but it just felt a bit false to me, everybody dressed up to the nines in church and maybe not being one bit religious in their lives. It wasn't that I went all out to become an atheist but by the time I was twenty I couldn't do it any more. I just didn't believe it. To me, when you die, you die, but what is important is to leave a legacy of being a decent person. We don't go to church now. I don't want our children to be taught religion as if it is fact. I want them to be taught this is what different people believe.

'Robin goes to the integrated school. She's learning about lots of different religions in her class. She mixes with Catholic children and Muslim children and children from families with no religion. My husband is an Orangeman but he is probably the most rubbish Orangeman there is because he's into integrated education and he's pro-choice and he's pro-equal marriage and he's all the things they really don't approve of. The area we live in now is mixed and we love it. The Protestant/Catholic discussion does not feature in our lives at all.

'I'm thirty-three now so I was born in 1986 and I can vividly remember the Drumcree time. I remember watching it on TV and learning a new word, quagmires, because they were digging them around the church and the Chinook helicopter flew over our house and me and my friends were outside playing and it was so low and it was so loud and you could see every propeller. And army checkpoints and soldiers with guns waving you down with red torches, and roads closed. Whenever I hear a helicopter now I get really anxious, whereas back then it didn't even take a fizz out of you.'

Ashleigh's life had taken a devastating turn in 2014. The experience had radically changed her, and turned her into a prominent feminist activist. 'Six years ago, I was pregnant with my first baby. Everything had been fine till we went for a twenty-week scan on Valentine's Day, and suddenly instead of us going for breakfast to celebrate, we were being told by a consultant, "It appears that your baby has a fatal fetal abnormality."' Ashleigh and her husband had to wait ten days for a second opinion. 'We shared a waiting room with people getting scans and coming out all excited with photos. The doctor confirmed the baby could not survive. I said, can I have a termination? And she said, I would sign it off for you but the approval has to come from your own hospital.'

'That night, my husband and I talked for hours and we decided that a termination would really be our only option because I just didn't think I could go through with the pregnancy. But when we said this to the next consultant they said, "Well, that's not going to happen. We don't do that here." I said, "What about the impact on my mental health?" And the reply was, "The psychiatrist is not signing off on it either." I said, "Are you telling me that you've made an assessment of my mental health before you've even met me?"

'It was awful. I got very angry. Looking back, I think they were afraid in case they would be prosecuted because the Attorney General had just come up with some new thing that stillbirths and late miscarriages had to be investigated,' she said. This 'chill factor' meant medical professionals might be excessively cautious in their advice. 'I was devastated. So I rang a clinic for advice. I said, "I need a termination." And the person said, "How far along are you?" And I said, "I'm twenty-three weeks." And she said, "I'm sorry, we can't help you because the procedure needs to be carried out before twenty-four weeks." So I hung up the phone and just thought, that's it. I did learn, six months later, that I could have had a termination but no one here was able to tell me that.

'So I just had to wait until the pregnancy naturally came to an end, which actually was thirty-five weeks. My boss at work was brilliant, totally supportive. I tried to get on with normal life but it was difficult because I was obviously pregnant and people in Northern Ireland are friendly – when they see a woman with a bump they want to know when you're due and what you're having. Mostly I played along because I would have felt guilty ruining their day, and I hated that look of pity.

'Honestly, my overarching feeling was relief when the baby's heart stopped. I felt like I could breathe. They brought me in to the delivery suite. You could hear babies, and women in labour. They did try to shield me from it. One of the midwives was great – she didn't treat me like I was broken. She and I are actually still friends. We dressed the baby, Katie, and did handprints and footprints and then we got to hold her but it was weird.' Talking about the lost baby still makes Ashleigh cry but she does it because 'It keeps her spirit alive'.

'I'm a totally different person now than who I was then. And in a way, I'm grateful for the experience because I lived a very naive life, you know, up until the 13 February 2014. I had no idea of what difficulties some people in Northern Ireland face. The first time I went to an Alliance for Choice meeting, I was bricking it. I walked into this room wearing jeans, a white vest top, and this coral pink cardigan and I was platinum blonde back then too. And it was quite an edgy crowd. I was like, Ashleigh, you do not fit in here. Then there was talk about maybe going to prison for taking pills and I thought, shit, I can't get arrested, what am I doing here? But then we started talking about fatal fetal abnormality and I spoke up and everybody turned and started to listen and I said, we have to do something about this. After I stopped speaking I was shaking. They were brilliant. They didn't look down on me. They just accepted me.

Ashleigh went on to play a key role in bringing about the legal changes that finally brought abortion legislation to Northern Ireland in 2019. 'The next thing I did was the judicial review for the fatal fetal abnormality with the Human Rights Commission. I had to write my affidavit and that was the start of the High Court proceedings. I was anonymous back then because I was still afraid of my name getting out there and the anti-choicers coming to your door and putting paint up it or something like that. Doing media stuff, I was guided by Alliance for Choice because they respected me and my story but they were savvy and I wasn't. They knew who the dead-on people are and the ones just looking for a sensationalist headline.

'Being in the High Court case was bonkers. It's only maybe last year that I believed I actually am an activist. Back then I just felt like I was playing dress-up, that I was an imposter. I take my hat off to the selfless people that have been fighting this for years. In my grief, I wanted to do something good with the pain. I also want to make sure nobody has to go through what I did. Now that I've got two girls I want to make sure they grow up in a world where they can make decisions about their reproductive life without anybody dictating to them.

'I have met wonderful people. I remember sitting in the High Court and I was pregnant with Robin and I was snuffling chocolate out of my handbag for morning sickness, and Dawn Purvis came in and sat behind me. She tapped me on the shoulder and whispered, well done. I was star-struck. She is such a legend, a powerhouse of a woman.

'Before all this, as far voting went for me, it was always, one, two, three, DUP. That's all I knew about politics because that's Portadown – it's ingrained into you. That's all changed. The DUP just make me angry now. Especially the women. They have no compassion. I mean Arlene used to be pro-choice. It leaves a bad taste in my mouth that we got our rights from Westminster because our local politicians were not at Stormont. We should have got our rights because our own politicians responded to all our years of campaigning. Now when I go to vote I read all the manifestos carefully. I just want a better life for my family and whoever's going to give me that will get my support.'

Ashleigh told me in March 2021 that she was 'exhausted with anger' when the DUP brought a bill to the Assembly to try to limit the abortion rights provided for by the new law. Just twelve MLAs voted for women's rights to be upheld. 'It just feels like we are being punished again,' she said. A few days after the vote, the Secretary of State Brandon Lewis intervened, ordering the Northern Ireland Executive to implement the law.

'I'M NOT ASHAMED OF MY COMMUNITY'

'It was always a big deal if Paisley came to Tobermore. He was our man, our saviour. Everybody turned out,' said Debbie Watters. 'I was keenly aware of what it meant to be Protestant, loyalist and unionist. Growing up in a village that was 99.9 per cent Protestant has definitely shaped who I am.' Tobermore lies in deep countryside close to the Sperrin Mountains and the north-western shores of Lough Neagh. Tom Paulin wrote about driving through this area during the Paisley times. Desertmartin is the next village along the road from Tobermore:

It's a limed nest, this place, I see a plain
Presbyterian grace sour, then harden,
As a free strenuous spirit changes
To a servile defiance .../... it shouts

For the Big Man to lead his wee people
To a clean white prison, their scorched tomorrow.[2]

Watters is the director of Northern Ireland Alternatives, a community-based restorative justice group, and vice chair of the Northern Ireland Policing Board, but spoke to me just as herself. She is a striking figure, tall and willowy, always in elegant clothes and heels, always impeccably made-up and coiffured. She loves good clothes, and her appearance is important to her, she told me. She works out in the gym. She has a stash of classy chocolate in her desk drawer, but admitted as we scoffed it that she would be skipping dinner. For years she worked in a tiny office in a terraced house at the top of the Shankill Road. Then Atlantic Philanthropies funded the purchase of a fine modern building near the peace line.

'The highlights of my year were my birthday, Christmas, Easter, the Eleventh Night and the Twelfth,' she said. 'My dad was involved in the loyalist workers' strikes. I was always an intense child and very independent. I left the Presbyterian Church for the Baptists because they had a good youth movement. I came to believe the way to live out your faith was social justice, and a social gospel. I passed the 11 plus and went to a school where there were Catholics who became my friends, so that was the end of "them and us". And my family found that very difficult. Christianity took me outside of the loyalist and the unionist boxes. Faith still shapes a lot of the decisions that I make.

'My dad was an Orangeman,' she said. 'There's a harshness that comes with extremism and it didn't sit well with my Christian faith. Overt sectarianism was the world that I grew up in. You know: "Don't sell your land to a Catholic", and even the awful, "The only good Fenian's a dead Fenian." My own family did not think that way or talk that way. People try to tell me those things weren't said. But they were. When I go home to Tobermore, there's still an element of that.' But her attitude to her community had changed. 'I wanted to leave behind where I had come from. I felt loyalism was dirty,' she said. 'But I understand now that this is how people act when they feel they're under threat. There's this myth that unionism was cold – unable to reach out and sectarian – and that republicanism wasn't. In reality, the sectarianism just took a

---

2 Tom Paulin, 'Desertmartin' *New Selected Poems*, Faber, 2014, p. 44

different format, people acting like there were no good Protestants. It didn't serve any of us well. I have come full circle now. I'm not ashamed of my community. It gave me good things, like a strong work ethic, and a sense of values. Unionism has a lot to offer.'

She got involved in restorative justice work while living in the US. 'I married an American, from the Mennonite tradition, the liberal wing of the Amish. They are pacifists. I moved back to Northern Ireland in 1997 and was very pro-agreement. My family were still DUP supporters. They thought it was a sell-out. I thought it enshrined the whole constitutional issue, protected it, and probably firmed up the unionist identity within this jurisdiction. We had arguments,' she said. When Paisley changed his mind about power sharing, Watters' parents were, she believes, among the traditionalists who felt betrayed. 'I think they saw the DUP going into government in 2007 as a sell-out too,' she said.

'They're still very much British and great supporters of the royal family. They'd have supported leaving the European Union. I say to my mum now, we wouldn't be here in this bad situation if you had voted remain. The Brexiteers have put us in this space; the majority of people in Northern Ireland did not,' she said. In the 2016 EU referendum 56 per cent of those who voted in Northern Ireland wanted to remain in the EU. However a survey conducted at the time found that there was a sharp religious divide in the vote, with just 38 per cent of Protestants voting remain, compared with 85 per cent of Catholics. The DUP and the TUV consistently supported Brexit. The UUP wavered. Its pro-remain position before the vote was unconvincing, and since the leave side won, it has increasingly aligned itself with the DUP.

Watters is one of those politically stranded by the fact that she is pro-union but not unionist. 'It's important that Northern Ireland remains part of the union, but there isn't a unionist party that I'm comfortable voting for,' she said. 'For me the issues that are important are poverty, mental health, equality, human rights. If you look back to the whole trade-union movement, which was very strong within working-class loyalism, I'm not sure how we've ended up here. Part of it is because republicans have seen human rights and equality as a platform, and unionists have sat back and allowed them to hijack it. They're scared to use the narrative, in case they're seen as being wishy-washy unionists.'

In times of perceived crisis, unionist leaders tend to exhort their people to be more manly – to stop crawling on their bellies, to get off their knees or at any rate cease bending them, to stand up like men. Negotiation, compromise, changing your point of view – all were seen as 'appeasement'. Arlene Foster's crocodile insult to nationalists was turned against her, when she was subsequently accused of turning into the 'chief crocodile feeder'.

'Republicanism and nationalism have seasoned politicians who have come from the grass roots. What is missing within unionist politics is activism,' said Watters. 'We have politicians that know how to manoeuvre, but they are disconnected from the people. They go straight for the Orange card but the social issues have been neglected. The people who are disadvantaged by this vote unionist, to keep republicans out. The quality of their life hasn't truly changed since the Good Friday Agreement. They feel angry and abandoned. So they blame the agreement.' This was the point that Joel Keys had also made. I have been to many public meetings in Northern Ireland at which the only political representation is from nationalists and republicans, even though unionists have been invited, and the issues under discussion are relevant to the entire community.

'Personally, I think the union is quite secure,' Watters said. 'But unionism and loyalism need to start thinking about what might happen fifteen or twenty years ahead. What would unionism look like in a united Ireland? There's no point burying your head in the sand. People need to start changing their psyche. Also, this is about more than two communities now.' Former DUP leader Peter Robinson had several times urged unionists in this direction. Writing in the Belfast *News Letter* in October 2020 he spoke of a 'predictable showdown' and accused 'border poll deniers' of 'complacent and dangerous thinking'.[3]

'I will probably never not be hopeful,' said Watters. 'Because I always think there's good work to be done. I believe in the union. But if my sense of identity and my family's sense of identity was respected, if I could live the same quality of life, if there was a health care system and an education system that I didn't have to pay for outside of taxes, I think I could be quite relaxed about a united Ireland.'

---

3 Peter Robinson, 'We have to be ready to fight our case in a border poll', *News Letter*, 23 October 2020

'MORE LEVELS TO THE DUP THAN MEET THE EYE'

Kyle Black's family have been subjected to a lot of callous abuse since 2012, when his father, David Black, was ambushed and murdered as he drove to work. The dissident republican faction known as the New IRA was responsible. Young people, including children, under the influence of this group use the occasion of bonfires commemorating internment in 1971 to burn placards with David Black's name, and those of other members of the security forces murdered since 1998, painted on them. When the family went to lay flowers at the scene of the ambush in 2020, there was IRA graffiti on a road sign at the site. 'It is sickening and Mum finds it really hard to take,' Black told me. His mother is a nurse.

'When Dad was murdered I had just turned twenty-one and my sister was seventeen,' he said. 'It's really difficult to put into words the impact his death in that way had, and continues to have on us. He was a prison officer and had been for about thirty years. He'd worked in the Maze, in Magilligan and Maghaberry. Prior to that, he was in the UDR. There were a lot of security force connections within my family, whether it was the UDR, RUC, or Prison Service. Dad had come through the worst years of the Troubles and he was about to retire. I think that made it even more difficult to deal with.'

The poet Gail McConnell has a long poem about the death of her father, the prison officer William McConnell, who was blown up when she was three, his death witnessed by her and her mother. In 'Type Face' (so called because the reports published by the Historical Enquiries Team were printed in the Comic Sans font) she describes the difficult search for the right words and the painful impact of those chosen by others. In one book that refers to her father's death, the authors state that he was 'executed', the etymology of which is 'follow up, punish', implying he brought it on himself. She finds the 'crazed portrait' in another book 'hard to bear'. She tries to avoid 'murdered', choosing instead 'died, was killed … lost'. She describes, 'This wish for solid ground. This vulnerable/ testimony – darkness, storms and floods/ frailty, nakedness, sheer exposure – and a love/ that answers choral calls for some foundation.'[4]

---

4 Gail McConnell, 'Type Face', published in Blackbox Manifold, issue 17, 2016
http://www.manifold.group.shef.ac.uk/issue17/GailMcConnellBM17.html

'Mum and Dad were married in 1989,' said Black. 'They built their family home in Cookstown. They gave us every opportunity they could. Dad really encouraged us to further ourselves and do well. They got me involved with rugby because they saw it as a very cross-community type of sport, and that was important to them because we attended pretty much a solely Protestant school, and then church organisations like the Boys' Brigade. Embarrassingly to say, we also took piano lessons, and they got us involved with pipe bands and drumming. We were brought up to respect people. Dad was proud of who he was. He was from a unionist background and in the Orange Order and the Black and Freemasonry as well. But he was also very tolerant of people from other backgrounds.

'The shock, and sense of disbelief to an extent, is still with me today. It's still very hard to comprehend. Not only have you lost your father, but the fact that somebody went out to do this, made a decision to target Dad and take his life for some sort of political ideology. Trying to put your life back together is a very difficult thing to do. It made you aware that there were people out there that wanted to cause you and your family harm. And that made you more guarded than you'd ever been before in your personal life and your professional life. It changes you as a person in a way.'

He said he struggled with a new reserve that had entered into his feelings towards Catholics since the murder. 'I'm not naive. I know there are people from a loyalist background that have also targeted security forces in the past. But nowadays these attacks are mostly from dissident republican groups. So it did make you suspicious of Catholic people to an extent. But whilst I say that, we have some very close Catholic friends who are very supportive of us. I don't have a grudge against Catholic people and none of my family does.

'We got boxes of cards and letters from people right across the world. Within that, there were letters and cards from inmates in Maghaberry, and some of them were republicans, and people that had served time previously that probably were connected with the IRA. They had come across Dad within prison and were saying they were disgusted at what had happened. They had always found him to be fair and respectful. They said he had treated them with integrity. So I think they were sort of ashamed about what had happened. It was actually quite nice for us to read as a family and we were pleased that they took the time to contact us.'

Black spoke about the decision the family had taken to decline deputy First Minister Martin McGuinness's offer to attend the funeral. They had appreciated his unreserved condemnation of the murder: 'We gave it a lot of thought as a family. Sinn Féin have obviously gone in a different direction since the signing of the Belfast Agreement, and I think that can only be welcomed. They have moved away from violence and they condemn the actions of so-called dissident republicans. I'm not taking away from that. But at the same time, there were so many members of the security forces and ordinary members of the public that were murdered at the hands of the IRA prior to 1998, and there has been no apology from Sinn Féin. They did not express remorse and they didn't see what they'd done as being morally wrong. They continue to justify it. There were thirty prison officers that were killed. So to have members of Sinn Féin at Dad's funeral to sit beside other members of the Prison Service and people that had lost loved ones at the hands of the IRA, we as a family felt that was wrong.'

In September 2019, Sinn Féin MLA and former IRA man Gerry Kelly, a member of the Policing Board, had Tweeted jokily about the anniversary of the escape in 1983 of thirty-eight IRA prisoners, including himself, from the Maze prison. Black was appalled. He pointed out that one prison officer had died during the escape, and another had survived having been shot in the head. Describing it as 'gloating', he asked republicans to consider how hurtful it was to the families of those and other officers.

'After Dad was killed, there were offers made to get me involved in politics,' he said. 'But I felt it was for the wrong reasons. I was quite aware my personal circumstances could be exploited and I didn't want that to happen. But politics has always interested me. It affects nearly every area of your life in some way, shape or form. So I saw it as a way potentially to try and give something back into the community and to do something positive out of something so bad that had happened. And I suppose after Dad was killed, it sort of made you, in a way, evaluate life. Standing last year in the local elections was something that I did off my own bat.

'I got on fairly well. I was happy with how things went. I stood in

Carntogher – it's a very rural area my mother comes from – and I got elected, so now I am a part-time councillor with a full-time job on top. Free time is a thing of the past. I met my girlfriend when we were both working in Asda as students. Then shortly after Dad was killed we ended up getting together. She has been with me ever since, every step of the way, and been very, very supportive.'

He stood for the DUP. His attitude to the party is nuanced. 'The DUP is the mainstream unionist party. The others don't carry the same weight or have the same level of influence. Am I naive about the fact that people maybe see the DUP as being the political wing of the Free Presbyterian Church? No. I'm not. But I don't see a time when the DUP aren't going to be the largest unionist party, and I think it's important for younger people to become involved who maybe aren't your typical, traditional DUP-style person, to actually make the party more varied at representative level,' he said. 'There are still people within the party that would be Free Presbyterian-minded, but I was surprised at the amount of people, especially at council level, that are not that stereotype. There are people within the party that come from different backgrounds, and maybe aren't religious and don't subscribe to the very conservative policies that the party would have. I was pleasantly surprised that there are more levels to the DUP than meet the eye.'

Black believed the party has to be responsive to these changes. 'There isn't any getting away from the fact that there is a deeply conservative element. But I think that any party has to continuously look at its voter base, and look at what they are telling them. Now that we are the leading party of unionism in Northern Ireland, we have to realise that we represent a broad range of people and we need to try and represent them as best as we can. It's actually a strength of unionism in the longer term. So people that see it as a sell-out or a betrayal and things like that, I think they need to see the bigger picture. Unionism has to be reflective of our diverse society. You have to keep an open mind on the direction that you take. Alison Bennington stood in East Antrim. She's openly gay, and she felt comfortable as part of the LGBTQ+ community to be able to stand for the DUP and she got support and got elected to the council.'

Elected to Antrim and Newtownabbey council in May 2019, Bennington had found herself compelled to choose between competing loyalties before the summer was out. The Alliance Party proposed that the Pride movement's rainbow flag be flown at a local civic centre. Bennington did not speak during the stormy debate that followed, and she voted with fellow DUP councillors against the motion. It was passed by the other parties on the council. DUP leader Arlene Foster has said that, like all members, Bennington has 'signed up to the policies of the DUP'.

Black said that people from a Christian background were entitled to their views. 'But at the same time, they shouldn't be vilifying other people if they choose to lead a different lifestyle,' he said. 'Again, personally for me, I think diversity in a society is good.'

He said a balanced view was needed. 'I think it works both ways – I mean, did I support the Ashers in that case? Yes, I did.' The 'gay cake' case to which he referred had begun in 2014 when a gay man, Gareth Lee, ordered a cake iced with the words 'Support Gay Marriage' from Ashers Bakery in central Belfast. The owners, Daniel and Amy McArthur, refused to supply it, citing their Christian beliefs. Lee sued, alleging discrimination, and won. He was supported by the Northern Ireland Human Rights Commission. The McArthurs appealed, and lost. However, the Supreme Court reversed this in 2018, ruling that there was no evidence the bakers had discriminated against Lee because of his sexuality. In 2019 his lawyers announced they were taking the case to the European Court of Human Rights.

'It's not because I think that things should be denied to people from an LGBT background. It's about mutual respect and not beating people over the head to fall into what your outlook is,' said Black. 'In the same way, gay marriage is now legal and that should be accommodated within Northern Ireland. But if somebody went to, say, get married within a church, should there be protection for a minister of a faith as to what he believes? Yes. I think it's about a common sense approach in these things so that we can coexist peacefully. In constitutional terms, that means moving beyond the Orange and the Green. Mid Ulster is still a very divided area. It's the only council in Northern Ireland that now does not have an Alliance representative.

'As far as politics goes, I'm more hopeful for the future in Northern Ireland than I have been probably over the last three years. Obviously Stormont is back up. There are certain elements that aren't happy. But from my point of view, I am proud of my identity but I have no issue with people of a different identity or culture, Irish speakers or whatever else, being accommodated within Northern Ireland. And if unionism makes them feel comfortable here, they're less likely to want to go down a different path, to a united Ireland, in the future.'

No one was convicted of David Black's murder. Two trials collapsed, the second in 2018. Black believes that families bereaved in the conflict have been neglected. 'Legacy was the main thing to me that wasn't addressed in the Belfast Agreement,' he said. 'The people that committed the crimes got out of prison but there was nothing there for the people that actually suffered on the other side of it.' Although a majority of people in Northern Ireland say they want to 'deal with the past', there are fundamental disagreements that have, to date, scuppered all efforts to agree a set of mechanisms, including the pension for the severely injured. Chief among these is the definition of who can be considered a victim. Black shared the view that the current definition of a victim equated 'terrorists' with 'innocent victims' and that this was morally indefensible. Reforming this would be necessary before the legacy of the past could be investigated fairly.

He does not, however, agree with those who believe there should be any kind of amnesty for members of the security forces. 'There is a tendency to try and discredit what the security forces did. But if you say that a security force member who did something wrong shouldn't be prosecuted, it actually allows people to claim that the security forces as a whole were corrupt,' he said. 'Whereas I think that if somebody did something wrong and they are prosecuted, it's that person that takes the brunt of the illegality and the organisation they belonged to is not tarnished. But 90 per cent of murders were carried out by paramilitaries and there has to be proportionality when it comes to investigations.

'There is still a lot of healing to do within Mid Ulster. But to talk about healing when there hasn't been a recognition of the wrongs that were done, or the pain and hurt that was inflicted on families, is putting the cart before the horse,' he said. 'You can do all the cross-community projects you want, but until you address that fundamental underlying issue it is really difficult to try and move our society forward.'

'ONE BLESSED MAN'

People kept telling me I had to meet the faith healer. But when I met Davy Robinson, he told me that was not what he was at all. 'I'm one blessed man,' he said. 'All I am is a servant of Christ. The reality is, Jesus said, all that have belief shall lay hands on the sick and they shall recover. So anybody who believes in him can do what I do. It's very simple. There's no magic in this, you know. People come for prayer, they have a need and Christ fills that need. It's not me that does the healing, it's Christ.' He's a big, bearded man with a grand, preacherly exuberance about him. He lives with his wife in a modest bungalow down a long lane among lush fields and gardens between Portadown and Armagh.

'I was born and bred in Armagh town in 1942. Mum raised six of us because my dad left when I was six years of age, and she did a tremendous job in very trying circumstances. I was abused at the age of eight by a man who was like a father figure to me. That set the scene really for a very up-and-down life, for the want of a better word. I started drinking heavily from the age of eighteen and booze took me over eventually. My whole interest in life was making money and I became quite successful at that.

'Then I was seriously injured in an accident. My foot was shattered. My son said to me, when are you going to catch yourself on, Dad? I said, what do you mean? He said, have you a Bible in the house and I said no. He went and got his Bible and he opened it up at 1 Peter 2:24. I hadn't read a Bible for years. It says, "Speaking of Jesus, who his own self bare our sins in his own body on the tree, that we, being dead to sins, should live unto righteousness." Which is fantastic – but it finishes off, "by whose stripes ye were healed". I threw the Bible to the far side of the room in my arrogance and foolishness. He picked it up and brought it back and said, Dad, that's God's Word. God doesn't lie, he doesn't have to. He's God after all.

'I knew it was God speaking to me, so I went up to a dear pastor, Pastor Bob Baines, away up in Darkley,' he said. This was the Mountain Lodge Pentecostal Church, where, in 1983, INLA gunmen had opened fire on the congregation, killing three elders while they sang about the blood of the Lamb. 'Bob was well known as someone who prayed for the sick and saw many miracles. So he sat down at the table with a cup of tea and we chatted about how God was good, and then he thumped the table and said, it's time for a miracle. And I thumped the table back and I said it's past time, and if anyone needs a miracle it's me. He sat me down on the chair in the middle of the floor and his wife and his family got round me and they prayed their heart out to this God I despised all those years. Within minutes I knew I was healed. I gave the crutches to my wife, and we walked out of the place.

'I went to the hospital the next morning and the wee nurse took the big scissors and cut the plaster off. There was this sharp intake of breath and she ran out. My foot was perfect. Every bone was back in place. So the doctor came in and he scratched his head and said, "Where on earth have you been?" And I said, "I haven't been anywhere on earth. I went to my heavenly father and he healed me." And he said, "I don't believe in miracles." And I said, "You don't have to, I do."

'God, when he grabs a hold of you, he just doesn't quit. I would be sitting watching *Tom and Jerry* and the tears running down my face. Every sin I ever committed in my life was like a video in front of me. So I went to a Church of Ireland church in Portadown. I never heard the preacher – I just bawled my eyes out. When I got home I opened the *Sunday People* and there was a massive article by Billy Graham [the American evangelist] and the last paragraph was Revelations 3:20. It says, "Behold, I stand at the door and knock: if any man hear my voice, and open the door, I will come in to him, and will sup with him and he with me." At that moment, I opened the door, and my son was on the other side and he took me to the Elim service in the town hall in Portadown and the preacher said, is there anyone here would like to receive the Lord Jesus as their personal saviour and I threw my two hands up. And that night I gave my life to Christ and my entire life changed.

'I fell in love with the Mountain Lodge Pentecostal Church at Darkley. Three weeks later, they had a convention, and Pastor Baines said to me, go down and pray for that lady and I said, you're joking. He said, do as you're told. He passed away a number of years ago, but Pastor David is his son-in-law that took his place. He's in Burma at the minute or Myanmar, out there speaking. So, anyway, I had seen this wee woman carried in and I knelt down beside her and I said, I have to tell you, I have never prayed for anybody in my life. And she said, son, you do the praying, I'll do the believing, and between you, me and Jesus we'll get it healed. And I started to pray and the next thing she jumped up and was completely healed. And that's been going on ever since.'

Robinson said he had brought God's healing to thousands of people. 'I've done missions in Africa and South America, America, Russia. Our meetings are in town halls and community centres. I don't pitch big long-winded messages. Most people, all's they're interested in is getting healed and getting home. The Lord himself had a very simple message and that was, we brought miracles and signs and wonders. I have the simplest job in the world. My wife would have been Church of England, she's a Sussex girl. She's a cracker. All my family have come to know the Lord is our saviour.' His small office is heaped high with crochet blankets his wife has made for the missions.

He lives in an area once known as 'the murder triangle', where the Glenanne Gang and its successor in the 1990s, Billy Wright's LVF, preyed upon Catholics. I asked him about the Troubles. 'Yes it was brutal round here,' he said. 'But you can either focus on the garbage or you can focus on what God does. In 1985 there was a blind woman crippled with arthritis and the Lord healed her and she went out and did a marathon and gave her testimony in church. After that there were that many people coming, they had to get the police out there to do the traffic. It just was staggering. We were often left with hearing aids, crutches and sticks. The local paper wrote this article: "Miracles happen in murder triangle." What a heading!'

Robinson had sent me a link to some testimonies from people who had got saved. Many gave their names, along with a note on the affliction from which they had been released. These included: gambling, drinking, violent marriage, demons, suicidal feelings, fear and fighting. Some declared themselves 'prodigal sons'. A few mentioned paramilitarism and bigotry. After an introductory bar or two of gospel country and western, the testimony would begin. One man gave a shocking insight into the social lives of his paramilitary circle. Shortly before he found God, he went to a party at which he and his friends took cocaine and, 'thinking it a good laugh', watched videos of men beheading other men in Iraq.

One of the testimonials was Alan Oliver's. Though he made no reference to this, he was reputed to be one of Billy Wright's hardest men. The respected and intrepid journalist Mandy McAuley had approached him in 2019 as part of a BBC documentary. 'I have nothing to say,' he told her. This had always been his response to journalists. Security sources told her however, that Oliver had indicated to the HET that he might talk – if he got immunity from prosecution. He told them he no longer considered himself 'protestant, loyalist or unionist', no longer believed in sectarianism and regretted the Troubles. A spokesperson for the Elim Pentecostal Church in Portadown where he worked responded to questions with praise for his 'exemplary service'.

'The peace process is ridiculous,' said Robinson. 'This idea of trying to find out why, wherefore, who did this and who did that. It is all totally irrelevant. The only question needs to be answered is whether you forgive. People suffered horrendous things. Our problem is not what happened, it's that we will not forgive the past. We're born in sin. The Bible says Christ came to set people free of that. I was a sinner right up to the age of forty-two. Now, I'm a sinner saved by grace. Christ's last basic last words were, "Father, forgive them, they don't know what they're doing."

'Jesus said, if you confess your sins, he will forgive and cleanse you of all unrighteousness. So whatever your part was in the Troubles, it is of total irrelevance. What is important is that you confess it and repent of it. It's very simple. If God forgives you, it doesn't matter what other people's opinion is. If someone came to me and they had killed or harmed, I would lead them straight to Christ,' he said. 'When you stand before God, he's not going to ask you, did you go to law? There are always two people hurting, you know. There's the killer and the one who suffered from the death of a family member. Both of them have to reconcile. It's what you do with what happened to you that actually makes you free or puts you in jail.'

He had asked me if I had received Christ into my life. I said no. As I was about to drive off he banged the roof of my car and called after me, 'Don't leave it too late!'

THE BORDER

CHAPTER 9

Shifting Ground

'NOT TO PROTESTANTS, ANYWAY'

Death had undone so many, and so brutally, among these soft hills in South Armagh. Impossible to drive these narrow roads and not remember.

Twenty years ago, the late Willie Frazer had taken me on a tour, showing me the lanes and ditches, the fields and the farmhouses where Protestants, including his own father, members of his family, and neighbours, had been murdered. He had also pointed out houses where, he said, their killers lived. He called them nests of rats. He named names. He had no hesitation when it came to speaking of collusion, one of the most contentious of the legacy issues. He saw it as common sense: 'You take a UDR man. He is in fear of his life. He knows who these boys are … He knows the government won't do anything about it. What does he do? He passes it on to the loyalist paramilitaries.' He'd challenged me: 'If you were in the UDR and your brother was shot, are you telling me you wouldn't?'[1]

He had no qualms about the British army's practice of shooting to kill either: 'See if a Paki comes from India and kills a Provo? I'm going to shake his hand.' He was often in the company of people I knew to be paramilitaries, including Billy Wright ('a right lad'), Mark 'Swinger'

---

1 Susan McKay, *Northern Protestants: An Unsettled People (3rd edition)*, Blackstaff Press, 2021, pp. 188–9

Fulton, some ex-prisoner pastors and a former member of the Glenanne Gang. He had praised them to me for, as he saw it, having defeated the IRA. He was one of the staunchest supporters of the Orange Order at Drumcree. I met him there the morning after the night the three Quinn children had been burned to death and asked him what he felt about calls for the protest to be abandoned. His response was ugly. He claimed he had it on good authority that there had been no petrol bomb, and that the fire had been started inside the house.

I got another chilling glimpse into the extreme sectarianism of the world he inhabited in 2000. Two Protestant teenagers had been taken out into these hills, where someone had cut their throats and then flung their bodies by the roadside. It was immediately (and correctly) suspected that local loyalists had been responsible. The boys, David McIlwaine and Andrew Robb, who had no paramilitary involvement, had spent their last evening at the nightclub Frazer was then running in Markethill. 'There's none of the local boys would be capable of doing that,' he'd told me. 'Not to Protestants, anyway.'[2] By 'boys' he meant paramilitaries.

At that time, Frazer was, he told me, planning to give up running the club. He had got saved, and selling liquor didn't sit well with his religion. In the years that followed, I'd often met with him. He ran Families Acting for Innocent Relatives (FAIR) and became one of the best-known advocates for 'innocent victims'. For Frazer at least, that meant, for the most part, those killed by republican paramilitaries. He had opposed the release of republican prisoners under the terms of the Good Friday Agreement, but when the broadcaster David Dunseith asked him on BBC Radio Ulster's *Talkback* programme about the release of loyalists at the same time, he replied, 'They should never have been locked up in the first place.'[3] Some of those who shared his views on 'innocent victims' saw him as their champion; others felt he diminished their cause. He campaigned for justice for the victims of the IRA's Kingsmills massacre. FAIR was substantially funded by the EU through its PEACE funds but in 2010, having been alerted to Frazer's anti-peace process commentary, a thorough audit was conducted and the funding was withdrawn. In the same year, a prominent member was convicted of rape. Frazer stood down in 2012 and went on to found the

---

2 Ibid., p. 360
3 Ibid., p. 188

Families Research and Policy Unit. In 2019 the Victims and Survivors Service withdrew funding from this organisation because of financial irregularities. Frazer had himself been turned down more than once when he applied for a personal protection weapon, because the police said there was credible evidence he had links with paramilitaries.

Frazer was perpetually alert to signs of new betrayals. He maligned decent people on Facebook and doggedly promoted conspiracy theories. His public behaviour was at times bizarre. In 2013, after he was arrested for a public order offence connected to the flag protests, he turned up in court dressed up as the radical Muslim cleric Abu Hamza, accompanied by Jamie Bryson in a long black wig and jeans.

Another time he protested about the flying of the Irish flag at a Catholic primary school, speculating that the children might be learning how to use guns. The flag was in fact Italian and was being flown as part of an EU friendship project. He disrupted public consultations of the Eames/Bradley commission in 2009 on how to deal with legacy, shouting down the voices of others. People felt for Frazer, because the IRA had inflicted such appalling violence on his family. They hesitated to challenge his bitter excesses. You could not fail to see that he was unstable, nor that he had been deeply, irreparably hurt.

In 2019, Frazer had cancer, and was dying in hospital. He sent for Mandy McAuley and told her that he wanted the truth to be known about his role in 'taking the war to the IRA'. He did not wish to be remembered as a clown, he said. He proceeded to tell her that he had distributed weapons for Ulster Resistance, the body set up in 1985 by the Reverend Ian Paisley to fight the Anglo-Irish Agreement. (The DUP had distanced itself when the rhetoric got translated into guns.) The weapons in question had been used in around seventy sectarian murders all over Northern Ireland.

'THE DIFFERENT STARS'

'Whenever William was in hospital before he died, he was so full of morphine that he thought Gerry Adams was under his bed. There's no way he was involved with guns,' said Molly Carson. 'I would have known. My mother was Willie Frazer's mother, but I grew up with my grandparents. I got a letter there from the police saying at no stage was William ever questioned or arrested in relation to guns or anything like that. When he was younger, he was just a young boy playing Gaelic, going about with his Catholic friends. He did take a bit of a drink as he got older, but he never harmed anybody. The harm that he did would've been to himself. I'll tell you the kind of carry-on of him: we were both at a wedding one time and I had a pair of red shoes on me and he followed me round till he got the shoe off me, and he was letting on he was drinking out of my shoe at the bar.'

He did, she acknowledged, change. 'He got involved with victims groups. If you are a weak person, you'll take that all on, the hurt. It became personal to him. He felt bitter. I think it all got to him. And then he was influenced by certain preachers that I wouldn't consider very Christian,' she said. I had seen Willie in tight huddles with certain evangelical men who had formerly been paramilitary killers. 'Personally, I go to Elim in Portadown,' said Carson. She runs FAIR now, and has struggled with the legacy of its loss of funding and reputation during Frazer's time. 'I'll never forget walking into a room full of victims and everybody was sitting in it with faces on which there was no expression. They were just like zombies. That was their reaction to life. It's because living on the border they have so much mistrust – of Catholic people, of anybody, of strangers coming to the door.' She said therapies and counselling are now more widely available, but that they could not cure the longing for justice.

'On the legal side, in my vision, it's very unbalanced. I condemn loyalist and republican terrorists. I do not support or have sympathies for either side and never have. They do the same bad deeds. We have a quilt at FAIR that we did for the murders at Darkley church and it shows an open Bible with the commandment embroidered on it: "Thou shalt not kill." But there are a huge number of republican families that have got reviews and got lots of money spent on them, and our people, particularly the families of people that served their country, feel that they died for nothing. The people that were trying to keep law and order don't even get a mention,' she said.

Carson is a former UDR soldier and also worked for the police. 'I served for twelve and a half years, out on the ground, and really the abuse that we got was horrendous. People spitting on you, biting you, throwing bricks at you, threatening to vomit on you. Sometimes they called you a queer, claimed you wanted to grope around them when you were searching. And I lost colleagues. One was a great man for walking and talking and knew all about the stars and when you were to be on duty with him on a foot patrol he would have been pointing out the different stars to you. A car bomb took his two legs off. He's dead now. It shortened his life tremendously.'

The Glenanne Gang consisted of loyalist paramilitaries and members of the security forces. Following an appeal court ruling in 2019, senior British police officer Jon Boutcher was appointed to head a new inquiry into its activities.[4] Carson said she did not believe it had ever existed. 'Any of the people I ever came across in the UDR, the RUC and the PSNI were far more professional than to even contemplate doing something like that. I haven't seen any evidence,' she said. Frazer had always denied that his father, Bertie, a part-time UDR man, was in the UVF. Carson reiterated this. 'They blame a lot of things on Willie Frazer's father. That man was the most decent man you could ever have met. He was an innocent sort of man. A very Christian man. Looking back I can see he wouldn't have been the sharpest person. But there is no way that man ever did anything. The police verified that in writing to us, that his record was completely clear,' she said. (Among those who were sceptical about this was the SDLP's Seamus Mallon, who had once told me that he was far from reassured when the person sent out by the council to do a check for security risks on his house was Bertie Frazer.)

Carson had been subjected to a torrent of abuse after Frazer's death. 'They got so low, you wouldn't believe it. I received numerous phone calls. Willie Frazer's da was now in the slurry tank, old Willie Frazer's dead. Hahaha. Sexual comments. It went on and on.' I had seen some of these vile messages on social media. 'I said to one young man, "It's time you were in the confession box telling the priest exactly what you're doing",' said Carson. 'Finally I turned on them. I said, listen, you cowards. That's what you are. That's what the IRA is. You have to cover your faces with masks. You have to crawl about and plant bombs in the dark. You have to kill innocent people who are unarmed and can't defend themselves. So don't keep ringing in here because, you know what, you didn't win the war. There never was a war. It was a cowards' game. So that stopped it. That's the truth.'

---

4 The inquiry is ongoing.

'WHO WILL DIE TONIGHT FOR VENGEANCE?'

I had asked Carson if I could meet some of FAIR's clients, and she invited May Quinn to come in and talk to me. Carson brought us tea and shortbread. May is an elderly woman. 'My brother was driving the Kingsmills minibus. Bobby was my parents' first child and he was called from my father, Robert,' she told me. 'The first I knew it was on the television. It said a minibus had been stopped and the workers had been shot. I was sitting in my own house when I heard it. The neighbours had a phone and they came and told me it was the Glenanne minibus.

'One of my brothers, he went up to the scene of the crime and he was told our brother was dead, and he had to come back and tell us. Then there were all the funerals in Bessbrook and Tullyvallen. I can still hear them singing "The Lord's my Shepherd". Every time that psalm is sung since it annoys me. People say you forget but you don't forget. It takes me back to that whole loss. If you love somebody, you know what it is. Daddy didn't survive a year. He had never spoken about it. He died of a broken heart.'

The IRA carried out the sectarian atrocity, though it initially denied it. It has been compared with the Altnaveigh massacre of 1922. There had been a series of sectarian murders in the area, and the night before Kingsmills, the UVF attacked two local Catholic families, the Reaveys and the O'Dowds, leaving six people dead.

After immense delays, an inquest into the murders of the ten Protestant workmen who were lined up and shot began in 2016. Further delays and setbacks followed and, utterly frustrated, family members walked out of the inquest in early 2020. The sole survivor of the massacre, Alan Black, began proceedings to have two IRA men who were allegedly involved named.

'We know who did it,' said May. 'We got it from a man in the barracks. But there's nothing we can do. One of them is outside in Newry. I worked there fifty years. I haven't seen him, but there was a person with me one day and he saw him. When we got home he says, May, I wouldn't tell you that it was him, because, he said, I don't know what you would have done. But I wouldn't have let myself down. I would love to meet them. I always said that from day one. I would tell them that our Bobby would never have done it on them. We were brought up to respect everybody. You honoured your father and your mother.

You kept the ten commandments, you didn't tell lies and you didn't kill anybody. If you could do a good turn well then you did it. And anybody that came into my house always got tea and my mother was a great baker.'

Her brother had referred to the murders of the O'Dowds and Reaveys, she said. 'Everybody was very annoyed about it. Bobby called in to my mother every day before he lifted the Glenanne workers and that day he stood with his back to the fire and he says, "Who knows who will die tonight for vengeance?" That was the last words he said to my mother.'

'There was a whole lot of things went on but people daren't open their mouth because they'd be afraid of being shot. Protestants would have told the police and the army, and so would good Roman Catholics. But if you had the real republicans, they would not do it. There was a fear in the Roman Catholics – they shot their own as quick as anybody else.'

May shared Molly Carson's view that the Glenanne Gang was a myth. 'James Mitchell was a Christian man. He had two sisters. They were lovely people. I don't think they would lift a gun to anyone. I lived across the fields. They would have sung in all the churches and choirs and everything. They were Covenanters.' The Covenanters, now more commonly known as the Reformed Presbyterians, had arrived in Ulster fleeing religious persecution in Scotland in the seventeenth century. Mitchell, a member of the RUC Reserve, was found by an Irish government inquiry led by Mr Justice Henry Barron to have kept arms and maintained a base for the Glenanne Gang at his farm.[5]

May believed the security forces had not been allowed to defend the community from the IRA. 'The UDR was not let out to keep the law. They had to account for every bullet used. They weren't allowed off the lead,' she said. According to the Barron Report, the 'theft' of arms and ammunition from UDR and Territorial Army bases was rife, and many were not so much stolen as handed over to loyalists.

'My mother never got over it,' said May. 'I looked after her for eight years. If she fell out with you today it would be somebody else

---

5 Alan Brecknell, whose father was one of the Glenanne Gang's victims, painstakingly charted the ballistic history of many of these weapons, and his findings were incorporated into Anne Cadwallader's chilling book, *Lethal Allies: British Collusion in Ireland*, Mercier, 2013. For links to the Barron reports and other documents see https://www.patfinucanecentre.org/glenanne-questions-and-answers.

tomorrow. I'm eighty-five. I looked after my husband until he died and I am looking after my sister at the minute. That's just the way it is. But the Roman Catholic neighbours up the road were always great. They still come to my house every Christmas. Times I'm all right, times I'm not all right. They're bringing out all these things now for trauma and all the rest of it. It's a heap of nonsense. No such thing then. You just got up and went to work in a couple of days and that was it. Now they're giving them all money. I think it's a heap of bull.

'There's good people in this country and there's other people out to destroy it. They could all work together because there comes a day they'll all die and they've got to face their Maker. Those that have done good are Christian people and they know where they're going, but the ones that have not done right, they know where they're going too.'

'LESSER BREEDS'

Five Mile Hill Full Gospel Fellowship church is a small, plain hall with crazy paving walls, perched on a hillside close to Glenanne. A framed notice by the door confirmed that Sunday Worship was at eleven, but the concrete car park was empty. A bunch of keys hung from the side door and I looked inside. This was where Willie Frazer had found God, his spiritual guide the minister, Pastor Barrie Halliday. He had presided over Frazer's funeral here at the end of June 2019, just before the marching season. He said Frazer had been 'one of the best sons Ulster ever had'.

All of the leaders of unionism attended the funeral. First Minister and DUP leader Arlene Foster, Robin Swann, who was then the leader of the Ulster Unionist Party, and Jim Allister, leader and sole MLA of the Traditional Unionist Voice. Halliday had stood, unsuccessfully, for election for the TUV in 2011. The party represented 'old-fashioned unionist Protestant views', he said then, and claimed he was representing 'good people that are sick of everything they see'.[6] Leaders of Orangeism, including Grand Secretary Mervyn Gibson, were also at the funeral, their sashes a slash of orange against the vivid green of the summer countryside.

Foster, who had been Frazer's solicitor before she became a full-time politician, spoke at the service. She spoke fondly of him. He had been

---

6 https://www.youtube.com/watch?v=HPhqU8xLACc

'fearless', he had 'fought the good fight'. She said, 'I will very much miss William for many reasons.' She implied that he was what is known in Northern Ireland as 'a character'. She did not comment on any of his extremist views. She was accompanied by her special adviser, former DUP MLA Emma Little-Pengelly, whose father had, like Frazer, been involved in Ulster Resistance. Noel Little was arrested in France during an arms procurement exercise.

An associate of Frazer's who disapproved of his evangelical turn had told me Frazer was buried 'in the back garden' of Halliday's house, and I was curious. I walked around to the farmhouse behind the hall and was about to knock when a car sped in and slammed to a stop beside me. A man, red-faced from rushing, jumped out, Bible in hand, shirt and tie askew, and bounded to the door beside me. He explained that the breaking of the bread on the Sabbath morning was held in the house. I followed him into the big kitchen. Pastor Barrie Halliday sat at the end of a long table with a Bible in his hands. A woman was busying about the sink behind him, and a man who looked like Halliday's brother sat at the other end of the table.

There were a few huge, plush armchairs around the room along with some hard kitchen chairs, on one of which a man sat reading his Bible. An elderly lady in a long dress stared frankly at me with a big smile. There were two other older women who also smiled at me, curious and pleased, it seemed, to see someone new. I took one of the armchairs, then regretted it, imagining it was probably someone's regular spot. A dark-suited man came in with two little girls, the older of them shy and staring at the ground, the younger in rainbow-coloured tights that brightened the room.

As I was so obviously the stranger, I asked if I should introduce myself. Halliday said, 'Oh we know you, Susan.' I heard myself declare that I had been a friend of Willie Frazer's. This was far from true, though we had always been civil and he had told me after *Northern Protestants: An Unsettled People* came out that, although he had not liked the book, I had fairly represented him and his mother. 'Yes, indeed,' said the pastor. 'William often spoke of you. He would have said, "She's hard but she's fair",' he said. The people seemed satisfied by this.

There were prayers, for which I closed my eyes; a hymn, which I vaguely remembered and stumblingly sang; and a Bible reading. Then a man brought round a tray with squares of sliced pan bread and little plastic cups of what I assumed was not wine. 'No thanks,' I said, when he offered it to me, 'I'm not saved.' I cringed. What a ridiculous thing to say. After the service, the old lady came straight over to me and took my hands and said I was very, very welcome. She asked me where I was from. 'Londonderry,' I said. I never call it that. The woman from the top table offered me tea, and I burbled about how we were both wearing the same colour of nail polish. Halliday introduced her as his wife. The man who looked so like him was his brother, and the smiling old lady was his mother.

Then I asked Halliday if he would direct me to the cemetery. He led me out to what appeared to be the back garden. And there it was, a modest grave against the wall, with a few wreaths laid on the grass. The gravestone would be erected at a later date. I could only see one other grave, which was a Halliday family one. There were some old stone stumps on the lawn and I asked if they were old graves. Halliday said no, they might have been for tethering horses.

Seamus Mallon had just died, and I mentioned to Halliday that I was going to call in and pay my respects at his house in Markethill. Halliday said stiffly that Mallon had been 'sore on the UDR'. He had himself been in the regiment, he said. He invited me to come and visit the museum at the Families Research and Policy Unit, which was also in Markethill. (Frazer had already given me the tour – it was mostly uniforms, flags and guns.) I wanted to ask Halliday about its funding issues, and about his own – he and his brothers, Ronald John Sinclair Halliday and Richard Jonathan Kris Halliday, had been convicted of fraud and forgery in 2017 after Her Majesty's Revenue Commissioners conducted a four-year investigation into VAT repayments of £140,000. The pastor pleaded guilty, and received a suspended sentence.[7] But I quailed.

Pastor Halliday had taken over Frazer's Facebook page, though it retained its deceased owner's name.[8] He posted videos of himself on it, often from among a thicket of flags, with the queen's portrait gazing from over his shoulder, or from the gospel hall, speaking to 'God's own people in Ulster', the 'most persecuted and maligned' people

---

7 https://www.agriland.ie/farming-news/farming-brothers-sentenced-for-tax-fraud/

8 https://www.facebook.com/william.frazer.58

in the world. Mostly he was drably dressed in denim jeans with an open shirt under a fawn-coloured jumper. In one video he addressed Frazer's deathbed confession to the BBC. For a start, he said, it was not a confession, because that was not a Protestant practice. 'Catholics sin away to a minute to midnight and then take themselves to the priest and make a confession,' he said. He was in any case unperturbed. 'All I can say is if someone is pointing the gun, why wouldn't I point the gun back?' he said. 'I'm not concerned about the rabble. I'm not worried about the lesser breeds.' He pointed to the Union Jack and said that it might let 'the brotherhood and sisterhood of Ulster' down but the other flag, and he fingered the Ulster flag, would not. If Willie had defended it, 'that's fine'.

One video was filmed in the darkness beside Frazer's grave, around the time that I had spoken with him. 'Friends, listen,' he said. 'There's no tears here on the top of the hill for Seamus Mallon's passing. He's away. I'd imagine the devil has him. I don't gloat on it but … I'd rather deal with the Shinners any day than the likes of him.'

In another video he lamented that the godless of Ulster were murdering the unborn, and gave a garish account of people in China opening parcels from America out of which the heads of dead babies stared as if crying out, 'You killed me in my mother's womb and here I am.' There was praise for Donald Trump who had 'fulfilled one of the last prophecies in the Bible prior to Jesus's return' by moving the US embassy in Israel back to Jerusalem. There was a warning that 'Jesuits and lesbians' were translating the Bible. He called the GAA 'Fenian, dark, and hellish' and those who attended its games were 'oul Sabbath-breakers'. The border, he said, 'was defended by the gun and will be maintained by the gun'. One sermon concluded that we should be glad there had been 'rats taken out' already. 'More's the pity some of the ones up at Stormont wasn't taken too,' he opined. 'Be still and know that I am God.'

Halliday used the Facebook page to lay out his full manifesto in the summer of 2020. He began by addressing those who had taken part in Black Lives Matter protests in Northern Ireland. 'It may have been boats brought youse here 300 or 400 years ago and youse were brought under duress and against your will,' he said. 'But there's boats sitting there empty at the minute, doing nothing. Youse are welcome to get on them and go back home if you think we're so bad.' He compared them to Catholics who fifty years ago had been 'rabble-rousing' that they were badly treated. 'Friends listen, see when you go to visit someone in their house you abide by the rules of the man that owns the house, the man who built the house.' He was not a racist, he said before declaring, 'Youse have shown yourselves to be lesser breeds ... You'd need to have a bit of manners, a bit of respect. We are a white civilisation, a Christian culture.'

'NO BIBLE THUMPERS'

Terry runs a small business on the border. It has been in his family for generations. 'The agreement was signed in April 1998 and my daughter was born in June,' he said. 'Paisley said there were to be no integrated schools, so we sent her to one, and she also went to a school run by the Quakers. She's away with a scholarship now to Paris. I sponsored school GAA tops as well as rugby ones. My daughter plays both. I was born in Mid Ulster. My parents were no Bible thumpers and I preferred playing golf with my granda than going to church.

'The DUP has brought on a united Ireland. Under Brexit, as a businessman, all my stuff is going to be more expensive – I get my supplies from Dublin but the products are from Britain and it comes up the road to the North then. May's deal that they rejected was far better. But the DUP didn't want a deal. They wanted a border. The Good Friday Agreement brought peace but that wasn't what they wanted either. I live in the South now. The people here voted to remain. Scotland wants out of the UK and to stay in the EU.

'Arlene Foster is a failed politician. Diane Dodds is a useless politician,' he said. Dodds was a former DUP MEP, and was co-opted into the Assembly as MLA for Upper Bann in 2019 after Carla Lockhart became an MP. Foster appointed Dodds as Minister for the Economy. 'From a business point of view the DUP didn't listen to anyone,' said Terry. 'The farmers warned them, business leaders warned them. The DUP thought they were somebodies – they played straight into Sinn Féin's hands. Everyone knew Boris was going to shite on them. Thatcher ruined the country too. Johnson would have us away in the morning if he could. My parents would have voted Ulster Unionist. I'd like to see Naomi Long as First Minister. She knows what she is at.'

Terry was an ex-fireman and had witnessed the ugly side of the Eleventh Night bonfires. 'My mother lived among other pensioners in a terrace of houses facing on to a bonfire site. The fire was higher than the treeline,' he said. 'The paint melted on their doors. All the pensioners' houses had to be boarded up – the home helps couldn't come in. My mother and all her neighbours were stressed out and very afraid. These hooligans start building the fires from April and they are there till eleven or twelve at night drinking and carrying on and making a racket. The DUP environment people wouldn't come down. When you rang the DUP about the bonfire they said, it's traditional,' he said. 'This is a sin for me to say it but do you know when that'll all stop? When someone falls off the top and gets killed.' At one bonfire in her constituency an effigy of Sinn Féin MP Michelle Gildernew was burned in 2015. 'She helped us and was the only one that did, so I voted for her when I lived in the North,' Terry said.

He felt there was a lack of honesty about the reason the bonfires were so important within unionism. 'They are about religion. It's the Orange Order and the paramilitaries that drive them. They're trying to show "we are loyal and true and we don't care". The police stay clear. They won't go against the Orange Order – don't want their own houses burned. The Orange isn't as strong as it was during Drumcree. Burned its boats.' Terry was another of those who believed it was the fury of the electorate, particularly over the treatment of the nurses, that had broken the political impasse and forced the DUP and Sinn Féin back into the Executive. 'They went back into Stormont because they were afraid,' he said. 'I'm back and forth across the border all the time. Our whole working infrastructure depends on it being open. The DUP won't even agree to improve the road from Derry to Dublin. We'd be better off in a united Ireland.'

A NIGERIAN INVASION

When Ngozi Njoku was appointed by the Church of Ireland as rector to a scattered cluster of remote parishes on either side of Fermanagh's borders with Leitrim and Donegal, she was inspired by a the spirit of a Scottish missionary who came to her native Nigeria in the nineteenth century. 'She was called Mary Slessor and she stopped the killing of twins. In eastern Nigeria they thought twins were an abomination. I felt, if she could do it, what was stopping me? I felt liberated. I had a car, a phone. I didn't know about North and South in Ireland, or Catholic and Protestant. My impression was the Twelfth of July and looking at the television thinking, "What is wrong with these Orange people – are they mad? Look at that water cannon!" I began to read about Northern Ireland. I wrote to my bishop and he suggested I get *Modern Ireland* by Roy Foster.[9] So I started to read it online. I came across the phrase, "troubled time in Ireland".'

That was in 2013. Since then she has been serving as rector to congregations in and around Garrison, Slavin, Belleek and Kiltyclogher, small villages straddling the border, some in the North, others in the Republic of Ireland, all part of the Church of Ireland diocese of Clogher. There are many lakes and forests and boggy hills in this westerly part of Fermanagh. It feels remote and half-deserted. 'When I came here first I was looking around and thinking, where is the filling station? Where is the bank? What am I doing here?'

She invited me to the rectory for dinner. It was easy to find the big old house outside the village. Tall, painted white and with distinctive blue windows, it was surrounded by a lovely garden running a bit wild. Ngozi told me there were five bedrooms, but it was cold and draughty, so she kept the kitchen and her study warm and lived there in the winter. She wasn't lonely, she said. She kept in touch with her family on social media. She cooked pasta for us from a recipe book written by the church organist, Joy Graham.

Ngozi's father was the first in his family to become Christian. 'His parents were crop farmers, but my father liked to be clean and if you are lazy like that you go to the white people, the missionaries, and so he became a minister,' she said. 'We grew up during the Biafran civil war. When we were out playing the fighter jets would fly over and people shouted, take cover, take cover! When I was in Germany in 1990 during the Kuwait war I realised it was there in my subconscious and it was awoken. It was a profound shock.'

She wanted to study theatre but theology was what was available. She trained in Europe, and had a partner. 'Unfortunately it was an abusive relationship. When a man lifts his hand to hit a woman he says he loves, he is explicitly saying she is a slave. Less than a dog,' she said. She left,

---

9 Roy Foster, *Modern Ireland: 1600–1972*, Penguin, 1992

trained in the Anglican Church, and was ordained in 2010, serving first in England.

'Relations here are good. My neighbour here brought a Mass card and I signed it for him. When he gave it to the person they looked at it and said, you've had this signed by a Protestant! I was in one Catholic house and I put my collar down on the table and the woman cleared the table and put it in the bin. The undertaker is a Catholic, well respected by the whole community. When the two of us are together people joke, oh no, these are the people you don't want to see! People want me to be here for them, for weddings, babies, funerals and burials. I am blessed to have them. My parishioners have experienced troubles and lost people. I touch, I feel, I am where it happened. I never imagined how much history is alive.'

She said being a Black woman in an area in which there was very little diversity had not been an issue. 'In Monea in Fermanagh there is another Nigerian minister – actually we come from the same area. In Manorhamilton in Leitrim there's another. Oh! We are invading Ireland, North and South!' she said.

The next day I went to Ngozi's service in the little stone church in Garrison. There were about thirty people there on the wooden pews. Ngozi looked striking, vividly unlike the standard white, male Northern Irish minister. She had her hair in cornrow plaits and tied in a bun at the side of her head, and she wore black and white vestments with a scarf embroidered with flowers. She spoke of beatitude and Brexit, of peace-making and 'the upside-down world of God's wisdom'. She spoke, too, about St Paul and the book of Corinthians. She said there was a need to distinguish between things that were in the Bible because of the culture of the time, and things that represented the principles of Christianity.

It was early January 2020, the beginning of the Brexit transition period. Ngozi acknowledged that some in the congregation would be celebrating, some would be disappointed. God had listened to the politicians, Ngozi said, though she added, 'Maybe not all of them.' Brexit would be felt keenly in this area – looking out across Lough Melvin you could see Leitrim in the Irish Republic, the border invisible under the choppy grey waters. The Boundary Commission of 1925 proposed transferring Garrison to the Free State. 'We pray in transition times. We pray for those who are leaving the UK because of the Brexit. We pray for all the foreigners who don't know where to turn to,' she said. 'We pray for rain in Australia.' Terrible bush fires were raging in Australia at this time.

After the sermon, the children came in from Sunday School. Four little boys played tambourines, cymbals and a triangle while plates were brought round for the offerings. I looked through the hymn book, which included hymns by Tomás Rua Ó Suilleabháin in Irish. There were memorial plaques on the walls. Facing each other across the church was one to Thomas Carson of the Irish Guards, 'killed in action' in 1915, aged seventeen years, and one to Thomas John Fletcher of the UDR, 'killed by terrorists' in 1972. Troubled time in Ireland.

Afterwards, Joy Graham, the organist and author of the cookbook, and her husband Eddie, who had been sitting in the pew behind me, leaned forward to speak with me. 'All over the Troubles this church has never been locked,' said Joy. 'There is a really good community spirit in the area, Eddie, wouldn't you say?' 'Absolutely, yes,' Eddie replied. Ngozi had told me that their seventeen-year-old son had been killed in a tragic accident. 'We had great support when we lost Neil,' Joy said. 'Yes,' said Eddie. 'It really came to the fore at that time. We always were conscious that we lived in a very good area, but especially when we had to come through such a horrendous time.' 'You're completely lost,' said Joy. 'You don't know what way to turn. Everybody rallied round, especially through the church here. We are such a small church, it is like a family.' They said that local Catholics had also stood by them.

'Ngozi prayed with us, sat with us, cried with us, listened to us. She had just had a tragedy of her own. Her brother was killed in a car accident in America and his remains had been brought back to Nigeria for burial. She was away for ten days and on her way home from the airport, the first thing she did was call us again. She's been tremendous,' said Joy. 'If I didn't have faith, I don't know if I'd be here today. God gives us the strength to get up every day and get on.' 'It also tested me,' said Eddie. 'I kept asking, why was this allowed to happen? But we have a strong enough faith that we do firmly believe that we will see him again.'

They show me the new stained-glass window dedicated to their son in the church porch. It has dogs and tractors and hens and the lush green hilly fields that characterise the area. The family told the designer all the things their son had loved. The golden retriever he'd persuaded them to get for him has since had eleven puppies.

As we spoke, I realised I knew Joy's brother, Ken Funston, who works with the victims and survivors group, South East Fermanagh Foundation (SEFF), and conducts tours pointing out places where local Protestants were murdered by the IRA. Joy's family was from Pettigo, which is split in two by the border. 'Yes,' she said. 'Our brother, Ronnie, was murdered on the home farm in 1984. He was ex-UDR. We moved away from the border then. The farm was sold and we moved to Kesh, to the next village. Then I met Eddie at a dance in Ballinamallard. I fell in love and got married and moved back to the border in Garrison.' 'I always say to our children I am so thankful they didn't experience any of that tension or that fear and dread,' said Eddie. Joy said it was like 'history repeating itself' for her to lose a son, as her mother had before her.

I felt that Joy would not have told me about her murdered brother if I had not made the connection with her campaigning brother, Ken. But once we started talking about it, both of the Grahams said they believed the IRA had deliberately set out to drive Protestants back from the border. Eddie said that after Johnny Fletcher was killed in 1972 a lot of families left. This was the Thomas John whose plaque I'd seen in the church. He was a hard-working man. He had a small farm that straddled the border, he was a forestry worker, a part-time member of the UDR and an Orangeman. I asked the Grahams if the cross-community spirit they had spoken so warmly of had survived those times. 'You know, it never really was extinguished in this part of the world,' Eddie said. 'Nobody knew what to do or where to turn. But that spirit was always there and it grew, actually, and I suppose it's brought us to where we are today. In other places it was completely wiped out, that sort of communication between people, but that always stayed here.' I had been in the sort of places he was describing, places in which terrible things had happened and that had a blighted feel to them, as though they had been unable to recover let alone thrive.

The Grahams said the Good Friday Agreement had transformed the area. 'This is a fantastic place for young families,' said Joy. 'But we could do with more jobs brought to the west. Our own daughter would love to come back if she had work.' 'This half of the country has been very badly neglected down through the years. There has just been no infrastructure spending at all,' said Eddie.

Eddie is a farmer, Joy a civil servant. Both voted for Brexit. 'I think it will be better for the country,' said Joy. 'I work in the North. We go across the border and buy our diesel, which is cheaper. That won't change.' Eddie said he was not concerned at the loss of EU subsidies. 'The population of the world is obviously growing and food will always be needed,' he said. 'You have to make the best of whatever happens.'

In October 2020 Ngozi left Fermanagh and Leitrim to move to a parish in London. In her farewell address she said that what had pleased her most was the number of baptisms she had carried out. A new generation was growing up in the church.

'A HAUNTED QUALITY'

Jean Bleakney is a poet, and a fine one. She had told me how devastated she had been by the murder of Lyra McKee. 'Not least because it seemed so starkly to epitomise how much my generation has failed the next,' she said. She is in her sixties. 'It triggered feelings of guilt and a depth of despair that I haven't experienced in decades.' She told me Lyra had written to her asking if she could use Bleakney's poem, 'Postcard', in the book she was writing about boys who had disappeared during the Troubles. 'Postcard' was written after the Omagh bomb in 1998. The last verse reads: 'In rain that is commensurate with tears/ another generation learns to grieve./ On this, the hardest summer here in years,/ we count the maimed. We name the disappeared.'[10] Bleakney showed me what Lyra had written to her: 'The poem left me chilled in all the right ways. It's so beautiful but also disturbing. There's a haunted quality to it.'

Bleakney told me that her late father, who was a customs man, had come from Garrison. Her family's graves are in the Church of Ireland graveyard. We planned to walk the road along Lough Melvin from Garrison in spring, but lockdown had delayed us, so it was a late summer afternoon when she brought me to her family places on that now quiet corner of the Fermanagh border. She showed me how her great-grandparents' grave is inscribed with a line from the Song of Solomon: 'until the day break', while on more recent family graves it is 'breaks'. 'As a poet it does bother me, slightly,' she said.

---

10 Jean Bleakney, 'Postcard', *Selected Poems*, Templar Poetry, 2016, p. 19

She talked about Johnny Fletcher. 'He was a good friend of my uncle's,' she said. 'They got him out of his car and demanded guns. They said he'd be all right and then they took him away and shot him.' She said when she mentioned Fletcher to her mother, her mother had remembered the thunder and lashing rain on the day of his funeral. I read that slates had been blown off the roof of the church during his funeral. He was buried during heavy snow, colleagues from the UDR firing a gun salute. One of them packed up and left with his family two days later. Bleakney spoke of the families who moved. There were certain towns, further north, like Kesh and Ballinamallard, that were retreated to, because they were at a distance from the border and had predominantly Protestant populations.

We walked out along the road by the grey lake, the houses on the far shore blurred by drizzle. As we left the village we passed a plaque in memory of Bobby Sands. The IRA prisoner had been elected MP for Fermanagh-South Tyrone in 1981 by 51 per cent of the population, just weeks before he died on hunger strike.

Bleakney stopped by a square brown farmhouse with a half-hipped roof facing out across the lough. I told her I had always liked this house. I used to walk here when I lived in Enniskillen. This road was cut off with dragon's teeth and had gone extravagantly wild. 'This is the family homestead, where my father was born,' she said. She remembered every stone and tree, a family story from 1921 of bullets fired into the house that lodged in the clock. 'My grandfather was in the Special Constabulary. He was shot at as he put in the spuds in a field along the road and had to move away for a while.'

We walked a few hundred yards further along the road to a stone bridge. 'This is the Kilcoo River, which was also called the County River. It marks the border. When I asked Mum about Garrison, she mentioned "that poor fella Plumb. It was awful what they did to him." I've looked at records and this was an ambush just here in 1922. Plumb was hit.' Edwin James Plumb was a special constable and a former British soldier who lived on the northern side of the border. His body had been recovered on the other side.

Willie Frazer's mother Margaret had spoken to me about the murder in 1975 of RUC reservist Willie Meaklim. 'See the death they gave him …' she said, before detailing the torture she believed the IRA had inflicted on him, despite the evidence of a pathologist.[11] People believed Plumb was tortured too, though the priest and the minister who attended the scene said otherwise.[12] Perhaps people exaggerated what was already awful because they felt their suffering went unnoticed. Bleakney said they were angry that generations of the IRA had been able to 'stroll back over the border' after these attacks. 'We had a reminder in our house of the IRA's 1950s campaign – there was a lump of metal in the sewing box that was money that melted when the customs post at Killeen was attacked,' she said, and later she sent me a photo of it.

'In 1967 Dad was running a one-man customs post in south Armagh and we lived on the square in Crossmaglen – not exactly a hard border! He spent a lot of time chatting with fishermen, who included RUC officers.' She had loved playing in the big attic bedrooms of the house, their dormer windows overlooking the square. In the 1970s, an IRA sniper had crouched at one of these same windows to shoot dead a British soldier.

'We moved back to Newry and lived in fear and anger. In 1972, we had to move, first of all to a Protestant part of town, later on to Lisburn. So I lost my home town.' She had terrible memories of what Newry was like for its Protestant minority in the early years of the Troubles, and had gone back to read the local paper recently to see if it was that bad. 'It was,' she said. She felt this experience was being written out of history. She showed me an opinion column from the nationalist *Irish News* in 2018. In it, Tom Kelly wrote about how Protestant businesses had 'disappeared' from Newry. He referred to Mitchell's shop, which used to have a portrait of the queen behind the counter. 'Today it's my favourite Chinese takeaway,' he wrote.[13]

Bleakney had been wounded by what he left out. 'Disappeared!' she said. 'I felt sick to think that he was either ignorant about the fate of Bob Mitchell or didn't consider it worth mentioning. That between the portrait of the queen and the Chinese takeaway there was an assassination. Bob was a Justice of the Peace and an Orangeman. He had retired by 1977 when the IRA came to his house and shot him in front

---

11 McKay, p. 195

12 http://irishhistory1919-1923chronology.ie/april_1922.htm

13 Tom Kelly, 'Chipping away at the "them and us" narrative many of us are stuck in', *Irish News*, 10 December 2018

of his two elderly sisters. Not a word about this. I just felt, dear God, our stories are just going to go unrecorded and forgotten.'

In 2019, historian Henry Patterson had addressed a meeting in the Orange Hall, which had been named after Mitchell. He spoke of the difficulty of getting the authorities in the Republic of Ireland to tackle the IRA, and of the erasure from history of the reason why the border was so heavily policed on its northern side. Arlene Foster made the same point during a television interview that year after dissident republicans tried to kill police officers along a country road in Fermanagh. Sinn Féin's Michelle Gildernew was beside her, but they faced slightly away from each other, and Foster tutted and shook her head when Gildernew spoke about the need to avoid reimposing a hard border. Foster responded angrily. It was the IRA who caused the security forces to have to militarise the border. Brexit would not.

Bleakney had voted 'yes' for the Good Friday Agreement but had rapidly become disillusioned. 'First we had the disbandment of the RUC and then the vilification of it and of the UDR. It is an insult to unionism that we have to thole in silence, not because of shame but still because of fear.' Writing in 'The Belfast Agreement: Twentieth Anniversary Issue' of the journal *Irish Pages*, she said she had realised 'the GFA was never fit for purpose. It institutionalised a two-tribes mentality. What was not factored in was human nature, a particularly nasty algorithm hereabouts.'

Her outlook remained gloomy. 'The school I went to in Newry closed, and the other state school has only 40 per cent Protestants now. Newry has a population of 27,000 but only around a dozen Protestant children now enter education there every year. The 2021 census will reveal the greening of south and east Belfast, Lisburn, and elsewhere. The wealthier areas are no longer exclusively Protestant and indeed I would say they are increasingly mostly Catholic. Being forced to move has possibly engendered rootlessness in the Protestant community. Offspring have gone elsewhere, leaving their greying parents here.'

This sense of continually being driven back had caused Bleakney to make a dramatic political switch. 'I was one of the panicked surge of people who voted DUP in the Theresa May election,' she said. 'I felt the ground shifting. I voted for Emma Little-Pengelly – I didn't want Máirtín Ó Muilleoir of Sinn Féin sneaking in. Before that I used to vote SDLP and before that for the Ulster Unionists.' Pengelly had been elected to Westminster in Belfast in that 2017 election (she lost her seat to the SDLP in 2019, after which she was appointed as a special adviser to Arlene Foster.) 'Arlene's hapless crocodile remark fuelled a surge to Sinn Féin in the Assembly, and there was Brexit. Hackles were up. It felt like a runaway train. There needed to be a steadying of unionism, and the DUP being the only show in town, that is where my vote went. I wasn't alone. They put on 100,000 votes in that election. Unionism feels aggrieved, isolated and anxious.

'The crocodile thing was half-remembered from Churchill who allegedly said, "an appeaser is one who feeds the crocodile hoping it will eat him last". The media never interrogated that, the genuine fear that underlies concession after concession. Poor Arlene – not allowed to use metaphors or even adjectives, like blonde and blood. Should the border disappear, unionists will morph into whipping-boy Brits, which would be hard to thole. One of these days I will say to one of my soft nationalist friends, 'Ah well, sure, in twenty years or so Ireland will be back under British rule.' And then I'll say, 'How did that make your gut feel? How did that make your head feel? And then I'll say, "Welcome to my unionist world!"'

'A BITTER TASTE'

I met Margaret Veitch at the meeting in memory of Edgar Graham in Belfast. When she saw that I was writing in a notebook, she leaned over to me and said, 'You know where the innocent victims went wrong? We never made a fuss. They never did *that* for us.' She snapped her fingers, meaning they did nothing. 'They have forgotten all about us because we are no threat. I have nothing but my tongue and no matter how much I voice my opinion or I've talked about it or express my hurt and devastation and despair, they're doing nothing.' She told me that her parents, Billy and Nessie Mullan, had been killed in the Enniskillen bomb in 1987, and invited me to come and meet her and her sister, Joan Anderson. We met at Margaret's house in the suburbs of Enniskillen. 'I was living in America and I got the call from my brother-in-law and I've been devastated ever since,' said Joan. 'For a long time I could not speak. Then I spent my life in just utter despair and crying.'

'I was in Africa,' said Margaret. 'I had won a window-dressing competition. My husband read about a bomb in Enniskillen in a paper in Kenya and we phoned home to be told the horrific news. It took years and years for me to ever to be normal again.' Their sister, Ruth, had been away on an overnight trip. She came back to roadblocks and sirens and news of the bomb.

'I'm not looking for compensation,' said Margaret. 'I'm looking for justice. But then when you see the way some victims are treated – like Bloody Sunday – there was £300 million spent on them. I'm not saying those people should have been shot, but the army did not go out that day with an intent to shoot. I reckon it was a reaction at the moment.' 'And the people that went out on Bloody Sunday had a choice,' said Joan. 'They could have stayed at home. Yet they received that whole inquiry.' 'That money would have built a hospital,' said Margaret. 'So do you understand how it makes us feel? The British government has done nothing for us British citizens that lived in hell for thirty-five years. It was a slaughter match around Fermanagh and right around the border. Those twelve victims in Enniskillen are every bit as important as the Bloody Sunday victims.

'My father and mother deserve not to be kicked into the grass and forgotten about. Now you hear me at the minute, I'm angry. Every single thing we have asked for, the door has been closed. I lived my life running. We renovated our shop the year after the bomb, and what hurt me was people assumed we got money for the bomb. We got nothing. It's festered on and on with us. Now, after all these years, with the peace process and everything, they are rewriting history. But Martin McGuinness had a choice to be in the IRA, a choice to go into politics. My father and mother had no choice. The Enniskillen bomb was premeditated murder. The gardaí in Cavan said they lost evidence in a flood. We'd been to the police to ask about DNA because DNA is supposed to be so wonderful. No, there's no DNA.' 'To our faces, they said that,' said Joan.

'They want us to die off and go away and forget about it,' said Margaret. 'The day after the bomb there was to be a boys' parade and a girls' parade at Tullyhommon, and the IRA had set a bomb for it. They say a cow triggered it off and the bomb didn't go off. That would have been a slaughter match of young children and it was an absolute disgrace. They said Enniskillen was a mistake. Well, you don't really go with a bomb to make a mistake. You go deliberate. A bomb isn't a tea party. Three thousand death certificates should be put on the British government's desk and they should be asked, what are you doing about three thousand innocent victims?'

'The IRA have now got themselves into government,' said Joan. 'And we have to look at people who have blood on their hands, that plotted and murdered their neighbours. People that caused the most vicious harm and ruined people's lives are being applauded now and all of a sudden they've got the right qualifications to be a minister of education or a minister of health. And if they want something they whine till they get it. Like this Irish language act. It is just appeasement.'

'Our government of unionists are all oh so pleasant and nice,' said Margaret. 'And they're being pushed down all the time. The IRA, the more they shout and scream, the more they get. We grew up in a housing estate. Everybody in Northern Ireland had all the same opportunities. Children were educated. If you had the brains, you went to university. And yet they started looking civil rights and went on and turned it into terrorism and our lives were ruined and still are being ruined.'

'My parents were good Christian people. We lived in Cornagrade among all our neighbours – Roman Catholics, Protestants. My mum used to say that they've all gone off to church to pray to the same God. If my parents couldn't see the good in you, they wouldn't see the bad in you, but this has left a bitter taste in my mouth. After the bomb, I was inundated with my Roman Catholic friends. They told me, "the IRA didn't do it in my name". Yet they voted en masse for Bobby Sands and they're still voting for Sinn Féin.

'My father was not born with a silver spoon in his mouth. He worked night, noon, and morning. We all lived within our means. But then there was a certain faction saying, oh we want the same as them, but they weren't prepared to work for it and an awful lot of people wanted to live off the British government. We had neighbours that had sixteen children. How on earth can anybody bring up sixteen children? But the people thought it was their right. I'm sorry, I'm getting frustrated.' 'It's the truth,' said Joan. 'As children, we saw it every day, we saw the priests going in and telling these women, and the next thing nine months later they had another child. We saw it; it went on non-stop. And we were living in amongst that. We weren't living in some high place and not knowing what we're talking about.'

'And now they are pursuing this poor soldier, Soldier F as they call him,' said Margaret. 'He was only following orders. What about the IRA that lay in ditches up in the border regions of Fermanagh and they've all snuck over the border and they were protected?'

The sisters were also angry that they had no say in how the Enniskillen bomb was commemorated. 'While we were out of our minds with grief, they built the Clinton Centre,' she said. 'And a thing around the war memorial that looked like crazy birds,' said Joan. 'Crows,' said Margaret. 'And then thirty years later we finally got a respectable, decent memorial that stated the people were murdered and they wouldn't let us put it up. It got carted away on a flatbed truck. The Catholic Church owns the land and the priest said there was no planning permission.' 'I think there was something going on behind the scenes with the priests, and I'm sorry, I am being truthful,' said Joan. 'There was something sinister going on that they didn't want this to go up.'

Other Enniskillen families who had also been angry about the memorial that had been put up, and by the inscription that said the people 'died' in the bomb. The memorial Joan approved of was a large black slab with the names of the victims and a clear statement that the IRA had murdered them. Planning permission was given in 2019, but the memorial had still not been put up. 'But there's memorials to terrorists round the countryside with no planning permission,' said Margaret. 'This is what they call equality. And this is the way we are treated.' 'Another door closed,' said Joan. 'Another door closed in our faces.'

'FRIENDS WHO ARE GAY'

Debbie Erskine is one of the new young politicians in the DUP. She brought me into a big plain office at the back of the DUP's constituency headquarters down by the River Erne in Enniskillen. She sat down in the big leather office chair behind the desk in the back office. I asked her if it was Arlene Foster's chair and she giggled and did a swivel around in it. 'Yes,' she said. 'This is Arlene's office. She's at a committee meeting in Stormont today. I used to canvass for her and now that I'm on the council, I work here. Having her as leader has been great. Women no longer make the tea in the DUP. You are given opportunities. I'm the only woman in the DUP group in our council. I don't believe in quotas though. It should be on merit.' The office is sparsely furnished, with plaques on the wall as you enter commemorating local UDR soldiers and police killed in the Troubles.

'I'm from Sixmilecross and now I live in Fivemiletown,' said Erskine. 'My dad was a Church of Ireland minister, and our house was a safe house for members of the security forces. Mum used to make soup and sandwiches and they'd call in when they were out on patrol. Mum and dad said there used to be IRA checkpoints and army checkpoints on the roads around where we lived. Dad took a notion to move to Richhill in County Armagh. It is not far from Portadown. I was born in 1992 so I was a wee girl during the Drumcree years. We were very much into the Orange Order – my brother would have marched around the garden with the toilet roll draped over him like the sash. I remember helicopters and barricades.

'I was in the Girls Friendly Society – it was like the Girl Guides only they were into crafts, which wasn't me. I was delighted when I could join the Scouts and go camping. I didn't know what my friends' parents did. Later on, I realised they were police and army families. Mum and dad were politically minded. They'd have been traditionally Ulster Unionist until the Good Friday Agreement. They found the prisoner releases hard – terrorism is terrorism – and that goes for both sides. After that they looked more towards the DUP. That was a big turning point for unionism.

'I was in the town hall in Portadown in February 1998 doing speech and drama, and the police came and said there was a bomb outside and we were evacuated. I was put in a car and I saw the bomb go off. It really affected me. I was a deep thinker as a child and I thought the IRA was after me personally. When the Omagh bomb went off later on that year I thought they'd been out to get me again. I'm on the Fermanagh and Omagh District Council now and just recently there was a whole debate about Liam Campbell,' she said. 'It was truly shocking and upsetting, especially the way it was brought up under AOB just out of the blue.'

No one has been convicted in the criminal courts in connection with the twenty-nine people who were killed in the Omagh bomb, but in

2009, a civil court found Campbell and three other men liable for the atrocity. In 2016 Campbell was arrested in County Louth in the Republic of Ireland on foot of a European Arrest Warrant served by the Lithuanian authorities who wished to question him about alleged arms smuggling for the Real IRA. There are 'Free Liam Campbell' banners across roads, and in the summer of 2020, Sinn Féin and SDLP councillors on the policy committee at Fermanagh and Omagh Council voted to support a letter to the taoiseach urging that Campbell should not be extradited.

Relatives of some of those killed in the bomb expressed hurt and anger at the proposed move. The SDLP later apologised for backing it. 'His only connection with Omagh was the bomb so why did they see fit to bring it to our council? The debate caused a furore and it has brought in quite a bitter feeling to our council,' said Erskine. 'There's a lot of the old Orange and Green coming up again. In 2020 we shouldn't be looking at things through that prism. For me, the debate also really brought it all back, that feeling when I was a child.

'I went to the University of Ulster and did English literature and journalism and absolutely loved it,' said Erskine. 'I got a job with the *Ulster Herald*, which is perhaps seen as a more nationalist paper but they were very kind to me and let me do stories about the Orange Order and the Royal British Legion. After a few years I realised it was hard to be as political as I was and be a journalist – it was like fighting for air all the time. So when a job came up in the DUP press office, I went for it. It was daunting. I was now working for politicians I had grown up listening to on the TV. I was young and female – I don't think they had ever had a female before, not that it should matter.'

Her parents were living in Clabby, a small town in Fermanagh, and she commuted up and down to Belfast. 'I just love Fermanagh. I love the people – they are so easy-going. There is such a good community aspect and the neighbourliness just shines through,' she said. She met her future husband when they were at secondary school. 'When I got married I moved to Fivemiletown because my husband is from Ballygawley in Tyrone and that was as far as he was willing to move,' she said. It takes twenty minutes to drive between the two villages. 'A lot of my generation did leave but they are coming back now to have their families,' she said. Staying close to home, or returning to settle, are still strong features of life in Northern Ireland.

Erskine was elected to the council in 2019. 'I'm glad devolution is back up and running. The atmosphere had got very tense. Communities were pitted against each other. It was all about waiting. But Northern Ireland has changed so much in my lifetime. People want hospitals and schools and good roads and tourism. They just want Northern Ireland to work and be a success. For some people who lived through the darkest days, what happened is so awful they will never fully heal. For my generation it is about acknowledging that two wrongs don't make a right and looking forward. Brexit is the biggest issue. When I was out canvassing I was taken aback by the amount of admiration people had for the stance the DUP had taken.

'People hark back to a negative view of the DUP but there is a younger generation now and the party has moved forward quite a lot. Arlene has gone to GAA matches and a PinkNews event.' At this event in 2018 Foster was warmly welcomed. She had asked the gathering of LGBTQ+ people to respect her opposition to same-sex marriage. 'The DUP is a socially conservative party and I am quite happy with that,' said Erskine. 'But I have friends who are gay. The UUP is struggling to position itself. Jim Allister has the luxury of being a one-man band who can say what he likes. That hard-core-attack mentality isn't where unionism is going now. I'm hopeful. After the Omagh bomber thing in council someone from the other end of the political spectrum emailed me to see was I all right. When I was getting married, some of the Sinn Féin women wanted to see photos of the dress.'

'ROSES IN THE GARDEN'

Violence that was politically motivated, the violence of bombs and bullets, was often referred to as 'the violence', but there was another kind of violence, which was overshadowed during the Troubles, and which has persisted. In the winter of 2019 there were almost three hundred women and one hundred children on a waiting list in Fermanagh for the domestic and sexual violence organisation, Women's Aid. This at a time when the local newspaper, the *Impartial Reporter*, was raising awareness of these crimes, signalling that an even greater need for the underfunded service might be anticipated.

Journalist Rodney Edwards had been publishing accounts brought to him by people who had never spoken out before about horrific abuses, some of them recent, some having taken place years or even decades before. Many of the alleged perpetrators and those who had facilitated them were men of the respectable classes, some of them even so-called pillars of society. I went with him to a meeting in a hotel function room in Enniskillen in the winter of 2019. It had been organised by people in the area who had experienced this violence.

Caroline Wheeler, herself a survivor, chaired the meeting. She said that because of what had happened to her, she had been viewed as 'a rebel without a cause, vocal, contentious, seen as trouble'. A spokeswoman from Women's Aid said the organisation had been in Fermanagh for twenty-five years. It was going to take at least three months before they got to see some of those waiting for their support.

Letters were read out from politicians who had been invited to the meeting and had been asked for their support. The DUP's Lord Morrow sent apologies and said he stood with the survivors and urged the PSNI to move investigations forward. His colleague Ian Paisley Jnr's response had been to note snidely that 'your MPs chose to gag themselves by abstention, something that is no use to the victims', a reference to the fact that the MP for Fermanagh is from Sinn Féin and the party does not take its seats at Westminster.

People at the meeting paid emotional tributes to Edwards, calling him their champion for enabling them to speak out. A man said that his brother, who had never got that opportunity, had drunk himself to death. Edwards won an Amnesty International award for the work.

I arranged to meet Ellen at her home in a small town close to the border. Ellen is not her real name and I have changed some details of her story. 'I grew up on a farm on the northern side of the border in the 1960s,' she said. 'My father was very involved in his church, the Orange Order, the Royal Black Preceptory and the Masonic. He was a part-time member of the security forces and he had inherited a farm that was basically bankrupt. A good number of extended family members lived with us, and everyone was flat broke. My father would go in to the village in the morning and all these men would stand in the line outside the courthouse. You picked how many men you wanted to come to do a day's work. You didn't pay them though. It was jaw wages. These were people from very poor families that needed fed, so they worked for their food.

'After the Troubles kicked off, my parents didn't pay us much attention. My mother had to go about the farm with the shotgun guarding my father because the IRA wanted him dead. We had flares attached to the chimney and if the house was attacked you pushed the button, which was in my bedroom, and this flare went up and you hoped that anybody saw it. We didn't have a telephone. We didn't have a bathroom. At one stage the British army was billeted in our haysheds.

'When I was a child it just seems there was a never-ending stream of standing in the church singing in the choir and watching coffins go past. We'd relatives that got shot, good friends shot, businessmen we knew got shot. It was a rough time and we were really well-trained kids. One day I came home from school late, my hair a mess, my knees cut, I was all dirt, my buttons were missing off my blouse, and I had been raped. I tried to tell Mum and got shouted at for dirty talk and told to get upstairs, get washed and changed and ready for dinner. End of conversation.

'Growing up during the Troubles here you relied 110 per cent on your Protestant neighbours or members of Protestant organisations. For support, for information, for giving you lifts, helping you out. You trusted them. There was no talk of child abuse back then. I'd never heard the word paedophile. I'd never heard the word alcoholic mentioned either, but both these things seemed to be at every institution that I was linked to through my family growing up, all Protestant organisations. There were people within all of them who were abusing children.

'At band practice we would have played games, just boys chasing the girls and catching them and tickling and whatever. Then on the instruction of a few of the older men, the younger boys – and you're talking eleven, twelve-year-old boys, were told that the game now was that they had to catch us, remove our underwear and then climb on to the roof of the Orange hall and hang our knickers on the flagpole. If some of the cars outside were open, we'd jump in and lock the doors, and then they'd start rocking the cars and we would be screaming.

'The boys were at secondary school, hormones raging, and the girls were still at primary school. Then the other girls moved away. I became the centre of attention. It became more sexualised. When I was caught, it was like the fox and the hounds. All these boys touching me, pulling me, kissing, poking. And they had adults telling them, encouraging them, to do stuff: older men not getting involved but managing, watching and giving these younger boys ideas of what they can do.

'The Orange hall was out in the countryside. You could practically see the border from it. A lot of the people in the band were in security force families so when the security alert was high, they wouldn't allow us to have band practice there. So we would meet up in the Orange hall in a village. I have memories of running up the side of it and being cornered. And one of the men hanging out of the window shouting instructions to six or seven boys who were pinning me on the ground. It felt as if I was being torn in several pieces.

'The thing was, I had been sexually abused by others already, men in my extended family. I taught Sunday School and I played the church organ and I went horse riding and to piano lessons. And there was a man sometimes gave me a lift was abusing me as well. So in my mind already, by the age of about ten, I had figured out that whatever I wanted to do, I had to pay and the price was sex with the men. I didn't really question it.

'One of my abusers started feeding me drink. I had insomnia and nightmares. I was, and still am, very aggressive. I'm moody and temperamental and all sorts. I was put on Valium when I was twelve. There were acts of constant terror. At fifteen I met and got engaged to a man who was a heavy drinker. Even though he was abusive to me, I thought I could manage one person, and to be honest, he was the first person that ever told me that he loved me and I thought as long as he loved you, it was going to be the roses in the garden. We moved in together but soon it wasn't rosy at all. He'd be in the pub and I was drinking at home.

'One time he spent the day in the pub and when he came back he brought one of his mates and, in front of him, he grabbed me by the throat. The other man dragged him off me and they went back to the pub. I took the children and drove to my mother's. There were a whole lot of hunters there that had been out shooting pheasants. They were having a sing-song and we were hardly noticed.

'I left him and moved in with a friend on the far side of the county but her husband was a policeman and he was a drinker too. I remember walking into a room and a mountain of weapons lying in the middle of the floor, and the people that owned them all drunk. Other times,

I saw boys having to leave him home in the police car, and they were all carrying loaded weapons. I couldn't stay there. It got worse for my friend after I left. Once, he lined her and her children up in the house with his loaded pistol and asked them which one of them wanted to go first.

'I was still a mess. My father asked me why I was drunk all the time and I said, "Do you want to know? Well, I'm drinking because I was abused as a child." And I started naming people, some of them his friends, some his family, and others members of the very organisations that were the mainstay of him, and of my mother, because she was also involved in the church and in the Orange Order. It was too much for him. He walked away. Then I had suicide attempts and admissions to psychiatric hospitals and zillions of tablets and drugs I bought on the street, but nothing was killing the pain.

'What finally got me through was six years of counselling, three of psychosexual counselling and three of cognitive behavioural therapy. I haven't had a drink now for twenty years. I think I'm almost sober.

'After Rodney printed my story, a senior figure in the church contacted me through the *Impartial* and said I'd been in her thoughts and her prayers. She sincerely apologised that the church had not helped me. There cannot be justice for what happened to me. No. The best that I can hope for is that these people will be named and shamed and parents will know who they are and keep their kids the hell away from them.

'The big bogey is the Orange Order that has supposedly held Northern Ireland together through the Troubles. The backbone of the whole Protestant community! God bless us, if we didn't have all these good upright Christian men our whole society would fall apart.'

CHAPTER 10

Loyal to People

'NOT THE WILD FRONTIER'

The first thing he had to deal with every time was the name. No, said Davy Crockett, with a patient sigh. No, he wasn't named after Davy Crockett, 'king of the wild frontier'. The question was irresistible, though, for the journalists and film-makers who had, since Brexit began to be spoken of, trekked to his farm in the rolling hills at Coshquin, on the border between Derry and Donegal. Davy dealt with it with good humour. He had the crinkled eyes of a man who laughed a lot. I arrived in on a stormy winter night into a flurry of wet sycamore leaves from one of the big trees at the front of the old pebble-dashed farmhouse. Crockett ushered me into the living room where a huge log blazed in the fireplace. Throughout our conversation he poked and stirred at it, enjoying the spectacle of the sparks flying up the chimney. It was one from one of his own trees that came down in a storm, he said. There was a large photograph on the wall, showing him out in the fields working with his son, a vast western sky behind them. It was strikingly good: a gift, he said, from one of the big international news companies. He brought tea, and Rebecca, his sixteen-year-old daughter, joined us. Davy spoke first.

'We are just outside Derry here, or should I say Derry/Londonderry,' he said, with that slightly mocking, slightly embarrassed tone that people from the city often adopt when getting over the cumbersome official compromise reached after centuries of stubborn disagreement over the name of the place. 'My grandfather purchased the farm in 1912 and at that time it was part of Ireland, and part of the United Kingdom. And then in 1922, the country was divided and the farm was divided. So that's where we're coming from. You don't know what is going to happen until it does, and that's when we'll know what Brexit is, when it actually happens.

'My grandfather had a milk run in the town, in Derry. And he went to bring the cows in for milking one day and the policeman had a customs post set up between the gate and the yard. And one side was Donegal and one was Derry. The policeman said to him, that's the last time you do that. That's a different country now. My grandfather took it badly. He was used to working the land from both sides, and now he had to fence it off. There was a sign put up. The road became an unapproved road and if you went across with a horse and cart or smuggled goods you would have been arrested. But in my father's time and my time, we've grown up with it. We just work with it, I suppose. Anybody else thinks it's strange, but we knew no different.'

Some of his land is now in the Republic of Ireland, some in Northern Ireland. 'We have nearly all sheep. We have no beef cattle simply because there's no money in it. Then the other crops we grow out in Donegal. We grow oats and some of that goes for making porridge. We grow barley and some of that goes to make beer. Then we have wheat and that goes into producing milk that we sell to milk farmers. So it's all used in Ireland, all used locally. We don't export anything,' he said.

He was appalled at the prospect of Brexit and shocked at how ignorant people are about the border. 'It's total madness leaving Europe. I said to someone, "They will be putting a border down through my fields." He said, "Sure Ireland's united now, the Good Friday Agreement took away the border." I said, "No, no, no, no. There's still a border there." "No, not at all," he said. I said, "England's going to vote the whole lot of us out of Europe." He said, "Oh no, that couldn't be right." The day of the referendum I put my father in a wheelchair and took him in to vote to stay in Europe to stop the hard border as I talked about. He hadn't voted in years.'

Crockett had done plenty of training courses and was as prepared as he could be for Brexit. He knew that having separate VAT rates and such would impact on his business. 'It's all a whole lot of bother, a whole lot of expense, laying out money and getting money back again,' he said. He believed no consideration was given to the particular plight of people in Northern Ireland. 'You know, that's a terrible thing, nobody wants us. The South doesn't want us and Britain doesn't want us. Nobody wants us. I think now the border will be up the Irish Sea.' Here it was again, this melancholy view, a frequent variation on which is, 'Britain doesn't want us, the South can't afford us.' Davy did not want a border at all, but if there had to be one, he had his own preference. 'The business I'm doing is throughout Ireland so I would rather have a border up the Irish Sea than across the fields of mine,' he said.

'It was Europe did away with the customs on the border but we had dragon's teeth at the bottom of the lane because of the Troubles and they stayed. I grew up with the Troubles. The army were coming up and down that road every day, you know, from the mid-seventies. They'd turn in the yard and sometimes did a search of the building and one thing or another like that. I took it as normal. You know, that's a terrible thing. Things become normal. Soldiers with guns and SLRs [self-loading rifles] and all the equipment. We would have walked down to get the bus at the army checkpoint and all the empty shells would have been sitting at the bottom of the lane. We sold them in the school to the girls to make necklaces with them.'

He remembered the aftermath of the 'human bomb' when, in 1990, the IRA forced Derry man Patsy Gillespie to drive a bomb into the checkpoint just below the house, beside the small Coshquin housing estate. Gillespie worked in the kitchen at Fort George army base in Derry. The IRA deemed him a collaborator, a legitimate target. The explosion killed him and five soldiers. Crockett spoke more slowly, staring into the fire. 'It blew the front door open and broke the glass on the front of the house. We had to go down the next day to help a neighbour who had the shop down there. It was eerie, the things you saw. You wouldn't want to even repeat what you saw. Like, limbs and everything else. Awful, terrible altogether, for no reason, no reason at all. What good did it do?

'It was aimed at the security forces. Nobody died in the estate, but there were older people died after, with shock and one thing or the other. If you were a Protestant in a border area, no matter what you did or what you didn't do, you were a legitimate target. The IRA thought you'd be telling things to the British army. We never saw anything so we had nothing to tell. But if somebody was smuggling you didn't say anything. No. You couldn't, you wouldn't, you know. You kept yourself to yourself. And, like, we just had neighbours: we had no Roman Catholic neighbours or no Protestant neighbours, we had just neighbours. And it was just a community, and a good community, and we got through it.

'We are part of the Presbyterian Church. We started off in Derry, and then that church closed and we joined Burt Presbyterian Church, my mother's church. She was a Donegal woman.' Burt is just across the border in the Republic. I asked Crockett if he was involved in the Loyal Orders. 'No, no, no, no,' he said, laughing. 'I'm British, but if it comes that I'd have to get an Irish passport, it won't bother me. Most people around here would feel the same. And if they weren't happy they'd just move. Four or five farmers around here sold their property and bought ground in England, Scotland, Wales and even Canada. You could sell fifty acres here and buy three hundred acres in Scotland.'

He was against segregated education. In his schooldays in the 1970s, a bus brought local teenagers into Derry, then the Catholics and Protestants went their separate ways, meeting again on the bus home. 'The school that my father went to and I went to, Oakgrove, it turned integrated. I would've been on the board of governors at that time and I'm all for integrated education. That's the total way forward. They're looking for extra money in Stormont and it would save them over a billion a year if they would change to just integrated education. That is the future.' He looked at his daughter. 'I think when you hear from Rebecca you'll find her schooling did her no harm,' he said, with a proud and loving smile.

'I'M JUST FROM THE BORDER'

Rebecca listened intently to her father while he spoke. 'There are a lot of things that you don't hear,' she said. 'Some of those stories I've never heard before. You don't ask. I think if you sat down in front of someone from the older generation and said, tell me about the Troubles, it would be a bit disrespectful because it's their lives you are talking about. It's not a history lesson. These are things that actually happened to them. And it might've been normal for him growing up and it might've been everyday life, but for me, it's very much removed from what I'm used to. So it's quite strange to hear about like a war that happened right here where we're sitting.'

'The idea of Patsy Gillespie,' Rebecca continued. 'I knew about that story. I know what happened, but to think it was at the bottom of our road … I can't even fathom what it would have been like to have an atrocity happen just down the road from me. It's not something that my generation luckily has any relation to. I was born in 2002 so I wasn't even alive in a time when there wasn't a Good Friday Agreement. I'm the generation after the Troubles, the legacy generation. What I know about the Troubles is based on what people tell me. There's always going to be two sides of it and it's important not to be biased, to listen to every account, because everybody was affected by it and there were no good sides.

'I had a happy childhood growing up here. It's a border community, it really is, we are all each other's neighbours. When people ask me where I'm from, there's nothing that identifies me as either side of the community, whereas in Derry your postcode can give you away, so to speak. But for me, I've been through integrated education all my life, primary and secondary. I'm from here. I wouldn't really identify as Donegal or Derry because it isn't either. I'm just from the border really. I don't have any connection to England and I don't really have a connection to Ireland. I'm Northern Irish. I wouldn't say I'm loyal to a flag or a government or anything. I'm more loyal to people.

'I didn't even think about the fact that we cross the border every Sunday to go to church. I obviously knew it, but it never crossed my mind. It's interesting in Northern Ireland, how when you're talking about being a Protestant or being a Catholic, it's not even about religion. If you're a Protestant and you haven't been to church for years and years and years, you're still a Protestant. That's all you'll ever be to anybody.

'I don't think that way. It doesn't come into your head. A lot of my friends are Catholic, or some of them are atheists, some of them are whatever. It doesn't come into the conversation because I think we have more respect for each other than to reduce each other down to what you've grown up believing. I have friends that live across the border in Burnfoot and Killea, and then I have friends that live in Top of the Hill and in Shepherds Glen and Tullyally. It doesn't matter because at

Oakgrove we have buses coming from all over the place.' The places she names are all in and around Derry, on both sides of the border.

'My only problem with integrated education is that because they don't want to cause any drama, they don't teach us the history of the Troubles. It's also a problem in segregated schools. I think the government needs to sort out and create a legitimate curriculum that will teach the facts and let people decide for themselves what they believe. By not teaching us, that leaves the people at home to teach us their version of it. They should be teaching us so that it doesn't repeat itself again, so we don't shy away from our differences, but talk about them and about our own views.

'I'm interested in politics because of where I live and because it affects me. Brexit and the rise of Trump have made our generation more politically aware. And it's led to movements like the climate movement here and around the world, and the anti-gun campaign in America and the March For Our Lives. Past generations might've seen it as an excuse to riot or be violent, whereas we look to make change peacefully and properly. The climate movement is definitely the most important one for me, because it's an issue of now or never. If we don't do something, that's it, there's nothing we can do if we have no planet. And I think every other movement should be directly linked to the climate movement, because nothing can change if we aren't here to change it.' Northern Ireland remains the only region in the UK without legislation on climate change. The DUP opposed a bill brought by the Green Party in 2021.

'LOOKING FOR A CONFIDENT HOME'

Although suburban housing estates of big, confident detached houses have now nearly reached it, the border zone between Derry and Donegal retains its own distinctly unsettling atmosphere. There is a wreath of artificial flowers on the wall where the checkpoint used to be, marking the spot where Patsy Gillespie and the five soldiers were blown up. A concrete hotel, long abandoned, still moulders, though the wreck of a car that used to sit outside it has gone. The busiest traders operate from vans in lay-bys, while the various showrooms and shops look as though they could be gathered up like Monopoly properties at a moment's notice. At weekends there are queues of northern cars heading to Muff in the Republic for petrol. The beautiful mountains rise in the distance, Muckish and Errigle to the west, Sliabh Snaght to the north on the Inishowen peninsula.

Off a winding side road, and up a wooded drive, Phillip Gilliland's house is a handsome Georgian farmhouse. It is in Northern Ireland, though when Gilliland and his wife, Karen, step outside to walk their dog, they are within three hundred yards of the border, invisible as it is, whichever way they set off. Both work as solicitors in Derry. He served me the most amazing cup of tea, in which a single gnarled leaf gradually softened and unfurled, releasing its potent flavour. 'Protestant Ulster has spent its life for the last four hundred years looking for a confident home – it has this kind of wandering Old Testament culture,' he said. 'A hundred years ago, it threw its lot in with the United Kingdom, but what has that actually delivered? A substantial population decline, and economic decline. A hundred years ago, a huge proportion of the GDP of the island of Ireland was in Protestant Ulster. Now we're a bit embarrassed about the fact that one out of every three pounds of public expenditure in Northern Ireland is a gift from the English taxpayer.

'We've become this really provincial, conservative people. Yes, Home Rule did mean Rome rule and, economically, the South was backward. But over the space of a hundred years, oh my God, how has this changed. Where is the socially conservative part of Ireland? Well, it's up here. Where do we find liberal Ireland? It's in the South. The border, in my head, absolutely does not exist in any cultural sense whatsoever,' he said. My Church of Ireland diocese, Derry and Raphoe, straddles the border, and there are many more Protestants on the southern side than there are on the northern side.

He grew up in one of Derry's most famous houses, Brook Hall. 'It's a very elegant Georgian villa with a commanding view overlooking the Foyle,' he said. 'But it felt normal to us, a lovely place for children, a warm house and a happy house.' The house was built by a member of the 'Anglo-Irish kleptocracy that ran Ireland', and infamously one of its owners was the man who arrested Wolfe Tone in Buncrana after his capture during the 1798 rebellion. Gilliland's great-great-grandfather bought the house. 'He was a totally self-made guy from Donegal. I am sure the aristocracy regarded him as absolutely nouveau riche. He was a proper industrial revolutionary. His sons and his grandsons ended up going to Harrow and Cambridge and were part of the establishment, as is the way history goes.

'My father was a gentleman farmer – he rarely got his hands dirty. He was also a solicitor,' Gilliland said. His late parents divorced when he was seven. His father got remarried to the writer Jennifer Johnston. 'Derry in the seventies was a pretty hot and heavy place, particularly if you're wandering around, living in a landed estate with a public school accent,' he said. 'My father presented like some eccentric, public school Englishman, but he never ever felt remotely English. He felt absolutely 100 per cent Irish, which he was.' Gilliland was sent off to boarding school in Coleraine when he was ten. 'Thirty miles away, a different planet. When you look back on it now, you think, Jesus, we were being bombed out of Derry for being Protestants, and then you go to Coleraine and you're accused of not being Protestant enough. We were in the middle of a sectarian war, but escaping to a Protestant hinterland was actually worse. Coleraine's east, looking towards Belfast, and Derry's west. The cultural frontier is at the top of the Sperrins. Most people's forebears in Derry came from Donegal, Protestant or Catholic.'

Gilliland became a corporate lawyer in London and Brussels but unexpectedly found himself nostalgic for home. 'It was just what a Protestant person in Northern Ireland did; if you were educated, you emigrated,' he said. He came back, married Karen, a Catholic from County Kerry, and settled a mile from Brook Hall. He was 'euphoric' over the Good Friday Agreement. 'Some pretty difficult things had to be swallowed. A lot of bad boys and girls had to be released from prison. But that was the deal. It stopped the fighting. It also allowed people to talk openly about what they are and what everybody else is. As a Protestant, it is paradoxically more challenging to have a political conversation with somebody from your own tribe.

'I've never actually been a unionist. I could never find anything attractive in a deeply nihilistic – not quite nihilistic, but almost – vision of politics. "What we have, we hold" does not inspire the soul. I would describe that as a pretty thin diet for the soul. The soul requires a degree of hope and optimism, and a bit of expansiveness – and unionism has never done that. I regard political unionism as equally culpable for the decline in the Protestant population as the IRA. Because educated kids would say, I don't like militant republicanism, but my own lot offer me nothing. I want something progressive and all I'm getting is conservative, reactionary cant, and I'm embarrassed by it and I'm leaving. Naomi Long has done a superb job with the Alliance Party. She's a tough politician. She has shunted the party away from soft unionism to become a party that is agnostic on the union and is explicitly about trying to build a shared society,' he said.

He was 'dead against' Brexit. 'Northern Ireland is being booted out of the union by the English political establishment,' he said. 'The only parts that voted for Brexit were the bits furthest away from the border. Belfast could become isolated, like "the Pale" around eighteenth-century Dublin. The DeSouza case has got people seriously talking about identity. There's been a significant change in the Protestant zeitgeist here over the last three years. Obviously a distinct majority of Protestants will vote to remain in the UK. But they wouldn't die in a ditch if the vote went the other way.'

Emma DeSouza is a young woman from County Derry who battled the British government to prove that the Good Friday Agreement respected her right to be Irish in Northern Ireland, and a citizen of the EU for immigration purposes. The British Home Office had tried to force her to seek residency for her American husband, Jake, as a British citizen, or to renounce her British citizenship and apply as an Irish citizen. In May 2020 the Home Office amended its immigration legislation to include the Good Friday Agreement's definition of a person of Northern Ireland as British, Irish, or both. All would be able to apply for resident status through the EU Settlement Scheme.

Gilliland felt that if Northern unionists had anxieties about a border poll, there were plenty in the Republic of Ireland who had misgivings too. 'The prospect of a referendum has put the fear of God into a lot of people in the South, who are thinking, goodness me. You know? I was at a rugby match with a Fianna Fáil chum and we were talking about this and he said it will be fifty years away. And I said, no, a lot sooner than that. There may be a lack of enthusiasm but it would be hard for the South to turn its face against the national myth. A united Ireland is going to happen. It's just a question of when and how. Protestant Ulster has been a deeply insecure place culturally for quite some time. You have to just find a way to bust through that, that state of mind.'

'WHAT HAPPENS IF WE SAY YES?'

Derry is a city of two sides, the Cityside, which has a Catholic majority, and the Waterside, where the majority of the city's Protestants live. The River Foyle curves languorously between them, widening into a lough on its way to the Atlantic. The city has three bridges now. The oldest of them is Craigavon Bridge, named after James Craig, Lord Craigavon, Northern Ireland's first Prime Minister. Halfway across there is a plaque with the city's coat of arms, featuring a seated skeleton, elbow on knee, skull resting on hand, in a dungeon. The Foyle Bridge, arching tall and cantilevered over a wide stretch of the river, links Derry with Belfast along a rackety, dangerous country road that was for decades a symbol of Stormont's neglect of the North's second city. It is finally being upgraded to a dual carriageway. Sadly, volunteers from Foyle Search and Rescue must patrol the river between the bridges, since the highest point of the Foyle Bridge has become a place all too often chosen for suicide by desperate people, most of them young men.

The Peace Bridge, for walkers and cyclists, was built in 2011 with European PEACE funding. Stretching from the old British army base, Ebrington Barracks, to the Guildhall and the old walled city, it has a self-consciously symbolic design. There are two half bridges, each suspended from an elegantly tilted steel pylon, with the pylons overlapping in the middle of the river to form, as the architects put it, 'a structural handshake'. Walking across it with my mother one day from the Waterside, we met a woman coming in the opposite direction with a terrier that had sat down precisely half way across and was stubbornly refusing to go any further. The woman said that this always happened. My mother said the dog must have strong politics, and the two of them laughed.

Kenny McFarland works in the village of Newbuildings, a few miles south along the river from the Waterside, on the road to Dublin. He is a big, friendly, bearded man, who runs the Ulster-Scots community association. His office has a distant view of the spires of Derry. 'It used to be in this city, a boy walked in that door there with a fiddle under his arm – he's a musician. A boy walked in with a side drum or a flute – he's a bigot,' he told me. 'We set up the Londonderry Bands Forum to change that.' He is the forum's chairman. 'I was always drumming mad. I'm from a family of drummers. I'd uncles and grandas who played, and I played the side drum. So when they started a flute band in Newbuildings way back in 1974, to me that was the dream. And that was how I got to know Northern Ireland, travelling around in a bus with the band.'

Ulster Scots was not something that was talked about, McFarland said, before the Good Friday Agreement gave it status. 'We didn't even appreciate half the words that we talked, that nobody else in the world knows about, like "redding up" and "thran" and stuff like that,' he said. 'Redding up' means vigorously tidying or sorting out. 'Thran' means stubborn, determined, wayward. Used pejoratively it means mulishly obdurate. 'We were never taught any local history at all so we never knew about the Scottish influence in the city,' McFarland said. 'We had no concept of who the hell came over here, and what actually happened.' The Bands Forum was set up in 2010 to promote Ulster-Scots culture, and got EU PEACE funds as well as grants from the International Fund for Ireland and the Irish Department of Foreign Affairs.

It was all a far cry from the small band McFarland joined when he was a boy, suddenly 'dumped' with his family in a place he now describes as having been 'a well-built refugee camp'. His Protestant family had been living in a gate lodge close to the edge of the Catholic Bogside, which became an epicentre of the Troubles from 1969 onwards. 'I suppose it was sort of exciting for an eight- or nine-year-old. But in '71 we had to move. There was madness going on. The back door was booby-trapped, the Scout hall was attacked, and then just the bombs, the rioting, the shootings,' he said. 'I remember someone saying, "Your mother nearly had a nervous breakdown." One day I went out to play and a woman came out of her house and said, nobody's allowed to play with you.

'Then one day I was at school and somebody came into the classroom and said, Ken McFarland, go to the office and take your bag. And when I went in my father was standing there. I said, what's wrong? He said, we have a house in Newbuildings. I didn't even go back to class. We just disappeared. I woke up in one house and went to bed in another.' A lot of the family's new neighbours were also Protestants moving out of the Catholic side of Derry. 'There was nothing here. It was sad for people.' Newbuildings was essentially a new town for displaced Protestants. Over the years it gained a bad reputation for sectarianism. During the Drumcree years there were some ugly incidents, including one in which a man and his son were dragged from their car as they passed through the village on their way to Derry. In the summertime there are a lot of flags. McFarland said that the reputation was undeserved, the flags were well managed and that he did not accept that they were intimidating.

Joining the band had given him a sense of purpose, he said. 'People don't realise, bands just want to be the best. You can call us Orange "B"s all day, that'll not really bother us. But if you turned round and called the William King a better band than ours, that would enrage us. People say, why do you burn Lundy? It's really nothing to do with us. We get hired and we just turn up for the parading. Some bands are connected to the Orange but a lot of the bands would be independent: bands like the Churchill that has been going 185 years. The Hamilton and the Britannia have been going over 150. Yet people treat us as if we only started twenty years ago to annoy Catholics.'

He said the 'kick the Pope' bands that specialised in thumping out rowdy sectarian tunes, preferably when Catholics were in earshot, were a thing of the past. 'The band community has moved on. Those rough-and-ready bands that are untidy and drunk, they're not even tolerated in their own community. People want to portray a positive image with discipline and good music. At the end of the day, we do it because we love music. We love the marching. What we were doing in the community was a lot more positive than what anybody was ever saying. You know, we had young people who had real problems and then they came into the band, and it was about discipline and it was about respecting yourself, your family, the band and your community.'

The 2013 All-Ireland Fleadh in Derry had been a great turning point. Fleadhs were a nationalist tradition. The organisers had invited unionist bands to participate. 'It was really strange going into a meeting that republicans had asked you to. I was thinking, you are the people that wrecked this city. Then we were talking about it among ourselves after, and we were saying, look, we have incredible musicians and this is about music. When they asked us they more than likely expected us to say no. What happens if we say yes? So we did, and it really showed how powerful culture can be if it's used positively, because it changed this town,' he said. 'It showed that the people are twenty years ahead of the politicians.'

McFarland said that because some major funders for community initiatives require projects to be cross-community, Protestant activists were in high demand. 'In this council area it is 20 per cent Protestant and when a group needs 48 per cent Protestant involvement, we get a lot of invitations,' he said sardonically. He was involved in other cultural initiatives, including the New Gate festival. I attended one of its debates in a big church hall in the Waterside, at which Sinn Féin's Mary Lou McDonald was the key invited speaker. 'There's never been a great thing within Protestantism about debating, not even amongst ourselves never mind with other people. And it is a missing element. We really need to sit down and ask ourselves who we are, and what are we about,' he said.

'When I was going to school I used to see written on a wall: "Do not forsake the blue skies of Ulster for the grey mists of the Irish Republic." But that's all I learned. Even today I don't think there's enough debate within the controlled education sector about getting young people to think and be challenged. We do a lot of talks but it's mostly in the maintained sector.' Controlled schools are state schools largely attended by Protestants; maintained schools are managed by the Catholic church. 'Our leaders have always taught us working-class people that we need to know our place, and it is at the bottom. We still struggle to break that, and it leaves our community at a massive disadvantage. I was one of the people who was marched up to the top of the hill with the DUP and Paisley and marched down again. That makes me sad.' Paisley had been known as the Grand Old Duke of York for this infamous practice of riling people up to militancy with fearful warnings, only to abandon them.

'But things are better now. Not perfect, but a hell of a lot better. We are living in a different world. There's a generation coming through who see social issues as important, and they're not interested in the constitutional question,' he said. He believed the DUP had lost a lot of votes in Derry and elsewhere because people were angry and frustrated about how the nurses and other workers had been treated. 'We want normal politics. That's what the politicians should be fighting about. I mean, I have family who'll maybe never vote for a united Ireland, but they'll not vote for the DUP either.

'When I was a teenager here in Newbuildings, we wouldn't have gone across the river into the town. I used to say to my kids when they were going over there, watch yourself, and they had no idea what I was talking about. Nowadays we have people who go out and do a band parade, go home and get changed and go out to a bar in Waterloo Street or go across the town and it's the most natural thing in the world.' Waterloo Street is a steep street leading into the Bogside from the city centre. It is where the bars are that play Irish music. During the Troubles there was a checkpoint on it. Protestants rarely went there.

'It took me to get to a certain age to realise some of the nonsense we went through,' McFarland said. 'What's really good is that there are a lot of people out there saying, see fighting and war and all that? We have done that, boys, don't go down there. I think there's a different mentality in this city than in Belfast. There's a great pride down here about coming from here, whether we call it Londonderry or Derry. People just were fed up with the wrecking and tearing. That's why you hope they actually get their act together and govern this country and make it something, because it's young people that you worry about. Where do they go from here?'

'HOW SWEET THE SOUND'

In May 2019, student nurse Brittany McArthur sang at the bedside of eighty-seven-year-old Nellie Barr in a ward at Altnagelvin Hospital in Derry. She sang 'Amazing Grace' and her rendition of it was so ethereal, so beautiful, that Nellie's grandson, a local SDLP councillor, recorded it on his phone and shared it on social media. Coming as it did just weeks after the death of Lyra McKee in the hospital, it seemed powerfully healing.

'I've been singing since I was tiny,' she told me. 'I was Mary in the nativity play. I learned to read music when I was three or four. I learned to sing and read music by ear. My granny recognised that I had a voice. She always wanted me to take lessons and after she passed away I did. I love it. I would have sung solos in the church regularly, though I hated singing in front of people, and I am still not keen. I get very nervous. I'm a trained classical singer. I taught myself piano, guitar and ukulele. In school I played cornet and euphonium. I learned ukulele in half an hour. I learn things practically, by doing them.' She lists her talents not boastfully but in a matter-of-fact way.

'I was born in the Altnagelvin hospital and now I work there. I sing at work on a regular basis. You'd be surprised how much it helps, especially with dementia,' she said. 'That particular day I was working in a thirty-one-bed ward and it was an elderly lady who wasn't well. I had never met her before. I just sang for her. I didn't know it was being filmed. I went on my break and there were all kinds of messages. Her grandson thanked me and said, I hope you don't mind me sharing this. I hate attention and I nearly died when I saw the video and saw it had 10,000 views. It was shown in America, Australia and Canada; the *Derry Journal* had it, the English papers and the TV. There were over 140,000 views of the original and 181,000 when it was on Fox news. I got an approach from an agency in England but I'm far too self-conscious to sing professionally. Anyway, it would take the fun out of it. And I want to be a nurse, not a singer.

'I was brought up to respect other people's views. Like, I call the town Derry or Londonderry – whatever. But at work I usually ask them what they prefer because some people take exception. Especially if someone has a head injury. Mum's dad was from a mixed family, half-Protestant, half-Catholic; Dad was Protestant. I was brought up Church of Ireland. I was a worship leader at church. I moved to a more contemporary church recently – it is non-denominational. I grew up in Ballykelly, which was very definitely a community sort of place. Doors were never locked, we lived in a cul-de-sac and there were lots of children so you just played out. Ballykelly Primary School was very mixed. We had army kids from the barracks too and I was friends with some of them. A family from Slovakia moved in and I am still in touch with the girls. It makes no odds to me what religion anyone is or where they are from. It doesn't come up for me – I honestly never think about it. You are still a person, regardless of your religion – I don't see why it matters.

Ballykelly, stretched out along the road between Derry and Coleraine, is a mixed town. During the Troubles the British army took over a 1941 RAF base and set up Shackleton Barracks, with a fenced-in and guarded housing estate for soldiers and their families, and another, with bigger houses, for officers. The estates were abandoned when the army left. The fortifications removed, in 2010 people queued for days to buy the houses, which were strikingly cheap. Among those who moved in were a couple who had been homeless and living in a tent. A new bar

and restaurant called The Well has been built on the site of the Droppin'
Well bar, scene of the 1982 atrocity.

It was a great town to grow up in, according to Brittany. In her
remarkable memoir, *Thin Places*, Kerri ní Dochartaigh describes it with
similar warmth. Her parents' marriage had been mixed, although, she
wrote, 'The truth is, we had *never* been either of these things – Protestant
or Catholic – and to live in Derry in the '90s and to have neither of
these words to fall back on left you in a harrowing hole of a place.'[1]
Once her parents divorced, the family was 'not Protestant' and got
burned out of the estate in the Waterside where they had been living.
But ní Dochartaigh relates that when they moved to an estate on the
other side of the river they found that because her mother had married
a Protestant, they were no longer Catholic enough either.

As 'nothing other than other' her mother moved with the children to
Ballykelly. 'It was like a whole other world entirely,' wrote ní Dochartaigh.
'It was quiet there, and calm, a kind of place I had never known before.
Everyone knew each other, and friendships there seemed to be above
any idea of difference.'[2]

'I was always in everything. I love working with people,' Brittany said.
'I went to Sunday School and taught at it after confirmation when I was
twelve. I was in Rainbows, Brownies, and Guides senior section – I've
done them all. I did kick-boxing too. All these things were available in
Ballykelly or up the road in Limavady. My parents were very open-
minded – they encouraged me to try everything. I was in Irish dancing
for eleven years – I only left because I'd reached the highest level. My
brain needs a challenge. I have to be the best. One time I remember I
only got a pass in something and I was beside myself. I couldn't be lived
with!

'I was the first in my family to go to grammar school and university.
I went to Magee in Derry to do nursing. I applied to go to Scotland
and England, but we couldn't have afforded for me to go away. My
bursary wouldn't cover rent so it was stay at home or go into debt. So
I didn't get the "uni" experience but I got what I went for – to train as
a nurse. I'd started working once I got my national insurance number
at sixteen, and when I went to college I was working in Tesco on stock

1 Kerri ní Dochartaigh, *Thin Places*, Canongate, 2021, p. 66
2 Ibid., p. 90

control, and banking at the hospice and at Altnagelvin with a company. At sixteen I wanted a car – I saved up and paid my insurance.' (Banking means doing shift work.)

'I always doubt myself. I am an overthinker and I find it hard to make decisions in my own life, but as soon as I started I knew it was definitely for me. At Magee you cram a four-year course into three years, doing eighty or ninety hours a week in uni or on placement. I'm really determined. When I set my mind on a thing I am going to do it. At the end of first year I had a really bad car accident and lost movement in my left arm. I didn't take time out. I got physiotherapy and all during the summer I worked my backside off. I never missed a day and I qualified with my class. After that I re-evaluated everything. I could have been dead at nineteen. I realised I don't know if I'll be here tomorrow – I need to live my life today, stop putting things off, do the things I want to do. I'd spent my life in church. I hadn't done the things my friends had done. I was very mature for my age – I grew up too quickly. I am too hard on myself. I still am but I have cut back a bit.

'After uni I went straight into Altnagelvin. You come across difficult situations – you need to know how you are going to react. I am working in trauma and orthopaedics, and in all my placements I have never found something I wouldn't do. I want to work in cancer care and palliative care but it is so intense emotionally and physically. It might be I need another set of skills. I'll do what I'm doing now for at least a couple of years – I am getting a grounding. There is no typical day. On Christmas Day we had a woman with spinal fractures – we have road-traffic accidents, work accidents, elderly people who have fallen.

'Nurses don't get recognition for what they do,' said Brittany. 'I was striking with the rest of my colleagues – we did everything to make sure people were safe. We went on the pickets for an hour at a time and all the time you were out you were thinking, oh my goodness, I hope so and so is okay. The main issue was staffing levels – there is no legislation on what is safe. There are days if you have really sick patients you have to prioritise tasks rather than the nice things. If we had more staff we could give a higher level of care.

'We didn't want to do it but it made people listen. None of us went into nursing for the pay. I know people who have a handful of GCSEs and they make double what I get without having had to spend all that time training. There are nurses going to food banks and working their backside off. I work four days one week and three the next, doing twelve-hour shifts, 8 to 8, morning or night. You don't always get two consecutive days off. It can vary. You don't get full breaks if you feel you need to do something, and you know, nurses are good-natured – I am in at 7.10 and doing handover at 7.30 for a shift that starts at 8,' she said.

I had attended one of the pickets. My notes got spattered with icy rain but the atmosphere was buoyant. The level of public support was obvious. Passing drivers blew their car horns and waved, and there was a stream of people arriving with boxes of food and flasks for the nurses. 'We can't do our job properly,' said one senior nurse. She was holding a placard that said, 'Save staffing, save lives'. 'This dysfunction has been years in the making. It is heartbreaking and we are tired. Nurses are leaving their shifts in tears.' A local DUP politician had turned up at the picket that morning and had been photographed, smiling beside the strikers. 'It is interesting to see politicians who voted for absence of parity standing as if in solidarity,' Brittany said with a wry smile.

'We are nurses because we care,' she said. 'It takes at least three years to train a nurse and I am continually learning while I work. There is never a day I go into work that I don't find someone with something new to tell me – there are always new medications, new people, new procedures. For the first six months you do courses. There is a shortage of nurses. It takes a while to increase numbers – you have to have a mixture of newly-qualified and experienced people. Nurses who were off duty came on the pickets. Everyone was behind us. We got pizza and tea and food all day. The patients were all so supportive.'

She was abashed at all the attention she got after the video of her singing went viral. 'It makes me out to be really great but I'm not – lots of nurses and carers do these things. It is the small things that matter to people when they are in a bad way. They remember,' she said. She quoted the poet Maya Angelou: 'I've learned that people will forget what you said, people will forget what you did, but people will never forget how you made them feel.'

Nine months after I met with Brittany, with one wave of the COVID pandemic over and another one building, a doctor at the hospital said it was 'like a war zone' and a union representative had said staff were approaching breaking-point.

'WE TRY TO COUNT OUR BLESSINGS'

Beth arranged to meet me after her shift but warned me she couldn't always tell what time she'd finish. She is a critical care nurse and has recently been promoted. 'I now manage a very weary team of orthopaedic nurses who've been moved around to deal with staff shortages and who are drained,' she said. 'Everyone is weary, me included. We try to count our blessings – after all, we are employed. The NHS might kill us, but at least in the meantime it pays us!'

A major survey by the Royal College of Nurses in August 2020 found that 76 per cent of nurses had experienced increased stress during the pandemic, while 33 per cent were working longer hours, mostly without getting paid for them, and the same proportion had been required to take more responsibility, again without extra pay. Asked what was needed to make them feel more valued, the main issues were those that the strike had been based on – pay and staffing levels.[3]

'A lot of staff are sick or shielding, so the only way to manage is to redeploy people,' said Beth. 'Every day is a roller coaster. You go through all the emotions. Sometimes you think, oh, today is going to be upbeat, and then by 11 a.m. you are exhausted and it just all seems impossible. But you have to get on with it. I'll be sixty in a few years and I'm tired but I won't be able to afford to retire for quite a few years yet. I've a mortgage to pay, I'm divorced, and I've children still at secondary school. I had what they describe as a mild case of COVID myself very early on. I was as sick as I have ever been.

'I'm from Derry and I spent my childhood here, though I have also worked in most of the hospitals in Belfast over the years. My parents were working-class people, Protestants living on a street where a lot of their neighbours were Catholics. They just believed in being neighbourly. Nothing was instilled in us in terms of sectarianism or anything like that. My parents were Alliance voters. They were kind, quite timid people. They'd never had any ambition to be rich. As a child I always wanted to be a nurse or an archaeologist.

'I nursed during the Troubles, which, looking back, was pretty horrific. We were dealing with gunshot wounds and burns from explosions. I remember a young guy who had been shot through both elbows and

---

3 https://www.rcn.org.uk/news-and-events/news/UK-Passionate-but-pushed-to-the-limit-COVID-19-200820

both knees and he was just screaming and screaming and cursing and his mother was with him. What do you say? It was a very different situation back then – you had no aftercare for nurses, no debriefings after major incidents. You never even showed your fear. You just did what sister told you to do. You just got on with it. Nowadays there is more recognition that people need to talk and process these experiences.'

Beth had found her experience in one hospital quite soul-destroying. 'The team that I was in was great but it began to get more and more stretched. We all just had too much responsibility and for patients who needed intensive care. It became dog eats dog. Our Accident and Emergency Department was closed. Our specialities were taken away. It all became overwhelming. I left for a better-paid job in a private clinic but I didn't like it. The NHS is where it is at. It's a high-tech environment and it is where lives are saved.

'It is a bit horrendous right now with cuts and huge waiting lists and pretty awful working conditions, and that is very stressful. We really do have to go over and beyond the call of duty. Sometimes you don't have time to take a toilet break. There are afternoons when I suddenly realise I have had nothing to eat but a banana and I haven't drunk any water all day. Sometimes you meet a colleague in the corridor and ask her how she is and she just starts ranting. Then maybe a day or so later she asks you the same and you let loose a rant yourself. There is a lot of ranting. People have no idea how hard we have to work to keep the whole system running. Then you get an MLA ringing demanding to know why their constituent isn't getting their operation. The waiting lists weigh heavy on the NHS. We are under pressure, never mind new waves of COVID.

'There is a lot of anger. The nurses were out on the picket lines looking for equal pay and a safer NHS and there is no doubt but that the public supported them. People were disgusted. You had the Assembly lying empty and MLAs drawing huge salaries and not working while the nurses were slogging their guts out in the hospitals. I think a lot of nurses were on a bit of a high when the strike ended because they got a bit of a pay rise, but COVID has wrecked us. When I was a young nurse you didn't answer back – now young nurses want a better work-life balance and they are not getting it.

'I got married at twenty-one,' she said with a big sigh. 'We would have been Christians.' She laughed. 'My husband's family was Presbyterian and they saw my family as half-Catholic because we were Church of Ireland. At that age you think you are going to change the world and you are going to do this and do that.' She shook her head. 'I stopped going to church long ago but I went through a wee phase of going back to church when the children were younger. One of those trendy churches with flags. I thought about Buddhism too. But then I realised, no, I don't believe in any of this. It is hard to relinquish that old Protestant guilt – but it is actually a release when you do.

'I don't describe myself as unionist. I'm not British and I'm not Irish. I'm Northern Irish. I don't see myself as part of the UK, really. I don't have much of a problem with the idea of a united Ireland. The NHS is the only thing. It is a bit horrendous but you don't realise how good it is until you look at other countries that don't have it. I'd never vote for the DUP or the UUP, oh gosh no. I would vote socialist if there is someone to vote for. My children are far more middle class than me. I call them yuppies. My son is a unionist and my daughter *says* she is but I don't see it in what she says. They are very smart and opinionated. They fight about politics and I had to ban all talk of politics at dinner because of the rows about Brexit. I was sick of having to be the peacemaker.

'Before COVID I thought life was pretty good here. I envied my children, the life they had, able to go into the city and drink coffee and go dancing. I went to an exhibition of Troubles photography with my daughter and it made me so angry and upset to remember, getting trailed through town through bomb scares, all the fear and the terrible things that were happening all the time. Our lives were so ruined, so stunted. If I'd had more freedom I wonder what I might have done with my life.' She stopped, laughed ruefully. 'Our generation has a lot of mental health issues, especially people who were involved in the Troubles. We have a lot of suppressed rage.'

'I CAN STAND NO MORE'

The first Saturday in December is known to the Apprentice Boys of Derry as 'Lundy's Day', though this is something of a misnomer, since Lundy is not celebrated but hung on a scaffold and burned. This is the anniversary of the day in 1688 when the thirteen apprentices shut the gates of the city, starting the siege. The 'Relief of Derry' parades are held in August to mark the ending of the siege in 1689. In 2019 the August event had been marred by the provocative behaviour of the Clyde Valley Flute Band from Larne, which had worn armbands with Parachute Regiment emblems. The Apprentice Boys had apologised for the incident and the Larne band had been instructed to stay away in December. The trial of Soldier F, now in his seventies, was still pending, and was to be held in the courthouse, which overlooks the spot where Lundy is burned.

The atmosphere was subdued as people gathered on stately Bishop Street, which has some of Derry's most elegant Georgian houses as well as the courthouse, Saint Columb's cathedral and the Bishop's Palace. A robed chaplain looked nervously about the assembling crowd. As usual, there were excitable youths with cans of lager, but I saw just one empty Buckfast bottle in a gutter. There was nothing like the level of drunkenness I'd witnessed in 1999 when I had last attended the burning of Lundy. White gloves and bowler hats; banners from deepest Ulster places, like Plumbridge and Caw, Blackskull and Castlederg; the bands with their archaic names – the Burntollet Sons of Ulster, the Dungiven Crown Defenders, the Red Hand Defenders Newtownstewart. I saw Dale Pankhurst looking proud and happy in the hat he had described to me with its remarkable sideways hackle, like a spurt of orange flame. The girls in one band wore glittery reindeer horns. One man marched with a little bag from a Derry jeweller's shop in his hand.

Lundy dangled on the scaffold, gazing down Shipquay Street across the city to the River Foyle where the blockade had been. The dignitaries returned from laying wreathes at the war memorial and it was time for the annual Apprentice Boys church service. The cathedral has a display of cannonballs, including the one thrown into the city with the terms of the proposed, and duly rejected, surrender. They also have the tattered remains of a crimson flag that was hung from the tower during the siege, to signal distress. I was ushered into one of the last seats, a velvet upholstered chair meant for a dignitary, with a fine view of the vaulted grandeur of the place, solemnly hung with vast old faded flags.

The service was taken by the Reverend William Orr from Portadown. He had brought young people from his Flute Band Church, which he had set up, he explained, after realising that many of the young boys in his community had no fathers to guide them. He spoke of Moses in the book of Exodus, who had murdered the taskmaster at forty and then spent forty years as a shepherd. 'He thought his days were over. How could you use a murderer at eighty?' he said, and then talked about the men who he said come to him in his study to confess their violent pasts. 'I say, if you repent, you can start again,' he said.

The children in the band struck up the music from *Popeye*, and then the minister quoted the rough and muscular cartoon sailor. 'When Popeye had enough, when he had been pushed over the edge, he'd say, "That's all I can stand, I can stand no more," and then he'd beat someone up,' he said. He compared this to 'holy discontent'. 'Jerusalem is in ruins,' he quoted from the book of Nehemiah. 'I sat down and wept.' Orr referred to his own past as a bandsman. 'When I was running about wild and maybe with liquid refreshment, I was a believer but I wasn't saved,' he said, and he appealed to those present to assure their own salvation for which Jesus had died on the cross. 'Ask yourself, what have you got in your hand?' he said, and urged them to use whatever it was to help build the Kingdom of God.

Back out on the wide street it was time to deal with the traitor. The face of the effigy looked alive, its kohl-rimmed eyes scared and sorrowful, the crimson lips fixed in a lipsticked smile under the jet-black moustache. There was the scent of petrol, then a whoosh of flame. Agitated by the wind, bits of Lundy's blazing coat fluttered like fiery oak leaves out over the crowd. Bandsmen and boys posed for selfies, mobiles upheld, then swept sparks from their hair, laughing and cursing. Through the flames and the smoke and the heat haze, you could see the war memorial in the Diamond, lit up like the battle scene it depicted, the First World War soldier in his greatcoat plunging his bayonet into the body of an enemy.

In 2020 Derry was in lockdown for Lundy's Day, but the Apprentice Boys upheld the tradition nevertheless. A friend sent me a video. '*Handmaid's Tale* vibes', he captioned it. Thirteen men wearing Apprentice Boys sashes stood solemnly around the perimeter of a small car park between a steel fence and the city walls. The scaffold was on a parking space but Lundy had not been hoisted up so he appeared to be standing. There was sombre silence but for one sudden raucous burst of laughter from someone as the flames devoured the face and the dark hair of the traitor. Stripped of the bands and the crowds, it did indeed look like a scene from Margaret Atwood's dystopian novel about a biblically-driven patriarchy.

'LILLIBURLERO BULLEN A LA'

Catherine Pollock has been mad about Rangers football club since she was a child. She used to be happy to chant, 'We are the people!' with the rest of the fans, but nowadays, knowing it represents the supremacist boast that the Protestants of Northern Ireland are, like the biblical Israelites, the chosen people, it makes her uncomfortable. It no longer fits with the life she leads. If one of her brothers sends her a family photo with 'WATP!' under it, as they sometimes do, she knows it is meant affectionately, but always replies, 'Yes, we *are* the Pollocks.'

'We've developed a good model for parading and it is several years since there was any violence,' Pollock told me. 'Protestants in Derry are the minority, and at some point somebody in the Apprentice Boys must have realised, we need to have some kind of arrangement or this is unsustainable. So they worked with nationalist groups. At the Fleadh in 2013, Martin McGuinness stood on a stage in front of thousands of people and said the parades were part of the cultural fabric of the city and that the nationalist community had no problem with them continuing.'

Pollock is a community worker and was involved in the initiative to engage Protestants in the Fleadh. 'The bands were the most visible symbols of unionist culture in the city, and that's why they were asked,' she said. 'It was a bit tetchy at first but then it became about music, that's where the change came. During the Fleadh, this band got up on stage and they played 'Lilliburlero'. I remember this sort of almighty roar came from behind me, and people clapping. And these musicians were visibly a bit moved and a bit shaken by this really rapturous welcome that they got.' 'Lilliburlero' is mostly played as a rousing instrumental piece though it is a Williamite ballad, with the opening lines, 'Ho Brother Teague, dost hear the decree, Lilli Burlero Bullen a la, Dat we shall have a new Debittie …'[4] It is popular with loyalist marching bands. Scott McKendry, who has written about the song in his doctoral thesis, comments on the way the song uses a pastiche form of Hiberno-English to ridicule the Irish, and compares this with

---

4 https://ebba.english.ucsb.edu/ballad/31637/xml

Gregory Campbell's 'curry my yogurt' comment three centuries later. The ballad includes a line about cutting the throats of the English, but the Fleadh exchange between the musicians and their largely nationalist audience was entirely good-natured.

Pollock was born in 1981. 'Five days before Bobby Sands died,' she said. She remembers soldiers with guns and bomb scares and hearing about the IRA, but she was sheltered in the Tullyally estate in Drumahoe, a community that was almost entirely Protestant, on the outskirts of Derry's Waterside. The Greysteel atrocity, which happened when she was eleven, troubled her because she understood that the killers were from her people. 'It was the fear that you might know somebody who was involved in doing it,' she said.

At Halloween in 1993, a four-man UDA gang burst into the Rising Sun Bar in the small village of Greysteel, between Derry and Ballykelly. One of them shouted 'trick or treat' as they opened fire. Eight people aged between nineteen and eight-one were killed. It was one of the last multiple killings before the ceasefires of 1994. A photograph taken of one of the gunmen, Torrens Knight, after he was charged with the murders, became one of the most chilling images of the conflict. His mouth was wide open as he screamed abuse at those watching, his face distorted with rage. Although he has since become a born-again Christian, there are those who still celebrate the massacre on social media sites.

'Before that, it was very simple for me, as a child,' said Pollock. 'We were the goodies and they were the baddies, you know: the state, the police, the army were obviously good, and the IRA were terrorists. Then suddenly to realise an organisation that's supposed to be on the Protestant side could do something like that ... it made me uneasy.'

Pollock had also started grammar school by then. 'All of a sudden you had a community that was mixed, Catholics and Protestants. There were people who felt different to you and people with Irish names. I was mad about football, and I can remember one of the Catholic lads in the class being like, You only support Rangers 'cos you're Protestant. And I named him the fifteen people in the Celtic squad that season,' she said. He was properly impressed. Having grown up a church- and Sunday School-going Presbyterian, as a teenager she began to rebel against the conservatism of the church's social teaching. 'We were told we had to be virtuous: no drinking, no sex before marriage, gays were going to hell … I said to my mother, "I'm not going any more," and she said "That's fine," and I thought, after all these years, is that all it took?

'The version of history that we were taught at school was the bog-standard planter version: very British, colonialism and all the lovely things that "we" brought to the world,' she said. Then she went to university in England. 'I went to Middlesborough, which was very like Derry. On the up a bit, but still poverty everywhere, and this conflict between communities as well, of working-class people. There was a big influx of Pakistanis and Indians and obviously the whole history of the miners there. The politics was definitely Labour. Some of my lecturers were quite lefty and I learned about rehabilitative approaches to crime, that sort of thing. I didn't realise I had any politics of my own until I was talking with this guy in a bar after a student conference around the time Tony Blair was bluffing people into supporting the Iraq war, and I said, "Well, someone needs to go and save those people from that man," meaning Saddam Hussein. And he said to me, "I can't believe that I'm trying to explain to a woman from Northern Ireland why war is a bad idea." I began realising that actually governments lie and the police and the army are not always the kind of white knights that you think they are.'

She'd left Derry in 1999 and she returned in 2005. 'The place was very different, easier to move around and mix with people,' she said. Her first job was with an organisation that worked to resettle ex-prisoners on a community safety project back in her own area as well as in the neighbouring Catholic estate. 'The project looked at issues we had in common, like dog shit and streetlights, rather than focussing on the interface and how different we were. It's a good way of working. I loved it. It did really well for a couple of years, and then it didn't. Short-term funding's always an issue, because you lose people. There's no long-term strategy. And then people are so bound up in form-filling, that you stop doing the advocacy and the relationship building, and it just gets bogged down.'

One of her next jobs was in the Gasyard, a community facility in Derry's Bogside and Brandywell area. It was a Catholic area, and strongly republican. Again, she felt her cultural certainties shake: 'You realise there's another perspective. I think three out of four of my teammates had been in jail, had been in the IRA. Their politics were in ways probably closer to mine than loads of people I knew at home.' She bought a house in the Fountain estate, the last remaining enclave of working-class Protestants within the old walled city. There is a mural outside it that says, 'Londonderry West Bank Loyalists Still Under Siege No Surrender'.

'My mum and dad did worry that me putting my head above the parapet while living in a loyalist area like that was a bit risky. They worried about my windows coming in. There are times when things happen, and you feel really uncomfortable. Like when Parachute Regiment flags go up, or recently when they put up a banner saying: "Fountain residents support our troops". Well, actually I'm very anti-war and I am a Fountain resident.' She doesn't like political bonfires. 'I find them aggressive. I don't like the burning of peoples' faces and posters and effigies of people. And that's on all sides. I just don't like the atmosphere around them. Among young people who are disadvantaged and excluded from society, I can understand why that's a way of, you know, saying screw you to the system.'

She fears that after years of good work bringing about better relationships, old tensions are reappearing. Divisions over the issue of 'Soldier F' were deepening. 'Relationships were really frayed after the incident at the August Lundy parade, and some of the groups who've worked together for years are still struggling,' she said. 'The unionist side sees this really energetic campaign to have him tried, and they see it almost as a slight on their community. And the other side, the nationalist and republican side, are like, but this is about justice. You know, if he behaved criminally then he should face prosecution like anybody else. On most issues I can see people going, all right, we're at different places on that. This one, there just doesn't seem to be any kind of softening or acceptance that the other might have a legitimate perspective.'

Pollock works for the community group Cultúrlann now, which promotes culture through the Irish language. 'A lot of my close relations always vote DUP, and some might even vote UKIP,' she said. 'When the Irish language act became a big issue, on one hand I was arguing with my family or my friends or people from the unionist community that it was a language that belonged so us all, it wasn't some Trojan horse. And then I was going back into work and Irish language speakers were being really negative about how those people felt. And I was saying to them, no, but you have to understand how little they know about the language, how it's been portrayed to them for years, how they don't have any ownership of it, you know. I felt like I was just fighting with everybody for a while.'

It is time to get away from the old model of the two cultures, Pollock believes. 'I do think that structures, like government structures and community relation structures, have reinforced it: that's yours and that's theirs. So, *you* paint yourself that colour, and *you* paint yourself that colour. We need to start undoing that. We all have ancestors that spoke Irish, and all our families have had hybrid marriages. There are loads of people in the middle, like me. I think there are difficult things coming. The border and Brexit is going to be massive. It worries me that unionism is unprepared for the conversation about a united Ireland. I just want peace. The suggestion that loyalists could take to violence I find unacceptable. Because if you're a democrat and the democratic will of the people is to have a united Ireland, then so be it. I don't see much of a difference in Dublin or London, I think I'll be poor no matter if the border's there or not.'

She's learning Irish herself and her children go to an Irish-medium school. Her children also take part in music sessions organised by the Bands Forum. She described 12 August, the day the Relief of Derry is celebrated, 'You just see everybody you know, from your granny to your cousin to all of my friends and their kids … it's just the best day's craic. There might be a barbecue, they get chips, they get sweets, they get to bang a drum in someone's front garden. Like, what's not to love? I don't want my kids to feel they have to choose between one Derry and another. There are so many Derrys. I want them to know they can have all of them.'

EPILOGUE

'This Country'

On the first of July, Susan Clarke and her family move to London to start a new life. They've had enough is what Susan's mum says. She just can't take it any more. 'This country,' she says to my mum.

'This country,' my mum says back to her, and neither of them says anything else.[1]

This is the beginning of Lucy Caldwell's moving short story 'Thirteen'. Caldwell, from Belfast, living in London, wrote with clear-eyed sensitivity about what it was like to grow up in Northern Ireland in the 1990s, sparing neither the squalor nor the glory. During the conflict, that phrase, 'this country', served as a way of avoiding rows. It was generally accompanied by a deep sigh, a shaking of the head, and a tightening of the lips. The tacit agreement was that there was nothing further to be said, meaning there was far, far too much to be said, and it wouldn't make a bit of difference.

Today, given that political violence has, to a huge extent, stopped, 'this country' signals a less desolate but still persistent frustration. Tempers still flare too readily. Northern Ireland is now a place in which, as Jean Bleakney put it, the ground is shifting. There is a new border, in the Irish Sea, as well as the one-hundred-year-old one, across the country. Both are at the heart of campaigns for constitutional change. Unionism feels profoundly threatened. Yet while writing this book I met many people who are living reconciled lives as envisaged in the Good Friday Agreement, and who are determined to make this place

---

1 Lucy Caldwell, from 'Thirteen', in *Multitudes,* Faber, 2016, p. 11

work for its many communities, whatever the constitutional future. I think of Stephen Donnan-Dalzell's tattoo: 'Do not tell me there is no such thing as hope.'

Sarah Creighton referred to Caldwell's use of the phrase 'this country' in a blog for the website Slugger O'Toole.[2] Creighton is a young Belfast lawyer working for a housing rights organisation in Belfast, and an insightful political commentator. Her blog was about a struggle familiar to many who are eager to participate in democracy, but cannot readily find a political home in Northern Ireland. 'This country', she wrote, is 'wee, awkward, mad' and apparently 'stuck in the dark ages'. But, she added, 'Every time I leave Northern Ireland, I long to return. When I go to Britain, the "mainland", I don't fit in. They think I'm a "paddy"... I don't see myself in the Republic ... There's no place for me there.' So although she rages at it and hates it at times, she writes, 'I belong here ... I feel proud of it.'

Hers is a contemporary expression of the feelings John Hewitt expressed in 'An Irishman in Coventry' after Belfast's provincially-minded arts establishment effectively banished him to England in 1957 by declining to employ him. The poem rails against all the ways in which Ireland, in which he includes the North, defeats itself: 'endlessly betrayed/ by our own weakness'. But it ends, 'Yet like Lir's children, banished to the waters,/ our hearts still listen for the landward bells.'[3]

On the north-west border between Derry and Donegal, Rebecca Crockett talked to me about a very particular sense of belonging. 'I'm just from here,' she said. 'I'm just from the border, really. I don't have any connection to England and I don't really have a connection to Ireland ... I wouldn't say I'm loyal to a flag or a government or anything. I'm more loyal to people.' At seventeen, she had a strong sense of the need to respect the experience of those who, like her father, had lived through the conflict, while at the same time looking at urgent issues that need attention today. Foremost among them for her and many other young people is the climate movement: 'Nothing can change if we aren't here to change it.'

---

2 Sarah Creighton, https://sluggerotoole.com/2020/08/15/northern-ireland-centenary-this-country/

3 John Hewitt, *Selected Poems*, eds Michael Longley and Frank Ormsby, Blackstaff Press, 2007, pp. 53–4

One community activist who is doing transformational work in a typical working-class Protestant community – neglected by mainstream unionism, dominated by paramilitaries – told me that for her the constitutional issue was distorting what was important. 'It's a twentieth-century question for a twenty-first-century situation,' she said. Like Rebecca, she felt climate was the most urgent issue, but she also recognised that local community solidarity was a prerequisite for global change.

John Hewitt's magnificent poem 'The Coasters' describes the placidity and complacency of middle-class unionists in the years leading up to the Troubles. These were people who were prospering. They would vote without feeling the need to contribute to political thinking, secure in the knowledge that the outcome was a foregone conclusion: 'The government permanent, sustained/ by the regular plebiscites of loyalty.'[4] The DUP, having so convincingly routed the UUP, fell into that old complacency, taking for granted its position as the dominant unionist party, and the dominant party in the mandatory coalition at Stormont.

In his book on the renewable heating scandal, *Burned*, journalist Sam McBride made the point that the DUP's behaviour was evidence that the party's unionism was 'infused with Ulster nationalism' and always had been. 'The party prided itself on extracting what it could from London,' he said. It was a 'crude philosophy', based on a brazen sense of entitlement.[5] In the middle of a battle to try to get the government to accept that Northern Ireland must be governed in the same way as the rest of the UK, Foster had told Secretary of State Brandon Lewis to 'back off' when he demanded that British legislation on abortion be implemented by Stormont.[6]

The dominant narrative of post-Brexit Northern Ireland is that the unionist community is angry and alienated, has given too much and has been pushed too far, so that constitutional discussion that contemplates the possibility of change, particularly a poll on the border, is dangerous. One of the ugliest iterations of this was Peter Robinson's grim, and, he claimed, restrained, 'take care' instruction in a piece in which he claimed

---

4 Hewitt, pp. 71–73

5 Sam McBride, *Burned: The Inside Story of the 'Cash-for-Ash' Scandal and Northern Ireland's Secretive Elite*, Merrion Press, 2019, pp. 30–31

6 'Arlene Foster: Brandon Lewis should "back off" in Northern Ireland abortion row', *News Letter*, 25 March 2021

that there were 'forces' trying to 'advance a programme of constitutional change through stealth and propaganda'. He also claimed that 'unionists dwell under a cloud of injustice … they have gone beyond the second mile to facilitate a stable, peaceful and shared society'.[7] I thought of Gregory Campbell, MP, claiming that if nationalists got their desired Irish language act, he would use it as toilet paper.

Plenty of people from a northern Protestant background, including unionists, including even DUP unionists, are open-minded about identity and nationhood. That is because they are democrats, whether or not they support the GFA's commitment to recognising that, while substantial difference remains, people have the right to work on their 'equally legitimate political aspirations'. I was struck by DUP man Sammy Douglas's considered view that although people feared Irish unity, 'You could actually probably live quite peacefully in a united Ireland; it's just that the ten years of it becoming a united Ireland would probably be pretty awful.'

Feminists have long realised that they are seen by mainstream unionism as outsiders whose demands must be resisted, and that they, therefore, like Lir's children, still have no country in which to feel at home. In 2019, feminist unionist Sophie Long Tweeted a quote from Rebecca Johnson, the founding chair of the International Campaign to Abolish Nuclear Weapons, which won the 2017 Nobel Peace Prize. 'As a woman, my country is still being formed: by millions of feminist peacebuilders, sharing power and working for disarmament, peace, justice and – yes – control over our fertility and our sexuality, and over our minds and bodies.'[8]

On Belfast's Shankill Road, Eileen Weir and her colleagues are providing a chance for women who are rarely consulted about public decisions to develop their own ideas and gain the confidence to express them. She spoke with pride when she said, 'I think working-class women are streets ahead of anyone else when it comes to changing this place.' During the Easter riots of April 2021, I saw a photograph of a woman passing a bag of shopping to her friend under a newly locked gate on the peace line.

---

7 Peter Robinson, 'Unionists are more alienated than I have seen at any time in my 50 years in politics', *News Letter*, 26 March 2021

8 https://www.opendemocracy.net/en/5050/feminist-peacebuilding-courageous-intelligence/

Women are subverting patriarchal language that has for too long silenced them. On International Women's Day, 8 March 2021, I read a Tweet from courageous Toni Ogle whose father, Ian, had been murdered in 2019 by people from within his own loyalist community. She said she had been looking for a quote from a strong woman, and had then decided to speak out herself. 'If looking for justice for my father makes me a tout, I'm a tout,' she wrote.

'OLAF'

Political unionism is struggling with a crisis of identity. It ignored the poll that showed most Tories would rather 'get Brexit done' than hold on to Northern Ireland.[9] The 1921 lament of Edward Carson was widely quoted after the hard Brexit the DUP held out for brought about the border in the sea. Yes, unionists had been fools and puppets once again. They had allowed themselves to be used. The man whose statue stands in front of Stormont, still impatiently gesturing to the people to rise up, saw the six-county state as the failure of his ambitions. Tom Paulin, reviewing A. T. Q. Stewart's biography of Carson, described his famous speech as 'a spectacular example of the contradictory, self-pitying, childish and festering sense of grievance which is at the centre of the Loyalist mentality'.[10]

In 1985 the Ulster Unionist MP Harold McCusker described his reaction to the Anglo-Irish Agreement: 'I stood outside Hillsborough, not waving a Union flag – I doubt whether I will ever wave one again – not singing hymns, saying prayers or protesting, but like a dog and asked the government to put in my hand the document that sold my birthright.'[11] In 1986, Ian Paisley Snr got over 100,000 Protestants, unionists and loyalists out into the centre of Belfast to hear him declare that civil war was imminent and to call on God to take vengeance on Prime Minister Margaret Thatcher. He and his deputy, Peter Robinson, had donned the red berets of the movement they called Ulster Resistance.

In the last five years of the 1990s, the Orange Order presided over a protest at Drumcree that it described as its last stand, its Alamo. This was

9 https://yougov.co.uk/topics/politics/articles-reports/2019/11/11/four-ten-mainland-britons-dont-care-about-northern

10 Tom Paulin, *Writing to the Moment*, Faber, 1996, p. 49

11 HC Deb, 27 November 1985, c 912

an all-out bid to defeat what others saw as a peace process and what it saw as the appeasement of the IRA. Paisley Snr denounced the 1998 Good Friday Agreement as 'the mother of all treacheries'.

The civil war Paisley had predicted in 1985 had not happened. The Anglo-Irish Agreement remained in place until the Good Friday Agreement superseded it. The Orange Order's tolerance of the atrocious LVF at its protests caused the order irreparable damage. The sectarian murders of that time intensified the resolve of those working for peace. After failing to 'smash' the agreement, the DUP signed up to a slightly adulterated version of it in 2007.

The flags protests that started in 2012 began in anger, turned ugly and for a while looked menacing. Loyalists threatened to desert the DUP over its failure to get the Belfast City Hall flag decision reversed, but it is still in place. The Parades Commission, resented by the Loyal Orders, still has authority. In the winter of 2019, unionists and loyalists united for the 'betrayal act' rallies. After meditating about historical UVF gun-running, the hyperbolic blogger Jamie Bryson warned that if the UK tried to separate Northern Ireland from the mainland, the 'grassroots PUL resistance' that would follow would 'make the Anglo-Irish Agreement and flag protests look like small tremors'. Thus fired up, unionism entered a general election at which it lost key seats to anti-Brexit, pro-EU parties.

In December 2020, a sorry-looking parade passed almost unnoticed through Belfast's city centre, commemorating the eighth anniversary of the flags protests. The organisers had applied for fifteen people to take part, the maximum number allowed under pandemic restrictions, but just eight turned up. Several carried shopping bags. The parade was led, bizarrely, by Olaf the snowman from Disney's *Frozen*. Carrying a flag emblazoned with 'Loyal People's Protest', 'In Memory of All Who Fell' and 'No surrender', he waved, as though at a festival parade, as a police car herded the remains of the protest through the empty, locked-down streets. A few months later, Jamie Bryson was hoisted onto the top of a blue bin in Belfast to proclaim to a handful of men in hoodies that there would be no need for further protests if the DUP brought down Stormont.

'PEOPLE START TO LOOK FOR LUNDYS'

Amy from Mid Ulster was one of several people I met who lived in single-identity communities but had a cross-community outlook, and for that reason felt sufficiently at risk that they could not give their names. Amy felt she would be put out of the area. When I asked her why her family, friends and neighbours voted for Brexit she did not hesitate: 'a border as high as you can get it and all the foreigners out. And no United Ireland.' The DUP sold Brexit to those people as a way out of the Good Friday Agreement. It was never going to work – the agreement is an international treaty. It includes a set of cross-border relationships that were designed to soften the border between the two jurisdictions in Ireland. Over 70 per cent of people in Northern had voted for the agreement, and 56 per cent voted to remain in the EU.

When it was first mooted in 2019, Foster had called the Brexit protocol proposal 'serious and sensible'.[12] When others at the harder edges of unionism began to chafe, she said it was her responsibility to implement it.[13] She even suggested tentatively that there might be advantages in it for Northern Ireland.[14] After she was pushed into militant opposition to it by her party, she was asked on BBC Northern Ireland how unionism could realistically hope to get it overturned, given past failures and its current weaker position, she replied that one of unionism's problems was that when it was in 'difficult circumstances … they turn in on themselves and people start to look for Lundys' to blame. She knew. The party was looking for someone to blame. She was the obvious candidate.

In an interview with journalist Tommie Gorman on Irish television in early 2021 she repeated something she had said a few years before in a documentary. She said that if, after a border poll, Ireland was united, she would leave. It would be pointless to stay if she was no longer able to be British. Such helplessness in the face of history. Such abdication of leadership. Anyway, a former unionist leader in England would be just as likely as anyone else to be seen as "a Paddy". She also talked about how

---

12 David Young, 'Arlene backs new Brexit plan as "serious and sensible way forward"', *Belfast Telegraph,* 2 October 2019

13 David Young, 'Sammy Wilson at odds with Arlene Foster with comments over Brexit withdrawal deal', *News Letter,* 6 September 2020

14 Michael McHugh, 'Arlene Foster: Northern Ireland an "attractive location for US firms accessing EU and UK"', *News Letter,* 14 December 2020

she would like to be an MP.

It had long been obvious that Foster's leadership was precarious. Some of her politicians openly defied her. These comments suggested that she felt the ground shifting under her own feet. Some of the ugly graffiti that had appeared around Northern Ireland included 'DUP must go'. Some of it said 'Foster must go.' Edwin Poots was also called a Lundy for putting customs infrastructure in place at Northern Irish ports, though he tried to blame officials for this.[15]

While apparently sensing she was being set up as a scapegoat, Foster claimed, however, she had seen a 'coming together' of unionism. She joined with TUV leader Jim Allister in a legal challenge based on claiming the protocol breached the 1800 Acts of Union *and* the Good Friday Agreement.

Billy Mitchell, who had been in the UVF and latterly the PUP said to me when I interviewed him for *Northern Protestants: An Unsettled People*: 'We've sheathed the sabre, and they can't rattle it any more.'[16] Twenty years later, the DUP leader met the Loyalist Communities Council (LCC), a group most people had never heard of, to talk about the protocol to the Brexit deal. The LCC included representatives of proscribed paramilitary organisations. Although the group said there was no threat of violence, its chairman, David Campbell, a former UUP adviser said on BBC Radio Ulster that if loyalists had to go back to war, 'so be it'. Bryson Tweeted that, 'If the Brexit Betrayal has any positive outcome, hopefully it will fuel unionist resentment of the pernicious Belfast Agreement.' The fuelling of resentment is hardly a promising political strategy, nor one likely to end peacefully.

A 2021 poll showed the DUP's support had dropped to 19 per cent, below Sinn Féin on 24 per cent and just one point ahead of Alliance, which gained almost 9 per cent, while the TUV gained 7.4 per cent to reach 10 per cent. The formerly dominant party was in difficulty, losing voters at both ends of the political unionist spectrum.[17] A UUP motion to outlaw conversion therapy saw the DUP isolated, voting

---

15 Sam McBride, 'Documents show DUP minister Edwin Poots' officials building Irish Sea border – which he says he opposes', *News Letter*, 7 November 2020

16 Susan McKay, *Northern Protestants: An Unsettled People (3rd edition)*, Blackstaff Press, 2021, p. 60

17 https://www.lucidtalk.co.uk/single-post/lt-ni-quarterly-tracker-poll-winter-2021

for an amendment to protect the religious persecution of LGBTQ+ people. Foster abstained.

In the last week of April 2021, Foster's foreboding that she was to be Lundified became a reality. The Apprentice Boys rose up, the gates were closed. There would be no surrender. The party that claims loyalty as its supreme virtue humiliated its leader and effectively banished her. The despised media delivered the message. Sam McBride was first, revealing that a letter had been written by DUP politicians expressing a collapse of confidence in the First Minister. Later in the day other journalists found out that around 80 per cent of the party's elected representatives had joined in the coup. Foster was to be blamed for everything; the slide from biblical values, the Brexit Protocol, the bad opinion polls. Her holding statement was a Facebook post quoting Psalm 18. 'It is God who arms me with strength and keeps my way secure.' The following morning she announced her resignation. Like her predecessor Peter Robinson, she began, as she departed, to sound conciliatory and pluralist. 'I have sought to lead the party and Northern Ireland away from division … We must all learn to be generous to each other,' she said. She later said the party had changed and she would leave it. But it had not changed. It could not change.

The party signalled its retreat from the Good Friday Agreement with the cancellation by leadership contender Edwin Poots of a cross-border ministerial meeting. Jim Wells, poster boy for biblically-driven figures who had been marginalised, was invited to participate in discussions. Never mind the pandemic, the broken health service, the rioting children. The sorry quest for a new Big Man resumed as the DUP squabbled its way across the wilderness to its 'scorched tomorrow'.

When, in 2021, Sammy Wilson MP declared that unionists were embarking on a guerrilla war,[18] it reminded me of one of the historic postcards from the collection at the Linen Hall Library in Belfast. Printed over a century ago in the turbulent period leading up to the partition of Ireland, it shows a pugnacious boy in a red jumper and short trousers who is squaring up for a fight over the slogan, 'Who says we're to have Home Rule? Come to Belfast and we'll shew them.' Unionism is heartsick with nostalgia for the days of its dominance, but those days are never going to come back.

---

18 https://www.bbc.co.uk/programmes/p098cmnl

'THE WRONG SIDE OF THE GAZE'

In 1972, John Hewitt wrote that memory was a 'loaded word'. It remains so, and the legacy of inherited trauma continues to blight young lives. Kyle Black talked about the pain of seeing his murdered father's name burned in a bonfire and to find republican graffiti at the scene of the fatal ambush. It is hard to bear the glimpse Chrissie Quinn gave of the loneliness of her only surviving son, Lee, still traumatised by the murders of his little brothers when he was himself a child. There are social media accounts that daily post photographs of members of the security forces who were murdered by the IRA and other republican paramilitaries 'on that day' during the conflict.

Dolores Savage, whose British soldier son, Brett, died by suicide after traumatic service in Afghanistan told me that the army abandoned him to 'his demons' and offered neither him nor his family the support they needed. An event to honour Edgar Graham at Queen's did not dispel his sister Anne's hurt that the university failed to put up a plaque to commemorate him.

Gail McConnell spoke to me about her 2021 book *The Sun is Open* in which she explores the murder of her father, a prison governor, and her complex feelings about it. Her mother was guided by her Christian faith and forgave her husband's killers. Some presented Bill McConnell's death as a just execution. Having read accounts that judge him harshly, she struggles to find her own way to mourning, '… thinking from that side/ of things bad bastard screw/ in the mechanism the/ panopticon the architecture/ of brutality knowing the theory/ the cruel ingenious cage thinking/ shit that's him on the wrong side/ of the gaze'.[19]

For many of the bereaved, the Good Friday Agreement's pledge to honour those who died during the conflict through creating a society founded on respect and equality did not bring peace. A 2019 survey found half of the DUP's voters favour a 'truth and reconciliation commission', roughly the same as in the wider Northern Ireland community.[20] However, in reality, attempts to find a set of mechanisms that are acceptable have, to date, failed. In the New Decade, New

---

19 Gail McConnell, *The Sun is Open*, Penned In The Margins, September 2021
20 https://www.liverpool.ac.uk/histories-languages-and-cultures/news/articles/huge-shift-in-support-for-truth-and-reconciliation-across-northern-ireland-electors

Approach deal that restored the Northern Ireland institutions in 2020, the UK government promised 'within 100 days' to legislate for the implementation of the Stormont House Agreement of 2014. This included a range of bodies designed to answer the needs of victims and survivors.[21] The 100 days came and went.

There are politicians who stoke old grievances, groups that summon up their dead to accuse their enemies. There are also people who have simply suffered too much. Some of those I interviewed in this book are angry and bitter and it is hard to see how this can ever be resolved for them. I am horrified when I hear journalists and others ask people bereaved in the conflict if they forgive the killers. In the absence of wider societal agreement, people have been left to carve out their own paths to truth or justice, and many have been disappointed, their grief compounded.

'LESSER BREEDS' OR 'LOVE YOUR NEIGHBOUR'

It has traditionally been left to the churches to look after moral issues and ease people from grief into becoming reconciled with death. Religious practice is still important to many. However, Northern Ireland is steadily becoming more secular. When I was researching *Northern Protestants: An Unsettled People* in 1998, just 9 per cent of people from a Protestant background had no religion. By 2017 this figure was 19 per cent. In 1998, 52 per cent attended church, but by 2017 this had fallen to 43 per cent.[22] Several of the interviewees in this book spoke sadly about how more pews in their church were empty than full on a Sunday.

On the other hand, US-style evangelical churches appear to be thriving. Green Pastures in Ballymena was packed with hundreds of people on the few occasions I attended. The theological message was conservative, if somewhat incoherent. Perhaps it was the energetic way it was presented that appealed. It was depressing to hear the Reverend Godfrey Brown, a former moderator and in many ways a liberal man, defend the Presbyterian Church's exclusion of same-sex couples from communion, and say that 'just because a girl doesn't want to have

---

21 https://assets.publishing.service.gov.uk/government/uploads/system/uploads/attachment_data/file/856998/2020-01-08_a_new_decade__a_new_approach.pdf

22 Claire Mitchell, https://sluggerotoole.com/2018/07/01/doctrine-and-decline-irish-churches-and-the-conservative-turn/

a baby is not really, I think, a good enough reason for destroying a human life'.

It was unsettling to be welcomed into the home of Pastor Barrie Halliday for a religious service, having heard him speak of 'lesser breeds' who should leave if they refuse to know their place. This kind of commentary characterised early Paisleyism. David Porter pointed out that the notion of 'For God and Ulster' is actually idolatrous, and that the 'chosen people' is a heresy.

Writer Jan Carson was brought up within strict Presbyterianism and had left it but had taken with her a deep love of biblical language and stories. She had found a non-denominational church that allowed her to engage with the mysterious, without dictating to her imagination. Anton Thompson-McCormick had likewise left behind a church that rejected him as a gay man but had found a place for his 'religious sensibility' with the Quakers. Pastor Karen Sethuraman embraced Anabaptism with funky courage after the Baptist Church refused to ordain her because she is a woman. She preaches 'Love God, love your neighbour' and was one of the community leaders who put themselves in danger by walking out into the middle of the 2021 riots to try to persuade those throwing missiles to stop.

I was moved to hear Joy and Eddie Graham speak of how important the solidarity of their minister, the congregation of the small Church of Ireland in Garrison and the wider, religiously mixed community had been to them when their son was killed in an accident.

'NORMAL POLITICS'

'We want normal politics.' Kenny McFarland spoke for many with this heartfelt statement. Younger people in Northern Ireland were 'living in a different world,' he said, and they had the right to thrive in it without being held back by old divisions, rigid positions and self-defeating confrontationalism. Sarah Laverty spoke about finding it exhausting to feel the perpetual drag backwards when you wanted to look to the future.

Responding to Ben Lowry's report on the 'betrayal act' rally in Portadown in 2019 and specifically the claim by one speaker that 'threats to Protestants from 1641 had been resolved by "men on the ground"', writer and academic Claire Mitchell wrote on Twitter: 'Must our kids leave? Will there be jobs? What will we do about rising seas? About poverty, suicide, addiction? Threatening peace is a strange kind of love.'

Derek Mahon's magnificent poem, 'A Disused Shed in Co. Wexford', is about the aftermath of war. The poem begins, 'Even now there are places where a thought might grow'. The shed is in the overgrown garden of a burned-out hotel, a forgotten corner in a neglected outpost of empire. Mahon imagines opening a door to ghostly forms. Abandoned in civil war times, prisoners of 'the old regime', they long for deliverance. '"Save us, save us," they seem to say,/ "Let the god not abandon us/ Who have come so far in darkness and in pain."' Mahon invokes 'Lost people of Treblinka and Pompeii!' but admitted in an interview with Eamonn Grennan that, 'included in that are the dead of Dungiven and Magherafelt'.[23]

An only child, Mahon was born in north Belfast, his mother a former linen mill worker turned housewife, his father a shipyard worker. When I read that his mother had worried he might become 'an oddity' it reminded me of Scott McKendry's story about how his mother sent him off to Every Boy's Rally in the gospel hall because she feared he was on his way to being a 'weirdo'. Jean Bleakney has a marvellous poem called 'A Noddity', based on hearing, as a child, adults who 'corralled the wild-eyed, the loud,/ the cowed, the always head-scarved women,/ the hidden from view, the ill-at-ease with themselves.'[24]

As a young man Mahon had seen Northern Ireland as a society 'sick unto death'.[25] He loved the hymns he learned as a member of the choir, but did not even think about believing in God. 'I believe in the words and the tunes; that's quite enough for me,' he told Grennan.

Mahon could not wait to get away, escaping to Dublin just as the violence of the Troubles began. He hated his sense of complicity with his Protestant community, describing it in one interview as feeling perhaps as a drunk driver must feel on waking up after being involved in a hit-and-run accident. In 'A Disused Shed', the lost people address him as if he were God, but the poet, with the 'relaxed itinerary' about which they reproach him, is passing by and however stricken he may be

---

23 Derek Mahon, 'A Disused Shed in Co. Wexford', *The Poems (1961–2020)*, Gallery, 2021, p. 86; http://www.ricorso.net/rx/library/criticism/revue/Zundry_AZ/Grennan_E.htm

24 Jean Bleakney, 'A Noddity', *No Remedy*, Templar Poetry, 2017, p. 6

25 Paul Durcan, 'The world of Derek Mahon', *Magill*, 24 December 1984

by their plight, can offer no salvation. Still, 'A thought might grow.' All is not necessarily lost.

'THE GENEROUS NEGOTIATION OF DIFFERENCE'

Michael Longley's poem, 'All of These People' begins with the question, 'Who was it who suggested that the opposite of war/ Is not so much peace as civilisation?'[26] The poem is an elegy for people who died in the conflict, and a tribute to those who showed them respect, and to those who get on with providing for the needs of others in ordinary and extraordinary ways. The poem ends: 'All of these people, alive or dead, are civilised.'

In January 2021, a terrible incident led to a communal response which was truly, in Longley's terms, civilised. Arsonists attacked the Multi-Cultural Association's centre in a handsome old church building on Belfast's Donegall Road and succeeded in burning it down. The First and deputy First Ministers united immediately to call the attack 'despicable'. Amnesty International Northern Ireland set up a JustGiving page, aiming to raise £20,000. Within a couple of weeks over £70,000 had been donated. The centre had been acting as a hub to distribute food and clothing to people from all communities who were in need during the pandemic. Its trustee, Muhammad Atif, thanked the people of Belfast for their 'outpouring of love'.[27] It was a glimpse of a gracious, generous Northern Ireland.

When Anna McCallion heard it said openly that her nephew Anton Thompson-McCormick was gay, she disregarded her church's hostility and responded bravely with love. I was delighted by Sophie Long's reference to going 'full Lundy' by learning Irish in England, and by Stacey Gregg's proud, 'I've been emancipating myself from restrictions arising from shame.' Gregg's play *Shibboleth* takes that Hebrew word for othering and uses it to dismantle the idea that people 'live in a different world' and that walls can be built to keep them there. Stephen Donnan-Dalzell had also found their place among the Lundys. I admired the value they placed on empathy, when they said that whereas in the past they had railed against people, including close family members who have traditional

---

26 Michael Longley, *Collected Poems*, Jonathan Cape, 2006, p. 253
27 David Young, 'Belfast Multi-Cultural Association: Over £70,000 raised for food bank following devastating arson attack', *Belfast Telegraph*, 11 February 2021

DUP views, they now tried to understand, and to respect difference.

I was impressed to hear from Amy, a respected and accomplished professional woman, that she had shouted when she spotted one of the ignorant young men who had trolled her: 'Are you the wee fucker who has been targeting me online? Say it to my face. I'm standing here now. Come on.' No wonder, as she put it, 'he near shit himself'. I was full of respect for schoolboy DeeDee Kerr who has Tourette's and needed support to stop him falling out of education. Now doing well, he now knows how to recognise when others are struggling, and cares enough to intervene: 'You just say to them, are you okay? And then sometimes they might say, yeah or no. It's just having confidence in yourself and knowing that you can sort of help.'

I described in the prologue to this book the old habit of trying to find out a person's religion. Claire Mitchell has written affectionately about the opposite – the way that people today, suspecting that someone is one of 'the other sort', go out of their way to let them know it does not trouble them. 'The guy who cuts our trees thinks we're Catholic, as we send our kids to the local Catholic school. We're not (we're Lundys). We think he's Protestant, because of his name and the fact that we live in a majority Protestant area. Last week, I was surprised to hear my husband drop a "Londonderry" into the conversation – I assume to make the tree guy comfortable. And the tree guy comes back with a sentence containing five "Derrys" – quite an achievement – to signal back that all is well. This is Northern Ireland to me. The gentle, intricate and generous negotiation of difference. Using language, humour, silence – or whatever we need – to navigate the situation. Most of us do this on a daily basis. We're pretty good at it.'[28]

I am Northern Irish, my husband and my children are Irish. A unionist politician once wrote an article about me which began ominously with the observation that I 'was born into a Protestant home in Londonderry' and went on to criticise the BBC for using me as a commentator, presumably because he considered that my upbringing had been wasted on me. I am reconciled to my Lundyism. There are a lot of us, I like the company, and we are not planning to flee.

The DUP's new leader, Edwin Poots, had laid out his sectarian

---

28 Claire Mitchell, https://sluggerotoole.com/2019/08/25/is-northern-ireland-spiralling-out-of-control/

credentials when, during the worst days of the COVID pandemic in 2020, he disagreed with the Executive's policy of general lockdowns. He favoured localised restrictions, he said. He and his community were abiding by the rules, but people from the other community had seen them broken. (This was a reference to the attendance by Sinn Féin leaders at the funeral of republican Bobby Storey despite the agreed restrictions of the time.) The rate of infection was six times higher in nationalist areas than in unionist ones, Poots said. This was false. But these prejudices have deep roots.[29] Poots's late father, Charles, one of the DUP's founding fathers, had advised in 1975, when the Troubles were raging, that he would 'cut off all supplies, including water and electricity, to Catholic areas. And I would stop Catholics from getting social security. It is the only way to deal with enemies of the state.'

The urge to exclude based on denigration remains a strong imperative within unionism. I am sure that former First Minister Peter Robinson had people like me in mind when he wrote about 'that lazy and witless cadre of anti-unionist journalists', and I do not care.[30] To quote Mahon again, 'close one eye and be king.'[31]

I have interviewed Alan Black several times, including in my book *Bear in Mind These Dead*,[32] and have stayed in touch with him. He is the sole survivor of the IRA's sectarian Kingsmills atrocity. He is a profoundly humane person who has managed to survive the most horrific experience, while remaining, in his own words, 'just an ordinary decent bloke'. He had spoken to me about how he finds each anniversary almost unbearable, so in 2015 I sent him a recording of a radio documentary I had made about the daughters of the murdered musician Fran O'Toole so that he could listen to it on that day. It had some fragments of music in it that had never before been broadcast. He left a message on my phone to say that the programme was lovely and that it had helped him. That matters to me. I think of the valiant people who have given me their 'vulnerable testimony' for this book, and I am grateful, as always, for open hearts and open minds.

29 See, for example, McKay, pp. 203–5

30 Peter Robinson, 'Unionists are more alienated than I have seen at any time in my 50 years in politics', *News Letter*, 26 March 2021

31 Derek Mahon, 'Ecclesiastes', *Collected Poems (1961–2020)*, Gallery, 2021, p. 40

32 Susan McKay, *Bear in Mind These Dead*, Faber, 2008, pp. 81ff and 222–23

AUTHOR
ACKNOWLEDGEMENTS

My thanks to all of those who agreed to be interviewed for this book, especially those who felt it was risky to speak out but decided to do so anyway. My apologies to those whose interviews had to be cut when the book sprawled. Thanks also to those who gave me valuable insights behind the scenes. It has been a pleasure to work with my editor, Patsy Horton, at Blackstaff Press.

Thanks to friends, colleagues and sources of wisdom and inspiration of one kind or another, including Patsy Brady, Michael Patrick McDonald, Trevor Birney, Scott McKendry (and Gizmo), Ian Cobain, Phil, Eithne, Beth, Ernestine, Enda, Marianne, Alan McBride, Kieran McEvoy, Sandra, Sam McBride, Eoin Ronayne, Rohan Naik, Duncan Morrow, Katy Hayward, Trish Devlin and Rodney Edwards, David and everyone at No Alibis, and the late Lyra McKee, whose memory reminds all of us why we have to change this country.

Thank you to my mum, Joan McKay, and all the lovely staff who care for her at Rush Hall. Thanks to Chris, and to Sheila and Rachael for transcribing recorded interviews.

I am grateful to Jean Bleakney from whose interview I took the book's subtitle *On Shifting Ground*, and to Gail McConnell for allowing me to use lines from one of her poems as an epigraph, as well as lines from her forthcoming book. I am honoured to have one of my friend Trevor McBride's great Lundy photographs on the cover.

Very special thanks and gratitude to my friend Anton Thompson-

McCormick for reading successive versions of various chapters and making perceptive editorial suggestions. Also to my sister Ruth for sparkling moments and coffee.

I would like to pay tribute to Davy Crockett, who died in a tragic accident at his farm in 2020. He was a delightful and decent man and I am so glad to have his interview, along with his daughter Rebecca's, in this book.

Thank you to the Arts Council of Northern Ireland and to the Joseph Rowntree Charitable Trust. The funding they gave me for my next book also gave me the peace of mind to finish this one.

ACKNOWLEDGEMENTS

Grateful acknowledgement is made to: Gail McConnell, for permission to quote from 'Type Face' (Blackbox Manifold 17, 2016) and from her forthcoming collection, *The Sun is Open* (Penned in the Margins, September 2021); The Lifeboat Press, for permission to quote from Scott McKendry, 'Duck, Duck, Goose' and 'Keepers of the Pedigree', from *Curfuffle* (2019); Kerri Ni Dochartaigh, *Thin Places* (Canongate, 2021), (c) Kerri Ni Dochartaigh, 2021, reproduced with permission of the Licensor through PLS Clear; Merrion Press, for permission to quote from Billy Hutchinson with Gareth Mulvenna, *My Life in Loyalism* (2020) and Sam McBride, *Burned: The Story of the 'Cash for Ash' Scandal and Northern Ireland's Secretive New Elite* (2019); Gallery Press, for permission to quote from Derek Mahon, 'A Disused Shed in Co. Wexford' and 'Ecclesiastes', both from Derek Mahon, *The Poems (1961–2020)* (2021), www.gallerypress.com; Wendy Erskine and The Stinging Fly, for permission to quote from Wendy Erskine, 'To All Their Dues' from *Sweet Home* (The Stinging Fly, 2018); Michael Longley, for permission to quote from the poem, 'All of These People', from *Collected Poems* (Jonathan Cape, 2006); Templar Poetry, for permission to quote from Jean Bleakney, 'Postcard', from *Selected Poems* (2016), and 'A Noddity', from *No Remedy* (2017); Faber and Faber and the author, for permission to quote from Tom Paulin, 'Desertmartin', from *New Selected Poems* (2014); Faber and Faber and the author, for permission to quote from Lucy Caldwell, from 'Thirteen', from *Multitudes* (2017);

Fleet, Houghton Mifflin Harcourt and the author, for permission to quote from Phil Harrison, *The First Day* (Fleet, 2017); Blackstaff Press on behalf of the Estate of John Hewitt, for permission to quote from 'The Coasters' and from 'An Irishman in Coventry', from *John Hewitt: Selected Poems*, eds. Michael Longley and Frank Ormsby (2007).

INDEX